WITHDRAWN
UTSA LIBRARIES

LIEUT.-COLONEL ABD-EL-KADER.

CONTENTS OF VOLUME II.

CHAPTER VII.
ESTABLISH COMMERCE 250

CHAPTER VIII.
TREACHERY 285

CHAPTER IX.
THE MARCH TO RIONGA 327

CHAPTER X.
BUILD A STOCKADE AT FOWEERA 362

CHAPTER XI.
NO MEDICAL MEN 400

CHAPTER XII.
I SEND TO GONDOKORO FOR REINFORCEMENTS 429

CHAPTER XIII.
ARRIVAL OF M'TÉSÉ'S ENVOYS 461

CHAPTER XIV.
CONCLUSION 499

APPENDIX 515

INDEX 562

CONTENTS OF VOLUME II.

CHAPTER I.
                                          PAGE
THE ADVANCE SOUTH 1

CHAPTER II.
THE ADVANCE TO LOBORÉ 31

CHAPTER III.
ARRIVAL AT FATIKO 83

CHAPTER IV.
THE MARCH TO UNYORO 130

CHAPTER V.
MARCH TO MASINDI 176

CHAPTER VI.
RESTORATION OF THE LIBERATED SLAVES 207

Originally published in 1874
by Macmillan and Co., London

Reprinted 1969 by
Negro Universities Press
A DIVISION OF GREENWOOD PUBLISHING CORP.
NEW YORK

SBN 8371-1509-4

PRINTED IN UNITED STATES OF AMERICA

ISMAILÏA

A NARRATIVE OF THE EXPEDITION
TO CENTRAL AFRICA FOR
THE SUPPRESSION OF THE SLAVE TRADE

ORGANIZED BY
ISMAIL,
KHEDIVE OF EGYPT.

BY
SIR SAMUEL W. BAKER, PACHA, M.A., F.R.S., F.R.G.S.,

*WITH MAPS, PORTRAITS, AND UPWARDS OF FIFTY FULL-PAGE
ILLUSTRATIONS BY ZWECKER AND DURAND.*

IN TWO VOLUMES.
VOLUME II.

NEGRO UNIVERSITIES PRESS
NEW YORK

LIST OF ILLUSTRATIONS.

To face page

LIEUT.-COLONEL ABD-EL-KADER . . . . *Front*.

MAP OF ALBERT N'YANZA 1

PECULIAR TABLE ROCK AT REGIAF 16

AMARN 44

ON THE MARCH THROUGH THE BARI COUNTRY—ENTERING MOOGÉ . 47

NIGHT ATTACK UPON ABDULLAH'S DETACHMENT; THE BARIS CAPTURE THE GUN 58

VIEW OF THE NAVIGABLE NILE ABOVE THE LAST CATARACTS AT AFUDDO 74

MARCHING TOWARDS FATIKO 82

MUSICAL ENTHUSIASTS—THE WOMEN FLOCK TO THE BAND . . . 93

RECEPTION OF THE CHIEF OF FAIEERA—ROT JARMA 127

BOTTLE-GOURD OF UNYORO 147

KABBA REGA AND HIS GREAT CHIEFS RETURNING A VISIT . . . 185

SUDDEN HOSTILE DEMONSTRATION—THE TROOPS FORM A SQUARE 268

PLAN OF SMALL CIRCULAR FORT AT MASINDI, AND SECTION OF STOCKADE 280

LIST OF ILLUSTRATIONS.

To face page

BATTLE OF MASINDI—REPULSE AND DEFEAT OF KABBA REGA'S FORCES 297

NATIVES SET FIRE TO THE SOLDIERS' CAMP AT NIGHT 318

ATTACK ON THE REAR GUARD BY AMBUSCADE—DEATH OF A BRAVE SOLDIER 343

THE VICTORIA NILE—AT RIONGA'S ISLAND 371

RECEPTION OF RIONGA 372

THE SLAVE-HUNTERS' ATTACK AT FATIKO—THE ADVANCE OF "THE FORTY THIEVES" 394

DESTRUCTION OF LIEUT. COLONEL TAYIB AGHA'S DETACHMENT AT MOOGI 409

FORT FATIKO 434

FORT FATIKO—GROUND PLAN 438

VIEW FROM THE ROCK FORT OF FATIKO 438

NET HUNTING IN THE SHOOLI TRIBE 444

DRIVING THE PRAIRIE WITH FIRE 447

CHARGE OF A LIONESS 456

AFFECTIONATE RESULTS OF A SUDDEN FEMALE EMANCIPATION . 474

THE NEW STEAMER, "THE KHEDIVE" 476

GONDOKORO, OR ISMAILÏA 478

SACRED TO THE MEMORY OF EDWIN HIGGINBOTHAM 479

ISMAILIA.

CHAPTER I.

THE ADVANCE SOUTH.

MILITARY critics will condemn my arrangements for an advance south.

My original plans had been well laid. A line of fortified posts was to have been established throughout the country at intervals of three days' march. This would have assured an open communication with Gondokoro.

Unfortunately, my original force had been 350 men short of the number stipulated; and the 1,200 men that had once been reviewed at Gondokoro had been reduced to 500.

I could not leave a smaller force at head-quarters than 340 men, including the 52 sailors; thus I was left with only 212 officers and men to commence a long and uncertain journey directly away from my base, without the power of communication in the event of unforeseen difficulty.

I had already experienced the treachery of natives, upon whom no reliance could be placed.

My intention was to leave the Englishmen, with the steamer sections, at a station to be formed at Ibrahiméyeh on the navigable Nile, N. lat. 3° 32′, together with a small garrison.

I should then endeavour to form an irregular corps of some of Abou Saood's men, who would be thrown out of employment at the expiration of the contract. This was near at hand.

An irregular corps of 600 men would, in addition to my 200, enable me to complete the annexation of the country, and to finish my work before the re-inforcements should arrive from Khartoum.

On the other hand, the men of Abou Saood might refuse to enlist in government service. Already they had been rendered passively hostile by the influence of Abou Saood. They had secretly encouraged the Baris in their war against the government; they might repeat this conduct, and incite the tribes against us in the interior.

Should this occur, I should be placed in a dangerous position with so small a force, as it would be necessary to detach half the little body to march to Gondokoro for supports.

I could not defer my departure in the hope of receiving reinforcements from Khartoum, as their arrival would be quite uncertain, owing to the state of the river.

Should I delay at Gondokoro, the dry season would pass by; the ground, now baked hard by the sun, would become soft, and would render transport by carts impossible.

The torrents would become impassable during the rains, especially the river Asua, which in the wet season cuts off all communication with the south. This dangerous river was very important, as it would prevent a retreat should such a movement be necessary during the rainy season.

I was well aware of the difficulties of the position, but I had only the choice of two evils. If I remained at Gondokoro, my term of service would expire fruitlessly. I should simply have reduced the Baris, and have established the station. Abou Saood would remain in the interior among his numerous slave establishments, to ridicule my impotence, and to defy my orders that he should quit the country. He would thus continue in the heart of Africa until I should have returned helplessly to England. He would then have resumed his original work of spoliation. The expedition would have been a failure.

On the other hand, should my small force meet with defeat or destruction, both the military and the civil world would exclaim, " Serve him right! the expedition to the interior made under such circumstances showed a great want of judgment; a total ignorance of the first rules in military tactics. What could he expect, without an established communication, at a distance of three or four hundred miles from his base? Simple madness!— not fit to command!" &c. &c. &c.

I knew the risks and the responsibility; but if I remained passive, I should be beaten. I had often got through difficulties, and if risks are to be measured in Africa by ordinary calculations, there would be little hope of progress.

I determined to carry as large a supply of ammunition as could be transported, together with sufficient merchandize, carefully assorted, to establish a legitimate ivory trade in my old friend Kamrasi's country, Unyoro.

The Englishmen would be occupied in the construction of the steamer at Ibrahiméyeh, while I should accomplish my mission farther south.

I selected my officers and men, carefully avoiding

Egyptians, with the exception of my true friends and aides-de-camp, Lieutenant-Colonel Abd-el-Kader, Captain Mohammed Deii of the "Forty Thieves," and the faithful Monsoor.

The officers that had served in Mexico under Marshal Bazaine were—Major Abdullah; Captain Morgiān Sherriff; Captain Abdullah; Lieutenants Morgiān and Ferritch; and several sergeants, corporals, &c.

I also included three sailors belonging to my diahbeeah, as they would be useful in the event of boating excursions. These men were Jali, Mohammed, and Howarti; all of whom were armed, and fell into the line of rank and file as soldiers.

The No. 3 steamer had been packed with much care. The carts had been loaded with the heavy portions that could not be transported by carriers, and we had proved our capability of travelling provided the Baris of Beddēn would remain faithful to their promise. Every cart had therefore been dismounted, and the material for the expedition was stowed on board six vessels.

Our servants had much improved. The negro boys who had been liberated had grown into most respectable lads, and had learnt to wait at table and to do all the domestic work required. First of the boys in intelligence was the Abyssinian, Amarn. This delicate little fellow was perfectly civilized, and always looked forward to accompanying his mistress to England. The next was Sāat, who had received that name in memory of my good boy who died during my former voyage. Sāat was a very fine, powerful lad, who was exceedingly attached to me; but he was not quick at learning. Bellaal was a thick-set, sturdy boy of fourteen, with rather a savage disposition, but quick at learning.

My favourite was Kinyon (the crocodile), the volunteer.

This was a very handsome negro boy of the Bari tribe, who, being an orphan, came to my station and volunteered to serve me at the commencement of the Bari war.

Kinyon was tall and slight, with a pair of very large, expressive eyes. The name Kinyon, or crocodile in the Bari language, had been given him because he was long and thin. Both he and Amarn were thoroughly good boys, and never received either chastisement or even a scolding throughout a long expedition.

Jarvah was also a good lad, who went by the name of the "fat boy." I should like to have exhibited him at Exeter Hall as a specimen of physical comfort.

Jarvah had a good berth—he was cook's mate. His superior was a great character, who, from the low position of a slave presented by the King of the Shillooks, Quat Kare, had risen from cook's mate to the most important position of the household. Abdullah was now the cook! He had studied the culinary art under my first-rate Arab cook, who, having received his discharge, left the management of our stomachs to his pupil. Abdullah was an excellent cook and a very good fellow; but he was dull at learning Arabic. He invariably distinguished cocks and hens as " bulls " and " women."

The last and the smallest boy of the household was little Cuckoo (or Kookoo).

Cuckoo was a sturdy child of about six years old: this boy had, I believe, run away from his parents in the Bari during the war, and had come to Morgiān our interpreter, when food was scarce among the tribe. Following the dictates of his appetite, he had been attracted by the savoury smell of Abdullah's kitchen, and he had drawn nearer and nearer to our establishment, until at length by playing with the boys, and occasionally being invited to share in their meals, Cuckoo had become incorporated with the household.

Abdullah and the six boys formed the native

domestic corps. My wife, who was their commanding officer, had them all dressed in uniform. They had various suits of short, loose trousers reaching half-way down the calf of the leg, with a shirt or blouse secured at the waist with a leather belt and buckle. These belts were made in England, and were about six feet long; thus they passed twice round the waist, and were very useful when travelling in case of a strap and buckle being required suddenly.

Each boy wore the fez or tarboosh. The uniforms were very becoming. There was dark blue trimmed with red facings; pure white with red facings, for high days and holidays; scarlet flannel suits complete; and a strong cotton suit dyed brown for travelling and rough wear.

The boys were trained to change their clothes before they waited at the dinner table, and to return to their working dresses after dinner when washing up was necessary. In this habit they were rigidly particular, and every boy then tied his dinner suit in a parcel, and suspended it to the roof of his hut to be ready for the next meal.

There was a regular hour for every kind of work, and this domestic discipline had so far civilized the boys that they were of the greatest possible comfort to ourselves.

The washing up after dinner was not a very long operation, as half a dozen plates and the same number of knives and forks, with a couple of dishes, were divided among six servants.

Directly after this work, play was allowed. If the night were moonlight, the girls were summoned, and dancing commenced. During the day, their games were either playing at soldiers, or throwing lances at marks, &c.

Thieving was quite unknown among the boys, all of whom were scrupulously honest. The sugar might be left among them, or even milk; but none of the boys I have mentioned would have condescended to steal. They had been so well instructed and cared for by my wife, that in many ways they might have been excellent examples for boys of their class in England.

The girls and women did not appear to so much advantage as the boys. These comprised old Karka, young Dam Zéneb, Sallaamto, Fad-el-Kereem, Marrasilla, and Faddeela. They had learnt to wash, but could never properly fold the linen. Ironing and starching were quite out of the question, and would have been as impossible to them as algebra. Some of these girls were rather pretty, and they knew it. In moral character Dam Zéneb and Sallaamto were the best. Fad-el-Kereem was the most intelligent, but she was a young woman of strong passions, either for love or war, and required peculiar management.

They were all dressed in similar uniforms to the boys, with only a slight difference in the length of their blouses.

We had sent little Mostoora to the care of Djiaffer Pacha at Khartoum to be educated, before we left Tewfikeeyah. That clever little creature had learnt English and Arabic sufficiently to converse, and although not far removed from infancy, she was more intelligent than any of the adults. She was much too young for a long voyage . . . Everything was ready for the start. I left written instructions with the colonel, Raouf Bey, also with Mr. Higginbotham, respecting the conduct of the works during my absence. I also gave the necessary orders to Mr. Marcopolo; thus all heads of departments knew their positions.

I sent off a detachment of 150 men to drive a herd of several thousand cattle and sheep to a well-known rocky ravine, about six miles south, which was to be the *rendezvous*.

Before leaving, I made rather a pretty shot with

the "Dutchman" from the poop-deck of my diahbeeah at a crocodile basking on a sand-bank. The first shot through the shoulder completely paralysed it. A second bullet from the left-hand barrel struck only three inches from the first. Lieutenant Baker determined to measure the distance; thus he took the boat with the end of a long line, and we found it exactly 176 yards.

The "Dutchman" was the best rifle I ever shot with, and was quite invaluable throughout the expedition.

I had served out a month's rations to the men, and my last instructions to Raouf Bey were to look well after Livingstone, and provide for his comfort should he appear during my absence.

On 22nd January, 1872, we started at 8 A.M., when I took leave of my good friend and excellent engineer-in-chief, Mr. Edwin Higginbotham. I little thought that we should never meet again.

The wind was light and variable, and my diahbeeah soon overtook the heavier vessels. In the evening we all joined and concentrated our forces at the rocky ravine, with the detachment that protected the cattle.

On the following day, the 23rd January, we all started in excellent spirits. The soldiers knew the country, and every one appeared to share the enjoyment of adventure. The people had learnt to depend upon my guidance, and although the interior of the country was unknown to them, they were quite contented that I had had a personal experience of the far south, and that they were safe in my hands.

The stream was very powerful, and the wind was so variable that it was necessary to tow the vessels. This would have been easy work if the river had been deep in all parts, but unfortunately the water was rather low, and many extensive sand-banks necessitated long detours.

The men were then obliged to wade hip-deep, and to tow the vessels round the banks.

I never saw the people in such high spirits. They were not contented with a walking pace, but they raced with each other, splashing through the water, and hurrying round the points of the sand-banks, until they once more reached dry ground. Then even the women and boys jumped ashore, and laying hold of the tow-rope, joined the men in singing; and running forward along the hard bank, they made the diahbeeah surge through the water.

This fun had continued for some hours, and I rejoiced that all hearts seemed to have at length united in the work. I had no fanatics with me. The black officers were excellent fellows now that they were relieved from a certain influence at head-quarters. Abd-el-Kader was as true as gold. Monsoor was a Christian,—and my "Forty Thieves" were stanch, brave fellows who would go through fire.

Ali Nedjar was, as usual, revelling in strength and activity, and was now foremost in the work of towing the diahbeeah.

A sudden bend in the river had caused a small sand-bank. It was necessary to descend from the high shore to tow the vessel round the promontory.

Men, women, and children, jumped down and waded along the edge of the bank.

As the diahbeeah turned the sharp point, I noticed that the water was exceedingly deep close to the sand-bank, and the stream was running like a mill race.

Fearing some accident to the children, I ordered all who could not swim to come on board the diahbeeah. At that time the bow of the vessel was actually touching the sand, but the stern, having swung out in the stream, might have been about fifteen feet from the edge of the bank in very deep water.

When the order was given to come on board, many of the people, in the ebullition of spirits, leapt heedlessly into the water amidships, instead of boarding the vessel by the fore part, which touched the sand.

These were dragged on board with considerable difficulty.

The boy Sāat would have been drowned had not Monsoor saved him. In the confusion, when several were struggling in the water, I noticed Ali Nedjar, who could not swim, battling frantically with his hands in such a manner that I saw the poor fellow had lost his head. He was not three feet from the vessel's side.

My four life-buoys were hung on open hooks at the four corners of the poop-deck; thus, without one moment's delay, I dropped a buoy almost into his hands. This he immediately seized with both arms, and I, of course, thought he was safe : the buoy naturally canted up as he first clutched it, and, instead of holding on, to my astonishment I saw him relinquish his grasp !

The next moment the strong current had hurried the buoyant safeguard far away. A red tarboosh followed the life-buoy, floating near it on the surface. . . . . . Ali Nedjar was gone !—drowned ! He never rose again. . . .

I was dreadfully shocked at the loss of my good soldier—he had been much beloved by us all. We could hardly believe that he was really gone for ever. Who would now lead the song in the moonlight nights? or be the first in every race?

I had quickly thrown every life-buoy into the river, as Howarti, Mohammed, and others of the best swimmers had vainly plunged after him, and were now searching fruitlessly for his body, carried away by the powerful current. The boat was sent after them immediately, and they were brought on board.

The mirth of the diahbeeah had vanished; the general favourite had so suddenly disappeared from among us, that no one spoke. The women sat down and cried.

His knapsack and rifle were brought to me, and a list having been taken of his clothes and ammunition, I cut his name, "ALI," upon the stock of his snider, which I reserved for the best man I should be able to select. There was no better epitaph for so good a soldier than his simple name engraved on his trusty rifle.

That evening every one was sad, and my people all refused their food. . . .

On the following day, the wind and stream being adverse, we had much trouble in avoiding the sand-banks, and our progress was so slow that we only reached the base of the rocky hill Regiāf.

Here I resolved to wait for the heavier vessels, which were far behind.

The natives were now friendly, and on the 25th January, Lieutenant Baker accompanied me to the summit of Regiáf to take observations of compass bearings of all the various mountains and prominent points of the country.

At the western base of Regiáf there is a very curious rock supported upon a pedestal, that forms a gigantic table.

This great slab of syenite is one of many that have detached and fallen as the original mountain decomposed.

I obtained my measuring tape from the diahbeeah, which gave the following results :—

	Feet.	Inches.
Length of slab	45	4
Breadth of do.	45	8
Thickness of do.	4	9
Height from ground	10	5
Circumference of clay pedestal	69	0

This rock must have chanced to fall upon a mass of extremely hard clay. The denudation of the sloping surface, caused by the heavy rains of many centuries, must be equal to the present height of the clay pedestal, as all the exterior has been washed away and the level reduced. The clay

PECULIAR TABLE ROCK AT REGIÁF.

pedestal is the original earth, which, having been protected from the weather by the stone roof, remains intact.

The Baris seemed to have some reverence for this stone, and we were told that it was dangerous to sleep beneath it, as many people who had tried the experiment had died.

I believe this superstition is simply the result of some old legends concerning the death of a person who may have been killed in his sleep, by a stone that probably detached and fell from the under surface of the slab.

I examined the rock carefully, and found many pieces that gave warning of scaling off. Several large flakes, each weighing some hundredweight, lay beneath the table rock,—upon the under surface of which could be distinctly traced the mould of the slab beneath.

On 27th January, we arrived with all the vessels at the foot of the cataracts, in N. lat. 4° 38′. This is a very lovely spot, as the rocky islands are covered with rich, green forest; the verdure being perpetual, as the roots of the trees are well nourished by water.

Our old friend Beddēn met us with a number of his people, and came on board the diahbeeah. He professed to be quite ready to convey our baggage to the south, and I proposed that his people should go as far as Loboré, about sixty miles from this spot, where I knew we could procure carriers, as during my former journey the natives of Loboré were the only people who could be depended upon.

Beddén seemed determined to help us, and I really believed that our luck had arrived at last, and that I should be able to convey the carts, together with the steamer, to the navigable portion of the Nile in N. lat. 3° 32′.

I determined to be very civil to the great sheik, Beddén; I therefore arranged with him that the work should be entirely in his hands, and that he should represent the government as my vakeel. At the same time, I gave him a grand cloak of purple and silver tissue, together with a tin helmet, and turban of cobalt-blue serge; also a looking-glass, and a quantity of beads of various colours.

The country was dried up, and there was only scant herbage for my large herd of cattle, the half of which I promised to give Beddén if he would carry our baggage to Loboré.

The sheik, Beddén, returned to his village to make arrangements with his people for the journey.

Somehow or other, as he took leave and marched

off in his grand cloak of silver and purple, I had certain misgivings of his sincerity.

Although great numbers of natives thronged the country, and came down to the vessels, there was *not one woman or child.* The absence of women and children is a sure sign of evil intentions. My wife, whose experience was equal to my own, at once expressed her suspicions. Had the natives been honest and sincere, their women would assuredly have come to visit her from simple curiosity.

Not only was there an absence of women and children, but the cattle had been driven from the country. There were several small cattle zareebas within half a mile of the vessels, situated upon the high ground. I went to visit them, as though simply strolling for my amusement; the dung of cattle was fresh, showing that the zareebas had been occupied during the past night, but the herd had evidently been driven far away.

Beddēn's people had never been attacked by the slave-traders, as his tribe was considered too powerful; he had therefore no cause for suspicion.

Unfortunately, my past experience of the Bari natives had proved that kindness was thrown away upon them, and that nothing could be done with them until their inferiority had been proved by force of arms.

Beddēn had never suffered. He had promised to assist; but no promise of a native is worth more than the breath of his mouth. If he failed me now, the object of my enterprise would be lost. I should not be able to move.

All my care and trouble would have been thrown away.

I was very anxious; but, without mentioning my suspicions, I ordered all the heavy vessels to cross over to the east side of the river, to prepare for disembarking the carts and general effects.

On the following morning the sheik, Beddēn, arrived to visit me, with many of his people. I had erected a tent on shore in which I could receive him.

I was struck with a peculiar change in his manner, and after a short conversation he asked me, " Why I had sent the vessels to the east side ? "

I replied that they would begin to unload and prepare for the journey.

" *Who is going to carry all your baggage?* " continued Beddēn, as though the idea had occurred to him for the first time.

I was perfectly aghast at this cool and prostrating question. My suspicions had been well founded.

I explained to Beddēn that I had arrived according to his express invitation, given some time before, when he had promised that his men should convey my things as far as Loboré. I pretended that his question had now been asked simply to amuse me, and I begged him in earnest to lose no time in collecting his people, as I should require at least 2,000 carriers.

Beddēn continued in a cold, stoical manner, and declared that his people were determined not to work for me; they had never before carried for "The Turks," and nothing would induce them to engage in such a labour.

I begged him to remember the importance of his promise, upon which I had depended when making all my arrangements for the journey. If he failed me now, I should be entirely ruined; whereas if he assisted me, as I had relied upon his honour, we should always remain the firmest friends, and he would be benefited by a grand herd of cattle, and would receive most valuable presents.

He now declared "that his people had taken the matter into consideration, and they were quite determined. They would not listen to him, or be persuaded to anything they disliked. They never had carried, and they never would."

I had the two natives with me who had resided for some time in our station at Gondokoro. One of these men, named Pittia, endeavoured to persuade Beddēn to beat his nogāra (big drum) and to summon the tribe; he might then, in my presence, explain the work proposed, and his people would see the cows which they would receive as payment for their labour.

Beddēn looked very ill at his ease; but after some delay, he rose from his seat, and declared his intention of immediately beating his nogāra. He took leave and departed with his people.

From my experience of Baris, I felt sure that I should never see Beddēn again.

He had hardly left the tent, when Pittia exclaimed, "I will follow him and listen to what he says to his people. I believe he will tell them NOT to carry the loads." Pittia immediately disappeared.

Many natives had collected on the east side of the river, where my vessels had now formed a line along the bank; I therefore crossed over in the dingy to converse with them in the faint hope of securing carriers.

The natives were squatting about in small groups, and they listened coldly to all I had to say. The only answer I could obtain was, "that they belonged to Beddēn, and if he told them to carry our things, they would obey; but without his order they could do nothing."

This is the regular African diplomacy when work is required. The people say, "We must receive orders from our sheik." The sheik says, "I am willing, but my people will not obey me." It is this passive resistance that may ruin an expedition.

My first exploration in Africa must necessarily have failed had I not been provided with transport animals. The readers of "The Albert N'yanza" may remember that I could not obtain a single native, and that I started from Gondokoro by moonlight without even an interpreter or guide.

The horrible state of the White Nile had prevented all possibility of conveying camels from Khartoum. My carts and camel harness were prepared, but the invaluable animals could not be transported. I was thus dependent upon such rotten reeds as native promises.

No one who is inexperienced in African travel can realise the hopeless position of being left with a mass of material without any possibility of transporting it

The traveller may sit upon his box until he stiffens into a monument of patience and despair, but the box will not move without a carrier. There is only one method of travelling successfully, and this necessitates the introduction of transport animals, where the baggage is heavy and upon an extensive scale.

I felt perfectly helpless. My colonel, Abd-el-Kader, advised me to seize the sheik, Beddēn, and to tie him up until his people should have delivered all the effects at Loboré.

This I might have done, but it might also have occasioned war, which would prevent the possibility of securing carriers. I should also incur the responsibility of having provoked the war by an act that, although necessary, could hardly be justified according to civilized ideas.

I had very little hope, but I had so frequently seen a sudden ray of good fortune when all had looked dark and cloudy, that I went to bed at night with the hope that something might turn up in our favour to-morrow.

On 29th January, 1872, Pittia returned with bad news. Beddēn had sent me a laconic message that "he should not call again, and that his people declined to carry the baggage."

Pittia explained that the natives had all left the neighbourhood, together with their sheik, therefore it would be well not to allow the soldiers to stray far from camp.

This was the gross ingratitude exhibited by Beddēn and his people. Not only had I scrupulously respected all their property, but I had even placed sentries over their tobacco gardens to prevent the possibility of theft.

The absence of the women and children had been a certain sign of ill-will.

It was necessary to consider what should be done. We were perfectly helpless.

I had about 2,500 head of cattle and 1,800 head of sheep. These animals were driven every evening to the margin of the river, and were only protected at night by a line of soldiers who slept around them.

The conduct of the natives filled me with suspicions. The sight of so large a herd without protection might have excited their cupidity. They had expected my arrival with this grand supply of cattle, and instead of finding their villages occupied, I had observed that their own herds had been driven off for concealment; not a woman or child was to be seen in the country; the natives had refused to carry; and, lastly, their sheik and his people had absolutely absconded.

In the meantime my cattle were unprotected at

night, thus, should the natives make a sudden attack in the darkness, there would be a regular stampede, as the large herd would be seized with a panic at the red flashes of the muskets during the attack, and they would scatter all over the country, and never be seen again.

The natives had probably considered that, instead of carrying our loads, and thereby earning a cow per man, it might save them much trouble should they possess themselves of our cattle without the necessity of carrying the baggage.

From my knowledge of the brutal character of all Baris, I arrived at the above conclusion.

I at once gave orders to secure the cattle. At a distance of about half a mile, there were three small villages on the high sloping ground, situated about eighty yards apart, and forming a triangle. I instructed my men to make an inclosure, by connecting each village with a strong hedge of thorns.

The country was generally bare of trees, but fortunately there was a grove of hēglik not far distant; and the troops at once began to fell these trees, and to form fences by laying the prickly branches in the position I had selected.

The "Forty Thieves" were all provided with

small and sharp Canada axes, which they carried under the strap of their knapsacks; thus forty-eight axes were at work, in addition to the heavier instruments belonging to the expedition.

All the officers and men shared my suspicions, and they worked with great alacrity.

It was just dark by the time that the three fences were completed, and the herd of cattle were driven and secured within the inclosure.

I arranged a guard of sixty men: twenty upon each side of the triangle. They were to remain outside the fence, and to keep a vigilant look-out.

This work being over, I returned at night to the diahbeeah together with Lieutenant Baker. We found dinner ready on the poop-deck, where my wife had been rather anxiously expecting us. I sent for Colonel Abd-el-Kader, and gave him the necessary orders for the night.

My diahbeeah was a charming vessel, that had originally been sent from Cairo to Khartoum, when the former Viceroy of Egypt, Said Pacha, visited the Soudan.

The poop-deck was lofty and very spacious. This comfortable boat had been my home for two years, and she was kept in admirable order.

There were no mosquitoes during this season in

Beddēn's country, although they were very numerous at all seasons at Gondokoro, therefore, being relieved from these pests, the enjoyment of the evening was delightful.

The night was calm, as usual in these latitudes. Dinner was concluded. I was enjoying my evening *chibouque* with the best Ghebbelli tobacco, that soothes most anxieties. The troops were for the most part asleep, and all was quiet. My wife was sitting on the sofa or divan, and Lieutenant Baker had been recalling some reminiscence of the navy, when several musket shots in the direction of the cattle kraal suddenly startled every soldier from his sleep!

The shots were almost immediately succeeded by heavy firing from the whole force stationed at the cattle zareeba. The bugles sounded the alarm, and every man was quickly under arms.

Having arranged the men in position to defend the vessels in case of a general attack, I took twenty men of the "Forty Thieves," together with a supply of rockets. I was accompanied by Lieutenant Baker and most of the Englishmen, and we pushed rapidly forward towards the cattle zareeba, where the flashes of the muskets were distinctly visible.

As we approached the position, I ordered my bugler

to sound "cease firing," as I expected to receive a few bullets intended for the enemy.

We were quickly challenged upon arrival at the zareeba. We found the cattle all safe; only a few sheep had been killed by the heavy attempt at a stampede when the cows took fright at the musketry.

I was informed that the natives in considerable force had made a sudden rush upon the zareeba, and had thrown showers of stones in order to create a panic among the cattle, which they expected would break through the fence and scatter over the country.

It was fortunate that I had taken the precaution of securing them.

I was determined to clear the neighbourhood. The night was dark. I was provided with matches and port-fires, and I quickly made an excursion and sent several rockets into the nearest villages. The Hale's rockets, as usual, rushed through the houses without igniting them; but a few of the powerful Egyptian rockets that are used as fireworks, rapidly lighted up the scene, as the descending fire-balls ignited the thatched roofs.

These rockets were fired from an inclined rest of a soldier's fixed bayonet.

Having cleared the neighbourhood, I returned to the diahbeeah at midnight.

I find this entry in my journal :—

"*January* 29, 1872.—All the googoos or granaries abound with corn. The natives are so rich, both in dhurra and cattle, that they will not work, but they are only ready to sleep or steal. After all my kindness, they have wantonly attacked **my cattle** without the plea either of hunger or provocation.

"What can be accomplished with such people? I shall be obliged to return the steamer to Ismailïa (Gondokoro). It is heartbreaking work after all my trouble in having brought her to this distant point.

"Nothing can be done without camels, and these animals cannot be brought from Khartoum in the closed state of the river.

"My original plan included 200 camels, 200 cavalry, and fifteen large decked sloops. None of these necessary items have been sent from Khartoum, thus I am paralysed."

CHAPTER II.

THE ADVANCE TO LOBORÉ.

I DETERMINED upon a new plan. I knew the direction of Loboré, as I had been there formerly; the distance could not exceed sixty miles.

If the soldiers could draw the carts, I might yet manage to advance, as I should be able to procure carriers on arrival at Loboré; provided always that the natives were as friendly as when I left them some years ago.

It would be impossible to convey the steamer, as I could not expect to provide 2,000 carriers; but I might be able to penetrate south, establish the government, and open up a legitimate trade.

The first step necessary was to convey the large herd of cattle across the river, which was about 400 yards in width, with a very rapid stream.

The sheep were taken across in vessels, but the

cows were obliged to swim. This operation was very tedious, as they were necessarily taken in small batches, guided by men who swam ·by their side in the manner already described at Gondokoro.

Although the natives were avowedly hostile, they dared not face us in the open. They made another attempt by night to surprise the cattle kraal, but Colonel Abd-el-Kader immediately set fire to a few villages as a response and warning.

We were occupied four days in passing the cattle across the river. During the passage, we lost one taken by a crocodile, and three cows were wantonly seized and drowned by hippopotami. A herd of these creatures happened to be in the way as the cows were floating in large numbers down the stream, and several were seen to attack the cattle and seize them in their jaws. As the hippopotamus is not carnivorous, this was an unexpected attack.

My Englishmen had been busily engaged in erecting the carts, greasing the wheels, and attaching the ropes necessary for hauling. They were all loaded, and were arranged to be drawn by fifteen men each.

On the evening of the 5th February, while we were at dinner, I was astonished by the unexpected mustering of my whole force, excepting the "Forty

Thieves." The men were without arms or officers, but they marched to the margin of the river and formed a line two deep alongside the diahbeeah, which lay close against the bank.

I knew at once what all this meant, but I pretended to take no notice, and I continued eating my dinner.

I was quickly interrupted by loud cries from the men. "We can't draw the carts! that's not the work for soldiers; we'll fight, or do anything else you may desire, but we are not camels to drag the waggons."

The "Forty Thieves" immediately seized their arms, and marching quickly to the spot, they formed in line upon the bank, between the diahbeeah and the men who thus mutinously had appeared without their officers.

I at once ordered the bugle call for all officers, and at the same time I sent for all the Englishmen to come to the diahbeeah.

When all had arrived, and the shouts still continued, I rose from the table and addressed the troops in Arabic, from the poop-deck of the diahbeeah.

I recalled to their recollection how I had always led them successfully through every difficulty, and I assured them that the distance to Loboré was trifling, and that we should find good and willing natives to convey the baggage, if we could only once reach the desired tribe.

Cries of "there are no good negroes—they are all bad," interrupted my discourse. I nevertheless continued; but having a thorough knowledge of the African character, and knowing that if a negro gets an idea into his head, that idea can only be eradicated by cutting the head off, I was not fool enough to persist in swimming against a torrent. The "Forty Thieves" now joined the tumult by declaring that "*they* would draw the carts, or do anything that I should command."

I took immediate advantage of the occasion, and exclaimed, "You *shall* do all that I command. I have changed my plans, and I order you to take the carts to pieces at sunrise to-morrow morning. All those who are afraid to follow me shall return with the vessels and carts to Gondokoro. I never turn back; and my lady and I will go on alone with Mr. Baker. I only require orderly soldiers, who know their duty; if you have forgotten your duty, you shall return at once to Gondokoro."

This declaration was followed by loud shouts— "We won't let you go alone; the natives are treacherous; we will follow wherever you lead.

Are we not soldiers of the Sultan? are you not the Sultan's Pacha?"

I had them in hand; therefore I at once terminated the scene by commanding silence. I then gave an order aloud to the officers: "Return carts and all baggage on board vessels at sunrise to-morrow. All troops to be ready for the advance."

"Bugler! sound the retreat."

That peculiar habit of discipline yielded instinctively to the sound of the bugle. The officer gave the order, "Right, turn," and the late tumultuous crowd marched quietly to their quarters. This was ended; at the same time it was not cheering.

My Englishmen, who had been witnesses of this scene, were filled with indignation. They were men who thoroughly represented English determination, and they at once volunteered to carry their own baggage if I would only permit them to accompany me.

How often my heart has beaten with pride when I have seen the unconquerable spirit of the country burst forth like an unextinguishable flame in any great emergency!

I now had to quell the eagerness of my own good fellows, as I knew that if "the spirit was willing, the flesh was weak," and it would be impossible for

Englishmen to carry loads through a journey in a tropical country.

I saw the necessity of the occasion at a glance; and I gave the necessary orders.

The Englishmen, together with the steamer sections, machinery, &c., must return to Gondokoro. They must immediately commence the construction of the No. 2 steamer of 108 tons and 20-horse power, as this vessel, being provided with twin screws instead of paddles, would be able to pass through the narrow channels of the Bahr Giraffe, and communicate with Khartoum.

I gave the order to prepare to-morrow for a return to Gondokoro.

On 6th February, at sunrise, all hands were at work dismounting the carts, and returning on board the vessels all material connected with the steamer, &c. I altered all the loads, and made arrangements for a new plan of action.

I had determined to push on to Loboré with one hundred men, in heavy marching order, if I could only engage a few natives to carry the necessaries for the road. At Loboré I might be able to engage a few hundred porters that I should send back to the vessels with an escort of fifty soldiers, to bring up sufficient ammunition and material for an advance south. I knew the route.

It was therefore necessary to assort the baggage: much had to be returned to Gondokoro with the Englishmen.

I had a small invoice-book that had been carefully prepared by Mr. Marcopolo, which gave the numbers and contents of every box; therefore the difficulty of assortment was not great.

All the boxes were of block tin, painted; thus they could be piled like bricks one upon the other to form a wall. I arranged about 400 loads which were set apart for the carriers, should I be fortunate in procuring that number from Loboré.

On 7th February the carts were shipped. All the loads were perfected and ready for a start on the following day. Some of my men were endeavouring to train a few oxen to carry their baggage.

On 8th February the Englishmen, in very low spirits, started for Ismailïa (Gondokoro) in two vessels, with ninety urdeps of dhurra consigned to Mr. Marcopolo.

I had arranged that twenty-two boatmen should accompany me to Loboré, carrying such loads as were absolutely necessary for our party. They would then return together with the fifty soldiers who would escort the native carriers to the vessels.

I had given the Englishmen instructions to commence the building of the steamer immediately, and to confine their work to this vessel until she should be completed.

Having counted all the loads that were left in charge of Major Abdullah, I took a receipt for them, and gave that officer both clear and positive orders for his conduct.

I left with him 120 men, together with the field-piece and eight artillerymen. In addition to these men was the crew of the No. 10 steamer, all of whom were trained as soldiers. Thus with the armed crews of the different vessels he would have a force of about 145 muskets. It was highly probable that the natives would attack the vessels and the cattle in my absence, as they would have remarked the great reduction of force. Although the country was perfectly open, the ground was high and rocky, and rapidly rose to about 200 feet above the level of the river within a distance of a mile; thus the natives scattered about the heights could always observe our proceedings.

Before I quitted the vessels, I made every preparation for their security. All the metal boxes were built into a quadrangular breastwork, that would form a little fort for a dozen people.

I moored the vessels in line close to the mouth of a deep flat-bottomed ravine, which, although now dry and about thirty paces wide, had formed the bed of a river during the wet season. The perpendicular banks of this fosse would make a grand protection for the cattle; I therefore ordered a fence of thorns to be constructed across the ravine about a hundred yards from the river, so as to form a kraal, in which the cows would be confined below the level of the country.

Sixty men were to guard the cattle at night; thirty upon either bank. As this ravine ran at right angles with the river, the sixty men would enfilade an enemy attacking the vessels, and the guard of the vessels would at the same time enfilade an enemy should he attack the cattle on the north side.

I placed the gun in a convenient position about twenty yards from the margin of the river, on a piece of hard, flat ground, exactly opposite the centre of the line of vessels. This would sweep the approach in front and upon the left flank.

I ordered the officer to load with canister containing 250 small musket balls. Having served out a dozen Woolwich tubes, instead of the uncertain Egyptian articles, I gave positive orders that the gun was to be laid for a point-blank range of 200 yards every evening at sunset, with the tube in its place, the lanyard attached and coiled. A piece of raw hide was to cover the breech of the gun to protect it from the night dew.

Having given every instruction, and impressed upon officers and men the necessity of vigilance, I ordered Major Abdullah, in command, to remain in charge of the vessels and cattle until I should either send him carriers for an advance, or fall back myself, should I be unable to obtain them.

A tall old man of about seventy, or perhaps eighty years, had paid us a visit. From his appearance, and the numerous spells hung about his person, I judged him to be a rain-maker. His face was smeared with wood ashes, and there was a good deal of the ideal demon in his personal exterior.

I gave him a blue shirt, and a glass of Marsala wine, thus appealing at once to his exterior and interior.

It is always advisable to make friends with the rain-makers, as they are regarded by the natives as priests, and are considered with a certain respect. I therefore gave him another glass of wine; or, to be correct, he drank it from a tin that had contained preserved provisions.

This caused him to blink his eyes and smack his lips, and the old rain-maker grinned a ghastly smile of admiration. His wood-ash-smeared features relaxed into an expression that denoted "more wine." I thought he had enough, and there was none to spare; therefore, having opened his heart, I began to ask him questions.

That unfailing key, liquor, had established a confidential flow of conversation. The old fellow explained that he knew the entire country, and he had no objection to accompany us to Loborè for a small consideration in the shape of a cow. He assured me that if he were with us, the natives would be civil throughout the journey. Beddēn had behaved very badly, but he had got the worst of it, and the news had spread up the country.

I asked him whether he would keep the rain away during the journey, as it would be very unpleasant should the soldiers' kits get wet. He immediately blew his rain-whistle that was suspended to his neck, and looked at me as though I could no longer doubt his capability. I then sent for a German horn from my cabin. This was a polished cow's horn, fitted with brass, which I think had cost a shilling. I begged the old rain-maker's acceptance of this instrument, which might be perhaps superior to his whistle.

The wine had now so far warmed his old blood, that the ancient sorcerer was just in that state of good-will with all mankind which made him doubly grateful for so interesting a present. He blew the horn!—again, and again! He grinned till the tears ran down his eyes, and at once suspended the glittering toy around his neck. He now said, "I am a great sheik; there is no rain-maker so great as I; you will travel with me, and this horn shall keep you dry. Don't trouble yourself about the Baris, they won't molest you; but start as soon as you can."

We had thus gained a valuable ally and guide. Although I knew the direction of Loboré, I should have been obliged to travel by compass, therefore I was overjoyed that we had obtained so experienced an old fellow as the rain-maker. His name was Lokko.

At 3 P.M., on 8th February, we started, old Lokko leading the way, and waving a couple of thin, peeled sticks at a refractory black cloud that appeared determined to defy his rain-ruling powers. A few loud blasts upon the new horn, and a good deal of pantomime and gesticulation on the part of old Lokko, at length had the desired effect; the cloud went off about its business, and Lokko, having given his face an extra rub of fresh wood-ashes before starting, looked ugly enough to frighten any rain-devil out of his wits.

My people were heavily laden. At the commencement of the journey, an ox that Monsoor had been training, kicked off its load, and went off at full gallop like a wild animal, and we never saw it again. Poor Monsoor now shouldered the load that the ox had left helpless, and marched thus heavily laden up the hill.

My wife rode "Greedy Grey," which carried as much as could be hung upon the saddle. I rode the powerful chestnut "Jamoos." Lieutenant Baker mounted a very handsome light chestnut "Gazelle," and Colonel Abd-el-Kader rode the Zafteer. The latter was a fine old Arab that I had purchased of a zafteer (mounted police) in Cairo. I had ten donkeys which carried officers' effects, spare ammunition, flour, &c. The twenty-two boatmen carried boxes.

My wife and I, with Lieutenant Baker and an advanced guard of five of "The Forty," followed old Lokko, who led the way; and Colonel Abd-el-Kader and Captain Mohammed Deii were with the rear-guard, which drove 1,000 cows and 500 sheep. The cattle were in the charge of the Bari interpreter, Morgiān.

Our boys and girls all carried loads. Amarn looked like a small Robinson Crusoe, with a tanned sheepskin bag of clothes upon his back, upon which was slung the coffee-pot, an umbrella, and various smaller articles, while he assisted himself with a long staff in his hand. Little Cuckoo, who, although hardly seven years old, was as strong as a little pony, strode along behind my horse, carrying upon his head my small travelling-bag.

Everybody was in the best spirits, as the reaction from despair to success was delightful. We were really off at last, and were actually on the march to the interior.

That evening we halted at a village on the heights, only three miles from the vessels. The natives had deserted their habitations on our approach, and would not come near us. I ordered the troops to save their flour, and to eat from that discovered in the village, for which on the following morning I left two cows as a present. They were tied up in the native zareeba. The cows were worth at least fifty times the flour we had consumed; but I wished to adopt this plan throughout the journey to Loboré, in order to establish confidence, and to open up the road for the future.

AMARN,
The liberated Abyssinian slave-boy. From a photograph by MAYALL

On 9th February we started at 5.35 A.M., and marched two hours and a half through a very beautiful undulating country, diversified with rocks, streams, and handsome park-like timber.

We halted at a village called Kōojōk, beneath a large fig-tree (*Ficus Indica*). Our old friend Lokko appeared to be perfectly well known, and he at once introduced us to the natives, who received us without fear or suspicion. At this village I was able to hire five natives for as many cows, to ease my people (especially Monsoor) of their loads.

Thus relieved, we started at 2 P.M., and halted for the night at a village named Gobbōhr. The day's march was twelve miles. North latitude, by observation, 4° 28'.

At this spot the natives brought us a great curiosity, which they had purchased from the Baris of Belinian. This was no less than a shell of $8\frac{1}{4}$lbs. that had been fired at the Baris by our cannon, but the fuze had not ignited. It had been sold to the natives of Gobbōhr as a piece of iron.

I inquired the use of such a lump of metal to them. "Oh!" they replied, "we are going to hammer it into molotes (hoes)."

I explained to them that it was a loaded shell, that would explode and blow the blacksmith and his people to pieces, if he were to place it on the fire. They went away with their shell, evidently doubting my explanation.

On the 10th February, having as usual presented the natives with two cows, we started at 6 A.M., and marched ten miles. The country was even more lovely than before, comprising fine rocky scenery and beautiful park-like views. The undulations terminated in stony bottoms or water-courses; the rocks were all syenite, gneiss, and large masses of snow-white quartz.

Although at this season the ground was parched, the trees were all vividly green: the contrast of this bright green with the yellow turf was very remarkable.

At 2.50 P.M. we again started, and marched three miles, arriving at a village on high ground called Marengo, in N. lat. 4° 18'. Here I met an old acquaintance, who, of course, asked me for a cow. This was a very respectable man, named Nersho, who had, when a boy, been brought up by the Austrian missionaries at Gondokoro. I had met him during my former journey when in company with Koorshood's vakeel, Ibrahim. We slept at Marengo. The soldiers borrowed the natives' mats, cooking-pots, &c., but scrupulously returned everything according to orders.

February 11.—Nersho received his cow; and

ON THE MARCH THROUGH THE BARI COUNTRY—ENTERING MOOGÉ.

I left two in addition for the headman of the village.

We started at 5.35 A.M., and marched ten miles, and halted at a small ravine of running water among wooded hills.

Our old guide, Lokko, was at fault. After much trouble we succeeded in obtaining two natives, who told us, that in this spot they had killed a large number of the slave-hunters' people.

Other natives soon joined us, and we were led by a difficult rocky path through thick forest among the hills for five miles, to the pretty open country of Moogé.

Throughout the journey from the Nile, the country had been thickly populated. At Moogé we camped in a large village on the hill.

February 12.— We started at 5.25, and marched straight to Loboré, a distance of fourteen miles. The road was through forest, intersected at right-angles with deep watercourses from the mountain, called Forké, about a mile distant upon our left. This fine, rocky, and almost perpendicular hill is 2,000 feet high.

On arrival at Loboré we halted beneath a large tree, and waited for the cattle, which were some distance in the rear, owing to the difficulty in crossing the numerous steep ravines. Some work would be necessary on this road to render it possible for carts.

We had thus marched fifty-seven miles from our vessels without the necessity of firing a shot, although we were accompanied by so tempting a prize as a large herd of cattle and sheep.

The natives of Loboré soon began to collect, and the dragoman, Wāni, shortly appeared, who proved to be an old acquaintance in my former journey. This man, who had been an interpreter when a boy among the traders, spoke good Arabic, and we soon felt quite at home. Abbio, the old sheik of Loboré, appeared. This old fellow was half-blind; but he seemed very willing to assist, and, after I had explained the object of my visit, he assured me that his people would go to the vessels if accompanied by my soldiers, and that I need not be uneasy about my baggage.

The Loboré are not Bari. I was delighted to have passed the southern frontier at Moogé, and to have quitted that incomprehensible tribe. The language of the Loboré is a dialect of the Madi.

In the evening, the cattle arrived with the rearguard. I had requested the old sheik to have a zareeba prepared for them; this was quickly accomplished, therefore an ox was slaughtered as a reward for all those who had worked at the inclosure.

On 13th February "we held a regular market for the purchase of flour in exchange for sheep and goats. Many of these useful little animals were sickly, owing to the marches in the hot sun, which had created intense thirst. Upon arrival at streams upon the route, they had drunk too greedily, and some had died of inflammation.

"The natives purchased live goats at the rate of about 30lbs. of flour. This was an equal exchange in live weight of the animal; a pound of flour for a pound of goat.

"*February* 14.—The whole country turned out to hunt, and the natives returned in the evening, having only killed two buffaloes and a few small antelopes. Even the small boys are armed in this country with bows and barbed arrows, with which they shoot remarkably well.

"*February* 15.—The old sheik, Abbio, accompanied by Wāni, appeared early, together with a considerable number of natives. They selected 396 cows from my zareeba, and a similar number of men promised to start to-morrow with fifty soldiers to convey the material from the vessels.

"*February* 16.—After some delay the natives

assembled, and with horns blowing and much shouting and whistling, they at length started, together with our return sailors, and an escort of fifty soldiers.

"I shall thus, after much care and anxiety, be able to push on with a quantity of goods sufficient to open the path and to establish relations with the equatorial countries. I shall have 212 troops and a good supply of ammunition, goods, and cattle: thus there should be no insurmountable difficulty.

"I wrote to Mr. Higginbotham, also to Mr. Marcopolo, and sent the letters inclosed in a bottle.

"*February* 17.—A slight shower fell this morning. The sheik of Moogé arrived to see me last evening, and presented a fat goat.

"I am trying to persuade him and old Abbio to join in cutting the cart-road through the forest from Moogé. I gave Abbio a mixture of sulphate of zinc for his eyes, and put a mustard plaster on Wāni the interpreter's stomach. At first he said it was of no use, as it only felt like cold water, but when it began to burn, he was greatly amazed, and said the cold water had turned to fire.

"I then physicked Colonel Abd-el-Kader and Monsoor, both of whom were overheated.

"A judicious present of a few blue shirts to certain headmen put every one in good humour.

"*February* 18.—I took a stroll for some miles in the forest accompanied by Lieutenant Baker. Game was very scarce, but we at length came upon a fine herd of tétel (*Antelope Bubalis*). These having been disturbed by the noise we had made in walking over loose stony ground, dashed through the open forest, about 120 paces in my front. I shot one through the shoulder, and upon running up I found it in the act of falling.

"I then heard a shot from Lieutenant Baker on my left, to whom my shot had turned the antelopes. He had killed a very large bull by a good shot in the neck.

"This good luck was a windfall for the Loboré natives who had accompanied us; and a man immediately started off for assistance, as many men were required to transport the flesh and hides of such large animals.

"*February* 19.—The natives begged that we would again accompany them to hunt, and they started with a considerable party.

"Having formed a long line like skirmishers, with intervals of about ten yards between each, they advanced with their bows prepared, and the arrows on the string, ready for a shot on the instant should game start on foot. There were many boys of about twelve years old, all of whom were armed with bows and arrows, and they advanced in the same line with the men. There were too many people, and the game became scared; so that after a long walk, we returned to camp without having fired a shot.

"I found some very curious flowers, which issued from the ground in pods, without leaves; these burst and threw out beautiful compact silk balls in great numbers, not half of which could be returned to the pod that had scattered them.

"On 22nd February we had purchased and stored, in expectation of the arrival of the troops, 3,740lbs. of flour.

"I was determined to carry a large supply to the south, as the country had in some places been depopulated by the slave-hunters.

"*February* 23.—I went out with Lieutenant Baker, accompanied by some natives, and travelled over very likely ground, composed of forest, glades, ravines full of bamboos, &c., until we reached the base of Gebel Forké.

"We had passed over several miles and had only seen a few small antelopes, when upon ascending some rising ground in the very open forest, we caught sight of a herd of tétel bounding along through some high grass towards some low, rocky hills, a few hundred yards distant. There were many large trees growing out of the clefts of the rocks, and I proposed that Lieutenant Baker should go round the hill on my right, while I should creep quietly over the summit of the rocks, as I expected we should find the antelopes standing in some sheltered glade.

"When I arrived at the base of the small hill, which was not higher than seventy or eighty feet, and was composed of large masses of granite, I carefully ascended, without making the slightest noise.

"On arrival at the denuded summit, I was well concealed by a detached block of granite that lay upon a flat weather-worn surface of the same rock.

"I raised my head, and looked in vain for the antelopes. The ground was a beautiful park, characterized by numerous masses of granite, like ruined castles, among trees of all shades of green. The ground was covered with young grass about six inches high, which had sprung up after the annual fire that had destroyed the last year's dry herbage.

"I could see no game. Presently I observed the native, who was a few yards on my left, making eager gestures, and pointing with his finger in order to direct my attention. I at once perceived a family of wild pigs which had emerged from some bush, and were quietly feeding along the glade, so that they would shortly pass in front of me within sixty yards.

"The natives love pork beyond all other flesh, thus I had a good opportunity for showing them a little treat. With a quick right and left shot I knocked over two pigs, and reloading the "Dutchman" in a few instants, I rolled over a boar that had galloped off to about 120 yards' distance. This animal recovered itself and got away to some place of cover.

"Upon the arrival of Lieutenant Baker and the natives, we tracked the blood for about 300 yards to a small plot of high grass that had escaped the fire. I knew that we must find the wounded boar in this retreat. I therefore ordered the natives to beat it out. The boar soon broke cover and galloped off along the open, but quickly rolled over as a shot from the "Dutchman" struck it behind the shoulder. The natives were delighted with the success of the rifle, as it had produced three fine pigs for their service within a few minutes.

"February 24.—The whole of the troops and baggage from the vessels arrived safely to-day, together with the cattle and sheep, thus all my arrangements have, thank God, speeded, and I am now in possession of my force and material."

Major Abdullah delivered his report. As I had expected, he had been attacked in great force by the natives after my departure. The Baris, as usual, had employed treachery, which had very nearly succeeded.

A day or two after I had left the vessels, several natives had desired to communicate with Major Abdullah. These men declared that they had nothing to do with Beddēn, and that all the Baris of the east side of the Nile desired peace.

It would have been natural to suppose that after so recent an example of treachery on the part of Beddēn, Major Abdullah would have been keenly suspicious; he was nevertheless deceived by the specious promises of the wily Baris. This officer knew my wish for peace and good-will, and he trusted to be able to assure me, that after my departure he had been able to establish amicable relations with our late enemies.

The messengers returned to their villages, and natives visited the camp with fowls, tobacco, and various articles for sale. The soldiers were ready purchasers, as they were well supplied with beads, zinc mirrors, and various trifles which they had recently obtained from the government magazines. The fault of my men lay in their extravagance, and they quickly spoiled a market by offering too much. The trade commenced vigorously, and the now peaceable Baris thronged to the vessels, and mixed freely with the officers and troops.

On the night of February 17, 1872, the troops were fast asleep. Confidence had been thoroughly established, and there was no apprehension of coming danger. My officers and men were careless of precautions; the sentries were nearly all asleep. The cannon had been loaded with shell instead of canister. The Woolwich tubes had been put away so safely that they could not be found when wanted. The gun had not been sighted for close distance, neither had any of my most positive instructions been carried out. The artillerymen were sound asleep upon their mats around their neglected gun.

I have already described the tactics of Bari night attacks. There can be no doubt that their scouts must have crept close to the camp, and must have returned to the main body without having been observed by the sentries. The report that all were asleep, or off their guard, had been delivered.

It is supposed that some thousands of the enemy moved cautiously forward, concealed by the darkness, upon ground that otherwise could not have admitted a stealthy approach.

Fortunately for the expedition, one or two of the cattle sentries were awake, otherwise the entire force must have been massacred.

The Baris crept forward without being observed, until they arrived near the silent and sleepy camp. Then with sudden shrieks and yells they rushed forward in a mass upon the unsuspecting troops.

A slight impediment may check an assault during the darkness of night. The only protection to the position was a simple line of thorn branches laid in a row about twenty paces in the front, running parallel with the river. The naked legs of the first line of the enemy must have become entangled in this unseen obstruction for a few seconds, which caused sufficient confusion to destroy the momentum of the first rush forward.

The sentries by the ravine immediately fired, and the sixty men who formed the cattle guard quickly responded, and poured a fire into the enemy's flank.

The delay caused by the thorns was only momentary, but it had been sufficient to allow the troops to awaken and to clutch their muskets. Here was a glorious opportunity for the gun, if loaded with canister and ready at point-blank range!

The enemy were already at the muzzle. The Egyptian artillerymen forsook their piece and fled ignominiously to the vessels for protection. Only one fine fellow had stood by the gun, and he pulled the lanyard when the crowd of natives were almost upon him. Where were the unfailing English tubes? An Egyptian tube had been placed in the vent in spite of all my orders. It *missed fire!*

The gun that should have swept a clear road through the enemy was silent, and the gallant soldier who alone had stood faithful at his post was immediately speared through the body, and fell dead. The gun was in the hands of the Baris.

The troops, seized with a panic, fled on board the vessels, where they were with difficulty rallied by their officers so as to open fire from the protection of the banks of the river.

The Baris were prepared with fire to burn the ships; and they not only succeeded in throwing fire within the vessels, but they killed an unfortunate woman with a lance, who was on the fore part of a noggur.

Troops had rushed into the cabins and upon the

NIGHT ATTACK UPON ABDULLAH'S DETACHMENT; THE BARIS CAPTURE THE GUN.

Vol. ii. p. 53.

poop-deck of my diahbeeah, from which they now opened fire upon the enemy, who were at the same time exposed to a flank fire from the sixty cattle guards. This checked the advance, and the major, Abdullah, succeeded in leading his men forward and recapturing the gun. At length a tube was found and fitted in the vent. Fortunately the Baris were ignorant, and the lanyard was lying by the gun. Another tube missed fire, but after some delay, the gun at length spoke, but unfortunately not with canister.

It was already too hot for the Baris, who were between two fires, and two shots from the cannon settled the affair and determined the retreat.

I could not have believed in such negligence and folly had I not had a long experience of Egyptian troops, whether brown or black. These people can generally be surprised, unless their commanding officer is vigilant and most severe. Little or no dependence can be placed on the non-commissioned officers; these are ignorant, thoughtless people, who having learnt from their Mohammedan teachers to trust themselves to God, would seldom keep awake unless kept to their duty by their superior officers.

On the morning following this attack, the big drums of the natives were sounding in all directions upon both sides of the river. Thousands of Baris had congregated upon the various heights, and it appeared that a general attack would be renewed upon the camp.

It was not considered safe to drive the cattle out to pasturage.

There can be no doubt that with a force of 145 men, Major Abdullah should have anchored his vessels a few yards from the shore, and have then made a vigorous attack upon the Baris. He was provided with Hale's rockets in addition to the fieldpiece; and he should have given the enemy a severe example.

Instead of assuming the offensive, he remained inactive, which so encouraged the enemy that they gathered from every quarter, and naturally concluded that the troops had received a panic from the night attack.

At this critical time, the scarlet uniforms of my fifty men appeared in the rear of the natives, together with 400 of the Loboré. Some of my men belonged to the "Forty Thieves;" and the Baris upon seeing the arrival of so powerful a re-inforcement, immediately dispersed, with much blowing of horns and whistles in defiance of Major Abdullah.

It was declared that the Baris had suffered severely during the night attack; but I had ceased to pay much attention to the official reports of the enemy's losses.

Between the river and Loboré, the troops had marched without opposition, and they had followed my instructions by leaving cows for payment at every night's halting-place.

I now divided the flour into loads of sixty pounds each, packed in baskets covered with raw hide.

I thus carried 3,600lbs. by sixty porters. My troops were now relieved from much weight, as I engaged 500 natives for the journey to the interior; at the same time I ordered every soldier to carry six pounds of flour in addition to his knapsack and accoutrements. Every one of my men was provided with a small tanned goatskin stripped from the animal (like a stocking from the leg) and secured at one end like a bag. These little chorābs, or travelling sacks, were most convenient, and were well adapted for carrying flour, as they were easily strapped to the top of the knapsack.

I lost no time in preparing for a move forward. Wāni the interpreter was invaluable, as he superintended all the arrangements necessary for collecting the carriers.

The cattle were confined within the kraal waiting for selection. About 1,000 natives assembled, and they were allowed to enter the zareeba and choose their cows, in parties of four at one time, to prevent confusion.

This was a tedious operation, as the Loboré carriers were almost as particular in their selection of cattle as ladies are supposed to be in the choice of their dresses.

February 27.—The Loboré were exceedingly quiet and orderly in their conduct, and 500 cows having been received by as many natives, they returned to their homes to make arrangements for the journey to Fatiko. I find the following extract in my journal of this date :—

"The Loboré will be useful allies as they are enemies of the Bari, and their country is well situated, lying between Bari and Madi, on the route to Fatiko; thus they will be ready as carriers for both ends of the line.

"If I can obtain eighty camels from Khartoum, I can get the steamer along without any serious difficulty, as the Loboré natives can be engaged to make the road; but nothing can prosper until a regular camel transport service shall be established.

"I am sadly in want of troops and European officers. There should be 200 men in four parties stationed at intervals along the line to direct the natives in opening the road.

"A soldier deserted and ran away with his arms and ammunition to some distant village. I immediately called Wāni and the old sheik Abbio, to whom I explained that I should hold them responsible if the deserter were not captured. They sent out natives in all directions in search.

"*February* 28.—The natives returned, saying they had found the deserter about half a march distant, but they could not seize him alive, as he threatened to shoot them; at the same time they were afraid to kill him, as he was my soldier.

"I immediately sent a sergeant and three men of 'The Forty' to take him prisoner.

"In the evening the soldiers returned, having captured the deserter. I left him in irons to be kept at hard labour by the sheik Abbio at Loboré, until I should return to the country. This is a good lesson to the troops.

"The natives had a grand dance to-day; the

men and women as usual naked, leaping, and yelling wild songs to an extraordinary accompaniment of music, produced by beating a long stick of extremely hard wood with a short stick of the same substance. Some of the girls were pretty, but being smeared with red ochre and fat, they were not attractive. The natives were very civil, and although at least a thousand were present, they immediately made room for me upon my arrival, that I might have a good place to witness their performance."

I was much struck with a simple arrangement made use of by the old people to support the back in lieu of an arm-chair. Each person had a cord knotted by the ends so as to form an endless loop or hoop. The size depended upon the measurement required, so that if the hoop were thrown over the body when in a sitting posture upon the ground, with the knees raised, the rope would form a hoop around the forepart of the knees and the small of the back, which would thus be supported.

The Loboré are great workers in iron, which is used, generally in the manufacture of ornaments. Large rings of this metal are worn round the neck, and upon the arms and ankles. Many of these ankle-rings are of extreme thickness, and would suffice for the punishment of prisoners. I was interested with the mechanical contrivance of the Loboré for detaching the heavy metal anklets, which, when hammered firmly together, appeared to be hopeless fixtures in the absence of a file.

I required several irons to construct manacles for the deserter, thus I had purchased the massive ornaments which had to be detached from the ankles of the owner.

The man sat upon the ground. A stick of hard, unyielding wood was thrust through the ring beneath the ankle, so that each end of the stick rested on the earth. A man secured one end by standing upon it, while another placed a stone upon the stick thus secured, which he used as a fulcrum. The lever employed was a piece of Abdnoos, which worked upon the stone, and pressed down the base of the ring at the same time that it opened the joint sufficiently to allow it to be passed over the thin portion of the leg.

I never saw this ingenious application of the lever among other tribes than the Loboré. The usual method among the Madi is far more simple, but requires a certain number of men, and places the patient in an uncomfortable position. A rope is fastened to each side of the ring, upon which a number of men haul in opposite directions until they have opened the joint sufficiently to detach it from the leg.

On 29th February we were ready for the start. The loads were all prepared and arranged in separate divisions of twenty each, under the charge of selected officers and men.

The big nogāra had sounded, the natives collected, and each man stood by his load; thus twenty-five gangs of twenty each should have stood in line.

I now discovered that the vaunted honesty of the Loboré was of the same order as that of other negroes. Five hundred cows had been given to as many natives, for all of which the sheik Abbio had declared himself responsible. The big nogāra sounded in vain. After waiting for some hours, and sending numerous messengers to as many villages, only 433 carriers could be mustered; thus sixty-seven had eloped with as many cows!

No one can imagine the trouble of such a journey with so long a retinue of carriers, most of whom are dishonest, and only seek an opportunity to abscond upon the road.

The Loboré are immensely powerful men, and they carried the boxes of Hale's rockets as single loads, although weighing upwards of seventy-two pounds. At the same time they quarrelled among themselves as to the choice of parcels, and I could with difficulty prevail upon them to carry the zinc boat, although it did not exceed 130lbs. Four men actually refused to touch it, as it sat uneasily upon their heads.

This handy little vessel was made of zinc upon an iron framework, and would contain four people upon a pinch, but would easily convey three across a river. I had arranged it upon two stout bamboos so adjusted that four men should have carried it with ease. The natives demanded eight, but I at length compromised for six.

The delay caused by the non-appearance of the sixty-seven carriers was extremely dangerous, as it increased the chance of desertions. Already many had volunteered to search for their missing friends, which would have resulted in a search for them also, until my body of carriers would have melted away.

Fortunately I had made a considerable allowance for desertions on the road, and I could manage to start with the assistance of the soldiers and their wives, among whom I divided many baskets of flour.

At 3.25 p.m. we started.

There was no danger now that we had passed the Bari tribe, therefore we could push on with an advance guard of five picked men of "The Forty," who always accompanied us, and leave the charge of the march and baggage to Colonel Abd-el-Kader and the various officers.

We accordingly marched, at four miles an hour, through a rocky and hilly country, generally wooded, which would have been an awkward position if held by an enemy.

At 6 p.m. we halted at a rocky ravine where water had been expected by our guide. To our dismay we found it nearly dry, and it was necessary to dig temporary wells in the sand to procure a supply for ourselves, while the horses were forced to content themselves with the impure pool.

It quickly became dark, and the troops and baggage were far behind. We therefore gathered wood and made a blazing fire to show our position; at the same time a bugler and drummer who had accompanied us, made as much noise as possible from the summit of a small hill.

At 7.30 p.m. the cattle arrived by torchlight, together with the troops and baggage. Some of the Loboré carriers had already deserted on the road, which had caused much delay.

We had marched nine miles, but it was absolutely necessary to send four men back to Loboré, to insist upon fresh carriers being immediately sent to replace the runaways.

On March 1 we started at half-past six A.M., after a terrific scramble for loads by 400 Loboré carriers, who rushed in and tugged and wrestled for their packages like wolves over a carcase. Boxes were turned upside down, and carried in that manner with an utter disregard for the contents.

The inverted canteen was discovered upon the head of a brutal Loboré, whose body was being basted with Cognac and gin that showered from the loosened stoppers of the decanters.

I never saw such a wild pack of savages; they were only fit to carry the elephants' tusks of the traders; but any civilized baggage ran a risk of instant destruction.

The old sheik, Abbio, had given me his son to keep order among the people. This young man was about twenty-seven years of age, but, although respectable in appearance, he did not appear to have the slightest control over his people, and he regarded their desertions with seeming indifference.

I had a strong suspicion that he might quietly abscond at night, in which case every man would instantly follow his example. I therefore ordered a light thong of leather to be attached to the iron collar worn as an ornament upon his neck, and I trusted him to the surveillance of a couple of soldiers told off as his guard of honour.

We marched south for sixteen miles through a fine country of hills and low forest, where the villages of the Madi had been mostly destroyed by the slave-hunting parties of Abou Saood.

We passed large tracts of land that had formerly been in a high state of cultivation, and the charred remains of numerous villages bespoke the desolation caused by these brigands of the White Nile. The road was well watered by many small streams in deep gorges, until we descended to the Asua River. This was just twenty-five miles from our camp at Loboré, in latitude N., by observation, 3° 43′.

We happened to arrive at the spot where the river Atabbi joined the Asua. At this junction the Atabbi was perfectly clear, while the Asua was muddy, which proved that heavy rain had fallen in the Madi and Shooli countries, while the weather was dry in the mountains of Obbo.

The Asua flowed through a fine forest, but although the water was muddy from recent rains, the volume at this season was confined to a portion of the bed, in the deepest parts of which it did not exceed two feet six inches. The bed from bank to bank was about 120 yards in width, and the maximum rise of the river was about twelve feet. During the wet season this is a frightful torrent that acts as a barrier to any advance or retreat of troops encumbered with baggage.

Having waded through the river, we halted under the shady trees on the south side; here there was excellent herbage for the cattle, as the young grass after the annual fires was now about eight inches high, upon the rich soil near the river's bank.

Whenever we halted during daylight, I took a stroll with the rifle, accompanied by Lieutenant Baker.

We walked for some time along the banks of the river up stream without seeing any game, and I was struck with the absence of tracks of the larger animals, which coincided with my remarks on the Asua river many years previous, when I crossed it about thirty miles higher up, on my route from Latooka to Shooa.

I expected to return without seeing game, when we suddenly spied a few waterbuck in the sandy bed of the river, about 300 paces distant.

We made a good stalk, but I only wounded the animal at which I fired at about 150 yards, and they galloped off through the open forest. I heard the bullet from the left hand barrel strike a tree stem, which saved the antelope, but having quickly reloaded, I had a clear and steady shot at a long range as the large buck suddenly stopped and looked back. I put up the last sight for 250 yards and took a full bead. To my great satisfaction the waterbuck with a fine set of horns dropped dead. I could not measure the distance accurately as we had to descend a rocky bank, and then, crossing the bed of the Asua, to ascend the steep north bank before we arrived at tolerably level ground.

Upon reaching the animal, I found the bullet in the neck, where it had divided the spine. I guessed the distance at about 240 yards. Some of our Loboré natives, who had kept at a distance behind us, now came up, and in a short time the noble waterbuck was cut up and the flesh carried into camp. This species of antelope, when in good condition, weighs about thirty stone (cleaned).

On March 2 we started at 6 A.M., and marched at a rapid rate through a hard and excellent path, which inclined upwards from the river for about eight miles.

The bush was very open, and in many portions the country was a succession of deep dells, which in the wet season were covered with high grass, but at this time the young grass was hardly three inches high, having sprouted after the recent fires.

From an altitude of about 1,000 feet above the Asua river, we had a splendid view of the entire landscape.

On the east, at about fifty miles distant, was the fine range of lofty mountains that stretched in a long line towards Latooka. On the west, on the left bank of the White Nile, which now flowed almost beneath our feet, was the precipitous mountain Neri, known by the Arab traders as Gebel Kuku. This fine mass of rock descends in a series of rugged terraces from a height of between three and four thousand feet to the Nile, at a point where the river boils through a narrow gorge between the mountains. It is in this passage that the principal falls take place which I witnessed in my former journey. At that time our path led along the rocky bank of the river, and was both difficult and dangerous.

Eight miles from the Asua river now brought us to the top of the pass, and having stopped for a few moments to take compass bearings, we began the somewhat steep descent.

Walking was preferable to riding, and after a distance of a couple of miles had been accomplished, we rounded the rocky hill by crossing a ravine upon our right, and the view of the promised land burst upon us.

The grand White Nile lay like a broad streak of silver on our right as it flowed in a calm, deep stream direct from the Albert N'yanza; at this spot above all cataracts. No water had as yet been broken by a fall; the troubles of river-life lay in the future; the journey to the sea might be said to have only just commenced. Here the entire volume flowed from the Albert N'yanza, distant hardly one degree; and here had I always hoped to bring my steamers, as the starting-point for the opening of the heart of Africa to navigation.

I was deeply mortified when I gazed upon this lovely view, and reflected upon the impossibilities that had prevented my success. Had the White Nile been open as formerly, I should have transported the necessary camels from Khartoum, and there would have been no serious difficulty in the delivery of the steamers to this point. Two or three strong pioneer parties, with native assistance, would quickly have bridged over the narrow watercourses and have cleared a rough road through the forests as the carts advanced.

It was useless to repine. I still hoped to accomplish the work.

VIEW OF THE NAVIGABLE NILE ABOVE THE LAST CATARACTS AT AFUDDO.—N. LAT. 3°·32.

We now descended into the beautiful plain, to which I had given the name Ibrahiméyah, in honour of the father of his Highness the Khedive (Ibrahim Pacha).

This point is destined to become the capital of Central Africa.

The general depot for the steamers will be near the mouth of the Un-y-Amé river; which beautiful stream, after rising in the prairies between Fatiko and Unyoro, winds through a lovely country for about eighty miles, and falls into the White Nile opposite to Gebel Kuku. The trade of Central Africa, when developed by the steamers on the Albert N'yanza, will concentrate at this spot, whence it must be conveyed by camels for 120 miles to Gondokoro, until at some future time a railway may perhaps continue the line of steam communication.

It is a curious fact that a short line of 120 miles of railway would open up the very heart of Africa to steam transport—between the Mediterranean and the equator, when the line from Cairo to Khartoum shall be completed!

The No. 10 steamer that I had brought up to Gondokoro from Khartoum was originally built in England for the mail service (per Nile) between Alexandria and Cairo, at the time when the overland route was made by vans across the desert to Suez. This steamer had sailed from London, and had arrived complete at Alexandria.

It appears almost impossible that she is now floating at an altitude of nearly 2,000 feet above the sea level; to which great elevation she has actually steamed from the Mediterranean. Thus, starting from a base line, and producing a line perpendicular to the sea level of 2,000 feet, she has climbed up the Nile to her present high position.

Accepting the approximate length of the Nile in all its windings from the Mediterranean to N. lat. 4° 38', at 3,000 miles in round numbers; this will give an average rise or fall in the river of nine inches per mile; which easily explains the position of the steamer at her most remote point below the last cataracts.

I revelled in this lovely country. The fine park-like trees were clumped in dark-green masses here and there. The tall dolape-palms (*Borassus Ethiopicus*) were scattered about the plain, sometimes singly, at others growing in considerable numbers. High and bold rocks; near and distant mountains; the richest plain imaginable in the foreground, with the clear Un-y-Amé flowing now in a shallow stream between its lofty banks, and the grand old Nile upon our right, all combined to form a landscape that produced a paradise.

The air was delightful. There was an elasticity of spirit, the result of a pure atmosphere, that made one feel happy in spite of many anxieties. My legs felt like steel as we strode along before the horses, with rifle on shoulder, into the magnificent valley, in which the mountain we had descended seemed to have taken root.

The country was full of game. Antelopes in great numbers, and in some variety, started from their repose in this beautiful wilderness, and having for a few moments regarded the strange sights of horses, and soldiers in scarlet uniform, they first trotted, and then cantered far away. The graceful leucotis stood in herds upon the river's bank, and was the last to retreat.

I selected a shady spot within a grove of hēglik-trees for a bivouac, and leaving my wife with a guard, and the horses, I at once started off with Lieutenant Baker to procure some venison.

We returned after a couple of hours, having shot five antelopes. The native name for this part of the country is Afuddo. Our present halting-place was thirty-seven miles from Loboré. Formerly there were villages in this neighbourhood, but they had been destroyed by the slave-hunters. Fortunately I had prepared a stock of flour sufficient for the entire journey to Fatiko, as this country was quite desolate.

In my last visit to this country I had thoroughly studied its features; thus I felt quite at home, and I knew my route in every direction. The mountain of Shooa was distinctly visible, where I had camped for four or five months, thus it would be impossible for the Loboré people to deceive me.

Abou Saood had four stations throughout this lovely country, *i.e.*, Fatiko, Fabbo, Faloro, and Farragenia. I was now steering for Fatiko, as it was a spot well known to me, and exactly on my proposed road to Unyoro.

On 3rd February, we marched at 6 A.M., and continued along the plain towards the rising country that led to Shooa. At six miles from the halting-place we took bearings:

Shooa hill, about 35 miles distant, bearing $162\frac{1}{2}°$
Akiko ,, ,, 16 ,, ,, ,, $321\frac{1}{2}°$
Gebel Kuku ,, 9 ,, ,, ,, $299\frac{1}{2}°$

Our course lay towards the S.S.E., beneath a wall-like range of precipitous rocky hills upon our left, in no place higher than 200 feet. The guides were at fault, and no water could be found upon the road.

A herd of tetel (*Antelope Bubalis*) upon our right tempted me, and, jumping off my horse, I made a fair stalk and killed a fine beast with the "Dutchman" at 210 yards.

Every one was thirsty, as the sun was hot, and the wall-like rocks upon our left reflected the heat. At length we discovered natives squatting upon the very summits of the perpendicular cliffs, and after some trouble we succeeded in coaxing them down. Two of these people volunteered to lead us to water, and they took us to a steep rocky ravine, in the bottom of which was a pool of dirty liquid that had been bathed in by wild buffaloes. My men quickly began to dig sand-wells with their hands, until the main body of the troops and cattle arrived.

In about an hour, I heard a great hubbub, with a noise of quarrelling and shouting; every one was running towards the spot. It appeared that a wild buffalo, which was ignorant of our arrival, had suddenly visited his drinking-place, and had thoughtlessly descended the deep and narrow gorge to drink his evening draught. The Loborés had espied him, and they immediately rushed down and overwhelmed him with lances from the cliffs above. There was now an extraordinary scene over the carcase; four hundred men scrambling over a mass of blood and entrails, fighting and tearing with each other, and cutting off pieces of flesh with their lance-heads, with which they escaped as dogs may retreat with a stolen bone.

On 4th February we started at 6.25 A.M. The advent of the buffalo was a sad misfortune, as it had supplied the natives with sufficient flesh to feed them on the road home; thus thirty Loborés had absconded during the night.

Fortunately we had already consumed many loads of flour. I was now obliged to divide two days' rations among the troops as extra weight. The light loads were then doubled. Brandy boxes of twelve bottles were now lashed together, so as to form a load of twenty-four. Several boxes of gin had been entirely destroyed by the savage carriers, who had allowed them to fall upon the rocks.

Having crossed the bends of the Un-y-Amé river twice, we halted for the night in fine open forest on the south bank, beneath a large tamarind-tree, that yielded an abundant supply of fruit for all hands.

We had only marched ten miles, owing to the delay occasioned by the desertion of the carriers.

On 5th February I led the way, as the Loboré guide professed ignorance of the route to Fatiko. The fact was, that the Lorobés had wished on the previous day to take me to Farragenia, which is two days nearer than Fatiko. Had I been ignorant of the country, we should have been deceived.

I now tied the guide by the neck, together with the sheik's son, to whom I explained that they would be shot should another man abandon his load. This had the desired effect.

I steered through low open forest, the leaves of which had been scorched off by the fire that had cleared the country. Neither a village nor the print of a human foot could be seen. This beautiful district, that had formerly abounded in villages, had been depopulated by the slave-hunters.

Having taken the Shooa mountain for a steering point, we reached the spot where in former years I had passed five months in the camp of Ibrahim. This also had been destroyed, in addition to all the numerous villages of the mountain. We had marched fourteen miles.

I gave orders that on the morrow all the troops were to appear in their best uniforms, as we were only six miles from Fatiko, the principal station, where I fully expected to meet Abou Saood himself.

On 6th February we started at 6.10 A.M. We were now in the country where I had been well known on my former exploration—in the Paradise of Africa, at an elevation of 4,000 feet above the sea.

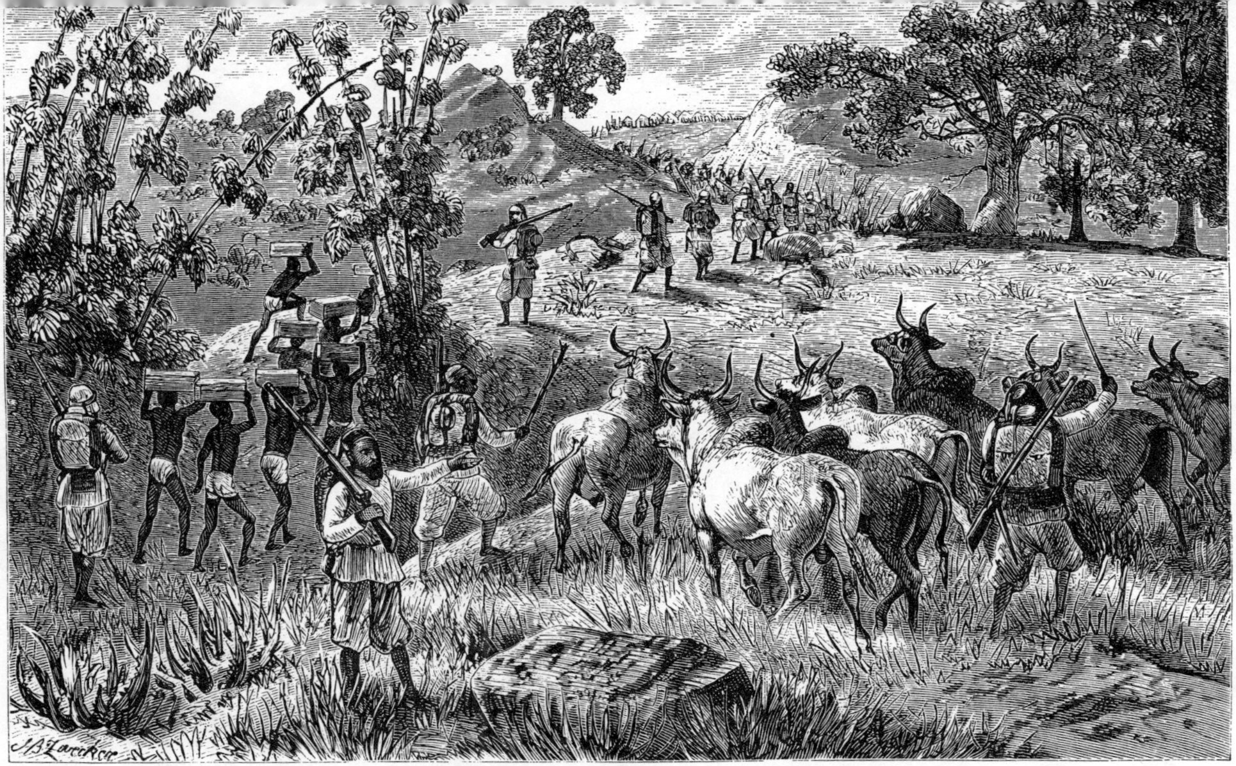

MARCHING TOWARDS FATIKO.

Vol. ii. p. 82.

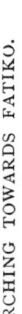

CHAPTER III.

ARRIVAL AT FATIKO.

On 6th March, 1872, we started from the bivouac at the base of the Shooa mountain at 6.10 A.M.

The troops were in excellent spirits, the air was fresh and cool in this elevated country, the horses had been well groomed, and the arms and accoutrements had been burnished on the previous afternoon, in order to make a good appearance before my old friends the natives of Fatiko and Shooa.

The bright scarlet uniforms and snow-white linen trousers of 212 men looked extremely gay upon the fresh green grass, which had lately sprung up throughout this beautiful park.

There was no enemy in this country. From a former residence of five months at Shooa, both my wife and myself were well known to the inhabitants, and I felt sure that our arrival would be hailed with gladness. In my former visit I had been a successful hunter, and had always given the flesh to the natives; thus, as the road to a negro's heart is through his stomach, I knew that my absence must have been felt, and that the recollections of past times would be savory and agreeable.

I had with me a herd of 1,078 cows and 194 sheep. No guard was necessary, and I intrusted the stock to the care of the three boatmen, and my Bari interpreter, Morgiān.

The line of march was thus arranged:—Myself, with my wife and Lieutenant Baker, on horseback in advance, preceded by the guard of five of the " Forty Thieves." Then came Colonel Abd-el-Kader and the remaining forty-three, composing the gallant " Forty." After which came the regiment, all necessarily in single file. Then came the baggage with 400 carriers, followed by the herd of cattle.

All our boys were dressed in their scarlet uniforms, and the girls and women generally had dressed in their best clothes. Little Cuckoo as usual carried my small travelling-bag upon his head, and kept his line with the other boys, all of whom assumed an air that was intended to be thoroughly regimental.

In this order the march commenced. The distance was only six miles. This was as lovely a route as could be conceived.

Magnificent trees (acacias), whose thick, dark foliage drooped near the ground, were grouped in clumps, springing from the crevices between huge blocks of granite. Brooks of the purest water rippled over the time-worn channels cut through granite plateaux, and as we halted to drink at the tempting stream, the water tasted as cold as though from a European spring.

The entire country on our left was a succession of the most beautiful rocky undulations and deep verdant glades, at the bottom of which flowed perennial streams. The banks of these rivulets were richly clothed with ornamental timber, the rich foliage contrasting strongly with the dark grey blocks of granite resembling the ruins of ancient towers.

We travelled along a kind of hog's back, which formed the watershed to the west. As we ascended, until we reached a large plateau of clean granite of about two acres, we broke upon a magnificent panorama, which commanded an extensive view of the whole country.

On the west, we looked down upon the magnificent country through which we had arrived, and the view stretched far away beyond the Nile, until it met the horizon bounded by the grey outline of the distant mountains.

No one could feel unhappy in such a scene. I trod upon my old ground, every step of which I knew, and I felt an exhilaration of spirits at the fact that I was once more here in the new capacity of a deliverer, who would be welcomed with open arms by the down-trodden natives of the country.

Having descended from the clean plateau of rock, we carefully rode across a slippery channel that had been worn by the sandy torrents of the rainy season, and once more arrived at level ground. We were now on the great table-land of Fatiko.

Upon our left, a mass of bold ruins, the skeleton granite remains of a perished mountain, which formed a shelter from the morning sun, tempted us to halt.

We had thus suddenly appeared upon the greensward of the plateau without the slightest warning to the inhabitants of Fatiko. About a mile before us stood the large station of Abou Saood, which occupied at least thirty acres. On our right we were hemmed in by a pure wall of granite, sloped like a huge whale, about three-quarters of a mile long and 100 feet high. The southern extremity of this vast block of clean granite was the rocky and fantastic hill of Fatiko crested with fine timber. To our left, and straight before us, was a perfectly flat plain like a race-course, the south end being a curious and beautiful assemblage of immense granite blocks, and splendid groups of weeping acacia.

A large village occupied the base of Fatiko hill. . . . The bugles and drums sounded "the advance." The echoes rang from the hard granite rock as the unusual sound gave the first warning of our presence.

I had dismounted from my horse, and was watching the slaver's camp with a powerful telescope, as the bugles sounded and the men fell into order.

A number of people ran out of the camp, and stared at the blaze of scarlet uniforms, which must have appeared as a larger force than the reality, owing to the bright contrast of red with the green turf.

In an instant there was confusion in the camp. I soon distinguished immense numbers of slaves being driven quickly out, and hurried away to the south. The slaver's drum beat, and a number of crimson flags were seen advancing from the camp, until they halted and formed a line close to the entrance of the village. I now saw natives rushing wildly from the villages, and appearing in all directions armed with spears and shields.

Some time elapsed before the cattle and baggage arrived. In the meantime I waited, perched on a block of granite, with my telescope, watching every movement. There was no doubt that our sudden arrival had caused intense excitement. I saw men running from the trader's station to the large village opposite, at the foot of the hill.

At length, I observed two men approaching from the trader's station.

We were not yet ready for a general advance, therefore, as the servants and carriers, cattle, &c., fell into order, the band struck up some Turkish airs, which sounded extremely wild and appropriate to the savagely-beautiful scenery around us.

In the meantime the two messengers approached. They were both filthy dirty, and appeared to be clad in dark-brown leather. One man seemed to hesitate, and stood about sixty yards distant, and demanded who we were. Upon hearing from Colonel Abd-el-Kader that it was "the Pacha," and that "he need not be afraid," he told us that Abou

Saood was at the station, and that he would run back with the news.

The other messenger came timidly forward, until he stood close beneath me. My wife was on horseback by my side.

Can it be possible?—*Mohammed*, my old Cairo servant of former years?

The grand dragoman of the lower Nile reduced to this! My wife exclaimed, "Ah, Mohammed, I am very glad to see you; but how wretched you appear!"

This was too much for the prodigal son; he seized my wife's hand to kiss, and burst into tears.

Poor Mohammed! he had gone through many trials since we last met. When I left him in Khartoum ill with guinea-worm in the leg, he was on his way to Cairo; but after my departure he had been tempted by the slave-traders to re-engage in the infamous but engrossing career, and he too had become a slave-hunter. He had never received any pay, as the custom of the slavers was to pay their men in slaves. Mohammed had never been fortunate in his domestic affairs; he was not a favourite of the ladies; thus his female slaves had all run away; his fortune had walked off, and he was left a beggar, with an overdrawn account in slaves.

Mohammed had never been a good English scholar, but want of practice during many years had almost obscured the light of his former learning, which was now reduced to the faintest glimmer.

The bugles now sounded the "advance," and we marched forward in admirable order, with the band playing.

In the meantime, several natives had approached, and having recognized Lady Baker and myself, they immediately raced back to the village with the news.

My men looked remarkably well, and the advance into Fatiko was a sight that was entirely new to Central Africa. We were in magnificent order for work, with a hardy disciplined force of 212 men, and a stock of cattle and merchandize that would carry us to any direction I might desire.

This arrival, in such perfect organization, was a fatal blow to the hopes and intrigues of Abou Saood. I was actually among them, in the very nest and hotbed of the slavers, in spite of every difficulty.

Abou Saood came to meet me, with his usual humble appearance, as we neared his station; and he cringingly invited us to rest in some huts that had just been prepared for our reception.

I declined the invitation, and prepared to camp beneath some grand acacias, among the granite rocks, about a quarter of a mile beyond, where I had rested some years ago. I accordingly led the way, until we arrived at a very beautiful spot, among some immense granite blocks, shaded by the desired foliage. Here the word was given "Halt!" and the tent was quickly pitched in a favourable locality.

We were now distant from the junction of the Un-y-Amé river 48 miles, from Loboré 85 miles, and from Gondokoro 165 miles.

Abou Saood ordered his people to bring a number of straw-roofs from his station, to form a protection for the officers. The men quickly housed themselves in temporary huts, and the cattle were placed for the night in a regular amphitheatre of rock, which formed an excellent position.

On 8th March, I reviewed the troops, and having given the natives warning of my intention, I had a sham-fight and attack of the Shooa mountain. Having fired several rockets at a supposed enemy, the troops advanced in two companies to the north and south extremities of the mountain, which they scaled with great activity, and joined their forces on the clean plateau of granite on the summit of the ridge. The effect was very good, and appeared to delight the natives, who had assembled in considerable numbers. After firing several volleys, the troops descended the hill, and marched back, with the band playing.

The music of our band being produced simply by a considerable number of bugles, drums, and cymbals, aided by a large military bass-drum, might not have been thought first rate in Europe, but in Africa it was irresistible.

The natives are passionately fond of music; and I believe the safest way to travel in those wild countries would be to play the cornet, if possible, without ceasing, which would insure a safe passage. A London organ-grinder would march through Central Africa followed by an admiring and enthusiastic crowd, who, if his tunes were lively, would form a dancing escort of the most untiring material.

As my troops returned to their quarters, with the band playing rather lively airs, we observed the women racing down from their villages, and gathering from all directions towards the common centre. As they approached nearer, the charms of music were overpowering, and, halting for an instant, they assumed what they considered the most graceful attitudes, and then danced up to the band.

In a short time my buglers could hardly blow their instruments for laughing, at the extraordinary

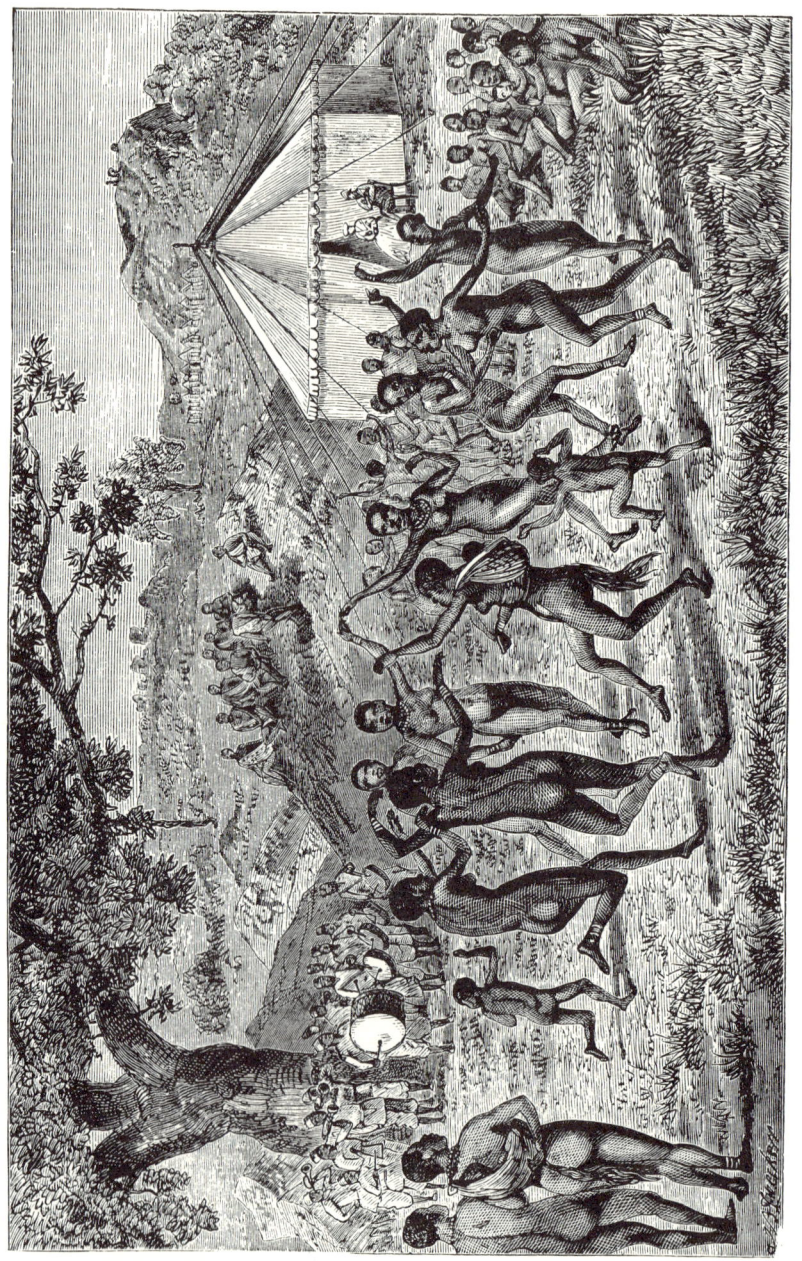

MUSICAL ENTHUSIASTS—THE WOMEN FLOCK TO THE BAND.

effect of their performance. A fantastic crowd surrounded them as they halted in our position among the rocks; and every minute added to their number.

The women throughout the Shooli are entirely naked, thus the effect of a female crowd, bounding madly about as musical enthusiasts, was very extraordinary. Even the babies were brought out to dance, and these infants, strapped to their mothers' backs, and covered with pumpkin shells, like young tortoises, were jolted about without the slightest consideration for the weakness of their necks, by their infatuated mothers.

As usual, among all tribes in Central Africa, the old women were even more determined dancers than the young girls. Several old Venuses were making themselves extremely ridiculous, as they sometimes do in civilized countries when attempting the allurements of younger days.

The men did not share in the dance, but squatted upon the rocks in great numbers to admire the music, and to witness the efforts of their wives and daughters.

The men of Shooli and Fatiko are the best proportioned that I have seen; without the extreme height of the Shillooks or Dinkas, they are muscular and well knit, and generally their faces are handsome.

The women were inclined to a short stature, but were very strong and compact. It was singular, that throughout the great Shooli country, of which Fatiko is simply a district, while the women are perfectly naked, the men are partially clothed with the skin of an antelope, slung across the shoulders, and covering the lower part of the body like a scarf. In other countries that I had passed, the men were quite naked, while the women were decently covered.

After the dance, I was visited by several natives who had known me in former years, among whom was my old guide, Gimōro, who had first led me to Unyoro. Another excellent man named Shooli now gave me all the intelligence of the country. Both these men spoke Arabic.

It was a repetition of the old story. The country was half-ruined by the acts of Abou Saood's people. The natives were afraid to resist them in this neighbourhood, as every adjacent country had been plundered, and the women and children carried off. Abou Saood had not expected that I could leave Gondokoro; but he had told the Shooli natives to attack me if I should arrive; thus on the day of my appearance, the natives, being ignorant of my presence, had considered the dreaded Pacha must be an enemy, until they had recognized my wife and myself as their old friends.

Upon that day, when I had observed the natives running to and fro with spears and shields, Abou Saood had told them to attack me at once, and he had promised that his people should assist the Fatikos; but when the natives saw our powerful force, they had known that an attack would be useless; they had accordingly sent men to discover our intentions, and these messengers had reported my return to their country in the capacity of Pacha commanding the expedition.

My old friends now assured me, in reply to my explanation of the Khedive's intentions, that the whole country would rally around a good government, and that all that the poor people desired was protection and justice. The fact of my return would give confidence throughout the country; and the news had already been carried to the great sheik, Rot Jarma, who had never visited Abou Saood or his people, but who would quickly tender his allegiance to me as the representative of the Khedive.

I told Gimoro and Shooli to inform the headmen,

and the people generally throughout the country, of my pacific intentions, and to have no fear now that the government was represented, as it would be impossible that the atrocities committed by the slave-hunters of Abou Saood should recur. At the same time I explained, that in about twenty days the contract entered into between Agād & Co. with the Soudan government would expire, and Abou Saood would be compelled to withdraw all his people from the country, which would then remain solely in the hands of the Khedive.

Throughout the subsequent expedition, I could always rely upon the fidelity of these two men, Gimōro and Shooli.

After their departure to spread the good news far and wide, I had a long conversation with my old servant, Mohammed, who I knew would give me every information respecting the acts of Abou Saood and his people, as he had been among them in these parts for many years.

He told me that my arrival at Fatiko was supposed to be impossible, as the Gondokoro natives were known to be hostile to the government; therefore it would be impossible to transport the baggage. Although the Baris were at war with the government, Abou Saood had about seventy of these natives at

Fatiko, armed with muskets, in his employ; thus he was openly in league with the enemies of the Khedive's government.

The report among the slave companies asserted that Abou Saood had been in league with Raouf Bey to frustrate the expedition; thus the conspiracy of the officers headed by Raouf Bey, which I had checkmated, was the grand move to effect a collapse of the expedition, and to leave a clear field for the slave-traders.

" Up to the present time, my arrangements have been able to overpower all opposition.

" The success of the corn collection at the moment of the conspiracy was fatal to the machinations of Raouf Bey, and secured me the confidence of the troops.

" The success of every attack that I have personally commanded has clinched this confidence.

"The trader's people are discontented with their leaders; they are without clothes or wages.

" Their parties have been massacred in several directions by the natives. Nearly 500 loads of ivory have been burned, together with one of their stations, by a night attack of the Madi, in which the slave-hunters lost thirty-five killed, and the rest of the party only escaped in the darkness, and fled to the forests.

"Thus I come upon them at a moment when they are divided in their feelings. A dread of the government is mingled with confidence in the arrival of a strong military force, which would be auxiliary in the event of a general uprising of the country."

I found several of my old men engaged as slave-hunters. These people, who had behaved well on my former voyage, confided all the news, and were willing to serve the government. Kamrasi, the former king of Unyoro was dead, and had been succeeded by his son, Kabba Réga.

Some few of the people of Abou Saood had been on a visit to the king M'tésé at Uganda. This powerful ruler had been much improved by his personal communication with the traders of Zanzibar. He had become a Mohammedan, and had built a mosque. Even his vizier said his daily prayers like a good Mūssulman, and M'tésé no longer murdered his wives. If he cut the throat of either man or beast, it was now done in the name of God, and the king had become quite civilized, according to the report of the Arab envoys. He kept clerks who could correspond, by letters, in Arabic, and he had a regiment armed with a thousand guns, in addition to the numerous forces at his command.

The Arab envoys of Abou Saood had been treated

like dogs by the great M'tésé, and they had slunk back abashed, and were only glad to be allowed to depart. They declared that such a country would not suit their business: the people were too strong for them; and the traders from Zanzibar purchased their ivory from M'tésé with cotton stuffs, silks, guns, and powder, brass-coil bracelets, beads, &c. The beads were exchanged by equal weight for ivory.

"Even at Fatiko the brass-coil bracelets from Zanzibar are now common. Some of Abou Saood's people are actually dressed in Manchester manufactures that have arrived *viâ* Zanzibar at Unyoro. This is a terrible disgrace to the Soudan authorities; thus the Zanzibar traders are purchasing by legitimate dealing ivory that should, geographically speaking, belong to Cairo.

"While fair dealing is the rule south of the equator, piracy and ruin are the rule of the north.

"Abou Saood and his people are now in a dilemma. For many years they have pillaged the country, and after having taught the natives to regard cows as the only medium of exchange for ivory, they have at length exhausted the cattle. Thus the transport of their large stock of ivory has for a time become impossible, as sufficient cows cannot be collected for the purpose.

"Every load from Fatiko to Ismailïa (Gondokoro) requires two cows; one to Loboré, and another thence to the journey's end.

"By the Nile traders' arrangements, the companies of Abou Saood receive as their perquisite one-third of all the cattle that may be stolen in successful razzias.

"The consumption of cattle by these brigands is enormous. All flour is purchased in exchange for flesh, while flesh is also necessary for food; thus the cow is being eaten at both ends.

"The frightful drain upon the country may be imagined by the following calculation, which is certainly below the truth :—

"If 1,000 loads of ivory must be carried to Ismailïa,

2,000 cows are required as payment of carriers;

To capture in a razzia 3,000 cows,

1,000 belong to the brigands as their perquisite;

300 are necessary to feed the native carriers and soldiers during the journey;

3,300 cows are required to deliver 1,000 loads of ivory a distance of 165 miles, from Fatiko to Ismailïa (Gondokoro).

A station of 350 men consumes daily . . . . 700lbs.

	In addition, they require to exchange for flour	350lbs.
	Daily consumption of flesh	1,050lbs.

"The oxen of the country do not average more than 170lbs. cleaned.

2,255 beasts are thus required annually.

5,555 oxen are necessary to feed and pay for the transport from a station only 350 strong; according to the customs of White Nile brigandage.

"It must be remembered that at least a thousand, and sometimes double that number of slaves, are prisoners in each station. All these must be fed. The same principle is adopted in the exchange of flesh for flour; thus the expenditure of cattle is frightful. Not only oxen, but all the breeding cows and young calves are killed without the slightest reflection. No country can support such wilful waste; thus after many years of ravage, this beautiful country has become almost barren of cattle. The central districts occupied by the slave-traders having been denuded of cattle, it has become necessary to make journeys to distant countries."

The slave-hunters of Abou Saood had recently suffered a terrible defeat, at the hands of the warlike tribe of Umiro, which was a just reward for the horrible treachery of their party.

A man named Ali Hussein was a well-known *employé* of Abou Saood. This ruffian was an Arab. He was a tall, wiry fellow, with a determined but brutal cast of countenance, who was celebrated as a scoundrel among scoundrels. Even his fellows dreaded his brutality. There was no crime that he had not committed; and as his only virtue was extreme daring, his reputation was terrible among the native population.

This fellow had waited upon my orders daily since my arrival at Fatiko.

At the death of the former vakeel of Fatiko, Ali Hussein had succeeded to the command of the station.

He had arranged to make a descent upon the Umiro tribe, about six days' march to the south-east.

He accordingly sent natives as spies, with specious messages to the Umiro, announcing his intention of visiting them to purchase ivory.

With a party increased by volunteers from other stations to a force of about 300 men, he arrived at Umiro.

The simple natives received him gladly, and showed extreme hospitality. The country was thickly populated, and abounded with vast herds of the finest cattle.

After a week's sojourn among the Umiro, during which he had received large presents of elephants' tusks, and seventy head of oxen from the confiding natives, the treacherous ruffian gave an order to his brigands at sunset. They were to be under arms an hour before daybreak on the following morning, to set fire to the adjacent villages of their generous hosts, and to capture their large herds of cattle, together with their women and children.

At the time appointed, while every Umiro slept unconscious of approaching danger, several villages were surrounded, and volleys of musketry were poured upon the sleeping inmates. The straw huts were ignited, and the flames rapidly spread, while a massacre commenced similar to the butcheries to which the slave-hunters were so well accustomed.

The Umiro, thus taken by surprise, and appalled by so dastardly a treachery, were easily defeated. Their children and wives were captured, together with large herds of cattle, which are celebrated for their size. All these were driven in triumph to Fatiko.

The success of this infernal scheme, raised the reputation of Ali Hussein to the highest pitch.

The reports of the vast pastoral wealth of the Umiro excited the cupidity of the various companies in the stations of Abou Saood.

It was determined to make a grand attack upon a people, who, in spite of their warlike character, had exhibited a total want of power to resist.

Ali Hussein sent an expedition of about 350 men, in addition to a large number of Fatiko allies. They arrived on the borders of Umiro, within about an hour's march of the villages doomed to pillage. The party were under the command of a notorious ruffian named Lāzim, whom I had known during my former exploration.

Upon arrival in the Umiro country, during the night after a forced march, he sent a party of 103 men, together with about 150 natives, to attack the villages by a surprise at dawn, and to capture the slaves and cattle in the usual manner.

The party started at the early hour of first cockcrow, while the main body under Lāzim waited for the result.

Hours passed, but the company did not return. A few shots had been heard in the distance.

The country was clear and open, but nothing could be seen. There was no lowing of cattle, neither did the heavy clouds of smoke, usual on such occasions, point out the direction of burning villages.

Presently, drums were heard in every direction, the horns and whistles of the Umiro sounded the alarm, and large bodies of natives rushed across the plain to the attack of Lāzim's party.

They had just time to form, and to post the men around the strong cattle kraal, which they had occupied, when the stream of enemies came down upon them.

Upon the open plain, the Umiro had no chance in attacking so well-defended a position, and the muskets, loaded with heavy mould shot, told with great effect upon the naked bodies of the assailants.

The Umiro were beaten back with some loss, and the slave-hunters held the position, although in a state of terror, as they felt that some terrible calamity must have befallen the party which had started to surprise the villages.

After dark, a Bari native cried out to the sentries to let him pass. This was a wounded man of their own party, the *only survivor* of all those who had left the main body on that morning.

The Bari described, that the Umiro, having gained information of the intended attack, had lain in ambush within high withered grass, in which they had awaited the arrival of their assailants.

The slave-hunters were advancing as usual, in single file, along the narrow track through the high grass, unsuspicious of an enemy, when the Umiro rushed from both sides of the ambuscade upon them.

Taken by surprise, a panic seized the slave-hunters, very few of whom had time to fire their muskets before they were speared by the pitiless Umiro, who wreaked wholesale vengeance by the massacre of the entire party of 103 of Abou Saood's men and about 150 of their allies.

The main body under Lāzim were completely cowed, as they feared an overwhelming attack that might exhaust their ammunition. The Umiro had now become possessed of 103 guns and several large cases of cartridges, in addition to those in the pouches of the soldiers.

Night favoured the retreat, and the remnant of the expedition under Lāzim returned by forced marches to Fatiko.

The defeat had spread consternation among the various stations, as it followed closely upon the destruction of a station belonging to Abou Saood in the Madi country.

DESTRUCTION OF JUSEF'S STATION.

This zareeba had been under the command of a vakeel named Jusef, who had exasperated the natives by continual acts of treachery and slave-hunting. They had accordingly combined to attack the station at night, and had set fire to the straw huts, by shooting red-hot arrows into the inflammable thatched roofs.

These calamities had happened since the arrival of Abou Saood in the Shooli country, and it was he who had given the order to attack the Umiro. His own people, being naturally superstitious, thought he had brought bad luck with him.

It appeared that when Abou Saood had first arrived at Fatiko from Gondokoro, the vakeels of his different stations were all prepared for the journey to deliver the ivory. They had given the cattle obtained in the first attack upon Umiro to the native carriers of Madi and Shooli, and the ivory had been arranged in about 2,000 loads for transport.

The sudden arrival of Abou Saood changed all their plans, as he immediately gave orders to return the ivory to the store huts; he did not intend to deliver it at Gondokoro that year. He also sent a letter to his Latooka station, nine days' march to the north-east, together with a party of eighty men, with instructions to his vakeel to deliver the ivory at the Bohr station below Gondokoro.

He thus hoped to defraud the government out of the two-fifths due to them by contract with Agād. At the same time, he had intended to remain concealed in the interior of the country until I should have returned to England; after which he had no doubt that affairs would continue in their original position.

It may be imagined that my sudden arrival at Fatiko had disconcerted all his plans.

In spite of his extreme cunning, he had overestimated his own power of intrigue, and he had mismanaged his affairs.

According to the agreement with Agād & Co., the representative of that firm, Abou Saood, had contracted to supply the government troops with all provisions at a given price, including even sheep and butter. He was also to assist the government expedition in every manner, and to supply not only carriers, but even troops, should they be necessary.

I read this contract to some of his principal men, who fairly laughed outright at the audacity of Abou Saood in subscribing to such utter falsehoods.

Not only had he secretly fraternised with the

enemy, instead of assisting the government, but he had cautioned the Baris not to carry our loads, and he had incited the Fatiko natives to attack us. The supply of food was too ridiculous. Instead of giving to the troops, he had been obliged to borrow corn from the government magazines at Gondokoro for his own people, and I had given him 200 cattle to save the men from famine.

The deceit and treachery of this man were beyond belief. He now came to me daily at Fatiko, and swore, by the eyes of the Prophet, eternal fidelity. He wished to kiss my hand, and to assure me how little his real character had been understood, and that he felt sure I had been influenced against him by others, but that in reality I had no servant so devoted as himself. He declared that he had only attacked the Shir and stolen their cows in order to supply the government troops with cattle according to contract.

In spite of these protestations, he could not explain his reason for having returned the ivory to store, instead of transporting it to Gondokoro. He therefore met the difficulty by a flat denial, as usual, calling upon the Prophet as a witness.

Only a few days of his contract remained, at the expiration of which he should have withdrawn his establishments from the country, according to my written orders that had been given many months ago.

He had entirely ignored these orders, as he had never expected my arrival; therefore he had concealed all such instructions from his people, in the hope that my term of service would expire fruitlessly at Gondokoro, and that, after my departure, he would have little difficulty in arranging for the future with his friend Raouf Bey, who would most probably succeed to the command.

I at once issued written orders to the vakeels of his different stations, that, at the end of the month Mohurram, the contract with Agād would cease, and that all future action would be illegal.

I gave all *employés* of Abou Saood due notice, that they must either quit the country, or become respectable subjects.

I gave them permission to settle at Gondokoro, and to commence farms on the fertile islands of the Nile free of all taxation.

Or, should they wish to enter the government service as irregular troops, I offered the same pay as the regulars, with the advantage of an annual engagement.

I met several headmen whom I had known in my

former journey. These men found fault with Abou Saood for having left them in the dark respecting the contract with the government; and they at once declared that they should be happy to serve as irregulars at the expiration of the agreement.

There was a great difficulty respecting the ivory which comprised in all the stations 3,200 tusks.

The cattle that had been given to the native carriers for the transport of the ivory to Gondokoro had only partially been returned by the disappointed Madi. Many of these people had killed and eaten the beasts, and had declared that they had died, when they found the necessity of restoring them.

It was now necessary to move the ivory, together with all the establishments, to Gondokoro. This would require at least 6,000 cows. It was a complete fix. There were no cows in any of Abou Saood's stations; they had all been consumed; and he now came to me with a request that I would lend him eighty cows, as his people had nothing to eat.

It was clearly impossible to move the ivory. Thus, in spite of my orders given to Abou Saood about ten months previous, the opportunity of moving had been lost, and the time of departure was reduced to *sine die*. This was a hopeless condition of affairs. There were no cattle in Abou Saood's possession, and without cattle, the ivory could not be moved. At the same time, it would be impossible for me to permit him to make razzias upon distant countries, as I had arrived to establish government, and to afford protection to all tribes that would declare their allegiance.

I now discovered that the principal vakeel of Abou Saood, named Mohammed Wat-el-Mek, had only recently started with a large force, by Abou Saood's orders, to invade the Koshi country on the west side of the White Nile, close to its exit from the Albert N'yanza.

This was a tribe that could not possibly have interfered with Abou Saood; but as the cattle had been exhausted on the east bank of the river, he had commenced a series of razzias upon the west. The Koshi were people with whom friendship should have been established, as they were on the navigable Nile that would eventually be traversed by the steamer, when constructed at Ibrahiméyah. It was thus that all tribes were rendered hostile by the slave-hunters.

Mohammed Wat-el-Mek (son of the king) was the man who had first discovered and opened up the countries south of Gondokoro. This person was a curious but useful character that I had always wished to employ, as he had great power with the natives, and he knew every nook and corner of the country.

I had known him during my former journey, and it appears that he had always wished to serve me in the present expedition. The slave-traders of Khartoum had been determined to prevent Wat-el-Mek from communicating with me; thus, when I had arrived in Khartoum, this important personage had actually been there; but he had been quickly sent by Abou Saood under some frivolous pretext, up the Blue Nile, to keep him out of the way.

On arrival at Gondokoro, he had studiously been retained on the west bank of the river, and his name had been kept so secret, that I had never heard it mentioned. Thus, although both at Khartoum and at Gondokoro Wat-el-Mek had been within a few hundred paces of me, I had always supposed that he was in Central Africa.

Abou Saood now declared that Wat-el-Mek had started many days ago from Fatiko to Koshi; but I subsequently discovered that he had only left Fatiko on the morning of my arrival, and that he was kept waiting at Fabbo station, only twenty-two miles west of Fatiko, for several days, while I had been told by Abou Saood that he had gone to Koshi.

Mohammed Wat-el-Mek was the son of a petty king far away up the Blue Nile, beyond Fazoklé.

He had in early life been a sergeant or choush in the Egyptian army; but having an adventurous disposition, he had taken to the White Nile, as the vakeel of Andrea Debono, a Maltese ivory merchant.

Mr. Debono, being a British subject, retired from the trade when the slave-hunting arrived at such a pitch that it became impossible for Europeans to continue business on the White Nile.[1]

Debono had amassed a considerable fortune entirely through the energy of Wat-el-Mek, who had pushed into the interior, and had established his stations with considerable forethought and skill throughout the formerly unvisited Madi country.

Wat-el-Mek was an exceedingly black man, about the middle height, and much pitted with the small-pox. While in the service of Debono, he had commanded the station of Faloro, where he had most hospitably received Speke and Grant on their arrival from Zanzibar. These great travellers were entertained at Faloro during many weeks, and were afterwards conducted by their host to Gondokoro, where I had the good fortune to meet them.

[1] The slave trade arrived at such a maximum that all European traders in ivory were driven from the White Nile, including Mr. Petherick, the British Consul.

CHARACTER OF WAT-EL-MEK.

Wat-el-Mek was a very courageous fellow; and although he would not perhaps have been considered a good character at a London police-court, he was a man who would be most useful to an expedition in Central Africa, where his vicious propensities could be restrained by the discipline of government.

When Speke parted from him at Gondokoro, he presented him with a beautiful double-barrelled gun by Blissett, in addition to other articles.

The worst vice of this man was drinking. When drunk, he could be induced to yield to any absurdity.

However, with all his faults, I should have been glad of Wat-el-Mek to command the irregular force.

In the days when Debono was the proprietor of the Madi station, Wat-el-Mek had been the sole vakeel; and although he was a tyrant, he was not disliked by the natives. Since Debono had sold his stations to the firm of Agād & Co., every separate camp was governed by an independent vakeel; thus there were many tyrants instead of one.

These numerous vakeels acted in opposition to each other in the purchase of ivory. If a native of Fatiko should take a tusk to sell at the station of Fabbo, he would run the chance of being shot upon his return; and this system of attempted monopoly was carried out throughout the country. This naturally resulted in anarchy. Although all the vakeels and companies belonged to one firm, they acted as rival companies. Thus, if slaves ran away from one station and took shelter with the natives of a village belonging to the people of another vakeel, an attack would be made upon the village that harboured the runaways, and their women and children would be immediately captured.

This onslaught on the village under the protection of a certain station would be quickly returned by a counter attack upon a village belonging to the encroaching vakeel. This system was purposely adopted, as it served to divide the country into opposing sections, which prevented the natives from forming a general coalition.

It may readily be imagined that my arrival was hailed with general satisfaction by the natives throughout the country. Should a stranger have filled my position, there might have been some suspicion in the minds of the natives, but I had been so well known during my former journey, that the people accepted the new government with thorough confidence.

Wat-el-Mek, who was always the discoverer of unknown lands, had lately visited a new country in the east.

It may be remembered by the readers of "The Albert N'yanza" that shortly before my return from Shooa (only six miles from Fatiko) a new country named Lira had been discovered by the vakeel of Koorshad Agha—"Ibrahim." Poor Ibrahim was dead, otherwise I should have had a good and dependable man.

The Lira country was rich in ivory, and the greatest prize discovered was the presence of donkeys, which are quite unknown in the White Nile districts.

Wat-el-Mek had now penetrated beyond Lira, and had reached the country of Langgo, which was exceedingly interesting.

From the description of the people, it appeared that the portion of the Langgo visited by them was entirely different from the country between Gondokoro and Unyoro.

The expedition *had crossed the Sobat river*, and had arrived in the Langgo about 130 miles due east of Fatiko. They described the country as similar to portions of the Soudan. Generally, flat plains of the rich grass known as negheel, which never grows high, and is the finest pasturage. The trees were for the most part Soont (*Acacia Arabica*), which is not met with in the White Nile countries south of the Sobat junction.

The Langgos were an immense tribe, but were, like the Baris, divided under many chiefs. These people were exceedingly large and powerful, and were esteemed as great warriors. They seldom ate flour, but lived upon the milk and flesh of their innumerable herds.

The cattle were as large as those of England, and were celebrated for the extreme size of their horns.

Wat-el-Mek had made a razzia with a very powerful force, collected from all the stations of Abou Saood, and he had succceded in capturing an enormous number of these fine animals, together with a large herd of donkeys.

These strange cattle would not live at Fatiko, as the herbage was quite different to that to which they had been accustomed. They died in such numbers, that in three months only three or four remained out of as many thousand. Thus all these beautiful beasts were wasted.

The river Sobat was described as flowing from the south, and was known as the Chol. The Asua river is only one day's march, or about twenty miles east of Fatiko. The Sobat is never dry, and is reported to be a noble river; this suggests that Speke's Victoria N'yanza, or the Bahr Ingo's eastern corner, must have an effluent in addition to the Victoria Nile, that flows from M'tésé's capital of Uganda.

Beyond Langgo there is a country called Lobbohr, which is said to possess camels. In the Lobbohr there is a river called Jooba. This is, I believe, the Juba that flows into the Indian Ocean, as the report continues that: "Arabs arrive at Lobbohr mounted upon camels, and armed with swords and pistols, but without guns." Horses and donkeys are also reported to exist in Lobbohr.

There can be no doubt that most important countries lie to the east of Fatiko, and should the story of camels prove correct, there will be no difficulty in opening up a commercial route.

It appears that at Langgo the value of beads is very great, as the natives work them into patterns upon their matted hair. Ivory has little or no value, and exists in large quantities.

The natives refuse to carry loads, and they transport an elephant's tusk by boring a hole in the hollow end, through which they attach a rope; the tusk is then dragged along the ground by a donkey. The ivory is thus seriously damaged. . . . .

Such was the position of affairs at Fatiko in March, 1872. New and important countries had been investigated, not by explorers or traders, but by the brigands of Abou Saood, whose first introduction was the unprovoked attack and carrying off of slaves and cattle.

Such conduct could only terminate in an extension of the ruin which a similar course had determined in every country that had been occupied by the traders of the White Nile.

I trusted that my arrival would create a great reform, and restore confidence throughout the country. The news had spread far and wide. The scarlet soldiers were regarded as a distinct species, and the report quickly circulated, that the "Pacha's troops were entirely different from any that had hitherto been seen, as their clothes were red, and their muskets were loaded from the wrong end."

I now determined to establish a station at Fatiko, to represent the government during my absence in the south.

Abou Saood had sworn fidelity. Of course I did not believe him, but as the natives had welcomed the government, I could not leave them without protection.

It was therefore arranged with Abou Saood that after the expiration of the contract, all operations should cease. He would simply remain on sufferance in the country, until he should be able to transport his ivory to Gondokoro. This could only be effected by the arrrival of carriers from his stations, about 180 miles west of the Nile, in the Makkarika country. His first step would therefore be to communicate with the vakeel Atroosh, who commanded about 600 men in the west station.

I ordered Abou Saood to disarm the seventy Baris who were in his service at Fatiko, as I would not allow muskets to be placed in the hands of natives who were hostile to the government.

This he promised to do, but of course he evaded the order,' by returning the arms to the Baris the instant I had departed.

It may appear to the public that having "absolute and supreme power," I was absurdly lenient towards Abou Saood, whom I knew to be so great a villain. I confess to one fault. I should have arrested and transported him to Khartoum when he first arrived at Gondokoro with the cattle stolen from the Shir; which caused the subsequent massacre of the five soldiers of the government.

At the same time that I admit this error, it must be remembered that I was placed in an awkward position.

"Absolute and supreme power" is a high sounding title, but how was I to exert it?

I was an individual possessing a nominal power, the application of which required extreme delicacy. I was determined to win, and with God's help I did win, but every step necessitated the coolest judgment. Had I adopted severe or extreme measures against Abou Saood, I might have ruined the expedition at the commencement.

It was impossible to know who was faithful. There was a general leaning towards his favour among all the officers, with whom he had been in close connection when in Khartoum. He was a man in a high social position in the Soudan, the partner of the great firm of Agād & Co., who commanded 2,500 armed men. He had worked for many years in company with the government, according to his connection by agreement with the governor-general.

I knew that I had him in my power, provided I should be supported by the authorities in Eygpt; therefore I gave him line, and occasionally held him tight, as though he had been a salmon on a single gut; but I was determined to land him safe at last, in such a manner that his greatest supporter should be obliged to acknowledge that he had received the fairest play. Abou Saood's Fatiko station was crowded with slaves. His people were all paid in slaves. The stations of Fabbo, Faloro, and Farragenia were a mass of slaves.

I did not enter a station to interfere with these slaves, as I knew that such an act would create irretrievable confusion.

I had only 212 men, and I wished to advance to the equator. Fatiko was in north latitude 3° 01′, and 165 miles from head-quarters. Had I attempted to release some thousand slaves from the different stations, I should have required a large military force to have occupied those stations, and to have driven out the whole of the slave-hunters bodily.

If the slaves had been released, it would have been impossible to have returned them to their homes, as they had been collected from every quarter of the compass and from great distances. If I had kept them, I could not have procured food for so large a number: as the stations contained several thousand.

Under the circumstances, I took the wiser course of non-interference with the stock in hand, but I issued the most severe orders respecting the future conduct of Abou Saood's companies.

I arranged to leave a detachment of 100 men, under the command of Major Abdullah, to form a station adjoining that of Abou Saood in Fatiko, together with the heavier baggage and the greater portion of the ammunition.

The government would be thus represented by a most respectable and civilized officer, who would give confidence and protection to the country; as I concluded that the *prestige* of the Khedive would be sufficient to establish order among his subjects, by the representation of one of his officers and a detachment of 100 troops.

I gave orders to Gimōro and Shooli to prepare carriers for the journey to Unyoro.

An untoward occurrence had taken place shortly after our arrival at Fatiko.

As has already been described, the Loboré natives had not only cheated us out of many cows that had been received, for which the carriers had not been forthcoming, but numbers had deserted on the road, which had caused the troops great trouble and fatigue, as they had been obliged to divide among them the abandoned loads. Upon our arrival at Fatiko, the son of sheik Abbio, of Loboré, would have absconded with all his people, had he not been retained by the troops. This man was responsible for the natives who had engaged themselves for the journey.

It would have been the height of imprudence to

have permitted the immediate departure of our carriers before I had arranged for the future, thus about eighty were secured by the soldiers, including the sheik's son, from a general stampede that took place.

I ordered them to be disarmed, as I considered that if unarmed, they dared not venture alone through the Madi country.

In the evening they were secured by a light line tied round each man's neck, and connected in gangs of five. A guard was placed over them in addition to the usual sentries.

At about 4 A.M. a signal was given. Every man had gnawed through his cord with his teeth during the darkness, and at the concerted cry in a language that no one understood, the entire party, of upwards of eighty men, knocked down the astonished guards, also the sentries, and rushed headlong over the rocks in the direction of Loboré.

It was a natural impulse and a soldier's duty to fire in the direction of the assailants, as the overturned sentries quickly recovered and joined the guard in a volley.

I was up in an instant, and upon arrival at the spot I was informed of the occurrence. It was pitch dark, therefore a lantern was brought, and after a search, three bodies were discovered of the rash and unfortunate Loboré. I was exceedingly sorry that such an event had happened, at the same time I could hardly blame the sentries. I was much afraid that if three were shot dead, others must have escaped wounded, and altogether the affair would have a bad effect at Loboré.

The sheik of Fatiko was named Wat-el-Ajoos. This name had been given him by the slave-hunters, meaning "Son of the old man." His village was not quite half a mile from our camp, and he frequently came to see me with his interpreter, accompanied by his wives.

Upon his first visit I gave him a long blue shirt, together with some yards of Turkey red cambric, to form a waist sash; also a red fez and two razors, with a quantity of beads for his wives.

Fatiko is merely a district of the great country of Shooli, which is governed by the sheik, Rot Jarma. This person had sent word that he intended to visit me, to tender his allegiance to the government.

On 16th March, a wild sound of many horns was the first introduction, and shortly after, a number of his people advanced chanting a peculiar low song, and dancing a solemn slow step. The great

sheik came behind them. He was quickly ushered into my presence beneath a shady acacia, close to my tent door. He was perfectly red from head to toes, having been freshly smeared with red ochre and grease for the interview. A well-dressed skin of an antelope was slung across his shoulder, and descending across his loins it constituted his scanty clothing.

His conversation was merely a repetition of the old story, being a series of complaints against the slave-hunters. He declared that he had never visited Abou Saood or any of his people, but that when he had heard of my arrival, he had determined at once to offer his allegiance, and he and all adjacent countries would serve the government faithfully, in return for protection and justice.

I assured him that he had nothing to fear from the slave-hunters in future, as I should leave Major Abdullah and a detachment of troops to represent the government during my absence. He was to supply them with corn, and to yield the same obedience to Major Abdullah as he would to me. I gave him nine yards of red cotton cloth, six pounds of beads, two razors, one comb, two horn snakes in boxes, one knife, one burning glass, one zinc mirror, two nickel spoons, three rods of thick brass wire, two finger-rings, two pair of ear-rings, two red and yellow cotton handkerchiefs.

The total value of this extensive present was about twenty-one shillings.

Before he had arrived, he had requested that a goat might be sent to be slaughtered at a stream before he should cross over; otherwise bad luck would attend his visit. Of course this was acceded to, and the goat was sacrificed and eaten by his people.

I gave him, according to my usual custom with all sheiks and headmen, seeds of the best Egyptian cotton, tomatoes, pumpkins, cucumbers, water-melons, sweet-melons, barmian, maize, &c., &c.

Before parting, I amused and shocked him with the magnetic battery, and he went away surprised and delighted.

I subsequently discovered that a large quantity of flour, together with some fowls which he had forwarded to me, had been stopped and appropriated by the renowned Ali Hussein. The intriguing spirit of these slave-hunters was extraordinary. It is their custom never to receive a sheik unless he brings a present. He therefore considered that if Rot Jarma should appear for the first time before me empty-handed, I should either not admit him, or perhaps be prejudiced against him; thus he had stolen the customary gift of introduction in order to create ill-will on my part towards Rot Jarma, who had never yet condescended to visit the station of Abou Saood . . . . .

Wat-el-Ajoos, with the assistance of Shooli and Gimōro, had collected 200 carriers, all of whom had received each a cow.

I had assorted the luggage, and although I had not the slightest suspicion of any fighting, nevertheless my ammunition formed a considerable portion of the heavier baggage.

Major Abdullah had received his instructions, and a site had been chosen for his station within a hundred yards of the south extremity of that of Abou Saood. This position was backed by a high rock, upon which I had already commenced to build a powder magazine of solid masonry.

Abou Saood having as usual sworn upon the eyes and head of the Prophet to do all that was right and virtuous, and the natives throughout the country being confident of protection, I prepared for the journey to Unyoro—a distance across the uninhabited prairies of seventy-eight miles from Fatiko, due south.

Our excellent and trusty friend Shooli was to be our guide. Gimōro was prevented from accompanying us owing to a wounded foot.

CHAPTER IV.

THE MARCH TO UNYORO.

On 18th March, 1872, we were all in order for the march to the south, under the direction of our guide, Shooli.

Having taken leave of Major Abdullah, I left him a good supply of sheep and cattle for his detachment, and at 2 P.M. we started for the prairie march to Unyoro.

The descent from the table-land of Fatiko was rapid for the first seven miles, at which point we reached a stream of clear running water, which is one of the channels of the Un-y-Amé river.

The limit of the inhabited country is about three miles from the camp at Fatiko, after which all is wilderness to Unyoro.

This fertile country has been left uninhabited, on account of the disturbance occasioned by the diversity of tribes. On the east it is bounded by Umiro, on the south by Unyoro, and on the west by Madi. This large tract of land, about eighty miles from north to south, is accordingly the resort of wild animals, and it forms the favourite hunting-ground of the various tribes, who generally come into conflict with each other during their excursions in pursuit of game.

We halted for the night at the clear stream of the Un-y-Amé, as the native carriers expected their wives to bring them provisions for the journey. It was only five o'clock, therefore I strolled along the banks of the stream accompanied by Shooli, and shortly came upon game.

At this season the country was very lovely, as the young grass was hardly a foot high. Stalking was extremely difficult, as the land was clear of trees, and the long sweeping undulations exposed every object to view when upon the face. I managed at length to get a tolerable shot at one of the beautiful teel (*Leucotis*), by creeping up the broken bed of a water-course until I arrived at a white-ant hill. On my way home I shot a gazelle, thus the natives all had flesh from the two animals on the first night of the march.

The wives appeared to be excellent women, as they

arrived in great numbers with a quantity of hard porridge made of dhurra flour, which was to form the commissariat for a journey of nearly 160 miles to Unyoro and back.

If a native travels through wilderness, he will always make forced marches, thus the Fatikos would only sleep one night upon the road of seventy-eight miles when on the return journey.

On the following morning, we were rather late in starting, as more women arrived with food, and certain farewells took place. The Fatiko natives appeared to be very superior to the Loboré, as not one man absconded. In fact, one native who had a swollen leg, which prevented him from walking, actually sent back his cow with an explanation of the cause of absence.

On 19th March we started at 6.50 A.M., all our carriers being well provided with food. The country was as usual a well watered, undulating prairie, abounding in game. At this season the march was very delightful, but when the grass is about nine feet high it is simply detestable travelling.

On the march, we, as usual, led the way. Lieutenant Baker dismounted for a shot at a splendid buck (*Leucotis*), which he wounded somewhere behind, and the animal made off in evident discomfort.

This was a signal for the natives, who immediately put down their loads and started off in pursuit, like a pack of hounds.

Although the animal was badly hit, the pace was very great, and it went along the face of the opposite undulation followed by the extraordinary runners, who, with their long springing strides, kept up a speed for about three-quarters of a mile that at length brought the leading native sufficiently near for throwing the lance. The next moment a crowd of hungry fellows fell upon the welcome game like starving wolves.

After a march of twelve miles we arrived at a rocky stream of clear water, which is another channel of the Un-y-Amé river, that carries off the entire drainage of this country. We halted to refresh the people and to have our breakfast on the clean rock that bordered the stream, and started for the afternoon march at 2 P.M.

During the march I endeavoured to stalk a large bull tétel (*Antelope bubalis*) but there was very little chance in so open a country. The animal galloped off exactly in a straight line from me at about 260 yards. I put up the last leaf of the sight, and I distinctly heard the bullet strike The next moment I saw the animal was wounded. It was just disappearing over the next undulation, and upon arriving at the spot, I saw the wounded bull standing about 200 yards before me.

I approached from behind until within 100 paces, without being observed by the tétel, who was evidently very bad. Moving slightly to my right, I was quickly seen, and the animal turned its flank preparatory to making off. A shot from the "Dutchman" exactly through the shoulder killed it on the spot.

I now found that my first bullet had struck the spine exactly above the root of the tail. This large animal was a good supply for the people, who quickly divided it and continued the march, until, having crossed another stream, we left the open prairie and entered a low forest. Halted for the night. The march during this day had been nineteen miles.

On 20th March we marched, from 6 A.M. till 9.45, through undulating forest, and halted upon high ground, which commanded a fine view of the mountain that borders the west shore of the Albert N'yanza, opposite Magungo, about fifty-five miles S.S.W. From our elevated point we looked down over a fine extent of country, and the Fatiko natives pointed out the course of the White Nile from the great lake, along which was a line of smoke, caused, according to their accounts, by the fishermen who were at this season burning the high reeds on the river's bank.

The natives were thoroughly conversant with the country, as they had on several occasions accompanied the slave-hunters in razzias along the river to Foquatch and Magungo. Just as we halted, a party of Umiro hunters came across our path, but immediately took to flight, as they supposed we were enemies. The day's march had been thirteen miles, and we were requested by our guide, Shooli, to halt for the night, as there was no water for a considerable distance to the south.

I immediately employed the soldiers in the construction of a cattle kraal, lest the prowling Umiro should endeavour to scare the animals during the night.

On 21st March we started at 6 A.M., and marched thirteen miles through forest. We at length reached water, but it was so thick with mud that the horses refused to drink it.

On 22nd March we were compelled to march twenty-three miles, as the water was quite undrinkable, the few muddy pools having been stirred into paste by the buffaloes and elephants.

We now reached the grand Victoria Nile, flowing beneath cliffs of seventy or eighty feet in depth, through magnificent forest. It was refreshing for all parties to obtain pure water after the miserable fluid we had been lately compelled to drink.

In the evening a sheik and several people, who had known me formerly, crossed the river from the Unyoro side, and desired an interview. They reported that the Khartoum traders had almost destroyed the country, and they begged me simply to judge with my own eyes.

I must now extract from my journal the entry of the date, as, although briefly written, it will convey the impression of the moment:—

"*March* 23, 1872.—We marched three miles east, along the banks of the beautiful Victoria Nile, through fine open forest, until we halted on a high cliff exactly opposite the last station of Abou Saood, commanded by a vakeel named Suleiman.

"It is impossible to describe the change that has taken place since I last visited this country. It was then a perfect garden, thickly populated, and producing all that man could desire. The villages were numerous; groves of plantains fringed the steep cliffs on the river's bank; and the natives were neatly dressed in the bark-cloth of the country.

DEPLORABLE CHANGE.

"The scene has changed!

"All is wilderness! The population has fled. Not a village is to be seen!

"This is the certain result of the settlement of Khartoum traders. They kidnap the women and children for slaves, and plunder and destroy wherever they set their foot.

"Suleiman and Eddrees, two vakeels, who were well known to me as forming a portion of Ibrahim's party on my former journey, now came across the river to visit me.

"The cunning Abou Saood has never told them of the expiration of the government contract with Agād & Co., neither had they any warning of my expected arrival.

"I explained the exact state of affairs.

"The principal sheik of the district, with many people, came to see me. The chief, Quonga, was one of my old acquaintances, and was formerly the favourite adviser of Kamrasi.

"Kamrasi died about two years ago. His sons fought for the succession, and each aspirant sought the aid of the traders. This civil strife exactly suited the interests of the treacherous Khartoumers. The several companies of slave-hunters scattered over the Madi, Shooli, and Unyoro countries represented only one interest, that of their employers, Agād & Co.

"Each company, commanded by its independent vakeel, arrived in Unyoro, and supported the cause of each antagonistic pretender to the throne, and treacherously worked for the ruin of all, excepting him who would be able to supply the largest amount of ivory and slaves.

"The favourite sons of Kamrasi were Kabba Réga and Kabka Miro, while the old enemy of the family, Rionga, the cousin of Kamrasi, again appeared upon the scene.

"The companies of Abou Saood supported all three, receiving ivory and slaves from each as the hire of mercenary troops; and at length they played out their game by shooting Kabka Miro, and securing the throne to Kabba Réga.

"They arranged with Rionga that he should be ostensibly banished to a convenient distance, to be ready as a trump card, should occasion require, against the new king, Kabba Réga.

"I explained the new reform to Quonga, and I gave him the following presents for Kabba Réga, who resides about six days' march south-west of this spot:—

"One piece entire of Turkey red cloth, one piece

grey calico, twelve pounds of beads of the finest varieties, three zinc mirrors, two razors, one long butcher's knife, two pair scissors, one brass bugle, one German horn, two pieces of red and yellow handkerchiefs, one piece of yellow ditto, one peacock Indian scarf, one blue blanket, six German silver spoons, sixteen pairs of various ear-rings, twelve finger rings, two dozen mule harness bells, six elastic heavy brass spring wires, one pound long white horsehair, three combs, one papier-mâché tray, one boxwood fife, one kaleidoscope.

"I proclaimed upon all sides that the reign of terror was ended. As I formerly, when alone, had defended Kamrasi, and driven out the invaders under Wat-el-Mek, by hoisting the English ensign, so now I would take the country under my protection with a powerful force.

"I gave Quonga and all his sheiks presents of beads, and shocked them powerfully with the magnetic battery, leaving a strong impression.

"*March* 24.—I wrote officially to Suleiman, the vakeel of Agād & Co., to give him warning 'that sixteen days hence the contract would expire, and that he and all his people must be ready to evacuate the country and return to Khartoum on that day. That any person who should remain after this notice would be imprisoned. That, should he or any of his people wish to enlist in the service of the government as irregular troops, their names must be handed in before the expiration of two days.'

"Suleiman declared his willingness to enlist together with Eddrees and several others.

"He told me that nothing could be procured in the country. Thank God I left a good reputation here seven years ago ; thus I shall be able to purchase food.

"This morning my old acquaintance, Keedja, formerly chief of Atada, came to see me with many of his people, and with perfect confidence they commenced a market, bringing provisions in exchange for beads. They promised to arrive tomorrow, and to establish a daily market at our camp.

"Keedja explains that he and his people have been obliged to fly from the depredations of the companies of Abou Saood, thus they have settled in the forest on the north side of the river, and have cultivated farms. They have very few clothes, as their barkcloth trees are on the south side of the river in their old plantations.

"All the people declare they will now return to their

old habitations and re-cultivate the land as in former days.

"I found that the natives who ran from us on the march, and dropped their elephant spears, were Keedja's people, thus I returned to them the three spears and an axe, to their great astonishment.[1]

"The elephant-spears were of a kind used from trees. The blade is about twenty inches long, the handle about twenty-four inches. The end of the handle is heavily weighted with a lump of several pounds, composed of clay, cow-dung, and chopped straw, and the weapon, beautifully sharpened, is dropped upon the elephant's back by a hunter from the branches of a tree. The constant movement of the heavy handle as it strikes the boughs when the elephant rushes through the forest, cuts the animal so terribly that it bleeds to death. The hunters follow on the blood track until they find the dying animal.

"*March* 25.—Suleiman, the vakeel, summoned his men to volunteer for the government service as irregular troops.

"I issued a written proclamation, that should volunteers enlist, the term of service would be annual, subject to three months' notice, should any officer or

[1] A party of native hunters had been scared during our march by our sudden appearance.

private wish to retire at the expiration of twelve months.

"The rank of the vakeel would be equivalent to that of major in the regular army.

"The pay would be equal to that of regular troops.

"If I can form a regiment of 600 irregulars I shall be independent of troops from Khartoum.

"*March* 26 —Quonga and many other sheiks arrived, and were quite delighted with the wheel of life.

"The natives are selling sweet potatoes and tobacco for beads, but flour is brought in very small quantities.

"*March* 27.—Provisions are coming in so slowly that we shall be short of food. Upon the arrival of Quonga and his sheiks, I made a hot complaint; he coolly told me that it would be better if the soldiers were to forage for themselves.

"I explained to him the rigid discipline that I enforced, and that, should I once permit thieving, the troops' character would be entirely ruined, and they would pillage throughout the route.

"He replied that this neighbourhood was in a state of anarchy; that many of the inhabitants were hostile to Kabba Réga, and they would not obey his orders.

"I told him that my troops were lambs if well fed, but they were like lions if hungry, and to prove their number I would summon them before him.

"The bugle sounded the 'taboor,' and upwards of 100 men immediately fell in with bayonets fixed, to the no small dismay of Quonga and his sheiks, who began to look very uneasy at the scarlet uniforms. By a *coup de théâtre*, I marched the men, with bugles and drums playing, round the numerous huts, so that they reappeared twice before the tent, and thus doubled their real number.

"At the halt and dismissal, they shouted their usual wild cry in Turkish, in honour of their commander.

"'Do you understand what they say?' I asked Quonga. To his negative reply, I answered, 'They say they will eat from the country if provisions are not supplied to-morrow!'

"Quonga and his sheiks started off immediately to give the necessary orders.

"Upon his return I told him 'to advise Kabba Réga to behave in a different manner to the conduct of his father, the late Kamrasi. I had returned to this country to bestow prosperity upon the land; that if Kabba Réga meant fair dealing and legitimate trade, he must act honourably and sincerely; if I should find any signs of unfairness, I should pass on direct to Uganda, the country of M'tésé, and he would receive the goods I had intended for Unyoro.'

"Negroes are great deceivers, especially the natives of Unyoro. I have beads, cattle, merchandize, and ivory, articles necessary to purchase flour and potatoes: nevertheless, our wants are not supplied. The cattle are dying, as the change of herbage does not agree with them; this is a sad loss.

"*March* 28.—The great sheik, Lokara, who is the commander-in-chief of Kabba Réga's forces, arrived. This man has left a large army on the banks of the Nile, a few hours' march up stream, ready to attack Rionga, who is settled, with his people, on an island in the river. Of course he is come to request military aid. This is the old story. Upon my last visit I was bored almost to death by Kamrasi, with requests that I would assist him to attack Rionga. I have only been here for a few days when I am troubled with the old tune.

"*March* 29.—Provisions are very scarce; the people have been fighting for so many years that cultivation has been much neglected, and the natives live principally upon plantains.

"I gave Suleiman, the vakeel, five cows yesterday. He declares that Abou Saood told him that my term of service with the Egyptian government had expired, therefore the entire country was now in his hands. This liar, Abou Saood, will some day reap the fruits of his treachery.

"I ordered the government flag to be hoisted in Suleiman's camp, and the vakeel, Suleiman, called upon all those who were willing to enlist in the service of the Khedive to assemble beneath the ensign. Sixty-one men registered their names.

"The only difficulty is the rate of wages. I offer the privates sixty piastres per month, *i.e.*, thirty piastres (or twopence-halfpenny per day) as equal pay to that of the regulars, and thirty piastres in lieu of clothes. Formerly these brigands nominally received fifty and fifty-five piastres, in addition to one third of all cattle that might be captured in razzias.

"Should I be able to establish a small irregular corps as a commencement, the expense would be considerable in proportion to the actual proceeds in ivory. The position is difficult.

"A radical change throughout the country is absolutely necessary. The companies have hitherto purchased ivory with slaves and cattle; thus all countries in which this custom has been established, must be abandoned until the natives will sell ivory in exchange for goods.

"The expenses will continue, or perhaps augment, while the ivory produce must decrease for the first twelve months, or until the people will understand and accept the reform.

"Without an irregular force it will be impossible to hold the country, and at the same time carry on the work of government. The force that I originally proposed, of 1,650, is absolutely required to occupy a chain of stations from Gondokoro.

"*March* 30.—The cows are dying in great numbers, and the natives are bringing large quantities of potatoes in exchange for the flesh, but there is no corn in the country.

"The days and nights are now cloudy and showery.

"Lokara and Quonga came this morning, but no messenger has yet arrived from Kabba Réga.

"I gave Lókara a blue shirt, a long red sash, and a crimson fez, to his great delight. The chiefs were much struck with the present intended for Kabba Réga; this consisted of three rows of Roman pearls as large as marbles, with a gilt shield, and onyx-pendant tied up with green satin ribbon.

"*March* 31.—I sent all the cattle across the river in charge of Quonga; two were carried off by crocodiles while in the act of swimming.

"The great sheiks paid me a visit, together with

BOTTLE-GOURD OF UNYORO. (FROM THE ORIGINAL.)

many of inferior rank. Lokara, Quonga, Matonsé, and Pittia, were among the principal chiefs of the country. As they were sitting before me, Lokara lighted a huge pipe and immediately commenced smoking. This is a great breach of etiquette, as smoking is strictly forbidden in the presence of Kabba Réga.

" My old Cairo dragoman, Mohammed, who was now thoroughly installed as one of the expedition, was well up in the customs of the country, and he quietly resented the insult of the pipe.

"He gently approached with a bottle of water, which he poured politely into the bowl, as though he was conferring a favour ; at the same time, he explained that in my presence every one smoked water instead of tobacco. The hint was immediately taken, and the huge pipe, thus summarily extinguished, was handed to a slave in attendance.

"We now entered upon geographical discussions. All the chiefs declared that the M'wootan N'zigé extends beyond Karagwé, and that it exceeds the Victoria N'yanza in size. The native name, in Unyoro, for the Victoria N'yanza is simply N'yanza, and for the White Nile, Masāba.

"There is a country called Baréga on the Albert N'yanza, south-west of Uganda, governed by a powerful king whose people are armed with bows, and arrows that are feathered. I have never yet seen feathered arrows among the White Nile tribes.

"The great mountain Bartooma is again mentioned, as on my former journey. I imagine it must be identical with the M'fumbiro mentioned by Speke.

"I shall send an expedition from Magungo to Ibrahimeyah by river to prove the capabilities of the route. I shall form a station at Magungo to trade with Malegga on the opposite shore. I shall then thoroughly explore the Albert N'yanza in boats, and afterwards proceed to King M'tésé of Uganda . . . .

"It rained last evening and during the night. Seven cows died. I have erected a comfortable stable for the horses.

"*April* 1.—The people belonging to Suleiman hesitate to accept the government pay, although a day or two ago they enlisted. I fear that these people can never be trusted. I shall give them a little time to consider, after which, if they refuse to serve, I shall turn them out of the country. Every camp or zareeba is of course full of slaves.

"There is a curious custom throughout Unyoro : a peculiar caste are cattle-keepers. These people only attend to the herds, and the profession is inherited from past generations. They are called Bohooma, and they are the direct descendants of the Gallas who originally conquered the country, and, like the reigning family, they are of an extremely light colour. If the herds are carried off in battle, the Bohooma, who never carry arms, accompany them to their new masters, and continue their employment. Nothing but death will separate them from their cattle.

"*April* 2.—The natives built a zareeba yesterday for the cattle ; but they are dying as rapidly as upon the north side of the river.

" I tried to do a little geography with the sheik, Pittia. He was the man who, some years ago, first gave me the information respecting the distance of the Albert N'yanza from M'rooli. He would say nothing without orders from the king, beyond telling me that you might travel for months upon the lake.

" It is very annoying in this country that no information can be obtained, neither can any work be commenced, without the direct order of the king. My patience is sorely tried. No reply has as yet been delivered to my message sent to Kabba Réga, although ten days have elapsed.

' My desire is to benefit the country by opening the road for legitimate commerce ; but the difficulties are great, as the king will endeavour to monopolize the market, and thus prevent free trade.

"*April* 3.—I sent for all the great sheiks to complain of Kabba Réga's conduct. This young fellow was evidently aping the manners of his father, Kamrasi, and attempting to show his own importance by keeping me waiting. The sheiks explained, that before my arrival, Suleiman had agreed to furnish soldiers to assist the forces of Kabba Réga in a united attack upon Rionga; and the army was now only a short distance from this spot, expecting the promised aid. My arrival had upset all their plans, as I had forbidden all action until I should have had a personal interview with Kabba Réga.

"The military operations were in abeyance until a reply should be received from the king. The return messengers were expected this evening.

"The sheiks declare that the ruling class in this country are all exceedingly light in complexion, 'because they do no work, but sit in the shade and drink abundance of milk.'

"The natives of Unyoro are very inferior in *physique* to the Fatiko. This is the result of vegetable food without either cereals or flesh. None of the general public possess cattle; thus the food of the people from infancy, after their mothers' milk has ceased, is restricted to plantains and the watery sweet potatoes. The want of milk is very detrimental to the children. The men generally exhibit a want of muscle, and many are troubled with cutaneous diseases.

"*April* 4.—The messengers are reported to have arrived from Kabba Réga. Last evening, at 8 P.M., we had a very heavy storm of rain with thunder. Fifteen cows died to-day, and I fear we shall lose the greater portion of the herd. All cattle that may be brought from the countries of Bari, Madi, and Langgo, are said to die on arrival in Unyoro.

"*April* 5.—The great sheiks, Rahonka and Kittākără, arrived together with Lokara and Quonga, and the smaller fry, Pittia and Malleggé. The latter was my guide to the Albert N'yanza many years ago.

"The 'Forty Thieves' and the band received them on arrival. The band was, of course, encored, all being delighted with the big drum and the cymbals. The latter were examined as great curiosities.

"Rahonka is Kamrasi's maternal uncle, and is great-uncle to Kabba Réga; and he can give more information than any man concerning the neighbouring countries.

"In reply to my inquiries about Livingstone, he says that two persons are living in a large house in Karagwé, which they have constructed in a different form to those of the natives. These people have no military escort, but they possess a large quantity of goods. This does not sound like Livingstone, unless he may have joined some Arab merchant.

"There are natives of Karagwé now visiting Kabba Réga at Masindi; thus I shall have a good opportunity of making inquiries. There are likewise envoys from M'tésé in this country; therefore I shall be able to send him a valuable present, and beg him to search for Livingstone in all directions.

"*April* 6.—Kabba Réga's messengers presented themselves with an offering of two cows, a parcel of salt, and some plantains.

"One of these cows is a splendid animal from Umiro. She is the size of a fair Durham—bright red colour—with immensely long and massive horns.

" Had I not had former experience in this country, and provided myself with a herd of cattle, we should have been half-starved, as there is nothing to be procured but beans, sweet potatoes, and plantains.

"*April* 7.—We all crossed the river in canoes. A heavy shower fell this morning. My improvident men have torn all their waterproof cloaks and blankets just as we have arrived in a country where they will be most required.

"*April* 8.—It now rains daily, more or less. The order was given by Kabba Réga that we were to be supplied with carriers for the journey to Masindi, which is to be under the charge of Rahonka. Suleiman and Eddrees have arranged with their men, all of whom now present in the camp have agreed to accept the government rate of pay, and to enlist for twelve months. I accordingly issued serkis, or certificates, for each man, with his name, date of engagement, and rate of wages.

"This is very satisfactory, as I shall now have a station in my rear on the river, with the command of boats, while I march up the country to Masindi. The irregulars in this station, which is in the district of Foweera, number sixty-five men. If they remain faithful, they will form a nucleus for the irregulars who will most probably follow their example. I understand that a small party of seventeen men are now staying with Kabba Réga. These people will join their comrades under Suleiman, and raise the strength of the Foweera station to eighty-two men. I shall thus be able to keep up a communication with my detachment at Fatiko.

"*April* 9.—At the expiration of Agád's contract there were 188 elephants' tusks in the zareeba of Suleiman. These will remain in his care.

"The natives collected were insufficient to convey all the loads. I therefore sent off a division, escorted by Morgiān Agha with ten men, to await my arrival at the village of Deang. The sheik, Rahonka, killed a man who attempted to evade the order to carry baggage.

"*April* 10.—Rain fell throughout the night, which makes everybody miserable. During the middle watch, having been awakened by the heavy shower, I heard the sentry outside my tent muttering a kind of low chant:—'This is the country for rain and potatoes; this is the place for potatoes and rain. Potatoes and rain, potatoes and rain; rain and potatoes, rain and potatoes.'

"Neither the rain nor the potatoes were esteemed by the troops. The roots were almost as watery as the rain, and their sweetness was excessive. A very uncomfortable result from this vapid food was extreme flatulence. The waist-belts of the boys were obliged to be let out by several holes at the buckles. As my men justly declared, 'They were uncomfortably full after a meal; but half-an-hour's march made them feel as though they had fasted for a day.'

"During the afternoon I was sitting beneath a shady tree, with my wife and Lieutenant Baker, when a naked native rushed wildly past the sentries, and, before he could be restrained, he threw himself on the ground and embraced my feet, at the same time begging for mercy by the Arabic ejaculation, 'Amān! amān!'

"He was immediately seized. On examination through an interpreter, it appeared that he was a native of Koitch, near Fatiko, and that he had attached himself to Suleiman's party at some former time, but now he had just escaped from the Foweera station, as Suleiman wished to kill him.

"In a few minutes Suleiman himself appeared: he was pale with rage.

"Suleiman was a thorough brigand in appearance. His father was a Kurd: thus his complexion would have been white had he not been for many years exposed to the African climate. He was a powerful dare-devil-looking fellow, but even among his own people he was reputed cruel and vindictive.

"He was so overpowered with passion that he approached and kissed my hand, at the same time imploring me 'as a favour, to allow him to cut off the native's head with his sabre.'

"Upon a trial of the case, I found that the native was a thief, and that upon a former occasion he had stolen a gun and two pistols from the camp, which, after some trouble, had been recovered. He was now accused of aiding and abetting at the escape of five female slaves from the zareeba during the past night, therefore he was to be beheaded without delay.

"As this was not my form of punishment, especially for the crime of *releasing slaves* that had been captured by force, I ordered the native to be secured in the zareeba until further orders, but upon no account should he be injured.

"Although I had heard from my old Cairo dragoman, Mohammed, that the prisoner was a bad character, I did not wish to punish him severely, as the effect would be bad among the natives of the country. He had run to me for protection, therefore, should he suffer, a precedent would be established that would deter others from appealing to me for mercy.

"The man was led away under a guard and was secured in the zareeba. Suleiman acknowledged that he was in an excusable rage, but that I had been just in my decision, and he would keep the prisoner in safe custody until further orders. Suleiman was to accompany me on the journey to Masindi on the following morning, as Rahonka had collected the native carriers.

"That evening, after a heavy shower, we witnessed one of those remarkable appearances of the winged white ants that issued from a mound within a few yards of our tent. Millions of these large fat insects struggled into their ephemeral flight, and were quickly caught by our people with lighted wisps of straw. The ant disengages its wings a few minutes after its appearance from the parent mound.

"The exodus from the ant-hill takes place annually at the commencement of the rainy season, and the collection of the insects is considered to be an important harvest throughout all Central Africa. The white ant, in this stage of its existence, is esteemed as a great delicacy when fried in a little butter.

"We tasted a considerable number, and found them tolerably good, but with a slight flavour of burnt feathers.

"On April 11 we were ready to start, but at the last moment the vakeel, Suleiman, who was to accompany us, excused himself until the next day, as he had some important business to transact with his people. I accordingly gave him permission to remain, but I ordered him to follow me quickly, as it would be necessary to present him to Kabba Réga in his new position as vakeel of the government." . . . .

It will now be necessary to explain the true position of affairs, which at that time I did not suspect.

Upon my first arrival at the river, when I had explained my views to Suleiman, he had immediately despatched a letter to Abou Saood at Fatiko. His party had travelled fast, and they returned with a reply.

I could never discover the actual contents of the letter, but I heard that it cautioned Suleiman not to part with the slaves, and to join Abou Saood with his ivory and all his people at the station of Fabbo, a day's march west of Fatiko.

Suleiman was in an awkward position. He had always held a high place in the eyes of Kabba Réga and his chiefs, and his alliance had been courted and obtained for a combined attack upon the old enemy, Rionga. The army of Kabba Réga had been waiting at the rendezvous in expectation of Suleiman's assistance. A fleet of large canoes had been concentrated at a given point for the invasion of the island; and Kabba Réga and his sheiks considered that at length their old enemy was in the snare.

My unexpected arrival had ruined the project, as I strictly forbade Suleiman to attack Rionga.

This disappointed Kabba Réga and his people, who could not understand how I could be the friend of his late father Kamrasi, and at the same time protect his enemy Rionga.

The attack on the island was a dangerous adventure, as it was surrounded by dense masses of papyrus rush that would prevent canoes from landing, except at certain places where narrow passages had been cleared. A few men concealed among the papyrus could massacre an attacking party at discretion, as they struggled through the narrow entrance in canoes. It had been proposed that Suleiman's people were to attack in boats and clear out the enemy by a sharp fire into the papyrus to cover the general advance.

Sulciman was in a dilemma, as he had already promised alliance, and had received a quantity of ivory in payment for his services. He had accordingly made the following secret arrangement with Rahonka and Lokara:—"Let the Pacha and his soldiers start for Masindi, and he will suppose that Suleiman will follow on the morrow. Instead of which, he will at once join Kabba Réga's forces, and attack Rionga, when the Pacha shall be several days' journey distant from the river."

On his return to Foweera from a successful invasion of Rionga's island, the commanders of the forces, Lokara and Rahonka, were at once to furnish carriers to transport Suleiman with all his people and ivory to the Fabbo station, according to the instructions received from Abou Saood.

I should thus be deceived, and be left at Masindi, 160 miles distant from my detachment at Fatiko, without the power of communication.

About a month previous, Abou Saood had himself visited Kabba Réga at Masindi, and had laid a snare that will be explained hereafter.

At 8.30 A.M. we were in the saddle, and started from Foweera. Suleiman came to kiss my hand at my departure. We rode at once into the low forest, and as the last man of our large party disappeared from view, Suleiman returned to his zareeba. He then prepared for vengeance, which through my presence had been long delayed.

He and his ferocious people dragged the prisoner (whose life I had protected) from the camp, until they arrived at a thick grove of plantains about 200 paces from the station. Rahonka, Lokara, Quonga, Matonsé, and other principal chiefs, were summoned to witness the impotence of the Pacha's power to save; and to see with their own eyes the defiance that Suleiman would exhibit to the orders of a Christian.

"Now let the natives clasp the knees of the Pacha and expect security from Suleiman!"

The ruffian drew his sabre, and with his own hand

in the presence of a crowd of witnesses, he hacked off the head of the unfortunate prisoner, and thus publicly ridiculed my authority.

In the meantime, while this murder was being committed, we were travelling onward without a suspicion of treachery.

Accompanied by Lady Baker, I rode at the head of the party with my usual advanced guard of five picked men of "The Forty." Lieutenant Baker walked on foot, as he wished to save his horse's back that was slightly galled.

We rode far in advance, as there was no danger to be apprehended in this country, and my five guards with knapsacks, small axes, and general accoutrements, kept the pace of four miles an hour for about twenty-one miles to Kisoona. The march had been through forest and grass about four feet in height, which was now growing vigorously after the recent showers. The large trees were covered with orchids, among which I noticed a peculiar species which hung from the boughs like an apron. This was exceedingly pretty, as the leaf was about eighteen inches in breadth, the edges were scalloped and of a copper-brown colour, while the upper portion was dark green.

The whole country had been desolated by civil war, in which the companies of Abou Saood had taken a prominent part, and had carried off a great number of the women.

Kisoona was a poor straggling place in the centre of the forest; but although the beehive-shaped nuts were far apart, there was the usual amount of filth and ashes that disgrace the villages of Unyoro. A very large plantation of bananas afforded food for the inhabitants, all of whom seemed to have disappeared.

Throughout Unyoro the soil is exceedingly rich; thus the tobacco gardens exhibited an extreme luxuriance, and the size of the leaves formed a great contrast to the plants in the hot soil of the Bari country.

I placed a sentry over the tobacco, and cautioned the troops against stealing or in any way damaging the crops.

A native of Umiro travelled as our interpreter. This man was a confidential slave belonging to Kabba Réga, and formed one of his regiment. Umbogo (or the "Buffalo") was a highly intelligent fellow, and spoke good Arabic, as he had been constantly associated with the Arab slave-traders. I had supplied him with clothes, and he looked quite respectable in a blue shirt belted round the waist, with a cartouche-pouch of leopard's skin, that had been given him by the people of the zareeba. Umbogo carried a musket, and was altogether a very important personage, although a slave.

The long march of twenty-one miles, through forest, along a rough and narrow path, had delayed the carriers and the cattle. Although my men had stepped along so briskly, the rear-guard did not arrive until the evening. A tremendous downpour of rain deluged the ground. This was a godsend to us, who were well housed and tented, as we caught a good supply of water with the mackintosh camp-sheets that was very superior to that of a small pool, which usually sufficed for the village people.

I always travelled with a large sponging bath, which was one of the household gods of the expedition. This was now full of pure rain-water. The value of this old friend was incalculable. In former years I had crossed the Atbara river in this same bath, lashed upon an angareb (stretcher), supported by inflated skins. Without extra assistance it would support my weight, and it was always used when crossing a small stream, assisted by two men wading, one of whom held it on either side to prevent it from overturning. Thus we could travel without the necessity of plunging into deep mud and water.

Such a utensil was invaluable for watering the horses; also for washing clothes, or for receiving a supply of rain-water, during a shower, from the camp-sheets suspended above the bath.

The neighbourhood of Kisoona was very populous, but the villages were all concealed in the forest, amidst vast groves of bananas.

There was a large tract of potato cultivation; a supply of these welcome roots was with difficulty obtained from the natives.

It appeared to be a repetition of my former experience in this country, which unpleasantly reminded me of the scarcity of food during my first exploration of Unyoro.

On the following morning (12th April), when the horses were saddled and we were ready to start, not a single native was forthcoming. Every man of about 200 carriers had absconded!

"Although Rahonka had assured me, previous to starting from the river, that food would be ready for the troops at every halting-place, nothing has been prepared. We are thus left as much neglected as during my former voyage in this detestable country. There is not one sheik with us, although three principal chiefs were told off to accompany us to Masindi. I therefore told our friend Pittia that I should not proceed farther, as I would have nothing to do with so miserable a king as Kabba Réga.

"I immediately sent Colonel Abd-el-Kader back to Foweera with thirty men, and a letter to Suleiman, ordering him to collect 300 men at once to return my effects to his zareeba. I tied Pittia, the guide, by a small cord attached to the neck, as I feared he also might escape. What can be done with these treacherous people?

"There is a report, now confirmed by the dragoman, Umbogo, that a plan had been arranged between Suleiman and Rahonka that I should be led out of their way, and they would then join their forces and attack Rionga.

"I do not believe that Suleiman would place his head in such a halter.

"Very heavy rain at 1 P.M.

"*April* 13.—The soil is wonderfully fertile—this is a chocolate-coloured vegetable loam. Among the crops is a species of esculent *solanum*, with large orange-coloured berries; both the fruit and leaves are eaten by the natives.

"I repaired my boots to-day with the milk from the indiarubber-tree. Julian (Lieutenant Baker) had fever. Colonel Abd-el-Kader and party returned at 2.40 P.M., having marched rapidly, and accomplished their mission and a journey of forty-two miles in twenty-seven hours and forty minutes.

"This excellent officer brought with him, secured by a small leather thong, by the neck, the great sheiks Kittākără, Matonsé, and several smaller fry.

"The royal sheik, Rahonka, escaped by breaking through the side of his hut.

"The report was as follows :—

"Colonel Abd-el-Kader and his party of thirty men had arrived at Suleiman's zareeba at about 8 P.M. He found the vakeels, Suleiman and Eddrees, surrounded by many of their men, apparently in consultation.

"Upon Abd-el-Kader's appearance, the men moved off, one by one, and quietly packed up their effects, preparatory to a general flight.

"Abd-el-Kader informed Suleiman of the flight of our carriers. He at once proceeded to the native zareeba, about 200 yards from the camp. He there found the principal sheiks in the hut of Rahonka.

"Abd-el-Kader immediately informed them of the purport of his arrival, and requested the sheiks to accompany him to the zareeba of Suleiman. Rahonka begged to be left alone for a short time to enable him to dress.

"Abd-el-Kader waited outside the door of the hut, and, becoming tired of so long a delay, he re-entered, and, to his astonishment, he found the dwelling *empty*. Rahonka had escaped by a hole in the straw wall.

"Suspicion being raised by the incomprehensible flight of Rahonka, the colonel placed the remaining sheiks under a guard, and led them to Suleiman's zareeba. He then applied to Suleiman for a guard of eight men to watch the sheiks during the night, as his own party required rest.

"Suleiman now informed him that he could not supply the men, as all his people had absconded from fear (of Abd-el-Kader).

"On the following morning the colonel perceived, from the smoke above our old camp on the opposite side of the river (which in this part is 500 yards broad), that Suleiman's people had escaped during the night, and had crossed the river with all their slaves and effects.

"This was the first act of my new irregular levy— they had positively run away from the colonel like a parcel of hostile natives!

"Suleiman and Eddrees declared that they could not control their men, who were afraid that I had ordered my officer to release the slaves that were in their possession.[1]

[1] There is no doubt that in truth they considered that I had heard of the murder of the prisoner committed to the care of

"Abd-el-Kader ordered Suleiman to accompany him to my halting-place at Kisoona. Suleiman declined upon the excuse that he had some business, but that he would present himself to-morrow.

"I can stand these scoundrels' conduct no longer. I have tried lenient measures, and I had hoped that by forming Suleiman's party into an irregular corps I might be able, by degrees, to change their habits, and to reduce them by good discipline into useful troops, but 'Can the Ethiopian change his skin, or the leopard his spots?'

"I immediately released and examined the captive sheiks, who one and all declared that the fault lay with Suleiman, who had previously arranged the plan with Rahonka: that when I should be led away a distance of two days' journey, he would assemble his men and attack Rionga in conjunction with Rahonka's army.

"The report of Umbogo, the dragoman, is thus corroborated by overwhelming evidence. This man, Umbogo, declares that Abou Saood wrote to Suleiman, instructing him to wait until I should have passed on, and then to bring all his slaves to Fabbo.

"I immediately sent Captain Mohammed Deii with

Suleiman, and that I had sent the colonel and his party to make inquiries.

fifty men, including twenty-five of the 'Forty Thieves,' with orders to liberate all slaves that might be discovered within the zareeba. He was to summon all the people of Suleiman, and to disarm those who had run away from the colonel, Abd-el-Kader.

" In the event of resistance, he was to use the force at his disposal, and at all hazards to prevent the escape of the slavers across the river.

" Suleiman and Eddrees were to be brought before me.

" A heavy shower fell just after the troops started.

" *April* 14.—Julian's horse, Gazelle, died last night; the poor animal had been ill for some days.

" Quonga, who is the sheik of this district, came this morning and excused his absence in rather a lame fashion, by saying that he had been collecting food for the troops, together with carriers, who are now ready to transport the baggage to Masindi. He declared that Kabba Réga was impatient, and had sent three of Suleiman's people to deliver the message to me, but these rascals had passed on this morning direct to the zareeba of Suleiman, without communicating with us on the way.

" Quonga not only corroborated the testimony of

the sheiks and the dragoman, Umbogo, against Suleiman, as having conspired to attack Rionga after my departure, but he gave additional evidence, that 'Suleiman had told Rahonka and the great sheiks that I, the Pacha, knew nothing about war, that none of the government troops could shoot, and that I should only travel and subsist upon the country, but that he (Suleiman) would join them and kill Rionga after I should have departed.'

"This I believe to be true, as a few days ago, when speaking of the troops, I had told Suleiman that the Soudanis were very hardy soldiers for marching and resisting climate, but that generally they were bad shots. Thus, in a treacherous manner, he has informed the natives that the soldiers of the government cannot shoot. In the afternoon, fresh reports reached me that Suleiman had, with his own hands, murdered the native to whom I had given protection. He had committed this horrible act the instant that my back was turned, and he had exhibited the crime before the great sheiks in derision of my authority!

"At 4.30. P.M. Captain Mohammed Deii returned with his party of fifty men, together with the vakeels, Suleiman and Eddrees, with six of their men who had been met upon their road from Masindi, and eight slaves.

"As I had expected to hear, the greater number of Suleiman's people had escaped with their slaves to Fabbo, when the colonel, Abd-el-Kader, had suddenly appeared among them, as his arrival had disconcerted all Suleiman's arrangements; and my detention at Kisoona had completely upset all his plans respecting an alliance with Rahonka's army. That cunning general had gone off straight to Kabba Réga after his escape through the wall of his hut.

"I summoned the great sheiks, Kittākără, Quonga, together with Pittia, and several others. These men gave their evidence most clearly as witnesses to the plan arranged by Suleiman for the attack upon Rionga ; and as eye-witnesses to the murder of the prisoner, whom they saw dragged by Suleiman and his men to the grove of bananas, where he was beheaded.

"I ordered Suleiman and his people to be disarmed, and secured both him and Eddrees in shébas.

"The sun had set, and, the sky being over-cast, it had become extremely dark.

"I proceeded at once to the trial of Suleiman and Eddrees, as the witnesses were all present.

"The bugler sounded the 'taboor' (assembly), and

the officers and troops quickly appeared, and formed in line two deep, facing the table at which we sat. I ordered half-a-dozen large port-fires to be brought; these were lighted and held by six men who stepped forward from the ranks. The blaze of red light illumined the whole neighbourhood, and cast a peculiar glow upon the dark foliage of the bananas, and the forms of the dusky chiefs who sat in a line opposite the troops.

"Suleiman and Eddrees were led by the guard, and appeared before the tribunal. Suleiman, although pinioned, retained the same haughty swagger that had always distinguished him. The charges against him were as follows:—

"1. For having conspired to attack Rionga in direct opposition to my positive orders.

"2. For treasonably speaking against the government of the Khedive to the native chiefs.

"3. For arranging and abetting the escape of the irregular new levy, who had enlisted in the government service, together with that of the slaves.

"4. For having murdered, with his own hands, a native whom I had confided to his care.

"After a careful trial the prisoner was found guilty upon every charge; and the second vakeel, Eddrees, was proved to have been an accomplice.

"I immediately sentenced Suleiman to receive 200 lashes upon the spot, as a first instalment of future punishment. Blue lights had been substituted for the port-fires that had burned out, and the effect of this change of colour heightened the theatrical appearance of the scene, as the haughty brigand, Suleiman, was laid upon the ground by the ready troops to receive his punishment.

"My ever-present attendant, Monsoor, volunteered to be one of the whippers, and the pride and haughtiness of the prisoner were soon exchanged for effeminate cries for pardon. It was this same man, Suleiman, who had flogged a poor boy nearly to death during my former journey, and the life of the child had, with difficulty been saved by the kind attention of my wife. When he now cried for mercy, I recalled to his recollection the unfortunate boy whose posterior he had literally *cut off* with a whip of hippopotamus' hide . . . .

"Eddrees was sentenced to receive 100 lashes, but when thirty strokes had been administered, the native chiefs interceded in his behalf, saying that the great blame rested upon Suleiman, and that Eddrees was not a bad man, but that he was obliged to obey the orders of his superior.

"They now continued, that Suleiman had ruined

the country, that he had kidnapped all the women and children, and that the natives had fled from their homes as the result.

"I was much struck with the straightforward, at the same time moderate, behaviour of the native chiefs. I accordingly spared Eddrees, who at once turned evidence against Suleiman, together with two of his own soldiers.

"They signed a declaration as witnesses of the murder of the native by Suleiman. This paper was formally witnessed and signed by Lieutenant Baker, Colonel Abd-el-Kader, and Captain Mohammed Deii.

"The punishment having been awarded and the prisoners withdrawn, but secured in shébas by the guard, I addressed the native chiefs, assuring them of my protection; and that in future the country should be governed with perfect justice; that property and the rights of women and children would be respected, and that any transgressor of the law would be punished. I explained that the object of the expedition was to bring prosperity; but, on the other hand, I should expect fidelity from Kabba Réga and his people. I told them that I should lead the prisoners in shébas to Kabba Réga, he must then summon a general assembly of his chiefs to hear and witness the truth.

"I now ordered the bugler to sound the 'destoor' (retreat), and the troops marched back to their quarters.

"The trial was over; the blue lights had burnt out, and we were now in comparative darkness beneath the banana foliage, with a feeble lamp glimmering on the table.

"The native chiefs declared their perfect confidence in the government, and that we should start on the following morning direct for Masindi."

CHAPTER V.

MARCH TO MASINDI.

"*April* 15.—The latitude of Kisoona was 2° 2′ 36″ N. We started at 11 A.M. till 1 P.M., reaching Kasiga— eight miles—through interminable forest full of fine ripe yellow plums and unripe custard apples.

"*April* 16—Started at 8.20 A.M. till 12—arriving at Koki—thick forest throughout the march. We passed several small villages, and made twelve miles, N. lat. 1° 59′. I gave various seeds of European vegetables to the headman; and I myself sowed the seeds of water-melons and sweet melons in his garden, and explained their cultivation.

"*April* 17—All the carriers have absconded. There is extensive cultivation in this district, and the tobacco is well attended, as the tops of the plants are carefully nipped off to prevent them from running too much into stalk.

"The chief, Kittākără, who is a kind of prime minister

to Kabba Réga, gave me this afternoon the history of the country.

"Kabba Réga is the sixteenth king since the original conquest of Unyoro by the Gallas. These invaders arrived from the East, beyond the country of the Langgos.

"To this day a peculiar custom is observed. Before a new king can ascend the throne, he is compelled to sleep during two nights on the east of the Victoria Nile. He then marches along the path by which his victorious ancestor invaded Unyoro, and upon reaching the river, he takes boat and crosses to the exact landing-place where the original conqueror first set his foot upon the frontier.

"*April* 18.—I purchased a quantity of excellent tobacco and divided it among the soldiers as a reward for their having respected the native gardens during the march.

"Kittākāra is the only gentleman that I have seen in the country, and he never asks for presents, thus forming an extraordinary exception to the rule of Unyoro society.

"I gave him a blue blanket, a zinc mirror, a spoon, comb, and four red and yellow handkerchiefs. To Quonga I gave a tarboosh (fez), and four yards of Turkey red cloth.

"*April* 19.—Fresh carriers arrived, and we started at 10.45 A.M., and halted at 4 P.M.—twelve miles. Forest and high grass as usual throughout the route, which would render this country highly dangerous in case of hostilities.

"The lofty mountains on the west shore of the Albert N'yanza are now about fifty miles distant. We halted at a populous district, and occupied a village at Chorobézé.

"There is an impression of general ruin in passing through this wonderfully fertile country. The slave-hunters and their allies have produced this frightful result by ransacking the district for slaves.

"The civil dissensions after Kamrasi's death were favourable for the traders' schemes. The two sons, Kabba Réga and Kabka Miro, contended for the throne. The latter was royally born by sire and mother, but Kabba Réga was a son by a shepherdess of the Bahoomas. The throne belonged by inheritance to Kabka Miro, who, not wishing to cause a civil war, and thus destroy the country, challenged his brother to single combat in the presence of all the people. The victor was to be king.

"Kabba Réga was a coward, and refused the challenge. The chivalrous Kabka Miro again offered terms:—Kabba Réga, as the son of the shepherdess, should take all the flocks and herds; and Kabka Miro would occupy the throne.

"Kabba Réga, like most cowards, was exceedingly cunning and treacherous, and, with the alliance of Suleiman's people, he shot his gallant brother, and secured both the throne and his father's flocks.

"*April* 20.—All the native carriers have, as usual, absconded. We are now about twenty-seven miles from Masindi, the head-quarters of Kabba Réga, and yet there are no signs of control.

"I ascended a small hill near the village, and sighted the waters of the Albert N'yanza, due west, about twenty miles distant.

"*April* 21.—About fifty natives collected. I sent off Colonel Abd-el-Kader with the prisoners to Kabba Réga to complain of the want of carriers and provisions. I ordered him to disarm all the traders' people, and the Baris in their employ, who might be at Masindi; as the news has arrived that the men belonging to Suleiman have returned to Foweera and are actually taking slaves in the neighbourhood.

"*April* 22.—More natives collected. I sent off 140 loads in charge of Morgiān Agha, with an escort of twenty soldiers, and the herd of cattle. The latitude of Chorobézé was 1° 57′ N.

"*April* 23.—The natives having collected, we

started at 10.5 A.M. I was obliged to walk, as my good horse, 'Greedy Grey,' is sick.

"The route was through forest and high grass as usual. We marched seventeen miles, and halted at immense groves of bananas at a place called Jon Joke.

"The baggage and cattle arrived after sunset, Morgiān Agha having been deserted yesterday by all the carriers. As usual, throughout the route the water is bad.

"Alas! my poor horse, 'Greedy Grey,' died to-day. He was the most perfect of all the horses I had brought from Cairo.

"*April* 24.—As usual, the native carriers have all bolted ! Last night a sergeant arrived with a letter addressed to me from Abd-el-Kader, who has carried out my orders by disarming the traders' party.

"*April* 25.—It rained throughout the night. The carriers sent by Kabba Réga arrived early. We started at 8.15 A.M., and marched ten miles, arriving at last at the capital of Unyoro—Masindi.

"This large town is situated on high undulating land with an extensive view, bounded on the west by the range of mountains bordering the Albert N'yanza, about fifty miles distant. The country is open, but covered with high grass. A succession of knolls, all more or less ornamented with park-like trees, characterize the landscape, which slopes gradually down towards the west, and drains into the Albert N'yanza, which is about twenty miles distant.

"The town of Masindi is, as usual throughout Unyoro, exceedingly neglected, and is composed of some thousand large beehive-shaped straw huts, without any arrangement or plan.

"I selected a position beneath a large banian-tree, which I had cleared from the herbage, and having pitched the tent, the natives tore up about an acre of the high grass, and we encamped upon the clean ground.

"Kabba Réga sent a present of twenty-nine loads of tullaboon (a small seed, *Eleusine Coracan*), a quantity of plantains and potatoes, and six goats.

"This spot is in N. lat. 1° 45′, and is seventy-nine miles, by our route from the river at Foweera. We are thus 322 miles by route from Ismailïa (Gondokoro).

"*April* 26.—I visited Kabba Réga officially, with the officers and troops in full uniform, and the band playing.

"I found him sitting in his divan; this was a large neatly-constructed hut, ornamented with some very common printed cotton cloths, which had arrived *viâ* Zanzibar. Kabba Réga was very well clad, in beautifully made bark-cloth striped with black;

he was excessively neat, and appeared to be about twenty years of age. He gave me the same account of the atrocious proceedings of Abou Saood's companies that I had already received from his chiefs, and he expressed his delight at my arrival, and that I had captured Suleiman and some of his people.

"I explained the intentions of the Khedive of Egypt, at the same time I lamented the terrible change that had occurred throughout his country since my former visit. I assured him that the future would be prosperous, and that, under the protection of Egypt, he would never have further cause for alarm. I then summoned the prisoners that had been captured and disarmed by Colonel Abd-el-Kader; and having explained the charges against them, they were publicly flogged in the presence of a multitude of Kabba Réga's people, while Suleiman and Eddrees were led away in shébas, to the astonishment and delight of all beholders.

"The slaves that had been discovered in the possession of Suleiman's people were now brought forward, and having been identified by Kabba Réga and his people as belonging to Unyoro, they were at once released, and I returned both young girls and boys to their country. One woman did not wish to leave the traders, as she had been married to one of the company for some years, and had several children.

"I explained that they were actually *free*—to remain with their captors, or to return to their homes, as they thought proper.

"This was a good opportunity for assuring both Kabba Réga and his people that I should restore all the slaves that had been carried out of their country to the various stations of Abou Saood at Fatiko, Fabbo, Faloro, &c.

"I described to the young king and his chiefs that I was determined to suppress the slave trade, and that I had hitherto forborne to interfere in the release of the slaves at the various stations, as it would have been impossible to have returned them to their distant homes, neither could I have supplied them with food. I was now at Masindi, beyond the farthest station of Abou Saood, and I should certainly insist upon the return of every slave that had been kidnapped from this country. This would at once prove to the inhabitants of Unyoro the benefit of the Khedive's protection.

"*April* 27.—Kabba Réga had arranged to return my visit.

"I had ordered a broad roadway to be cleared

from Kabba Réga's divan to my tent, which was pitched beneath an enormous fig-tree or banian (*Ficus Indica*). The troops were lined on either side of this approach in their best uniforms.

"The band was stationed near the tent, which was spread with skins and small carpets, all the sides being open.

"An hour and a half passed away after the first messenger had arrived from Kabba Réga to announce his arrival. One after another, messengers had hurried to assure me that the king was just now approaching; but still the troops remained in expectation, and no king made an appearance.

"At length, after this long delay, he sent Rahonka to say that 'if it was all the same to me, he would rather see me at his own house.'

"This unmannerly young cub was actually suspicious of foul play, and was afraid to enter my tent!

"I immediately told Rahonka that his king was evidently not old enough to have learnt good manners, therefore I should at once dismiss the troops, who had already been waiting for nearly two hours to do him honour.

"I ordered the bugler to sound the 'destoor,' and the troops at once obeyed the signal.

"Terrified at the sound of the bugle, which was known to be some mysterious order, Rahonka implored me not to be angry, and he would at once bring Kabba Réga to the tent. The troops resumed their position.

"In a few minutes a great din of horns, drums, and whistles announced his approach, and we observed him walking down the road with an extraordinary gait. He was taking enormous strides, as though caricaturing the walk of a giraffe. This was supposed to be an imitation of M'tésé, the king of Uganda, whose ridiculous attempt to walk like a lion has been described by Speke.

"Kabba Réga thus stalked along, followed by his great chiefs, Kittākără, Matonsé, Rahonka, Quonga, and a number of others. Upon arrival opposite the band, the bugles and drums suddenly commenced with such a clash of cymbals that he seemed rather startled, and he entered the tent in the most undignified manner, with an air of extreme shyness half concealed by audacity.

"He was trembling with nervous anxiety, and with some hesitation he took his seat upon the divan that had been prepared for him. His principal chiefs sat upon skins and carpets arranged upon the ground.

"A crowd of about 2,000 people had accompanied him, making a terrific noise with whistles, horns, and drums. These were now silenced, and the troops formed a guard around the tent to keep the mob at a respectful distance. Every now and then several men of Kabba Réga's body-guard rushed into the crowd and laid about them with bludgeons five feet long, hitting to the right and left. This always chased the crowd away for a few minutes, until, by degrees, they resumed their position. Everybody was dressed up for a grand occasion, mostly in new clothes of bark-cloth, and many were in skins of wild animals, with their heads fantastically ornamented with the horns of goats or antelopes. The sorcerers were an important element. These rascals, who are the curse of the country, were, as usual, in a curious masquerade with fictitious beards manufactured with a number of bushy cows' tails.

"Kabba Réga was about five feet ten inches in height, and of extremely light complexion. His eyes were very large, but projected in a disagreeable manner. A broad but low forehead and high cheek bones, added to a large mouth, with rather prominent but exceedingly white teeth, complete the description of his face. His hands were beautifully shaped, and his finger-nails were carefully pared and scrupulously clean. The nails of his feet were equally well attended to. He wore sandals of raw buffalo-hide, but neatly formed, and turned up round the edges.

"His robe of bark-cloth, which completely covered his body, was exquisitely made, and had been manufactured in Uganda, which country is celebrated for this curious production.

"This was Kabba Réga, the son of Kamrasi, the sixteenth king of Unyoro, of the Galla conquerors, a *gauche*, awkward, undignified lout of twenty years of age, who thought himself a great monarch. He was cowardly, cruel, cunning, and treacherous to the last degree. Not only had he ordered the destruction of his brother, Kabka Miro, but, after his death, he had invited all his principal relations to visit him; these he had received with the greatest kindness, and at parting, he had presented them with gifts, together with an escort of his body-guard, called bonasoora, to see them *safe home*. These men, by the young king's instructions, murdered them all in the high grass during their return journey. By these means he had got rid of troublesome relations, and he now sat securely upon the throne with only one great enemy; this was Rionga, the stanch and determined foe of his father, who had escaped from every treachery, and still lived to defy him in the north-eastern provinces of Unyoro.

"It was easy to understand that he would welcome my arrival with a force sufficiently large to assist him against Rionga, and at the same time to rid him of Suleiman's party. He made use of the latter force as mercenary troops, to which he was obliged to allow boundless licence; otherwise he might be invaded by the whole power of the combined companies of Fabbo, Faloro, Fatiko, and Farragenia. These companies might at any time change sides and ally themselves with Rionga, thus, could I clear the country of such doubtful allies, he would be relieved from all cause of alarm."

Notwithstanding these advantages, the young king sat uneasily upon his divan, and appeared timid and suspicious. According to Turkish etiquette, a handsome *chibouque*, trimmed with blue silk and gold, was handed to him. He examined the amber mouth-piece but declined to smoke, as "tobacco would blacken his teeth;" this was a curious excuse from a Central African dandy.

I begged him to accept the long pipe as a reminiscence of my arrival. Coffee and sherbet were then handed to him, but he declined both, and insisted upon two of his chiefs drinking the whole; during which operation he watched them attentively, as though in expectation of some poisonous effect. This was conduct that boded no good for future relations. My wife tried to converse with him through the interpreter, Umbogo. Kabba Réga then explained that he recollected us both, as he was one of a crowd when a boy on the day we started from M'rooli for the Albert N'yanza.

The conversation quickly turned upon Rionga, whom he declared must be either captured or killed, before any improvement could take place in the country. The young king assumed that it was already arranged that I should assist him in this laudable object. I now changed the conversation by ordering a large metal box to be brought in. This had already been filled with an assortment of presents, including a watch. I explained to him that the latter had been intended for his father, Kamrasi, in the recollection of his constant demands for my watch during my former visit. The new toy was ticking loudly, and it was of course handed round and held to the ear of each chief before it was replaced in the box.

Kabba Réga replied that "he knew I had been a great friend of his father, Kamrasi, and that I had now brought many valuable presents for him; but I must not forget, that, although the father was dead, the son (himself) was still alive, therefore I might at once hand over to him all that I had intended for his father."

This was a true son of his father in the art of begging. I replied, that "hens did not lay all their eggs in one day, but continued one by one; and that I hoped, when I should know him better, he would discover the advantage of commerce, as the various goods that had now been introduced were intended to exhibit the manufactures of my own country. These would continue to arrive in Unyoro to be exchanged for ivory."

I then exhibited the large musical box with drums and bells. This was one of the best instruments of its kind, and it played a remarkably good selection of airs, which quite charmed the audience. Among the presents I had given to Kabba Réga was a small musical snuff-box. This was now wound up and exhibited, but the greedy young fellow at once asked "Why I did not give him the large box?"

I gave him a regular lecture upon the advantages of commerce that would introduce an important change in this extraordinary country; at the same time I recalled to his recollection, that I had promised his father to open up a commercial route by which the productions and manufactures of the north should arrive in Unyoro, and render that country even more prosperous than Uganda. I had now arrived, as the lieutenant of the Khedive, according to my promise, and the whole of the equatorial Nile basin would be taken under his protection. No unnecessary wars would be permitted, but he (Kabba Réga) would remain as the representative of the government, and the affairs of the country would be conducted through him alone.

I assured him that no country could prosper without industry and a good government; that agriculture was the foundation of a country's wealth; and that war or civil disturbance, which interfered with agricultural employment, would ruin the kingdom. He replied that " Rionga was the sole cause of war; therefore it would be necessary to destroy him before any improvements could be made. If Rionga were killed and the slave-hunters expelled from the country, there might be some hope of progress; but that it was wasting breath to talk of commerce and agriculture until Rionga should be destroyed."

This was Kamrasi's old tune once more dinned into my ears. In my former journey I had been deserted by my carriers and starved for three months at Shooa

Moru, simply to induce me to yield to this repeated demand : " Kill Rionga ; or give me your men to assist me against Rionga."

From what I had heard I considered that Rionga must be a very fine fellow, and much superior to either Kamrasi or his son.

In my former journey I had accomplished a long and difficult exploration without firing a shot at a human being; and I had studiously avoided meddling in native politics, which is certain to involve a traveller in difficulty. It had always been a source of great satisfaction when I looked back to my past adventures, and reflected that I had never pulled a trigger at a native ; thus the arrival of a white man in these countries would be regarded without suspicion.

In my present expedition I had always endeavoured to preserve peace, but, as this work will show, I was in every instance forced to war in absolute self-defence. I was therefore determined not to attack Rionga, unless he should presume to defy the government.

In reply to Kabba Réga and his chiefs, who all had joined in the argument, I declared that I would find means to establish peace, and that Rionga would assuredly come to terms. Nothing would induce me to use force against Rionga or any other person, unless absolutely necessary. I suggested to Kabba Réga that he should for a moment change positions with Rionga. What would his feelings be should I wantonly attack him, simply because I had been requested to do so by his enemy?

No argument was of any avail. Kabba Réga replied, "You were my father's friend and brother: your wife was the same. You drove back the slave-hunters under Wat-el-Mek by hoisting your flag. Since you left us, the slave-hunters have returned and ruined the country. My father is dead; but Rionga is still alive. Now YOU are my father, and your wife is my mother: will you allow your son's enemy to live?"

It was quite useless to attempt reason with this hardened young fellow, who had not an idea of mercy in his disposition. As he had murdered his own relatives by the foulest treachery, so he would of course destroy any person who stood in his way. I therefore changed the conversation to Abou Saood.

Kabba Réga and his sheiks all agreed that he had arrived here some time ago in a very miserable plight, exceedingly dirty, and riding upon a donkey. He was without baggage of any kind, and he introduced himself by giving a present to Kabba Réga of an old, battered metal basin and jug, in which he washed, together with a very old and worn-out small carpet, upon which he was accustomed to sit. With these magnificent presents he declared that he was "the son of a sultan, who had come to visit the king of Unyoro."

Kabba Réga had replied that "he did not believe it, as he had heard that he was simply a trader."

Reports had reached Unyoro that I had arrived at Gondokoro, and that I was on my way to visit Kamrasi, and to explore the Albert N'yanza; therefore Kabba Réga had questioned Abou Saood concerning me.

"Oh," Abou Saood replied, "that man that we call 'the traveller?' Oh yes, he was a very good fellow indeed; but he is dead. He died long ago. The Pacha is a very different person; and I hope he will never be able to reach this country. If he does, it will be a bad time for *you*."

"Indeed!" replied Kabba Réga. "I heard that the Pacha and the traveller, the friend of my father, were the same person."

"You have been deceived," said Abou Saood. "The Pacha is not like the traveller, or any other man. He is a monster with three separate heads, in each of which are six eyes—three upon each side. Thus with eighteen eyes he can see everything and every country at once. He has three enormous mouths, which are furnished with teeth like those of a crocodile, and he devours human flesh. He has already killed and eaten the Bari people and destroyed their country. Should he arrive here, he will pull you from the throne and seize your kingdom. You must fight him, and by no means allow him to cross the river at Foweera. My soldiers will fight him on the road from Gondokoro, as will all the natives of the country: but I don't think he will be able to leave Gondokoro, as he has a large amount of baggage, *and I have told the Baris not to transport it:*—thus he will have no carriers."

This was the actual report that Abou Saood had given to Kabba Réga, as the dragoman Umbogo had been the interpreter, in the presence of Mohammed, my old Cairo dragoman.

I laughed outright at this absurdity: at the same time it corroborated all that I had already heard of Abou Saood's treachery. I immediately asked Kabba Réga if he was satisfied now that he had seen me? He replied, "Abou Saood is a liar, and you are Kamrasi's friend, and my father: therefore you will, I am sure, assist me, and relieve me from my great enemy, Rionga. I shall then know that you are indeed my true friend."

Once more it was necessary to change the conversation. A number of buffoons that were kept about the court for the amusement of the young king now came forward. The crowd was driven back, and an open space having been thus cleared, they performed a curious theatrical scene, followed by a general fight with clubs, until one man, having knocked down all the party, remained the victor. The scene terminated with an act of disgusting indecency, which created roars of laughter from the immense crowd, who evidently considered this was the great joke of the piece.

"Kabba Réga now took leave, and retired as he had before arrived, with drums, whistles, horns, flageolets, making a horrid din . . . ."

The spot that I had selected for a station was at the southern edge of the town, from which site the land sloped into a valley about a hundred feet below. I had at once commenced clearing away the high grass, and, as usual when first settling, I had broken up a few small plots, and had already sown seeds of English cucumbers, sweet melons, &c.

The soil was wonderfully rich, at the same time it was very easily worked. When the tall rank grass was torn out by the roots, a fine surface was exposed that resembled dark chocolate. This was a vegetable loam, with a minimum of two feet thickness, resting upon a bright red quartz gravel.

The quartz was not rounded, and appeared to be only the residue of decayed rock that had never been subjected to the action of running water. When washed, a handful remained of sharp and clear white fragments.

With such a subsoil the country must be healthy, as the heaviest shower drained rapidly through the gravel.

I employed the prisoners in clearing the grass, while the soldiers commenced cultivation, and dug up the ground with a number of hoes that I borrowed from Kabba Réga.

These implements are nearly the same in shape as those in Gondokoro and throughout the Madi country, but smaller, and the iron is very brittle and inferior. They are not used like the Dutch hoe, with a long handle, but are fixed upon a piece of wood with a bend of natural growth, so that the hoe can be used with a downward stroke like a pick-axe.

On 29th April I commenced building a government house and public divan.

The king of Uganda (M'tésé) has envoys throughout the countries which surround his dominions. One of these chiefs, who represented M'tésé at Masindi, paid me a visit, and gave me a good deal of information.

He described the M'wootan N'zige (Albert N'yanza) as forming the western frontier of Karagwé, from which point it turned westward for a distance unknown. This was a similar description to that given by Kamrasi some years ago.

I gave the envoy a red and yellow handkerchie to tie around his head. The man was neatly dressed in Indian clothes that had arrived from Bombay *viâ* Zanzibar.

On 30th April, Kabba Réga sent a present of twelve elephants' tusks, forty-one loads of tullaboon, twelve pots of sour plantain cider, and thirty-four cows. At the same time, he complained that some of Abou Saood's people were taking slaves in the neighbourhood of Foweera and Kisoona.

The principal chiefs, together with Kabba Réga, assured me that Abou Saood's people had been in the habit of torturing people to extract from them the secret of the spot in which their corn was concealed. Throughout Unyoro there are no granaries exposed at the present time, as the country has been ravaged by civil war; thus all corn is buried in deep holes specially arranged for that purpose. When the slave-hunters sought for corn, they were in the habit of catching the villagers and roasting their posteriors by holding them down on the mouth of a large earthen water-jar filled with glowing embers. If this torture of roasting alive did not extract the secret, they generally cut the sufferer's throat to terrify his companions, who would then divulge the position of the hidden stores to avoid a similar fate. This accusation was corroborated by Mohammed, the Cairo dragoman.

It is difficult to conceive the brutality of these brigands, who, thus relieved from the fear of a government, exhibit their unbridled passions by every horrible crime.

Umbogo, the interpreter, was now regularly installed in a hut within call of my tent. This man appeared to be exceedingly fond of us, and he was the main source of information.

He had a very lovely wife, a Bahooma, who was a light brown colour, with beautiful Abyssinian eyes; she had been given to him by Kabba Réga, with whom he was a great favourite.

Umbogo was very intelligent, and he took a great interest in all my plans for establishing free trade throughout the country: but he told me privately that he thought the idea would be opposed secretly by Kabba Réga, who would wish to monopolize all the ivory trade, in order to keep up the price, and to obtain the whole of the merchandize.

The great variety of goods much astonished him, and he advised me strongly to send for a large supply of soap, for which there would be a great demand, as a light complexion was greatly admired in Unyoro. He said that Mohammed, the Cairo dragoman, was several shades lighter since I had supplied him with soap; this was true, as he had been very filthy before my arrival; but Umbogo was persuaded that the difference between white and black people was caused by the fact of our ancestors having always used soap, while the blacks used only plain water. This ethnological fact having been established, I gave him a cake of soap, to his great delight, as he expressed his intention to become a white man.

I was always chatting with Umbogo and the various chiefs, especially with my favourite, Kittăkără, who was Kabba Réga's most confidential counsellor. They gave me a graphic account of the royal funeral that had taken place a few months ago, when Kamrasi was interred.

When a king of Unyoro dies, the body is exposed upon a framework of green wood, like a gigantic gridiron, over a slow fire. It is thus gradually dried, until it resembles an over-roasted hare.

Thus mummified, it is wrapped in new bark-cloths, and the body lies in state within a large house built specially for its reception.

The sons fight for the throne. The civil war may last for years, but during this period of anarchy, the late king's body lies still unburied.

At length, when victory has decided in favour of one of his sons, the conqueror visits the hut in which his father's body lies in state. He approaches the corpse, and standing by its side, he sticks the butt-end of his spear in the ground, and leaves it thus fixed near the right hand of the dead king. This is symbolical of victory.

The son now ascends the throne, and the funeral of his father must be his first duty.

An immense pit or trench is dug, capable of containing several hundred people.

This pit is neatly lined with new bark-cloths.

Several wives of the late king are seated together at the bottom, to bear upon their knees the body of their departed lord.

The night previous to the funeral, the king's

own regiment or body-guard surround many dwellings and villages, and seize the people indiscriminately as they issue from their doors in the early morning. These captives are brought to the pit's mouth.

Their legs and arms are now broken with clubs, and they are pushed into the pit on the top of the king's body and his wives.

An immense din of drums, horns, flageolets, whistles, mingled with the yells of a frantic crowd, drown the shrieks of the sufferers, upon whom the earth is shovelled and stamped down by thousands of cruel fanatics, who dance and jump upon the loose mould so as to force it into a compact mass; through which the victims of this horrid sacrifice cannot grope their way, the precaution having been taken to break the bones of their arms and legs. At length the mangled mass is buried and trodden down beneath a tumulus of earth, and all is still. The funeral is over.

Upon my return to Egypt I was one day relating this barbarous custom to a friend, when Mr. Kay, of Alexandria, reminded me of the curious coincidence in the description of the travels of Ibn Batuta, written A.D. 1346.

I am indebted to Mr. Kay for the following extract

from the work of Ibn Batuta, which will go far to prove the extreme conservatism of Africans in all that regards their rites and customs.

On his arrival at Khan Balik (Pekin), Ibn Batuta found that the khan, or emperor, was absent. His cousin had risen against him, and had been joined by most of the ameers, who accused the khan of having broken the laws of the Yassak, and had called upon him to abdicate.

The emperor marched against the rebels at the head of an army (which, Ibn Batuta says, consisted of a million cavalry and half a million infantry). A battle was fought, in which the khan was defeated and killed.

"This news reached the capital a few days after our arrival. The city was decorated, drums and trumpets were sounded, and games and rejoicings instituted, which continued for the space of a month.

"The dead body of the khan was then brought, together with the bodies of about a hundred men, his relations and followers.

"A large vault was constructed underground. It was spread with magnificent carpets, and the body of the khan was laid in it, along with his weapons and with the gold and silver vessels that were used in his household.

"Four female slaves and six memlūks were led into the vault, each provided with a drinking vessel filled with liquid.

"The entrance of the vault was walled up, and earth was heaped on the top until it resembled a large hillock.

"Four horses were then brought and made to gallop in the neighbourhood of the tomb until they stood still with fatigue. A large beam of wood was erected over the tomb, and to this the horses were attached, being impaled with wooden pales, passed longitudinally through their bodies and projecting through their mouths.

"The bodies of the khan's relatives, whom I have previously mentioned, were likewise deposited in vaults, each with his weapons and with the vessels used in his house.

"Those of highest rank were ten in number. Over each of their tombs three horses were impaled, and one horse over each of the others.

"The day was one of public solemnity, and no one abstained from its observance, neither man nor woman, Moslem nor infidel. All arrayed themselves in funeral garments—the infidels wearing white tailasans, and the Moslem white gowns.

"The empresses, wives of the khan, and his chief

followers remained in the neighbourhood of the tomb for forty days, living in tents. Some prolonged their stay up to a year, and a market was established at which provisions and every other necessary were sold.

"These are practices of the existence of which among any other people in these present times I have no personal knowledge.

"The Indian infidels and the people of China burn their dead. Others bury them, but without burying living men or women along with the corpse.

"But I was informed in the Soudan, by persons upon whose word full reliance may be placed, that among certain infidels in these countries, on the death of the king, a vault is constructed in which the corpse is laid, and along with it a certain number of his courtiers and servants; as also thirty persons, sons and daughters of the most distinguished men of the country. The fore-arms of these persons are first broken, as also their legs, below the knees, and drinking vessels are deposited with them in the tomb.

"I was informed by a person, one of the chief men of the Masuffahs, who dwelt in the country of Koobar, in the Soudan, and who was a favourite with the sultan, that on the death of the latter the people wished to bury my informant's son in the tomb along with those of their own children who had been chosen for the same purpose. He added: 'I remonstrated, saying, "How can ye do this? The lad is not of your faith, neither is he one of your children." 'Finally, I ransomed him,' he continued, 'with a heavy payment.'" . . . . . .

This is an interesting fact, that so long ago as the year 1346 such a practice was known to exist in Central Africa.

When the funeral rites of Kamrasi were over, Kabba Réga ascended the throne, and succeeded to all his father's wives, with the exception of his own mother. This is the invariable custom in Unyoro.

The throne is composed partly of copper and of wood. It is an exceedingly small and ancient piece of furniture, that has been handed down for many generations and is considered to be a cojoor, or talisman. There is also an ancient drum, which is considered with reverence as something uncanny, and the two articles are always jealously guarded by special soldiers, and are seldom used.

Should the throne be lost or stolen, the authority of the king would disappear, together with the talisman, and disorder would reign throughout the country until the precious object should be restored.

CHAPTER VI.

RESTORATION OF THE LIBERATED SLAVES.

THE work had now fairly commenced, and Kabba Réga and his chiefs were assured of a grand reform. Already the slave-hunters had been punished: the vakeel, Suleiman, was secured in the stocks, and the slaves that had been kidnapped had been restored to their homes in Unyoro. I now determined to insist upon the restoration of all the Unyoro slaves that had been carried away from this country, and were captives in the zareebas of Fatiko, Fabbo, Faloro, and Farragenia. From the descriptions of Kabba Réga and his chiefs, I considered that these prisoners amounted to about a thousand persons—women and children.

Umbogo, the interpreter, declared that Abou Saood's companies would attack the government troops, should I insist upon the liberation of the slaves. He had lived with these slave-hunters, and he had frequently heard them declare, that, "should the Pacha ever arrive in this country, and insist upon the suppression of slavery, they would shoot him rather than lose their slaves." I treated this idea as an absurdity.

At the same time that Kabba Réga and his people were eager for the restoration of the numerous women and children that had been stolen from Unyoro, they were themselves great slave-dealers.

M'tésé, the powerful King of Uganda, on the southern frontier of Unyoro, was in the habit of purchasing ivory in that country for the merchants of Zanzibar.

These purchases were made by an exchange of slaves, brass-coil bracelets, and long cotton shirts; which were either of British or Indian manufacture, that had arrived *viâ* Zanzibar.

M'tésé, with his usual sagacity, did not permit the merchants of that country to enter Uganda in force, but he received from them both slaves and merchandize, which he sent into the surrounding countries for the purchase of ivory. He thus monopolized the trade, and kept the price at a minimum.

In Unyoro there was an established value for a healthy young girl. Such a person was equal to a single elephant's tusk of the first class, or to a new shirt. Thus a girl could be purchased for a shirt, and she might be subsequently exchanged for a large elephant's tusk.

In the country of Uganda, where the natives are exceedingly clever as tailors and furriers, needles are in great demand. A handsome girl may be purchased for thirteen English needles! Thus for slave-traders there existed an excellent opening for a profitable business. A girl might be bought for thirteen needles in Uganda, to be exchanged in Unyoro for an elephant's tusk that would be worth twenty or thirty pounds in England.

Abou Saood's brigands had been far too lawless even for this innocent traffic, and in default of the merchandize necessary for such profitable exchanges, they had found it more convenient to kidnap the young girls, which saved much trouble in bargaining for needles and shirts.

In every African tribe that I have visited, I found slavery a natural institution of the country. I had at length discovered that it was bad policy to commence a dissertation against the slave trade generally; this attacked local interests, therefore it was more diplomatic to speak against the capture of women and children that *belonged to my hearers*, but to avoid a discussion upon the moral aspect of the slave trade.

The negro idea of the eighth commandment is this : " Thou shalt not steal—from ME ;" but he takes a liberal view of the subject when the property belongs to another.

I had been rather startled in the year of my arrival at Gondokoro, when, during the voyage, I landed and conversed with some sheiks of the Shir tribe. One of these headmen was loud in his complaints against the slave-hunters and against the slave trade in particular, from which his tribe had suffered. Many of the women and children had been carried off by a neighbouring tribe, called the Berri, on the east of the Nile. The sheik therefore proposed that I should join him with my troops and capture all the women and children that belonged to his enemies. This was natural enough, and was a simple example of the revenge that is common to uneducated human nature. The sheik and I got on famously, and I found a good listener, to whom I preached a touching sermon upon the horrors of the slave trade, which I was resolved to suppress.

The good man was evidently touched at the allusion to the forcible separation of children from their parents.

"Have you a son?" he asked.

"My sons are, unfortunately, dead," I replied.

"Indeed!" he exclaimed. "I have a son—an only son. He is a nice boy—a very good boy; about so high (showing his length upon the handle of his spear). I should like you to see my boy—he is very thin now; but if he should remain with you he would soon get fat. He's a really nice boy, and *always hungry*. You'll be so fond of him; he'll eat from morning till night; and still he'll be hungry. You'll like him amazingly; he'll give you no trouble if you only give him plenty to eat. He'll lie down and go to sleep, and he'll wake up hungry again. He's a good boy, indeed; and he's my only son. *I'll sell him to you for a molote!* (native iron spade)."

The result of my sermon on the slave trade, addressed to this affectionate father, was quite appalling. I was offered his only son in exchange for a spade! and this young nigger knave of spades was warranted to remain *always hungry*.

I simply give this anecdote as it occurred, without asserting that such conduct is the rule. At the same time, there can be no doubt that among the White Nile tribes any number of male children might be purchased from their parents—especially in seasons of scarcity.

Girls are always purchased, if required, as wives. It would be quite impossible to obtain a wife for love from any tribe that I have visited. "Blessed is he that hath his quiver full of them" (daughters). A large family of girls is a source of wealth to the father, as he sells each daughter for twelve or fifteen cows to her suitor. Every girl is certain to marry; thus a dozen daughters will bring a fortune of at least 150 cows to their parents in all pastoral countries.

In Unyoro, cattle are scarce, and they belong to the king; therefore the girls are purchased for various commodities—such as brass-coil bracelets, bark-cloths, cotton shirts, ivory, &c.

I was anxious to establish a new and legitimate system of trade in this country, which would be the first step towards a higher civilization. I accordingly devoted every energy to the completion of the station, in which we were assisted by the natives, under the direction of their various headmen.

The order and organization of Unyoro were a great contrast to the want of cohesion of the northern tribes. Every district throughout the country was governed by a chief, who was responsible to the king for the state of his province. This system was extended to sub-governors and a series of lower officials in every district, who were bound to obey the orders of the lord-lieutenant. Thus every province had a responsible head, that could be at once cut off should disloyalty or other signs of bad government appear in a certain district.

In the event of war, every governor could appear, together with his contingent of armed men, at a short notice.

These were the rules of government that had been established for many generations throughout Unyoro.

The civil war had ceased, and Kabba Réga having ascended the throne, the country had again fallen into the order that a previous good organization rendered easy.

The various headmen of the district now appeared daily, with their men laden with thatch-grass and canes for the construction of the station.

I commenced a government house, and a private dwelling adjoining for myself.

On my first arrival at Masindi I had begged Kabba Réga to instruct his people to clear away about fifty acres of grass around our station, and to break up the ground for cultivation, as I wished my troops to sow and reap their own corn, instead of living at the expense of the natives.

The system, both in Uganda and Unyoro, is bad and unjust.

Should visitors arrive, they are not allowed to purchase food from the people, but they must be fed by the king's order at the cost of the inhabitants. This generally results in their not being fed at all, as the natives quit the neighbourhood.

I had suffered much from hunger in Unyoro, during my former visit, in the reign of Kamrasi; therefore I wished to protect myself against famine by a timely cultivation of the surrounding fertile land, that was now covered with rank grass about nine feet high.

In a military point of view it was impolitic to sit down within a station incircled by a dense grass covert, and although I had not the most remote suspicion of hostility in this country, I preferred a situation whence we could enjoy an extensive landscape.

The Albert N'yanza lay distant about twenty miles on the west, in the deep basin which characterizes this extraordinary sheet of water. Immense volumes of cloud rose in the early morning from the valley which marked the course of the lake, as the evaporation from the great surface of water condensed into mist, when it rose to the cooler atmosphere of the plateau of 1,500 feet above the level.

The proposal of farming did not appear to please

Kabba Réga. It was explained that the men were not accustomed to labour in the fields, as all agricultural work was performed by the women, all of whom were now absent and engaged in preparing their own land.

Although Masindi was a large town, I was struck by the absence of females. The only women that I saw were two, one of whom was the pretty wife of Umbogo the dragoman. It has already been explained, that the absence of women generally denotes hostility, but as the rainy season necessitated hard work, I accepted the explanation.

The corn for the supply of Masindi was brought from a distance of two days' journey, and numbers of people were daily employed in going to and fro for the general provisions of the station.

The slave-hunters belonging to Suleiman, who were now prisoners under a guard, numbered twenty-five men: I employed these people daily to clear away the high grass, which was piled and burnt, the ashes were then spread, and the ground was hoed up and thoroughly prepared by the troops.

It was in vain that I urged upon Kabba Réga and his chiefs the necessity of cultivation for the supply of corn requisite for the troops. Every day they promised to clear away the grass, provided the soldiers would then dig and prepare the ground. This I agreed to do, but the natives showed no intention of working.

I began to suspect that Kabba Réga had an objection to a large open clearing. The tactics of all natives are concealment; if a man is frightened, he hides in the grass; in case of hostilities, the high grass is a fortress to the negro. It became evident that we were to remain surrounded by this dense herbage, which not only obstructed the view, but rendered the station damp and dreary.

I explained to the chiefs the folly of Kabba Réga in thus neglecting such magnificent soil, which, with a little labour, would produce all that we could require, and would save both him and his people the trouble of feeding us. At the same time I set all hands of my own people to clear a large space and to make gardens.

Unyoro had always been a country of cowardice and suspicion, and I could plainly see that we were narrowly watched. Kabba Réga usually sat in his public divan from about 2 P.M. till 4 daily, to transact public business. This large circular building was extremely neat, and the ground was carefully strewed with the long fringes of the papyrus rush, after the fashion of our ancestors in England, who, before the introduction of carpets, strewed the floor with rushes.

The young king informed me that, as he wished to be in constant communication with me personally, he should build a new divan within a few yards of my residence, so that we could converse upon all occasions without being watched by his people.

This was merely an excuse for erecting a building within fifty yards of my house, from which his guards could watch all that happened, and report everything to their master.

The new building was constructed with wonderful quickness, and prettily walled with canes inside to resemble basket-work.

Kabba Réga came to his new divan, attended by a number of his guards, or bonosoora, armed with guns. To give him confidence, I went to see him unattended, except by Lieutenant Baker and my ever-faithful attendant, Monsoor, who did not at all approve of my going unarmed.

The conversation quickly turned upon arms. Kabba Réga was delighted with the mechanism of Monsoor's snider rifle, which he at once understood and explained to his body-guard. He appeared to have quite lost his shyness, and he begged me to consider him simply in the light of my own son, and to give him all the merchandize *at once* that I had brought with me to establish a new trade.

I told him that fathers did not give their sons all their property at once; but that if I saw that he performed his duty to the Khedive, he need not fear. I had both the power and the good-will to reward him.

He continued the conversation precisely according to his late father Kamrasi's style : " I have no one but yourself to regard. Does not a father consider his son? You were my father's friend ; and I have always looked for your return. I knew that Abou Saood was a liar when he spoke against you; I knew that he was an impostor when he announced himself as the son of a sultan. Would the son of a sultan only give me a present of an old carpet and a dirty washing-basin ? I always said, ' Wait till the Pacha comes—Malleggé,[1] my father's friend. He is truly a great man, who does not travel empty-handed ; and he will bring me presents worth my acceptance— things that the impostor, Abou Saood, does not understand the use of.' By the by, there was a magic instrument by which you could find your way without a guide in strange countries, that you

[1] Malleggé, or the Man with the Beard, was my nickname in Unyoro during my former journey.

promised to send to my father; you have, of course, brought it for me?"

This demand amused me much, as I well remembered how Kamrasi had bothered me for my compass. I pretended that he meant a watch, which I had already given him.

At length I was obliged to promise him that if he would clear away the grass and cultivate the neighbouring ground, I would give him a compass.

I now explained to him the advantages of free trade, and I begged him to order his men to complete the government house without delay, as I could not unpack my numerous boxes until I had some place where I could exhibit the contents. I described the difficulties of the route from Khartoum, and the expense of transport from Gondokoro, owing to the unwillingness of the Baris to carry loads, and I explained my intention of erecting steamers on the Nile which would bring all kinds of merchandize to Unyoro *viâ* the Albert N'yanza in exchange for ivory, thus the Zanzibar trade would turn towards the north, and the elephants' tusks that were now purchased by M'tésé, would remain in Unyoro, until delivered to the Khedive's government in barter for manufactured goods.

The name of M'tésé seemed to make him uncomfortable. He replied: "You are my father, and you will stand by your son against his enemies. This M'tésé troubles me. In my father Kamrasi's lifetime he frequently attacked us, and carried off our herds, together with our women and children. He is too strong to resist single-handed, but now that you are here I shall have no fear. Don't let us talk about merchandize, that will come in due time; never mind trade; let us talk about guns and gunpowder. You must give me muskets and ammunition in large quantities; I will then arm all my bonosoora (soldiers) and with your assistance I will fight M'tésé. I will then fill your large new house with ivory for the Khedive."

"There is no time to lose; you *promised* to fight Rionga; my troops are all ready, your men have nothing to do. Keep a few here, and send the main force with my army to attack him at once, before he has time to escape to the Langgos."

I could almost have imagined that I had been speaking with Kamrasi, so thoroughly did his son resemble him in his diplomacy.

I answered him with caution, declaring that I could not allow any reckless acts that would plunge the country in confusion. He (Kabba Réga) had nothing to fear; but time was required to ripen my plans. I had promised that I would dismiss Suleiman and his people from Unyoro: at the same time I should liberate all the slaves that had been stolen by Abou Saood's companies, and restore them to their homes. This was my first duty, that would assure the natives of my sincerity, and establish general confidence in the government.

Fatiko was 160 miles distant. I should therefore send Suleiman and his people under an escort direct to Major Abdullah, the commandant, with orders to recover from Abou Saood all the slaves that had been captured from Unyoro.

Major Abdullah would then break up his camp at Fatiko, and march in charge of the slaves, with his detachment of 100 men, together with all effects, and join me at Unyoro. He would, upon arrival at the Victoria Nile, occupy the now deserted station of Suleiman at Foweera; thus he would be within a march of Rionga.

The old enemy of the family (Rionga) would then have an opportunity, either of declaring his allegiance and remaining at peace, or, should he become turbulent, a government force would be at hand to control him.

I therefore arranged that Kabba Réga should supply me with 300 carriers, who would accompany my escort to Fatiko and transport all stores, ammunition, &c., &c., so as to concentrate my force in Unyoro.

This plan seemed to delight Kabba Réga; he declared that the first step necessary was the banishment of Suleiman and his people from the country. The next move would be the attack upon Rionga. I explained to him that it would be quite useless for any enemy to retreat for security to the river islands, as the rockets would search them out in the middle of the dense canes, and they would be only too glad to escape; but at the same time, I should hope that Rionga would come to terms and avoid the necessity of a resort to force.

That evening, after we had dined, and I was smoking my customary *chibouque*, Kabba Réga astonished me by an impromptu visit; he was as usual attended by some of his followers armed with muskets. He sat down at the table, and having felt the table-cloth, he wished to know "why the table was covered;" he then examined the tumblers, and everything that was present, all of which he seemed to admire. I offered him some gin and water. This he smelt but would not taste, as he suspected poison; accordingly he poured it into wine glasses, and divided it among three of his people, who were obliged to drink it, while their master watched them attentively, in expectation of some ill effects. His people rather approved of the poison, and asked for more. Kabba Réga seemed to think that a larger dose was necessary; but as we could not afford to waste Geneva by experiments upon numerous attendants, all of whom were to be poisoned with our good liquor for the amusement of the king, I sent the bottle away and turned the subject.

Kabba Réga now minutely examined the lamps and glass shades. The principle was explained to him, and the candle was withdrawn from the tube and spring, and again replaced. He expressed a wish to have one, saying that he intended to have everything precisely as I had.

I assured him that this was my object; I wished to create new wants among his people and himself, which would tend to develop commerce. He might have everything in European style, and live in a civilized manner, now that the route was open from the north. Ivory was abundant in this country, and this would provide him with the means of purchasing all that he could desire.

I had ordered Monsoor to arrange a stake in the ground, with a large nail driven in the top at right angles to form a rocket-stand. I now asked

Kabba Réga if he would like to see a rocket fired.

The idea delighted him, and a few rockets having been brought, together with port-fires and blue lights, we exhibited the fireworks. There was no wind, thus the rockets did no damage, as they were inclined towards the north, in which direction there were no buildings.

Kabba Réga himself ignited a rocket with a port-fire, and although rather nervous at the great rush of fire, he seemed greatly interested at the fact that a town composed of straw huts could be destroyed from a great distance . . . .

On the following morning, Umbogo, the dragoman, told me that the natives had been very much frightened at the rockets, as they said, "the Pacha was going to set the sky on fire."

The station was progressing rapidly. The soil was of such extraordinary richness that the seeds sprang up like magic. On the third day after sowing, the cucumbers, melons, pumpkins, and cotton seeds, showed themselves above ground.

I had made a broad walk of red gravel from Kabba Réga's new divan, to the government house. The roads and approaches were finished, and all neatly laid with fresh gravel stamped firmly down. The borders of all paths and roads were sown with the best quality of Egyptian cotton, known in Egypt as galleené. My large tent was pitched beneath an immense banian-tree, close to which was the new government house. This grand-sounding name was given to a very solid construction of a most simple character. The divan was a building containing only one room twenty-eight feet long by fourteen wide, and about twenty feet high. It was carefully thatched with overhanging eaves, which formed a narrow veranda, and it was entered by a commodious porch; this was arched in the native fashion, and was so large that it formed a lobby, in which we sometimes dined. The inside walls of the divan were neatly made with canes closely lashed together.

There was a back door to this public room which communicated with a separate house by a covered way.

This was our private residence, which also consisted of only one room; but I had arranged it with extreme neatness, in order to excite the admiration of Kabba Réga and his chiefs, who would, I hoped, imitate the manners and customs of civilized life, and thus improve trade.

The room was twenty-four feet long by thirteen wide. The walls were as usual made of canes, but these were carefully hung with scarlet blankets, sewn together and stretched to the ground, so as to form an even surface. The floor was covered with mats. Upon the walls opposite to each other, so as to throw endless reflections, were two large oval mirrors (girandoles) in gilt metal frames. A photograph of her Majesty the Queen stood on the toilet table.

At the extreme end of the room was a very good coloured print, nearly life size, of her Royal Highness the Princess of Wales. The scarlet walls were hung with large coloured prints, life-size, of very beautiful women, with very gorgeous dresses, all the jewelry being imitated by pieces of coloured tinsel. A number of sporting prints, very large, and also coloured, were arranged in convenient places on the walls. There were fox-hunting scenes, and German stag-hunts, together with a few quiet landscapes, that always recalled the dear old country now so far away.

The furniture was simple enough : two angarebs, or Arab stretchers, which, during the day, were covered with Persian carpets and served as sofas, while at night they were arranged as beds. The tables were made of square metal boxes piled one upon the other and covered with bright blue cloths.

These were arranged with all kinds of odd trinkets of gaudy appearance, but of little value, which were intended to be asked for, and given away. Two native stools curiously cut out of a solid block formed our chairs. The guns and rifles stood in a row against a rack covered with red Turkey cloth; and a large Geneva musical box lay upon a table beneath the Princess of Wales.

Altogether the room was exceedingly pretty. It would have been vulgar if in England; but it was beautifully clean, and it shortly became the wonder of Central Africa.

I had brought the large gilt mirrors from England specially for M'tésé, the king of Uganda, and for Kamrasi. I knew that if they were arranged in my own house, the news would be carried to M'tésé immediately; and the fact of so great a curiosity and treasure being on the road to him would at once open a communication.

On 8th May, the prisoners of Suleiman's company, numbering twenty-five persons, came to the divan, headed by Ali Genninar, and supplicated forgiveness. They all declared their desire to be registered on the government books as irregular troops.

I had already witnessed an example of their duplicity, therefore I had no confidence in their professions, but at the same time I did not know what to do with them. The fact of their being in custody required twenty soldiers to relieve the necessary guards. I therefore determined to be magnanimous, as I was only too happy to be rid of such bad bargains should they run away. The only man that I trusted was Ali Genninar; he was a clever and plucky fellow that I had known in my former African journey, at which time he belonged to the company of Ibrahim.

After a good lecture I forgave them, and they all received their serkis (certificates) as members of the irregular corps. Ali Genninar was to have the rank of lieutenant.

I told them that it was my intention to hoist the Ottoman flag, and to officially annex the country in the presence of Kabba Réga and his people, therefore I did not wish any subjects of the Khedive to be in disgrace upon such an occasion, excepting only Suleiman, who would be sent to Cairo on the first opportunity, to answer for the murder of the prisoner at Foweera. I therefore divided a few pounds of beads among them for the purchase of new barkcloths, as I could not allow them to appear in their dirty clothes on the day of the ceremony.

They all went away rejoicing, and swearing fidelity, at the same time confessing their sins, and vowing that I had treated them better than they had deserved.

As usual, our proceedings were narrowly watched by the guards stationed at Kabba Réga's new divan, within fifty yards of my house. These spies immediately ran off to their master with the report that I had forgiven the slave-hunters who were lately prisoners, and that I had actually made them presents of beads.

This report was quickly confirmed, as the new and dirty members of the irregular corps, who were now at liberty, presented themselves in the town with their hands full of beads to purchase the necessary bark-cloths. These cloths are prepared from the bark of a species of fig-tree in a very simple manner, which I have personally witnessed.

A piece of bark about six feet long, and as wide as possible, is detached from the trunk of the tree. The outside rind is pared off by a lance-head used with two hands, like a cooper's drawing-knife. The bark is then laid upon a beam of wood on the ground, on which it is hammered with a mallet grooved in fine cuts, so that the repeated blows stamp the bark with lines somewhat resembling corduroy. This hammering expands the bark, which is repeatedly turned and hammered again, until at length it is beaten into a cloth of rather fine texture. The action of the air colours the bark, which, although white when first stripped from the tree, quickly assumes a delicate shade of brown, as a slice of an apple oxydizes upon exposure in our own climate.

The finest cloths are ornamented with patterns in black. These are simply produced by drawing the design with water from iron springs, which combining with the tannin of the bark immediately stains it black.

The sheets of bark-cloth are frequently dyed this colour by immersing them for a short time in springs of the same water.

The finest cloths are produced in Uganda, and all that are used for royal wear are brought from that country in exchange for ivory.

My new men, the late slave-hunters, who I hoped were "wicked men that had turned away from their wickedness," had succeeded in purchasing a quantity of new cloths ready for the day of annexation.

That night, at about nine o'clock, just before we were going to bed, we had remarked an extraordinary stillness in the town of Masindi. There was not a whisper to be heard throughout the capital, where generally the night was passed in the uproar of drunken singing and blowing of horns.

Suddenly this extraordinary silence was broken by the deep notes of a nogāra or drum. This sounded for a second or two, and ceased. Again all was still as death.

A sudden burst of hellish noise, such a I have never heard before or since, now startled every soldier to his feet, and without orders, every man armed and fell into position.

Colonel Abd-el-Kader, with his sword belted on and a rifle in his hand, came to me for orders on the instant. The ever-ready Monsoor was armed and by my side.

In the meantime the din of very many thousands continued, yelling and shrieking as though maniacs; I should imagine that at least a thousand drums were beating, innumerable horns were blowing, with whistles, fifes, and every instrument that would add to the horrible uproar.

At the same time not a human being was visible.

Mohammed, the dragoman, appeared, together with Umbogo. In reply to my question as to the cause of such a sudden irruption of noise, Umbogo laughed, and said it was "*to make me afraid*, and to exhibit the great numbers of people that were collected at Masindi."

This was all. I therefore at once ordered the band to play, as I determined to accept the carefully planned surprise as a compliment that I would return.

The band struck up, the cymbals clashed, the big drum thundered, and the buglers blew their loudest, while the regimental drums rattled away as hard as the sticks could roll upon the skins.

In a short time the noise of the town ceased, and the only sound was occasioned by our own band.

I ordered them to cease playing. Once more there was perfect stillness.

I ordered the sentries to keep a sharp look-out, and we all went to bed.

This was a practical joke that did not please me, as it smacked of distrust and defiance. It took place on the same day upon which I had liberated the slave-hunter's people, and engaged them as irregular troops.

On the following morning I sent several messengers to Kabba Réga to beg him to pay me a visit. They all returned, some saying that he was asleep— others, that he was drunk. It was the usual habit of this young man to get very drunk every night, and to sleep until about 2 P.M., when he dressed and attended at his public divan.

I now heard that native messengers had arrived from the country of Faieera, which formed one of the districts within nine miles of Fatiko, under the charge of the great sheik, Rot Jarma, who had sworn allegiance to the government, and was under the protection of Major Abdullah.

These messengers had brought some guns and ammunition to sell to Kabba Réga. They wished particularly to see me, as they had important news.

When they appeared in the divan, I at once recognized them as people that I had seen at Fatiko.

They informed me that since my departure, Abou Saood and his people had ridiculed the authority of my commandant, Major Abdullah; and to prove to the natives how powerless he was to protect them, Abou Saood had sent his men to attack Rot Jarma, and they had carried off his cattle and slaves.

The messengers declared that both Rot Jarma and all the natives were delighted with Major Abdullah and his troops, as they were very different from the slave-hunters, but the latter were too numerous and strong for Abdullah to contend against.

I told them that Abdullah was only waiting for

orders; but if such was the state of things " why had he not written a letter by this opportunity?"

The natives asserted that the slave-hunters of Abou Saood had lost five of their party, killed in the attack upon Rot Jarma; therefore they (the messengers) were afraid to go near the station of Major Abdullah. They had accordingly travelled fast to bring me the news (160 miles), at the same time they brought the guns for sale to Kabba Réga.

It was the old story of deception and rebellion. Before my face Abou Saood would cringe to the earth, but he became an open rebel in my absence. It was absolutely necessary to place this man under arrest. When the Baris were at open war with the government, he had not only associated with their chief, but he had armed parties of these natives with muskets, which he employed in his zareebas.

He now attacked, in defiance of government protection, those friendly natives of Faieera who had become peaceable subjects of the Khedive. This was the same spirit of defiance that had been exhibited by Suleiman when he slaughtered the prisoner to whom I had granted an asylum.

Unless I should arrest Abou Saood, it would be ridiculous to attempt the establishment of a government. This scoundrel knew the weakness of my military force. He had himself requested Kabba Réga to attack me upon my arrival in his country. He was now plundering and kidnapping the districts that were under government protection; this would immediately be known to Kabba Réga and his people, who would naturally conclude that my assurances of protection were valueless, and that Abou Saood was stronger than the government of the Khedive.

I determined to send orders to Major Abdullah to arrest Abou Saood if the reports were true concerning Faieera, at the same time he was to insist upon the liberation of all the Unyoro slaves, which he was to escort with his detachment to Foweera on the Victoria Nile.

There was no doubt that this fellow, Abou Saood, was confident of support from some Egyptian authority behind the scenes; he had therefore determined to be humble before my face, to avoid being pounced upon at once, but to have his own way when my back was turned, as he trusted that after the advice he had given to Kabba Réga I should never return from Unyoro. It would then be said that I had been killed by the natives, the affair would be ended, and the official supporters of Abou Saood would reinstate him in his original business or a sufficient *consideration*.

I made arrangements for the departure of my new irregulars. After many invitations I at length succeeded in allaying Kabba Réga's apprehensions, and he promised to pay me a visit on the 11th May. Lieutenant-Colonel Abd-el-Kader went to meet him, and escorted him to the new house.

On arrival in the divan he was much astonished and delighted. The room, twenty-eight feet by fourteen, was arranged with double rows of metal boxes on all sides, so closely packed that they formed either low tables or seats, as might be required. These were all covered with blue blankets, which gave a neat appearance, upon which, at the east end of the room, were exhibited samples of the various goods that I had brought for the establishment of a regular trade in Unyoro. There were tin plates as bright as mirrors, crockery of various kinds, glasses, knives of many varieties, beautiful Manchester manufactures, such as Indian scarfs, handkerchiefs, piece-goods, light blue serge, chintzes, scarlet and blue blankets, blue and crimson cotton cloth, small mirrors, scissors, razors, watches, clocks, tin whistles, triangles, tambourines, toys, including small tin steamers, boats, carriages, Japanese spinning tops, horn snakes, pop-guns, spherical quicksilvered globes, together with assortments of beads of many varieties.

"Are these all for me?" asked Kabba Réga.

"Certainly," I replied, "if you wish to exchange ivory. All these things belong to the Khedive of Egypt, and any amount remains in the magazines of Gondokoro. These are simply a few curiosities that I have brought as an experiment to prove the possibility of establishing a trade."

Among other things, the wheel of life attracted his attention. This had frequently been exhibited, but neither Kabba Réga nor his chiefs ever tired of the performance.

The magnetic battery was now called for, and Kabba Réga insisted upon each of his chiefs submitting to a shock, although he was afraid to experiment upon himself. He begged Lieutenant Baker, who managed the instrument, to give as powerful a shock as he could, and he went into roars of laughter when he saw a favourite minister rolling on his back in contortions, without the possibility of letting the cylinders fall from his grasp.

Every individual of his headmen had to suffer, and when all had been operated upon, the ministers sought outside the divan among the crowd for any particular friends that might wish to try "the magic."

At length one of the wires of the instrument gave way, as a patient kicked and rolled frantically upon the ground; this was a good excuse for closing the entertainment.

Kabba Réga now requested permission to see our private residence. I told him that only himself together with four of his chiefs and the interpreter, Umbogo, could be permitted to enter. These were Rahonka (his maternal uncle), Néka (his uncle, Kamrasi's brother), Kitākără, and Quonga. On that occasion the tall chief, Matonsé endeavoured to push his way through, but was immediately turned back by the sentry and Monsoor.[1]

The first exclamation upon entering the room was one of surprise—" Wah! Wah! "—and Kabba Réga and his chiefs covered their mouths with one hand, according to their custom when expressing astonishment.

The large looking-glasses were miracles. Kabba Réga discovered a great number of Kabba Régas in the endless reflections of the two opposite mirrors. This was a great wonder that attracted particular attention.

It was then discovered that every person was

[1] This little incident must be remembered, as the man took a dislike to Monsoor from that moment.

multiplied in a similar manner! This was of course "cojoor" (magic). It was difficult to draw them away from the looking-glasses, but at length the pictures were examined. The Queen was exhibited and explained, and I described her subjects to be as numerous as the white ants in Unyoro. The Princess of Wales was a three-quarter face; and they immediately asked "why she had only one ear?" The same question of unity was asked respecting the leg of a man in a red coat on a white horse.

Every lady's portrait was minutely examined, but to our great satisfaction, that of the Princess was declared by general consent to be the most lovely.

I was much struck with this exhibition of good taste, as the other portraits were pretty faces, but the hair and dresses were gaudily ornamented, whereas that of the Princess of Wales was exceedingly simple; the dress being an evening gown of white satin.

I should have expected that natives would have preferred the gaudy attire, without bestowing sufficient admiration on the features.

Kabba Réga now asked "why the women in the various portraits all looked at him?" wherever he moved, their eyes followed him.

His chiefs now discovered that the faces in the

pictures were also looking at them; and the eyes followed them whether they moved to the right or left! This was cojoor, or magic, which at first made them feel uncomfortable.

One of my wife's female servants, Wat-el-Kerreem, would not remain by herself in this room, for fear of "the eyes that stared at her."

Everything that we possessed was now minutely scrutinized. The guns and rifles of various breech-loading mechanism were all displayed and admired. Kabba Réga thoughtfully asked "which of them I had intended for him?" His uncle, Rahonka, exclaimed—" You have done wisely in bringing *all those guns* as presents for Kabba Réga." My visitors were quite charming. The musical box played various delightful airs, and it was remarked that it would be more convenient than an instrument which required the study of learning, as " you might set this going at night to play you to sleep, when you were too drunk to play an instrument yourself; even if you knew how to do it."

This was my young friend Kabba Réga's idea of happiness—to go to sleep drunk, assisted by the strains of self-playing melody.

Of course, the large musical box was asked for; and, of course, I promised to give it as a present from the Khedive of Egypt, if I found that Kabba Réga conducted himself properly.

My wife's trinkets, &c., were now begged for; but it was explained that such things were private property belonging to the Sit (lady). "The Sit! the Sit! the Sit!" the young cub peevishly exclaimed; "everything that is worth having seems to belong to *the Sit!*"

A small and beautifully-made revolver, with seven chambers, now attracted his attention. "Does this also belong to the Sit?" inquired Kabba Réga. "Yes, that is the Sit's own little revolver," was the reply; at which the young king burst out laughing, saying, "Do women also carry arms in your country? I see everything belongs to the Sit!"

My wife now gave him some of the finest Venetian beads, of which we only had a few dozen. These were much prized. He was then presented with a handsome gilt bracelet, set with four large French emeralds. This was a treasure such as he had never seen. He also received a few strings of fine imitation pearls.

After much delay and vexatious demands for everything that he saw, we at length got rid of our visitor.

I had explained to him the intended ceremony of

hoisting the flag in the name of the Khedive, and that the country would be in future under the protection of Egypt, but that he should remain as the representative of the government. He seemed highly pleased at the idea of protection and presents, and expressed himself as very anxious to witness the ceremony. . . . . . . On the 14th May, 1872, I took formal possession of Unyoro in the name of the Khedive of Egypt.

I recalled to the recollection of Kabba Réga and his chiefs the day when, many years ago, I had hoisted the British flag, and thus I had turned back the invading force of Wat-el-Mek, and saved Unyoro. I now declared that the country and its inhabitants would be protected by the Ottoman flag in the same manner that it had been shielded by the Union Jack of England.

There was a tall flag-staff fixed at the east end of the government house.

The bugle sounded the "taboor," the troops fell in, the irregulars (late slave-hunters) formed in line with that charming irregularity which is generally met with in such rude levies.

Kabba Réga had received due notice, and he quickly appeared, attended by about a thousand people.

The band played; Kabba Réga's drums and horns

CHAP. VI.] *OFFICIAL ANNEXATION OF UNYORO.* 243

sounded, and the troops formed a hollow square to listen to a short address.

Kabba Réga was invited within the square; and the men faced about with fixed bayonets, as though prepared to receive cavalry. It was now explained to the young king that this formation defended all sides from attack at the same time. He seemed more interested in getting out again, than in the explanation of military tactics. He evidently had suspicions that he was fairly entrapped when he found himself in the middle of the square.

The flag was now hoisted with due formality; the usual military salutes took place; volleys were fired; and the crowd at length dispersed, leaving the Ottoman flag waving in a strong breeze at the head of the flag-staff.

As a proof of his satisfaction, Kabba Réga immediately sent me a present of twelve goats.

One of the soldiers had been caught in the act of stealing potatoes from a native. This having been proved conclusively against him, I sent word to Kabba Réga to summon his people to witness the punishment of the offender.

A great crowd of natives assembled, and the thief having received punishment in their presence, was confined in the stocks, and was condemned to be sent back to Gondokoro. This strict discipline had a strong moral effect upon my men; as thefts which had formerly been the rule, had now become the exception. The natives were always assured of justice and protection.

On 19th May, my people were ready to start, with the post and the prisoner Suleiman, to Fatiko. Kabba Réga declared that the 300 carriers were in readiness with fifty loads of flour for the journey; and he said that he had already sent orders to Foweera to prepare the deserted zareeba of Suleiman for the reception of Major Abdullah and his detachment on their arrival.

The party was to consist of a serjeant and ten men (regulars), together with twenty-five irregulars under the charge of my old Cairo dragoman, Mohammed.

Ali Genninar had the military command in the place of the second vakeel, Eddrees, who was suffering from chronic dysentery. I had arranged that the party should start on the following day.

In the afternoon I had an interview with Kabba Réga in his private divan, within our garden. I was suddenly interrupted by Ali Genninar and a few of his men, who presented themselves in the face of Kabba Réga, to inform me that they could not start without their guns!

It appeared that on the day that Abd-el-Kader had ordered Kabba Réga to disarm the people of Suleiman upon his first arrival at Masindi, the young king had certainly ordered their disarmament, but he had himself retained their arms and ammunition, in addition to a goatskin bag with about 300 rounds of ball-cartridge. This had never been reported to me.

The mendacious young king had the audacity to deny this, in face of several witnesses; and he would at once have retired from the divan (and probably I should never have seen him again) had I not insisted upon his remaining until the affair had been thoroughly explained.

It was then discovered that he had returned all the muskets to Abd-el-Kader, except five; which were not forthcoming.

I requested him in future to adhere more strictly to the truth; as it was a disgrace for a man in his position to tell a falsehood, which would render it impossible for me to place implicit confidence in him; at the same time I insisted upon the immediate return of the guns, together with the cartouche-belts and ammunition.

The young rascal retired in great confusion and stifled anger with a promise that everything should be restored!

In the afternoon he sent five wretched old muskets that had been injured in the stocks, and repaired with the raw hide of crocodiles. These had never belonged to the irregulars; but he had kept their good guns, and hoped to exchange these wretched weapons, which had been given some years ago to Kamrasi by the vakeel, Ibrahim.

I spoke very strongly to Kittākără, his favourite minister; and explained to him the folly and discredit of such conduct.

Kittākără replied: " Is not Kabba Réga your son? Do you begrudge him a few good guns and ammunition taken from your late enemies, the slave-hunters?"

It was in vain that I endeavoured to explain that these people were subjects of the Khedive, and had now received forgiveness: therefore, as they were engaged as irregulars they must receive their arms. Kittākără simply replied: "Do you believe in these people? Do you think that, because they have now enlisted through fear, they will ever change their natures?"

I asked him "if soap would wash the black spots from a leopard's skin?" but I explained that I could strip the skin at once off the leopard, and that I should quickly change their natures.

Day after day passed, and the ammunition was only returned in driblets, after constant and most urgent demands.

On 21st May I sent word to Kabba Réga (who had declined to appear in public or private) that if he persisted in this deception I should myself be compelled to return to Fatiko, as it would be impossible for me to hold communications with any person in whom I could place no confidence.

In the event of my departure from Unyoro he knew the consequences. He would be ridiculed by Rionga, who would join the slave-hunters and attack him should I withdraw my protection. On the south he would be invaded by M'tésé, who would imagine that Kabba Réga had prevented me from visiting him; thus his country would be utterly ruined.

The chiefs, Néka, Kittākără, and Matonsé, to whom I spoke, appeared thoroughly to comprehend the position.

During the day the five missing guns were returned, together with the goatskin bag (chorāb), containing much of the missing ammunition—some of which had been abstracted.

On 23rd May I sent off the party to Fatiko,

together with the post—including letters to Egypt, Khartoum, and England, to be forwarded by first opportunity.[1]

I wrote to Wat-el-Mek to offer him the command of an irregular corps of 400 men, which he was to raise immediately from those companies that were now thrown out of employment by the termination of the contract with Agād & Co.

I sent written instructions to Major Abdullah to arrest Abou Saood, and to liberate all the Unyoro slaves in the possession of his people. He was then to forward Abou Saood, together with Suleiman, as prisoners, to the care of Raouf Bey at Gondokoro; and to march himself with his detachment and all effects, together with the liberated slaves, to Foweera.

Three hundred natives accompanied my party from Unyoro to transport the baggage of Major Abdullah.

I had not seen Kabba Réga since the day when he had lied concerning the possession of the muskets and ammunition. Whether from shame or anger I could not tell, but he declined to appear.

The party started with the post, thus reducing my

[1] These never arrived in England.

force by the departure of thirty-six men, including eleven regulars and twenty-five of the new irregular levy.

I was now left with one hundred regulars, four sailors, and four armed Baris.

CHAPTER VII.

ESTABLISH COMMERCE.

For some time past the natives had commenced a brisk trade with ivory in exchange for all kinds of trifles, which left a minimum profit for the government of 1500 per cent. A few beads, together with three or four gaudy-coloured cotton handkerchiefs, a zinc mirror, and a fourpenny butcher's knife, would purchase a tusk worth twenty or thirty pounds. I calculated all the expenses of transport from England, together with interest on capital. In some cases we purchased ivory at 2,000 per cent. profit, and both sellers and buyers felt perfectly contented.

I am not sure whether this is considered a decent return for an investment of capital among the descendants of Israel; but I am convinced that at the conclusion of a purchase in Unyoro each party to the bargain thought that he had the best of it. This was the perfection of business.

Here was free trade thoroughly established: the future was tinged with a golden hue. Ivory would be almost inexhaustible, as it would flow from both east and west to the market where such luxuries as twopenny mirrors, fourpenny knives, fourpenny handkerchiefs, ear-rings at a penny a pair, finger signet-rings at a shilling a dozen, could be obtained for such comparatively useless lumber as elephants' tusks.

Manchester goods would quickly supersede the bark-cloths, which were worn out in a month, and, in a few years, every native of Unyoro would be able to appear in durable European clothes. Every man would be able to provide himself with a comfortable blanket for the chilly nights, and an important trade would be opened that would tend to the development of the country, and be the first step towards a future civilization. Unfortunately for this golden vision, the young king, Kabba Réga, considered that he had a right to benefit himself exclusively, by monopolizing the trade with the government. He therefore gave orders to his people that all ivory should be brought to him; and he strictly prohibited, on pain of death, the free trade that I had endeavoured to establish.

The tusks ceased to arrive; or, if any individual was sufficiently audacious to run the risk of detection, he sent word beforehand, by Monsoor (who was known to be confidential), that he would bring a tusk for sale during the darkness of night.

This was a troublesome affair. Annexation is always a difficult question of absolute right, but, as I trust my readers will acknowledge, I had done all that lay in my power for the real benefit of the country. I had to make allowances for the young king, who now had become a vassal, and I determined to observe the extreme of moderation.

It was generally acknowledged that the conduct of the troops was most exemplary. No thefts had been allowed, nor even those trifling annexations of property which are distinguished from stealing by the innocent name of "cribbing." Not a garden had been disturbed; the tempting tobacco plantations had been rigidly respected, and the natives could only regard my troops as the perfection of police. They were almost as good as London police—there were no areas to the houses, neither insinuating cooks or housemaids, nor even nursemaids with babies in perambulators, to distract their attention from their municipal duties.

Among my men there was an excellent young man, named Ramadān, who was the clerk of the detachment. This intelligent young fellow was a general favourite among our own men, and also among the natives. He had a great aptitude for languages, and he quickly mastered sufficient of the Unyoro to make himself understood by the natives.

I arranged that Ramadān should become the schoolmaster, as it would be useless to establish commerce as a civilizing medium without in some way commencing a system of education.

Ramadān was proud at the idea of being selected for this appointment.

There was a son of Kittăkără's, of about nine years old, named Cherri-Merri. This nice little boy had paid us many visits, and had become a great favourite of my wife's. He usually arrived after breakfast, and was generally to be found sitting on a mat at her feet, playing with some European toys that were his great delight, and gaining instruction by conversation through the interpreter.

Although Cherri-Merri was a good boy, he possessed the purely commercial instinct of Unyoro.

He seldom arrived without a slave attendant, who carried on his head a package of something that was to be *sold*.

He was told that it was bad taste to bring articles for sale to people who had shown him kindness, at the same time no presents would be received. The little trader quickly relieved himself of this difficulty by marching off with his slave and package to the soldiers' camp, where he exchanged his flour or tobacco for metal buttons, which they cut off their uniforms; or for beads, or other trifles which they possessed.

Cherri-Merri was a general favourite, and he was to form the nucleus for the commencement of a school.

The station was now in perfect order. Altogether, including the soldiers' gardens, about three acres had been cleared and planted. Everything was well above ground, and was growing with that rapidity which can only be understood by those who have witnessed the vegetation of the tropics on the richest soil. English cucumbers, varieties of melons, pumpkins, tomatoes, Egyptian radishes, onions, Egyptian cotton, &c., were all flourishing. Also a small quantity of wheat.

Every cottage was surrounded by a garden; the

boys had formed partnerships, and, having been provided with seeds, they had beds of pumpkins already nearly a foot above the ground.

The girls and women-servants were as usual extremely industrious; they also had formed little companies, and the merits of the rival gardens were often warmly discussed.

Three acres of land, thus carefully cultivated, made a very civilized appearance. The cucumber plants had grown wonderfully, and had already formed fruit. Not a leaf was withered or attacked by insects, and both the soil and climate of Masindi were perfection for agricultural experiments. The thermometer generally stood at 62° at six A.M., and at 78° at noon. The air was always fresh and invigorating, as the altitude above the sea-level was nearly 4,000 feet.

An industrious population would have made a paradise of this country, but the Unyoro people are the laziest that I have ever seen. The days were passed either in sleep, or by the assembly of large crowds of idlers, who stood at the entrance of the broad, gravelled approach, and simply watched our proceedings.

The only excitement was produced by the sudden rush of Kabba Réga's guards (bonosoora) with big sticks among the crowd, whom they belaboured and chased, generally possessing themselves of the best garments of those who were captured, with which they returned to their quarters, as lawful prizes.

This daring system of thieving was considered as great fun by all those members of the crowd who had escaped; and the unfortunates who had been reduced to nudity by the loss of their garments were jeered and ridiculed by the mob with true Unyoro want of charity.

These bonosoora were an extraordinary collection of scoundrels.

The readers of "The Albert N'yanza" may remember the "Satanic Escort," with which I was furnished by Kamrasi for my journey from M'rooli to the lake; these were bonosoora. I could never learn the exact number that formed Kabba Réga's celebrated regiment of blackguards, but I should imagine there were above 1,000 men who constantly surrounded him, and gained their living by pillaging others.

Any slave who ran away from his master might find an asylum if he volunteered to enlist in the bonosoora. Every man who had committed some crime, or who could not pay his debts, could find a refuge by devoting himself to the personal care of the young king, and enrolling within the ranks of the royal guards. The general character of these ruffians may be easily imagined. They lounged away their time, and simply relieved the monotony of their existence by robbing passers-by of anything that attracted their cupidity.

Umbogo belonged to this celebrated corps, and he informed me that hardly a night passed without some person being murdered by these people, who would always kill a man after dark, unless he yielded up his property without resistance. The great number of vultures that continually hovered over Masindi were proofs of Umbogo's story, as these birds generally denote the presence of carrion. My men had, on several occasions, found bodies lying in the high grass, neatly picked to the bone, which had only recently died.

There was much to be done before the brutal customs of Unyoro could be reformed : and I was by no means satisfied with the conduct exhibited by Kabba Réga. He had promised faithfully that he would send a large force to clear away the high grass by which our station was surrounded; this was never fulfilled, neither could I engage the natives to work for hire.

I had observed for some time past that his people were rapidly extending the town of Masindi, by erecting new buildings upon both our flanks, which, although only a few yards from our clearing, were half obscured by the high grass; thus it appeared that we were being gradually surrounded.

Since the departure of the post with my escort and the irregular levy, nothing was done by the natives, except the usual lounging by day, and drinking and howling, with drums and horns as an accompaniment, throughout the night.

Kabba Réga had always declared that the natives would work for me and obey every order when the slave-hunters should have been expelled from the country. Although the people who were lately a portion of the slave-hunter's company had now been enlisted in the service of government, not one man remained in Masindi, as I had sent them all away to Fatiko, at the particular request of Kabba Réga.

The real fact was, that so long as the slave-trader's people were in the country, both the king and his people knew that we were independent of native guides, as Suleiman's men knew all the paths, from their long experience of the country when engaged in the civil wars. It was considered that in the absence of the new levy of irregulars we should be perfectly helpless to move, as we were dependent upon Kabba Réga for guides.

From the general conduct of the people since the departure of my party with the post to Fatiko, I had a strong suspicion that some foul play was intended, and that, when the 300 native carriers should have taken the people across the Victoria Nile, they would desert them in the night, and return with the boats. I therefore wrote a letter addressed to the second vakeel, Eddrees, ordering him to return at once to Masindi with the entire party if he had any suspicion of treachery.

I concealed this note in a packet of blue cloth, together with a few little presents for Shooli and Gimōro, at Fatiko; but I had written on the brown paper cover of the parcel, instructions that Eddrees or Mohammed, the dragoman, should search the contents, as a letter was hidden within. I gave this packet to Umbogo, telling him that it was a present for Shooli, and begging him to despatch a messenger without delay to overtake the party before they should have crossed the Victoria Nile. The native messenger, to whom I gave a small gratuity, immediately started: thus I should be able to forewarn my people in the event of trouble.

In the afternoon Kabba Réga sent for me to repair the small musical box that I had given him, which was slightly deranged. I replied that, until he fulfilled his promise of clearing the high grass from the neighbourhood, I could not think of attending to any request, as he had broken all his promises.

In half an hour after this answer he sent forty men, under Kittākără, to commence the clearing, as he was in despair about his musical box.

Two native merchants from the distant country of Karagwé, who had been sent by their king, Rumanika, to purchase ivory from Unyoro, had arrived at Masindi. These people were brought to me on 26th May, accompanied by Kittākără, together with Umbogo, the interpreter. I observed that Kittākără was acting the part of spy, to overhear and to report the substance of the conversation. Some excitement had been caused by the report that· two travellers were residing with Rumanika, and that these people had arrived from the M'wootan N'zigé. I was in hopes that one of these travellers might be Livingstone.

The Karagwé merchants were well-dressed, and very civilized-looking people. They stared upon arrival in the divan, and were shortly seated upon a mat before me.

After some conversation, I questioned them concerning the travellers, and I immediately wrote both questions and replies in my journal, which I now give *verbatim*.

"Have you personally seen the travellers?"

Answer: "Yes; one is tall, with a long beard and *white* hair. The other is a very black man (an African), and short."

Question: "How do they eat?"

Answer: "With a knife and fork and plate."

Question: "Have they a compass" (Compass exhibited)?

Answer: "No; but they have a small mirror like those in your possession."

Question: "Do they purchase ivory?"

Answer: "Yes. We are now sent by Rumanika to buy ivory for them."

Question: "Have they a large quantity?"

Answer: "An immense quantity. They have a large house, which is quite full."

Question: "How will they transport it?"

Answer: "They are building a vessel of iron on the M'wootan N'zigé, upon the borders of which they are now staying."

Question: "Do they know that I am commanding this expedition?"

Answer: "Yes; they have frequently asked 'whether you had arrived;' and they wish to go to Khartoum."

"There is no trace of poor Livingstone in their description. I imagine that some enterprising Portuguese trader is building a ship to trade upon the M'wootan N'zigé. God help him if he tries to transport his ivory by this route.

"I shall write to Livingstone by the first opportunity. Like all other of my informants, these native merchants told me that the M'wootan N'zigé extended to Karagwé, after a long turn to the west. It varied much in width, and at Karagwé it was narrow."

For some days I had conversations with these intelligent people. They brought me two elephants' tusks to sell, as they wished to show Rumanika the quality of goods that were now introduced from the north. I made them a few presents, after the bargain, to create a favourable impression, and I once more cross-examined them upon geographical questions.

Their description of the east shore of the M'wootan N'zigé was as follows :—

"South of Unyoro is a country—Kābbŏyū ;

,,	,, Kābbŏyū	,,	,,	Tambooki ;
,,	,, Tambooki	,,	,,	M'Pororo ;
,,	,, M'Pororo	,,	,,	Ruānda ;
,,	,, Ruānda	,,	,,	Băroondi ;
,,	,, Băroondi	,,	,,	Chibbŏgōra ;
,,	,, Chibbŏgōra	,,	,,	Watūta ;
,,	,, Watūta	,,	,,	Machoonda."

"Beyond the Machoonda they knew nothing, except that the lake extends for an enormous and unknown distance.

"On the west shore, opposite Kābbŏyū and Tambooki, is situated the cannibal country of Booāmba.

"The route to Karagwé from Masindi, *via* the M'wootan N'zigé (Albert N'yanza), is—take boat from Chibero (a day's long march from Masindi) to M'Pororo—at which spot you leave the boat, and proceed overland in one day to the Karagwé frontier.

"The Kittangūlé river passes through M'Pororo, N'Kolé, and Kishākka, and, after a very winding course, it cuts through Karagwé, and falls into the Victoria N'yanza.

"'Bǎroondi' must be Speke's 'Urundi;' as I find that many names that he has prefixed with 'U' are here pronounced as 'B.'

"By Speke's map Urundi is in about 3° south latitude. The M'wootan N'zigé is therefore known to pass through Ruānda, Bǎroondi, and the Watūta—or *beyond* the north end of the Tanganyika Lake.

"This looks as though the Tanganyika and the M'wootan N'zigé were only one vast lake bearing different names according to the localities through which it passes."

I have extracted this from my journal, as it was written at the moment that the information was given. I have no theory, as I do not indulge in the luxury of geographical theories; but I shall give my information in the same words in which I received it from the natives. Speculative geographers may then form their own opinions.

From the day when Kabba Réga had denied the possession of the guns and ammunition belonging to the irregular levy, he had never appeared at his new divan, neither had I seen him.

Upon many occasions I had sent to request his attendance, but he was always in the sanctuary of his own private house, or rather establishment of houses: these were a series of enormous beehive-shaped straw and cane dwellings in a courtyard of about an acre, surrounded by a fence, and guarded by many sentries, each of whom had a small hut built in the middle of the fence.

Since the departure of the irregular levy, I had noticed a decided change in the demeanour of the chiefs. Kittākără, who had been our greatest friend, could never look me in the face, but always cast his eyes upon the ground when speaking or listening.

The food for the troops was obtained with the

greatest difficulty, after constant worry and endless applications. It was in vain that I insisted upon the right of paying for a supply of corn; the chiefs replied : " Is not Kabba Réga your son ? can a son sell corn to his own father ?"

At the same time we never had two days' provisions in store, and we were simply living from hand to mouth. This looked suspicious, as though the troops were to be rendered helpless by the absence of supplies in the event of hostilities.

My few Baris consisted of my good interpreter Morgiān, together with three other natives, who had been for some years in the employ of Suleiman. I had kept these people with me, as they knew something about the country and the Unyoros. They were all armed and were tolerably good shots. One of these fellows (Molōdi), a native of the Madi country, was extremely useful and intelligent. He now told me that I could never depend upon Kabba Réga, and that he had simply begged me to send the irregulars out of the country in order that I should not hear the truth of his former conduct from them; also, in their absence, I should be quite ignorant of the paths that were now completely overgrown with immensely high grass throughout the country.

An incident occurred on the 31st May which caused me serious anxiety.

The station was in complete order : the cultivation was thriving, and the general appearance of the government settlement was a strong contrast to the surrounding wilderness of high grass, and the large and dirty town of Masindi.

My troops were now without occupation, therefore I instructed Colonel Abd-el-Kader to drill them every morning.

It had been the daily practice of the band to march up and down the broad approach, and to perform nearly opposite Kabba Réga's public divan.

There was no clear place in which the troops could be drilled, except in the public square at the back of Kabba Réga's divan; this was about the centre of the town.

The square was an open space of about two acres, and was the spot at which all public festivities were held, and where, upon many occasions, Kabba Réga delighted to sit, in a large open shed, to witness the absurd performance of his buffoons.

This open space was well adapted for the exercise of a company of troops. I therefore ordered the men on parade, and I accompanied them myself together with Lieutenant Baker.

The band played, as usual, at the head of the company, and we marched through the town to the open square.

Here the troops were put through their musketry drill, and commenced various evolutions.

To my astonishment, I saw the natives hurrying off in all directions. I was perfectly unarmed, as were also the officers (excepting their side arms) and Lieutenant Baker.

Almost immediately the huge war-drum sounded in the house of Kabba Réga, and the dull hollow notes continued to beat the alarm!

In less than ten minutes, horns were blowing and drums were beating in all directions, and with extraordinary rapidity, some five or six thousand men came pouring down from every quarter, fully armed with spears and shields, in a state of frantic excitement, and at once surrounded the troops. Fresh bands of natives, all of whom were in their costume of war, continued to concentrate from every side. The crowd of warriors leapt and gesticulated around my little company of men as though about to attack.

I immediately gave the order to form a square

with fixed bayonets. This manœuvre puzzled the natives extremely.

They danced around the square, within a few feet of the glistening row of bayonet-points, which were lowered so as to form an impenetrable fence.

The officers were of course inside the square. I gave the men strict orders not to fire under any provocation, unless I gave the word of command, and attended by Lieutenant Baker and Monsoor, the latter with his sword drawn, I left the square, and walked into the middle of the crowd, towards the three chiefs, Rahonka, Kittākără, and Matonsé, who were all standing with lances in their hands, and apparently prepared for action.

Although the situation was full of meaning, I thought the best policy was to appear amused. At this moment Monsoor struck up with his sword, a lance, which one of the frantic warriors, in the midst of his wild gesticulations, had advanced within a few inches of my back.

The interpreters (many of whom I knew well) were all armed with muskets, and the bonosoora were dressed in their usual fantastic manner when prepared for war; a considerable number were provided with guns.

The slightest accident would have caused a general

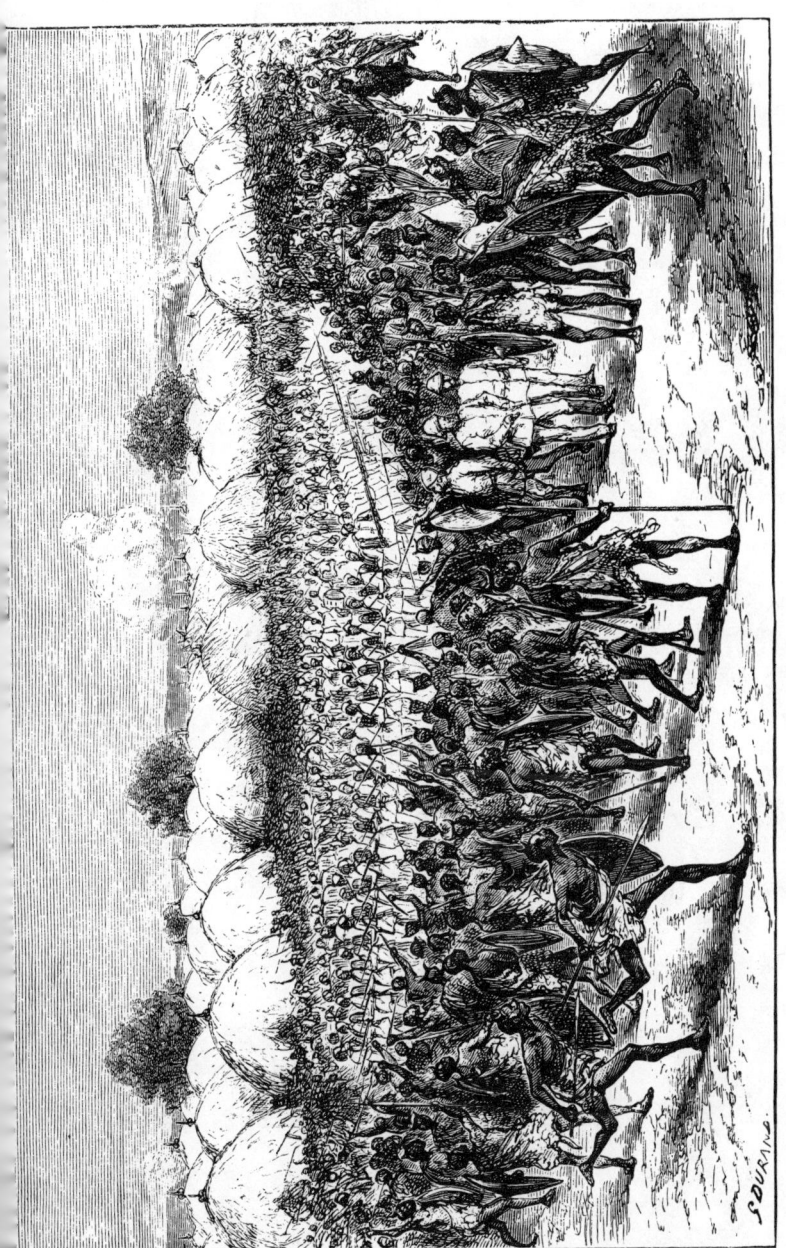

SUDDEN HOSTILE DEMONSTRATION.—THE TROOPS FORM A SQUARE.

Vol. ii. p. 268.

outbreak of hostilities. I had eighty men on the ground; the remainder of the force were at the station, about three hundred yards distant, where Lady Baker, and all stores and ammunition would have been in extreme danger, had an attack become general.

I at once walked up to Rahonka and Kittăkără, and calling an interpreter, named Kadji-Barri, who was standing near them, dressed in Arab clothes, with his musket in his hand, and his cartouche-belt on his waist, I burst out laughing, and exclaimed: "Well done, Kadji-Barri! this is famously managed; let us have a general dance. Ask Kittăkără if my band shall play, or will you dance to your own music?"

This was immediately translated to the chiefs, and my demeanour seemed to cause some hesitation. I at once ordered our band to strike up.

The instant that a well-known lively air commenced, I begged them to exhibit some native dance to amuse us. Seeing their hesitation, I inquired whether they would wish to see my men perform? After a few words between Kittăkără and Rahonka, the former agreed that it would be better for my men to commence the dance first.

I lost no time in explaining to Kittăkără that he

must at once address the crowd and assure them that the performance about to commence was intended for their amusement, and there was no cause for fear. At the same time, I begged him to order the crowd to stand back, and to afford space for my troops, who were about to advance with the bayonet.

In a loud voice Kittākără gave the necessary explanation.

I ordered the bugler to sound the advance, and the whole band sounded the charge with the bayonet (sinjāre dorān).

At the inspiriting call, each side of the square advanced at the double with bayonets at the charge. The crowd lately so demonstrative, fell quickly back, and, having thus cleared the square, I told Kittākără to order every individual of the crowd to sit down upon the ground.

The great mass of people obeyed the order with the discipline of soldiers, and my troops fell back and reformed their square as before. The little square, with a single line of front of twenty men, now occupied the centre of the clear space.

I lost no time in inquiring for Kabba Réga, whom I insisted upon seeing. After a short delay he appeared, in company of some of his bonosoora. He was in a beastly state of intoxication, and, after reeling about with a spear in his hand, he commenced a most imbecile attempt at warlike gestures.

Had my eighty men been armed with breech-loaders, I could have mown down hundreds by a fire from the square, had hostilities been forced upon us; but, as the greater portion were armed with old muskets, we might have been overwhelmed by a general rush, when reloading after the first volley.

Kabba Réga was so drunk that he did not appear to recognize me, but he continued to reel about for a short time, and thus to expose his idiotic condition, until his chiefs at length recommended him to retire.

Kittăkără now explained that, if I wished to have a general dance, they would prepare a grand entertainment at some future time; but he now begged me to withdraw the troops, as the sun was very hot, and the natives were fatigued.

I assured Kittăkără and the chiefs that the people had no cause for fear, and that now that my station was completed I should frequently bring the troops to the public square for musketry drill, as there was no other open space, unless Kabba Réga would order his people to clear away the high grass, which he had so often promised to do.

The band now struck up, and the troops, in single

file, marched through the narrow lanes of the crowded town. I walked at their head, and I was much pleased by seeing my little friend, Cherri-Merri, who ran out of the crowd, and, taking my hand, he marched with us as a volunteer, and accompanied us to the station.

Upon arrival at the government quarters, I found all hands armed and well stationed for the defence of the divan and powder-magazine, by my wife, who was commandant in my absence. She had placed rockets in readiness to fire the town on the instant of a volley of musketry being heard. My good little officer had also laid out a large supply of spare ammunition, together with every gun, rifle, and pistol, all of which were laid on a table in the divan, ready to repel an attack.

I now sent for Rahonka, who was supposed to be the general of Kabba Réga's forces.

The conduct of little Cherri-Merri was very gratifying, as he had adhered to his true friends in a moment of great uncertainty.

Rahonka shortly appeared. My interpreter, Umbogo, was absent on leave for two days to visit his farm; thus Rahonka was accompanied by Kadji-Barri, who was well accustomed to us, and had often received presents.

I now insisted upon an explanation concerning the sudden beating of the war-drum and the extraordinary assembly of the people armed for war. Rahonka looked foolish and nervous, as though he doubted the chance of a safe retreat. He could not give any satisfactory reason for the hostile display we had so recently witnessed, but he attributed it to the drunken state of Kabba Réga, who had sounded the alarm without any reason.

I assured Rahonka that such conduct would not be permitted; and that if such a scene should occur again, I should not allow the troops to be surrounded by thousands of armed men, in hostile attitudes, without immediately taking the initiative.

Rahonka retired, and in a few minutes we received twenty loads of corn for the troops, as a peace-offering.

Thus ended the month of May, which had nearly closed in bloodshed.

There could be no doubt that an attack upon the troops had been intended; and I could not help admiring the organization of the people, that enabled so large a force to be concentrated upon a given point in so few minutes after the alarm had sounded. My wife, upon whose cool judgment I could always depend, described vividly her apprehensions of treachery. She had witnessed the extraordinary energy which the natives had exhibited in rushing from the neighbouring villages, almost immediately when the war-drum had sounded. They had poured in streams past the station, and had brandished their lances and shields at her as they thronged at full speed within fifty yards of the government clearing.

Fortunately, when the big nogāra had sounded, both she and the troops understood the signal, and with praiseworthy speed she had placed every man in position to defend the station. Even the servants and our black boys were armed, and occupied the posts assigned to them. Without these precautions it is highly probable that the station would have been attacked, in which case it might have been at once overwhelmed by so immense a superiority of force.

I felt that on the whole we had narrowly escaped from ruin. My intention, when in the open square, had been to seize a rifle from a soldier, and at once to shoot Kabba Réga had hostilities commenced after his appearance ; but, even had we been able to hold our own, with a party of eighty men, we should have lost the entire station, together with all our ammunition, and every soul would have been massacred.

I had serious misgivings for the future. This

demonstration looked extremely bad after the departure of my thirty-six men with the post to Fatiko. If Kabba Réga and his people were treacherous, they could easily murder the party whom they were pretending to escort as friends.

On the other hand, I could not conceive why Kabba Réga or his people should be ill-disposed, unless he harboured resentment on account of the discovery of his theft of the muskets and ammunition from the irregulars, which I had forced him to restore.

My Baris and Molōdi all declared that he was suspicious because I had pardoned the slave-hunters and received them into government service. This merciless young villain, who had so treacherously murdered his own kith and kin, had no conception of forgiveness; thus he could not understand why I had not killed the slave-hunters when they were once in my power.

There was no doubt that discontent rankled deeply in his heart for some cause or other; as he had never appeared, or received visits for many days, but had sulkily shut himself up within his own court.

He only went out daily, at a certain time, to collect subscriptions for the pay of his beloved rascals, the bonosoora; but this led him through the town in the opposite direction to our camp, therefore we never saw him.

The collection of alms was a most undignified proceeding. At the hour of his exit from his house, a band of fifes or flageolets struck up a peculiar air which was well known as the signal for preparing to pay for the king's visit. The few notes they played was a monotonous repetition of:—

As his pipes played before him, Kabba Réga called at any houses that he thought proper to select, and received from the inmates of each, a few cowrie shells, which are used as the smallest coin in Unyoro. These shells were afterwards divided among his bonosoora as their daily pay.

My station had not been arranged for defence, as I had not considered that hostilities in this country could be even a remote possibility. Although black human nature is the darkest shade of character, I never could have believed that even Kabba Réga could have harboured treacherous designs against us, after the benefits that both he and his people had received from me. The country had been relieved from the slave-hunters, and my people were actually

CHAP. VII.] KABBA RÉGA'S DRUNKEN STATE. 277

on the road to Fatiko to liberate and restore to their families about 1,000 women and children of Unyoro. I was about to establish a school. No thefts had taken place on the part of the troops. The rights of every native had been respected. The chiefs had received valuable presents, and the people had already felt the advantage of legitimate trade.

At the same time that hostility appeared impossible, I could not blind myself to the fact of the late demonstration; it would therefore be absolutely necessary to construct a small fort, for the security of the ammunition and effects, which could no longer be exposed in simple straw huts, without protection.

I explained this necessity to my officers and men, all of whom were keenly alive to the evil spirit of Kabba Réga, from whom they expected future mischief.

This miserable young fellow was nearly always drunk; his time was passed in sucking plantain cider through a reed, until he became thoroughly intoxicated. We were, therefore, subject to any sudden order that he might give in a fit of drunkenness.

His people obeyed him implicitly, with that fanatical belief that is held in Unyoro respecting the person who occupies the magic throne (Bamba).

There could be no doubt that he was offended and insulted: therefore, according to the principle *in vino veritas*, he might pluck up courage to surprise us when least expected.

I determined to build a fort immediately.

I drew a plan of a circular stockade, surrounded by a ditch and earthen parapet. The ditch ten feet wide by seven deep. The diameter from scarp to scarp, sixty feet; diameter of inner circular court, thirty-six feet.

With the assistance of Lieutenant Baker I drew the plan on the ground, and my troops set to work with that vigour which always distinguished them.

There were numerous large trees of the fig tribe in the immediate neighbourhood. This wood was exactly adapted for the purpose, as it was easy to cut, and at the same time it was undying when once planted in the ground. Any log of the bark-cloth tree will take root if watered.

The axes with which the men were provided now came into play, and the clicking of so many tools at work at once surprised the natives. Rahonka, Kittăkără, and other chiefs came to inquire concerning our intention.

I explained the necessity of storing the gunpowder in a fire-proof building. Only a few days ago several native huts had been burnt; such an accident might endanger our station, therefore I should construct an earthen roof over a building of strong palisades. I explained that should the whole of the ammunition explode, it might ignite and destroy Masindi.

My men thoroughly understood their work. Immense logs, nine feet in length, and many upwards of two feet in diameter, were planted, close together, in holes two feet deep. Any interstices were filled up with smaller posts sunk firmly in the ground. The entrance to the little fort was a projecting passage, about twelve feet long, and only three feet wide, formed of two rows of enormous palisades, sunk two feet six inches in the earth, which was pounded closely down with heavy rammers. This passage was an important feature in the power of defence, as it added to the flanking fire. A reference to the plan will show that the arrangement of this small fort gave us four fireproof rooms for the protection of stores and ammunition, and for the accommodation of the necessary guard. Each of these rooms was formed of the strongest palisades, upon which I arranged a flat roof of thick posts, laid parallel, which were covered with tempered earth and chopped straw for the thickness of a foot.

The earth from the ditch would lie against the outside face of the stockade, at an angle of about 40° from the edge of the ditch to within eighteen inches of the projecting roof: thus the defenders could fire from the strong rooms through the interstices of the upright timbers.

We commenced this fort on the morning of 2nd June, and every palisade was in its place and firmly rammed down by the evening of the 5th; thus, in four days' hard work we had an impregnable protection in a position nearly half-way between the entrance of the main approach and the government divan.

The digging of the ditch was commenced, but this was a longer operation, as we were provided with the light Unyoro hoes, which were not sufficiently powerful to cut through the hard gravel subsoil.

The interpreter, Umbogo, returned on 3rd June. He could not in the least explain the hostile demonstration of 31st May. This added to my suspicion, as Umbogo must have known more than he chose to tell.

On the 4th June envoys arrived direct from M'tésé, the king of Uganda, with a letter of welcome, written in Arabic, addressed to myself.

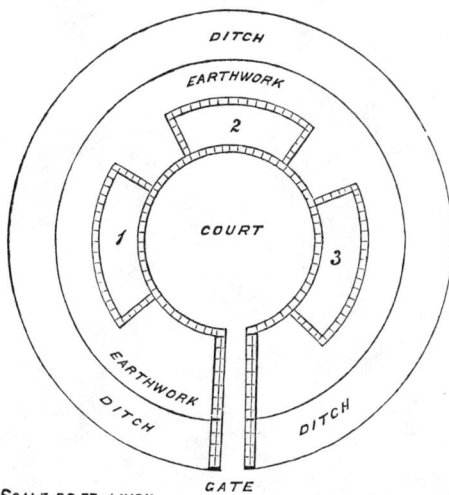

Plan of small circular fort at Masindi with fire-proof rooms; Ditch left unfinished.
Vol. ii. p. 280.

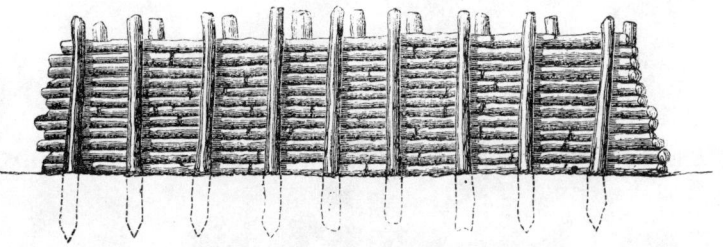

Section of Stockade where no heavy timber is procurable. Vol. ii. p. 363.

The principal messenger was one of M'tésé's headmen, named Wāysŏŏa. The commander-in-chief, Congōw, had also sent a representative, named Bōnněggěsăh; these people were accompanied by an interpreter named Bokāmba.

These envoys were remarkably well-dressed, in Indian clothes, and they appeared quite civilized, as though native merchants of Bombay.

They now delivered their credentials from King M'tésé : these were objects that had been given to him many years ago by Speke and Grant. A printed book (Kaffre laws), several water-colour drawings, including a picture of a guinea-fowl and a yellow-breasted pigeon; also a little folding-book with sketches of British soldiers of various regiments. These I carefully examined and returned to the envoys, who wrapped them neatly in a piece of calico as great treasures.

The general, Congōw, had sent a tusk to *sell!* I declined the offer, but I sent him a scarlet blanket as a present. I also packed up an assortment of handsome articles for M'tésé, including many yards of orange-coloured gold brocade, sufficient for a large flowing robe.

I gave presents to the envoys, and they appeared delighted, bowing frequently to the ground while upon their knees, with their hands clasped together, and repeating the word, "N'yanzig," "N'yanzig," "N'yanzig."

In reply to my inquiries, nothing had been heard of Livingstone. I sent M'tésé a letter in Arabic, begging him to use every exertion in a search for the great traveller, and to forward him to me, should he be so fortunate as to discover him. At the same time I wrote two letters, which I addressed to Livingstone; in these I gave him the necessary information. I consigned them to the care of M'tésé, to be forwarded to any travellers who might be heard of, far or near.

In my letter to M'tésé, I complimented him upon the general improvement of his country, and upon his conversion from heathenism to a belief in the Deity. I explained, that owing to his kindness to Speke and Grant, his name had become known throughout the world, and I begged him to show the same attention to Livingstone.

I described the object of the expedition, in opening up a trade from the north that would bring merchandize of every description to his kingdom; but I advised him to send his own carriers, as I felt sure that Kabba Réga was already jealous, and would endeavour to prevent the opening of the commercial road to M'tésé, as he would himself wish to monopolize the trade.

This was a little stroke of diplomacy that I felt sure would open a direct communication without delay, as M'tésé looked down with contempt upon Kabba Réga, and would at once feel insulted at opposition from such a quarter.[1]

Should I have any open rupture with Kabba Réga, M'tésé would at once attribute the cause to the obstructive and selfish character of the ruler in Unyoro.

I explained to the envoys all that I had written to M'tésé, and having exhibited the varieties of merchandize that belonged to the expedition, I took them into the wonderful private house, where they were introduced to the Queen, and the Princess of Wales, and the gaudy ladies, together with the fox-hunters and hounds, the large mirrors, the wheel of life, &c.; all of which were duly explained to them. A good shock with the magnetic battery wound up the entertainment, and provided them with much material for a report to their royal master upon their return to Uganda.

The geographical information afforded by these

[1] The good effect of this policy will be seen towards the close of the expedition.

people I shall extract *verbatim* from my journal, in which it was written at that particular time; thus, geographers will hear all that I heard, and they may form various opinions, which will perhaps add still further to the interest pertaining to the mysteries of Central Africa.

"The native name for the Victoria N'yanza is Nĕrraă Bāli. There are two lakes adjoining each other, one is Nĕrraă Bāli, the other Sessi; both of which are very large, and they are separated by a neck of land about a day's march across.

"On the Sessi Lake the natives live on floating islands, and subsist by fishing; exchanging their fish for flour, &c., upon the main land.

"There is a narrow water-communication through the neck of land or isthmus, which can be passed through by a canoe in one day."

On the 5th June the envoys returned towards Uganda, having been highly gratified with their visit. They had appeared much concerned at hearing of poor Speke's death; and continued to exclaim for some minutes, "Wah! Wah! Speekēē! Speekēē! Wah! Speekēē!"

CHAPTER VIII.

TREACHERY.

For some days past, Kabba Réga had frequently sent his interpreters with messages, that he wished to sell the ivory that he had collected for the government. We had noticed on several occasions many people laden with large elephants' tusks, who invariably marched towards the same direction. The dragoman, Kadji-Barri, daily brought ivory for sale for the account of his master; and exchanged tusks for all kinds of trifles, such as porcelain cups and saucers, small musical boxes, &c., &c.

On 6th June, twenty-one tusks were purchased from the messengers of Kabba Réga, and I thought that the young king was getting tired of his sulky fit, and that we should be once more friends.

The supply of food was always a trouble. Every day was passed in repeated applications to the authorities for supplies, which were at length grudgingly bestowed.

On 7th June, there was nothing for the troops to eat. Although on 31st May we had received twenty loads of corn, these were simply the long narrow packages which are so neatly made of the plantain bark throughout Unyoro, but which contain very little. Several times during the day Lieutenant-Colonel Abd-el-Kader, together with Monsoor, had been sent to the divan of Kabba Réga, to impress upon his chiefs the necessity of a supply of food. They explained my great annoyance, as this was precisely the result that I had foretold when Kabba Réga had neglected to clear the ground for cultivation.

At about 3 P.M., the tall chief Matonsé appeared, together with Umbogo, and several natives, who carried five large jars of plantain cider. These were sent to me from Kabba Réga, with a polite but lying message, that "he much regretted the scarcity of corn; there was positively none in Masindi, but a large quantity would arrive to-morrow from Aggūsé." In the meantime he begged I would accept for the troops a present of the five jars of cider.

I declined to accept the present, as I did not require drink, but solid food for the troops. The jars were therefore returned.

About sunset Matonsé again appeared, accompanied by Umbogo and natives with *seven* jars of cider, and two large packages of flour, which he assured me had been borrowed from Rahonka. He was exceedingly polite, and smiled and bowed, beseeching me to accept the cider, as plenty of corn would be sent on the following day, when better arrangements would be made for future supplies.

I could no longer refuse the cider, therefore I sent for Abd-el-Kader, and gave him five jars for the officers and troops.

It was at this time about seven o'clock, and we sat down to dinner in the divan, as it was too chilly to dine outside.

We had just finished dinner, when Abd-el-Kader suddenly entered the divan in a state of troubled excitement, to inform me that "many of the troops appeared to be dying, and they had evidently been *poisoned* by the plantain cider!"

I inquired "how many men had drunk from the jars?" He could not tell, but he feared that at least half the company had taken some portion, more or less. He had himself drunk a tumblerful, and he already felt uncomfortable, with a tightness of the throat, and a burning pain in his inside.

I at once flew to my medicinal arms. Independently of the large medicine-chest, I had a small box, about nine inches by five, which contained all that could be desired for any emergency. This little chest had been my companion for twenty-five years.

I begged my wife to get as much mustard and strong salt and water ready as she could mix in a hurry, and I started off with Abd-el-Kader and Lieutenant Baker. I immediately sent Monsoor to find Umbogo.

On arrival at the camp, which was about 120 yards distant, my first order was to double all the sentries.

I found the men in a terrible state. Several lay insensible, while about thirty were suffering from violent constriction of the throat, which almost prevented them from breathing. This was accompanied by spasms and burning pain in the stomach, with delirium, a partial palsy of the lower extremities, and in the worst cases, total loss of consciousness.

I opened the jaws of the insensible, and poured down a dessert-spoonful of water, containing three grains of emetic tartar, and, in about ten minutes, I dosed everybody who had partaken of the poisoned cider with the same emetic, while I insisted upon a flood of mustard and salt and water being swallowed. Fortunately we had everything at hand. The soldiers who were sound were all nursing the sick, and they poured down gallons of brine, until the patients began to feel the symptoms of a rough passage across the British Channel.

My servants always kept the lanterns trimmed—this was a positive order. The lights were now moving to and fro, and, having seen all the poisoned under the full effect of a large dose of tartarised antimony, with an accompaniment of strong brine and mustard, I returned to the divan, where I found Umbogo had just arrived with Monsoor, who had met with him at his own hut.

I sat quietly at the table as though nothing had occurred.

"Are you fond of merissa, Umbogo?"

"Yes," he replied.

"Would you like to drink some that you brought from Kabba Réga, this evening?"

"Yes, if you have any to spare," replied Umbogo.

I ordered Monsoor to fill a gourd-shell that would contain about a quart. This was handed to him, together with a reed.

Umbogo began to suck it vigorously through the tube. My wife thought he was shamming.

"Drink it off, Umbogo!" I exclaimed.

He drank with enjoyment—there was no mistake.

"Stop him!—that's enough, Umbogo! Don't

drink it all." The man was evidently not guilty, although he had been employed to bring the poisoned stuff.

Umbogo had only time to leave the divan and turn the corner, before he fell to the ground, with the same symptoms that had been exhibited among the men. He had drunk more than the others. His eyes were blood-stained, and nearly started from his head, as he strove wildly upon the ground and wrestled with those who endeavoured to assist him, in a state of total unconsciousness.

I was by his side immediately, and administered the same remedies.

I now ordered all the sick men to be either carried or led within the fort, from which they could not escape. Those who were slightly better, now endeavoured to wander about in delirium, and they would have been lost in the high grass unless I had thus secured them.

All that was possible had been done; the sick were secured, and the night guards for relief were all at their posts; with double sentries awake and on duty; thus no man would sleep within the station.

I sent Monsoor to call the chief, Matonsé, whose house was within 200 yards of the government divan.

Monsoor shortly returned without Matonsé. He

had brought an interpreter from this chief, in lieu of Umbogo, who was incapacitated ; and Matonsé had sent a message "that he could not come to me in the dark, but he would call on the following day."

In the meantime an ominous stillness reigned throughout the usually boisterous population of Masindi. Not a sound was to be heard, although the nightly custom of the people was singing, howling, and blowing horns.

My arms and ammunition were always in readiness, but I filled up my pouches to the maximum of fifty cartridges, and at midnight I went to bed.

I woke frequently to listen, as I was anxious, and therefore I slept lightly. The faithful Monsoor was under arms, and was pacing throughout the whole night before my door ; he never slept.

At about 2 A.M., there was a sound throughout the town of fowls crying, as though they were being disturbed and caught while at roost.

At about 3 A.M. the lowing of cattle was heard, as though Kabba Réga's cows were being driven off.

A little after 5 A.M. I got up, and went out at daybreak to visit the sick within the fort. I found Monsoor waiting by my door.

The emetics had counteracted the poison, and

my patients, although weakly, were quite out of danger.

Having examined them, I ordered the men to their quarters, and they all left the fort, with the exception of the night guard.

The two interpreters, Umbogo and Aboo Kooka, were secured by a thin cord fastened round their necks.

Having given all the necessary instructions, I ordered Monsoor to go to the chief Matonsé, with a message that I wished to see him, as the men had been ill after drinking the cider, and although now recovered, it would be satisfactory if he would examine the remaining jars.

Monsoor took his rifle, and, accompanied by a corporal, Ferritch Baggára, one of the best soldiers of the "Forty Thieves," started on his mission. Matonsé's house, as already described, was within 200 yards of the government divan.

It was now about 5.45 A.M. I noticed that Kabba Réga's divan, within fifty yards of the government house, seemed full of people, some of whom were washing their faces, as though they had just risen from sleep.

My wife had now joined me, and, according to my usual habit, I strolled up and down the broad gravelled approach and smoked a short pipe. We were conversing together about the present state of affairs, and were anxiously expecting the return of Monsoor with Matonsé, who would perhaps throw some light on the matter.

I was followed closely by a bugler and a choush (sergeant). The main entrance of the approach from the town was bordered upon either side by a dense plantation of castor-oil trees, which continued in a thick fringe along the edge of the garden, so as to screen the huts from our view, although they were within twenty paces of the entrance of the drive.

The castor-oil bushes were within five yards of the entrance, and gradually increased the distance, as they turned obliquely towards the private divan of Kabba Réga.

We little suspected that sharpshooters were already concealed within this dense covert.

My wife and I had reached the entrance of the approach. Nothing seemed to denote hostility on the part of the natives, no person being visible, except those guards who occupied the king's divan.

Suddenly we were startled by the savage yells of some thousand voices, which burst unexpectedly upon us!

This horrible sound came from the direction of

Matonsé's house, and was within 120 yards from the spot on which we stood ; but the town was not visible, owing to the thick covert of oil bushes.

The savage yells were almost immediately followed by two rifle shots in the same direction.

" Sound the taboor ! " Fortunately I gave this order to the bugler by my side without one moment's delay.

I had just time to tell my wife to run into the divan and get my rifle and belt, when the sharp-shooters opened fire at me from the bushes, within a few yards.

I had white cotton clothes, thus I was a very clear object. As I walked towards the divan to meet my rifle, the sergeant who followed close behind me fell shot through the heart.

The troops had fallen into position with extraordinary rapidity, and several ascended the roof of the fort, so as to see clearly over the high grass. A soldier immediately fell, to die in a few minutes, shot through the shoulder-blade. Another man of the " Forty Thieves " was shot through the leg above the knee. The bullets were flying through the government divan, and along the approach.

A tumultuous roar of savage voices had burst from all sides, and the whole place was alive a few instants after the first two shots had been heard. Thousands of armed natives now rushed from all directions upon the station.

A thrill went through me when I thought of my good and devoted Monsoor!

My wife had quickly given me my belt and breechloading double rifle, the "Dutchman."[1] Fortunately I had filled up the pouches on the previous evening with fifty rounds of cartridge.

The troops were now in open order, completely around the station, and were pouring a heavy fire into the masses of the enemy within the high grass, which had been left purposely uncleared by Kabba Réga, in order to favour this treacherous attack.

The natives kept up a steady fire upon the front from behind the castor-oil bushes and the densely thronged houses.

With sixteen men of the "Forty Thieves," together with Colonel Abd-el-Kader and Lieutenant Baker, R.N., I directed a heavy fire into the covert, and soon made it too hot for the sharpshooters. I had ordered the blue lights at the commencement of the attack. My black boys, Sāat and Bellāal,

[1] This beautiful weapon, I have already mentioned, was made by Mr. Holland, of Bond Street, London.

together with some soldiers, now arrived with a good supply.

Covering their advance with a heavy fire from the sniders, the boys and men rushed forward, and immediately ignited Kabba Réga's large divan.

These active and plucky lads now ran nimbly from hut to hut, and one slight touch of the strong fire of the blue lights was sufficient to insure the ignition of the straw dwellings.

I now sent a party of fifteen sniders, under Lieutenant Ferritch Agha, one of my most courageous officers, with a supply of blue lights, to set fire to the town on our left flank, and to push on to the spot where the missing Monsoor and Ferritch had fired their rifles.

Every arrangement having been rapidly carried out, the boys and a few men continued to fire the houses on our right flank; and giving the order to advance, our party of sixteen rushed forward into the town.

The right and left flanks were now blazing, and the flames were roaring before the wind. I heard the rattling fire of the sniders under Ferritch Agha on our left, and knowing that both flanks were now thoroughly secured by the conflagration, we dashed straight for Kabba Réga's principal residences and

BATTLE OF MASINDI—REPULSE AND DEFEAT OF KABBA RÉGA'S FORCES.

court, driving the enemy before us. Colonel Abd-el-Kader was an excellent officer in action. We quickly surrounded Kabba Réga's premises, and set fire to the enormous straw buildings on all sides.

If he had been at home he would have had a warm reception, but the young coward had fled with all his women before the action had commenced, together with the magic bamba or throne, and the sacred drum.

In a few minutes the conflagration was terrific, as the great court of Kabba Réga blazed in flames seventy or eighty feet high, which the wind drove in vivid forks into the thatch of the adjacent houses.

We now followed the enemy throughout the town, and the sniders told with sensible effect wherever they made a stand. The blue lights continued the work of vengeance; the roar of flames and the dense volumes of smoke, mingled with the continued rattle of musketry, and the savage yells of the natives, swept forward with the breeze, and the capital of Unyoro was a fair sample of the infernal regions.

The natives were driven out of the town, but the high grass was swarming with many thousands, who, in the neighbourhood of the station, still advanced to attack the soldiers.

I now ordered "The Forty" to clear the grass, and a steady fire of snider rifles soon purged the covert upon which the enemy had relied.

In about an hour and a quarter the battle of Masindi was won. Not a house remained of the lately extensive town. A vast open space of smoke and black ashes, with flames flickering in some places where the buildings had been consumed, and at others forked sheets of fire where the fuel was still undestroyed, were the only remains of the capital of Unyoro.

The enemy had fled. Their drums and horns, lately so noisy, were now silent.

I ordered the bugle to sound " cease firing." We marched through the scorching streets to our station, where I found my wife in deep distress.

The bugle sounded the assembly, and the men mustered, and fell in for the roll-call. Four men were missing.

Lying on the turf, close to the fort wall, were four bodies arranged in a row and covered with cloths.

The soldiers gathered round them as I approached. The cloths were raised.

My eyes rested on the pale features of my ever faithful and devoted officer, Monsoor! There was a sad expression of pain on his face. I could not help feeling his pulse; but there was no hope; this was still. I laid his arm gently by his side, and pressed his hand for the last time, for I loved Monsoor as a true friend.

His body was pierced with thirty-two lance wounds; thus he had fought gallantly to the last, and he had died like a good soldier; but he was treacherously murdered instead of dying on a fair battle-field.

Poor Ferritch Baggara was lying next to him, with two lance wounds through the chest.

The other bodies were those of the choush that had fallen by my side, and the soldier who had been shot on the parapet.

We were all deeply distressed at the death of poor Monsoor. There never was a more thoroughly unselfish and excellent man. He was always kind to the boys, and would share even a scanty meal in hard times with either friend or stranger. He was the lamb in peace, and the lion in moments of danger. I owed him a debt of gratitude, for although I was the general, and he had been only a corporal when he first joined the expedition, he had watched over my safety like a brother. I should "never see his like again."

Monsoor was the only Christian, excepting the European party.

The graves were made. I gave out new cloth from the stores in which to wrap the bodies of four of my best men, and they were buried near the fort.

My heart was very heavy. God knows I had worked with the best intentions for the benefit of the country, and this was the lamentable result. My best men were treacherously murdered. We had narrowly escaped a general massacre. We had won the battle, and Masindi was swept from the earth. What next?

I find these words, which I extract from my journal, as they were written at that moment:—

"Thus ended the battle of Masindi, caused by the horrible treachery of the natives. Had I not been quick in sounding the bugle and immediately assuming a vigorous offensive, we should have been overwhelmed by numbers.

"Since we have been in this country, my men have been models of virtue; nothing has been stolen, except a few potatoes on one occasion, when the thief was publicly punished, and the potatoes restored to the owner, neither have the natives been interfered with in any manner. I have driven the slave-hunters from their country, and my troops from Fatiko are ordered to restore to Unyoro all the slaves that have been stolen by the traders. The disgusting ingratitude and treachery of the negro surpasses imagination.

"What is to become of these countries? all my good-will brings forth evil deeds."

In the battle of Masindi nothing could have exceeded the cool, soldier-like bearing of both officers and men. Every man had done his duty. In the first onset, when about seven or eight thousand natives had suddenly attacked the station, the men had not only fallen into position for the defence of the camp with extraordinary alacrity, but they had behaved with extreme steadiness and coolness, and not a man had moved from his post without orders.

The attacking parties, formed exclusively of the "Forty Thieves," had exhibited an activity and *élan* for which this gallant little corps was eminently distinguished; and had they been European troops, their conduct upon this occasion, against such overwhelming odds, would have covered them with glory.

We had no newspaper correspondents, therefore I must give the due praise to my officers and men.

During the day I established patrols throughout the now cleared space lately occupied by the town.

In the afternoon Umbogo was able to call some natives who were within earshot. These men explained that the chief, Matonsé, was the cause of the outbreak, and that it was his people who, by his orders, had killed Monsoor and Ferritch.

Umbogo had been set at liberty during the fight, but I now secured him by the neck to a leathern thong in the hand of a sentry ; for, although a good man, I could not afford to lose him, and the devil might have tempted him to run away.

In the afternoon some natives cried out that Kittākără was coming, and Lieutenant-Colonel Abd-el-Kader, with a few men, immediately went out to meet him.

Kittākără would not approach within less than about a hundred yards, but he assured Abd-el-Kader that the outbreak was not the fault of Kabba Réga, but that the responsibility lay with Matonsé, who had escaped, and that he should be captured and delivered up to me.

He continued to assure Abd-el-Kader that Kabba Réga had already ordered provisions and a large number of elephants' tusks to be collected for us, and that, although for the present he was hiding through fear in the high grass, he would quickly rebuild his divan close to my own, so as to live in friendship.

It was impossible to credit one syllable in Unyoro. On the other hand, should I be unable to bring the enemy to terms, I should be utterly ruined, as it would be impossible to transport my baggage.

It was a terrible position. The treachery had been frightful, and I could only attribute it to Kabba Réga's orders, in spite of the protestations of Kittākără. If I should be right in my suspicions, what would become of Major Abdullah and his detachment?

Nothing would be easier for the 300 natives who had accompanied my people with the post, than to behave well on the route to Fatiko, in order to establish confidence. They could then carry all the effects and ammunition, in company with Abdullah and his troops, from Fatiko to Unyoro, and in the prairie wilderness, they might murder every man at night when asleep, and possess themselves of the arms, ammunition, and effects, with which they would rejoin Kabba Réga.

This was a frightful idea; and there could be no doubt that such treachery had been planned, if

Kabba Réga were guilty of the attempt to poison the troops and attack us by surprise. It was hard to disbelieve his guilt.

There were no means possible of communication with Abdullah. In case of necessity, there was only one move; this was to march to the Victoria Nile, and form an alliance with Rionga, the old enemy of Kamrasi's family, whom I had always refused to attack. I was sure that he must have heard of my refusal to ally myself with Kabba Réga against him : thus he would be favourable to the government.

I resolved that, if hostilities should continue, I would proclaim Rionga as the representative of the government, as vassal-chief of Unyoro, in the room of Kabba Réga, deposed.

Rionga would send a letter to warn Major Abdullah at Fatiko ; but how was I to convey my baggage and ammunition from Masindi to Foweera, without a single carrier, or even a guide ?

It was the height of the rainy season, and the grass was about nine or ten feet high, throughout a country of dense and tangled forest.

I had no interpreter of my own; Umbogo was Kabba Réga's slave, and although I fancied that he was fond of us, I had no faith in any one of these detestable people. This want of confidence was keenly felt at a time when I required an interpreter in whom I could absolutely trust. I was obliged to confide my plan to Umbogo, as I wished him to find some man among the natives who would take a message to Rionga.

I knew that many people hated Kabba Réga. Umbogo had frequently assured me that Mashudi, which was only two days distant from Masindi, to the south-east, had always been Rionga's stronghold; and that the natives of that district would rise in favour of their chief, should any reverse befall Kabba Réga.

The news of the defeat of his army, and the complete destruction of his capital, would run through the country like wild-fire. It was well known that Rionga had spies, who were disguised as friends, even at the court of Kabba Réga; these agents sent him information of all that occurred.

If Umbogo could communicate with one of these people, I might send off to Rionga, to beg him to send 300 men to Fatiko, with a letter from myself to Major Abdullah. Rionga's people would transport the effects instead of Kabba Réga's carriers, who would be seized and held as hostages. This would save Abdullah from the intended treachery, if it were done at once; but there was not a moment to lose.

Already fifteen days had elapsed since my party with the post had started, and by this time they should be near Fatiko,[1] unless they had been delayed upon the road, as was usual in Unyoro.

If I could depend upon Rionga, he would at once save Abdullah's party, and he would send a large force to communicate with me at Masindi.

Had I provisions, I could have held my now fortified position against a whole world of niggers; but with only a hundred men, I should be unable to forage in this country of high grass, and at the same time defend the station.

All depended upon the possibility of my communication with Rionga.

Umbogo declared that if I would only march to Mashudi, the natives would rise in Rionga's favour and join me.

I told him that if this were true, he could surely find some person who would run to Mashudi, and raise the malcontents, who would at once carry my message to Rionga.

Umbogo promised to do his best: at the same time he expressed an opinion that Rionga would not wait long in inaction, but that he would invade Kabba Réga directly that he should hear of the war.

---

[1] At that time they had already been treacherously attacked.

From my experience of natives, I did not share his opinion.

As Kittākără had apologized for the attack to Colonel Abd-el-Kader, and a truce had been arranged, a great number of natives spread themselves over the ruins of the town, to search for the iron molotes, which are generally concealed in the earth, beneath the floor of the huts. The natives were all prodding the smoking ground with the iron-tipped butt-ends of their lances to discover the treasures.

Umbogo now went among them with his guard, and conversed upon the cause of the late attack.

In the evening, Umbogo declared that he was not quite certain of the truth; he evidently suspected the sincerity of Kabba Réga. It was quite impossible to procure any messenger at present that could be trusted with a message to Rionga.

The memorable 8th of June happened to be my birthday. It had been the day of death to my lamented follower, Monsoor; but we had well avenged him.

Umbogo reported that the natives had given him the names of nine mătōngălés (chiefs) killed in the action, together with a large number of common people. A great many were still missing: these were probably lying in the high grass which had been raked by the hot fire of the sniders. Vultures were collected in immense numbers over many spots in this dense covert, which denoted the places where the "missing" had fallen.

I ordered the troops to abandon their undefended camp, and to sleep within the fort that night.

The morning of the 9th of June arrived—the night had passed in perfect quiet.

My troops were set to work with their sharp sword-bayonets, swords, knives, &c., to cut down all the high grass in the neighbourhood, so as to throw open the view, and prevent the enemy from attacking us by another surprise. They worked for many hours, and soon found a number of the missing, who were lying dead. Five bodies were discovered close together, as though they had been killed by a shell. This was in a spot where the "Forty Thieves" had been at work.

One unfortunate creature was found in the high grass with a smashed leg. He had been lying, thirsty and in pain, for about thirty hours in the same spot. My men gave him water and food, and his friends came and took him away. The wounded man seemed very grateful, and he told my soldiers that they were "better men than the Unyoros, who would certainly murder a wounded enemy instead of giving him food and water."

I had told Umbogo to make inquiries as to the safety of little Cherri-Merri. The boy was unharmed, as he had been taken away before the fight.

I now proved that the cows had also been removed during the night previous to the attack, as I had suspected.

During the day, vast numbers of people were collected at a large village, situated on a knoll, about 700 yards from our station in a direct line. This place, we were informed, was now occupied by Kabba Réga. The knoll was about eighty feet lower than our high position; therefore, as we had now roughly cut down the grass, we looked directly upon the village.

We lost no time in erecting the large astronomical telescope upon its stand. This was placed upon the flat gravel approach in front of the government divan, and through the powerful glass we could distinguish each feature, and the expression of every individual countenance of the crowd within the village.

During the day, messengers arrived from Kabba Réga with an official explanation of the misunderstanding. They declared that it was entirely the fault of Matonsé, who would be soon captured; that Kabba Réga desired them to express his deep regret; "Was he not my son? Did he not depend upon the protection of his father?" He only begged for peace.

The natives had been killed in great numbers; therefore "if we had lost a few soldiers, the Unyoro had lost many—so the affair was settled."

I told them that nothing could ever compensate for the loss of Monsoor, who had been so treacherously killed; at the same time, if Kabba Réga could prove that the guilt really lay with Matonsé, the simple plan would be to deliver him up to me.

I recalled to their recollection how I had passed ten months in Unyoro in the reign of Kamrasi, at which time I had only an escort of thirteen men, and no misunderstanding had ever occurred. I explained that the fault was not on my side. An attempt had been made to poison us collectively; we had then been surprised by a thoroughly organized attack, at a time when the troops were supposed to have been disabled by the poison.

Kabba Réga must clear his character. If he were innocent, I should be only too happy.

The mătōngălé or sheik, who was the principal messenger, assured me that Kabba Réga was quite in despair, and that he had given orders for provisions and a large quantity of ivory to be immediately collected, which would be sent to us on the day following, in charge of Rahonka and Kittākără.

The want of provisions was sorely felt; fortunately,

as our cows had been dying daily, the troops had some sweet potatoes that had been purchased in exchange for flesh. These would last for a few days.

A short time before the attack, I had promised to send Kabba Réga a porcelain *cache-pot*. I therefore took the opportunity of reminding the sheik of my promise, and I begged him to deliver the piece of china to Kabba Réga as a proof of my peaceful intentions, should he really be innocent of the treachery.

The handsome present was wrapped up in red Turkey cloth, and the messengers departed.

I watched them through the telescope, and, upon their arrival at the village below us, I distinctly witnessed, not only their reception by the expectant crowd, but the *cache-pot* was unpacked and held at arm's length above the head, to be exhibited to the admiring people.

This looked well. My officers began to believe in peace; and, although I still had strong suspicions, I hoped that the signal defeat that Kabba Réga's army had sustained had so far cowed them as to induce a termination of hostilities, which would enable me to communicate with Major Abdullah.

The luggage from the government divan had all been carried to the fort. This was now returned to our original quarters; my wife and her black maids working hard at rearranging the rooms.

The night passed quietly.

On 10th of June a mătōngălé and several natives arrived from Kabba Réga, with a most polite message and friendly assurances, accompanied by a present of two beautiful white cows.

The messengers corroborated the statement of the preceding day, that large quantities of provisions were being prepared for us, together with twenty fine elephants' tusks, which were to be delivered as a peace-offering by Rahonka and Kittākără in person.

Affairs looked brighter. It was my best policy to secure peace if possible.

I determined to send Kabba Réga, in return for his present of cows, the large Geneva musical box, with drums and bells, which he had always desired.

No one knew how to wind it up; and it was necessary that some person should accompany it with the native messengers.

The clerk of the detachment, Ramadān, who has already been mentioned as a favourite with the natives, and a good linguist, at once volunteered to be the bearer of the present. Since the battle of Masindi, Ramadān had been in frequent personal communication with the natives, and he assured me that there was a general desire for peaceful relations. He was supposed to be a favourite of Kabba Réga's, and it was therefore arranged that he should accompany the musical box, which was a good load for a fast-travelling native.

Hafiz, the farrier, whose occupation was nearly gone by the death of all the horses but two, volunteered to accompany Ramadān. I ordered them to go unarmed, as their peaceful mission would be at once understood; this fact would establish confidence among the natives.

It was about 3 P.M. when they started, and we watched their arrival in the village with the telescope, where they appeared to be well received.

In the evening they both returned with the musical box, accompanied by the sheik who was to be their guide, as Kabba Réga had retired to a town at which he had a residence, about half a day's march distant. It was arranged that they should start on the following morning.

On the 11th June, Ramadān and Hafiz, together with the musical box, started, and we watched their reception at the village with the telescope. I had released Umbogo, whom I had sent to Kabba Réga to explain all that he had seen of the outbreak, as he was one of those who had been poisoned by the plantain cider. Umbogo promised to return as soon as possible. The dragoman, Abou Kooka, remained with us in the place of Umbogo. This was a sullen-looking brute who had been a slave stolen from the Madi tribe.

I must now take an extract *verbatim* from my journal, as that was written on the day of the incident. Any warm expressions in this extract must be excused as a natural consequence, for which I trust due allowance will be granted:—

"I walked round the burnt town of Masindi, accompanied by Julian (Lieutenant Baker), Abd-el-Kader, and two guards of 'The Forty.' Neither Abd-el-Kader nor I carried guns, as I wished to establish confidence among the natives, who were searching among the ashes for molotes.

"I sent for the dragoman, Abou Kooka, and conversed with the natives, assuring them of peace, and that I had no ill-will against Kabba Réga, if Matonsé was the cause of the outbreak. At the same time, I told them to bring provisions for sale.

"They seemed very shy, and replied that 'all would be right when the messengers should arrive from Kabba Réga.' One by one they went away, until only two were left. Julian gave his gun to one of the guards.

"The two natives were standing on the edge of

the high grass, close to the ashes of the town, and they appeared more confident, as they conversed with us at about twelve yards' distance.

"Presently they said they would come close to us, were it not for their fear of the two sentries with their rifles, who were about forty yards in our rear.

"I turned round to order the sentries to retire a little. The instant that my back was turned, one of the treacherous brutes hurled his spear at me, which stuck quivering in the earth at my feet! At the same moment they bolted into the high grass, *accompanied by our dragoman, Abou Kooka*, and disappeared at once like fish in water.

"The treachery of the negro is beyond belief; he has not a moral human instinct, and is below the brute. How is it possible to improve such abject animals? They are not worth the trouble, and they are only fit for slaves, to which position their race appears to have been condemned.

"I believe I have wasted my time and energy, and have uselessly encountered difficulties, and made enemies by my attempt to suppress the slave trade, and thus improve the condition of the natives.

"It is now 4.40 P.M., and I am anxious about Ramadān and Hafiz, who have not returned.

"My men have been on half rations since the 8th

inst., and we have supplies only for to-morrow, after which we shall be obliged to forage, unless Kabba Réga sends the promised provisions.

"It is impossible to believe one word in this accursed country. At the same time that Kabba Réga declares peace and good-will, he may be planning a surprise. I do not think, however, that his people will be in a hurry to fight after the lesson they received on the 8th inst.

"Nevertheless, fighting is dangerous work in this country of high grass, where troops cannot see to manœuvre, and where the ground is everywhere favourable for native ambuscades."

When I returned to the divan with the spear that had so narrowly missed me, through the cowardice of the assailant (who should have made sure of me, had he not been nervous), my wife was not cheered by the little incident. She had had the same experience as myself in African natures, and she immediately declared against the pretended sincerity of Kabba Réga.

I had serious misgivings. Nothing can happen in Unyoro without the order of the king. The superstitious veneration for the possessor of the magic throne produces a profound obedience.

On the other hand, this attempt at murder might

have been only the revenge of an individual who had perhaps lost his house and property in the conflagration of Masindi.

The evening arrived without tidings of either Ramadān or Umbogo. I was now without an interpreter.

The troops, and their wives and effects, occupied the fort, and the officers' quarters and camp had been abandoned.

It was about 8 P.M., and dinner being over, I was smoking my pipe in the divan, conversing with my wife and Lieutenant Baker upon the situation of affairs, when a sudden bright glare attracted my attention.

An officer immediately reported that the abandoned quarters were in a blaze of fire!

I was of course ready in an instant, and armed, and accompanied by my wife and Mr. Baker, I really enjoyed the beauty of the scene in that moment of anxiety.

Without the slightest noise, or even an audible whisper, the troops were all in position, kneeling on the ground in open order around the fort and the divan, keeping the most vigilant watch for the appearance of an enemy. The flames from the camp rose about seventy feet high. There was not a breath of air; thus the fire danced and leapt up to its extreme height, and illumined the neighbourhood for a great distance.

Not an enemy was to be seen. The soldiers were like statues, and there was no sound except the roaring of flames.

Suddenly loud yells broke out from a distance of about 200 yards from the farthest side of the fort, as though from a considerable body of men. Not a soldier stirred or spoke.

I had cleared the grass around the fort and station, therefore it was impossible to approach us unobserved.

The natives must have crept up stealthily, and fired the abandoned camp in the expectation that the troops would have rushed down to extinguish the flames, and thus the fort and the divan would have been at the mercy of an attack from the dark side.

I immediately sent a strong patrol around the station, but not a soul was visible. The attempt had failed.

Once more the luggage, with beds, boxes, &c., was transported from the divan to the fort; and with the assistance of Lieutenant Baker, I built a quadrangular wall of boxes like huge bricks, to form a

NATIVES SET FIRE TO THE SOLDIERS' CAMP AT NIGHT.

protection for my wife, in the event of a night attack with fire-arms.

The night passed quietly. On 12th June, I watched the natives with the telescope, and I observed that many of the crowd were gesticulating in an excited manner.

I was almost convinced that we were again subjected to the foulest treachery, and I was extremely anxious about Ramadān and Hafiz. I could hardly believe it possible that these poor men, unarmed, and carrying a valuable present, would be cruelly murdered.

The day passed in hope and expectation of their return. Late in the evening, the act of incendiarism of the preceding night was renewed, and the deserted house of Colonel Abd-el-Kader was in a bright blaze without a native being visible.

No yells were heard, nor any other sound. The troops turned out with their usual quiet discipline, but not a shot was fired.

The 13th June arrived. Still there were no tidings of either Umbogo, Ramadān or Hafiz. I now felt convinced that the young villain, Kabba Réga, had played me false, and that he was only gaining time to collect and organize the whole force of Unyoro to attack us, and to line the path to Rionga with ambuscades.

It is impossible to this day to say whether Umbogo was true or false. I never saw him again; and the unfortunate Ramadān and Hafiz were wantonly murdered.

At about 10 A.M., 13th June, we were let into the secret of Kabba Réga's villainy. A sudden rush of natives was made upon the cattle, which were grazing within sixty yards of the fort! Poisoned arrows were shot, and we at once observed that a general attack was made upon the station. Guns fired; the bullets whistled over our heads, and I thought I recognized the crack of our lost sniders, (those of Monsoor and Ferritch) that were employed against us.

The curtain had now risen. When the actual fighting arrived, there was some little relaxation from the intense anxiety of mind that I had suffered for some days.

I at once ordered the men into line, and the bugles and drums sounded the charge with the bayonet—that I had always taught my men to depend upon.

The gallant "Forty Thieves" led the way, with drums beating and a hearty cheer, and dashed through the ruins of the town and straight into the high grass on the other side, from which the cowardly enemy fled like hares.

On our return to the station, I took a snider, and practically explained to the rascals in the village on the knoll what long range meant, sending several bullets into the midst of a crowd that scattered them like chaff. I at once ordered Colonel Abd-el-Kader to take eighty men and some blue lights, and to destroy every village in the neighbourhood. The attack was made on the instant. The large village, about 700 yards distant, which I had raked with the fire of a few sniders, while Abd-el-Kader descended the slope to the attack, was soon a mass of rolling flames. In an hour's time volumes of smoke were rising in various directions.

My active and gallant colonel returned, having driven the enemy from every position, and utterly destroyed the neighbourhood.

I had made up my mind. There could be no longer any doubt of the diabolical treachery of Kabba Réga. He had only endeavoured to gain time by specious assurances of good-will, combined with presents, in order to organize the whole country against us. The natives who shot arrows must have come from Magungo, as none of the other districts were armed with bows. The arrows that had been shot at us, which my men had collected, were thickly poisoned with a hard gummy matter.

It was now rendered certain that a snare had been laid for the massacre of Major Abdullah's party.

Kabba Réga had no doubt ordered the various routes towards Rionga's province to be ambuscaded.

I determined at once to push straight for the camp at Foweera on the Victoria Nile, as Rionga's island was about fifteen miles from that point.

Among the men of the "Forty Thieves," there was a soldier named Abdullah, who had an extraordinary instinct for finding his way. This man never forgot a path if he had ever travelled upon the same route.

I also depended upon my Baris and Molōdi, although they had not had any long experience of the path by which we had arrived from Foweera with the herd of cattle.

Unfortunately, the country had changed terribly by the immense growth of the grass and tangled creepers.

I felt sure that the route would be occupied by the enemy throughout the whole distance, and that we should have to fight every mile of the path at a grave disadvantage.

The question of a supply of food was vital. The men had mostly exhausted their provisions.

At this critical moment, when every man of the expedition felt the fatal truth, my wife confided her secret, that she had hitherto concealed, lest the knowledge of a hidden store should have made the men extravagant. She now informed the officers and men that in past days of plenty, when flour had been abundant, she had, from time to time, secreted a quantity, and she had now *six large iron boxes full* (about twelve bushels). This private store she had laid by in the event of some sudden emergency.

"God shall give her a long life!" exclaimed both officers and men. We had now enough flour for the march of seven days to Foweera, at which place there were regular forests of plantains.

My herd of cattle had been reduced to seventy, and I much doubted the possibility of driving them in a high grass country, as they would scatter and make a stampede should we be attacked; they would be scared by the guns.

I mustered my force and spoke to my men, to whom I explained their exact position, and my plan of action.

I should immediately divide among them, as presents, all the cotton stuffs that belonged to the expedition.

Each man would carry three pounds of beads in his knapsack, one-third of which should subsequently belong to him.

The line of march would be thus arranged—a Bari, who professed to know the path, would lead the advance-guard of fifteen sniders, commanded by Lieutenant-Colonel Abd-el-Kader, supported by myself with ten sniders in charge of the ammunition, accompanied by Lieutenant Baker, my wife, and two servants, carrying double breechloading elephant rifles. The rear-guard would consist of fifteen sniders. The few remaining sniders would be distributed along the line.

Neither the advance nor rear-guard would carry any loads beyond their knapsacks and a small bag of flour. Five of the sniders with me would also be exempted from carrying loads; but every other soldier, and every woman and boy, would carry either one of the metal boxes or some other package.

I explained to the men that they would be attacked throughout the route at a great disadvantage, but that success would depend upon the strict observance of orders for the march, combined with the utmost coolness.

Each man was to keep just near enough to be able to touch with his outstretched hand the knapsack of the man before him, and upon no account to widen this distance, but to keep the line intact. Should it be broken by the sudden rush of the enemy, we should at once be lost.

Should the attack be made simultaneously on both sides, alternate files would face to right and left, place their loads upon the ground, and fire low down in the grass, as the natives always crouched after throwing a spear from covert.

A bugler would accompany the colonel commanding the advance-guard, in addition to buglers with myself and the rear-guard; thus we should be able to communicate along the line, which would be concealed from view by the high grass.

On arrival at water, and in crossing either swamps or streams, no man or woman was to stop to drink unless the bugle of the advance-guard sounded halt.

No woman would be allowed to speak during the march, as profound silence must be observed.

The officers and men received their instructions, merely declaring that wherever I should lead them, they would follow me and obey.

I at once divided the effects that could be carried, into the requisite number of loads, which were carefully packed in metal boxes by my wife and her black maids. It was hard and anxious work. The strongest men were selected to carry the boxes of snider cartridges, which weighed 64lbs. each.

All the rest of the baggage I arranged in piles, and distributed in the government divan and the various houses. I spread my large tent over the luggage in the divan, and poured over it a quantity of nitrous ether, spirits of wine, lamp-oil, spirits of turpentine, and all the contents of the large medicine-chest.

I filled up my small chest, and took a good roll of adhesive plaster, a number of bandages, and a roll of lint.

Upon the tent-cloth, rendered highly inflammable by the saturation of spirits and oil, I laid about sixty rockets.

My two horses and three donkeys would be loaded with baggage.

I gave orders for the march early on the following morning. The rear-guard was to set fire to the station, which was the result of our industry and labour in this land of detestable savages.

CHAPTER IX.

THE MARCH TO RIONGA.

ON the morning of the 14th of June, 1872, at 9.30, the advance-guard filed along the gravel path, and halted at the extremity of the station at Masindi. The line was complete, according to the orders for the march. Not a word was spoken.

A light, drizzling rain fell, and the sky was a dull grey.

I looked back, and waited for the destruction of my favourite station. In our little house we had left pictures of my own children, and everything that was not absolutely necessary to our existence. Even the Queen and the Princess of Wales were to perish in the conflagration, together with much that was parted with in this moment of exigency.

The smoke now curled in thick, white folds from the government divan and our own private house.

Lieutenant Baker's new house was ignited. One by one every hut was fired. The rear-guard, having done their duty, closed up in the line of march.

I did not give the word " Forward ! " until the flames had shot up high in the air, and the station was in the possession of the fire. At this moment a loud report announced that all the rockets had exploded. The advance-guard moved forward, and the march commenced.

We soon entered the high grass, which was reeking with the light rain, and we were wet through in an instant.

My wife was walking close behind me with a quantity of spare ammunition for the " Dutchman " in her breast. She had a Colt's revolver in her belt. Lieutenant Baker was heavily loaded, as he carried a Purdy rifle slung across his back, together with a large bag of ammunition, while he held a double breechloader smooth-bore in his hand, with a bag of heavy buckshot cartridges upon his shoulder.

Suleiman and Mohammed Haroon (our servants) were close by with my two breechloading No. 8 elephant rifles. These carried picrate of potash shells that were immensely powerful. Very little would have been left of the body of a man had one of such shells struck him in the chest.

The cattle began to cause much trouble as soon as the march commenced, and we slowly descended the knoll upon which the station stood, and in single file entered the extremely narrow path which led down to a small swamp.

Crossing the swamp, through deep mud, we arrived on firm ground, and continued to march slowly on account of the cattle. I felt sure they would have to be abandoned. The cows strayed to the right and left, and Morgiān the Bari, and Abdullah Djoor the cook, who were the drovers, were rushing about the grass in pursuit of refractory animals, that would shortly end in being speared by the enemy.

We thus marched slowly forward for about a mile before a hostile sound was heard. We then distinguished the tumultuous voices of the natives in the rear, who had been attracted to the station by the general conflagration.

The slow march continued, through grass about eight feet high, and occasional forest. The rain now descended steadily, and I feared that the old muzzle-loading muskets would miss fire.

The sound of drums and horns was now heard throughout the country, as the alarm spread rapidly from village to village. We could hear the shouts of natives, and drums that were now sounding in the forest upon a hill on our right. These people were evidently in possession of a path unknown to us, which ran parallel to our route.

For seven hours the march continued with such frequent halts, owing to the straying of the cattle, that we had only progressed the short distance of ten miles, when, at 4.40 p.m., we entered the valley of Jon Joke. We saw before us the hill covered with plantain groves where we had slept when upon the march to Masindi.

The grass was very high, and the path hardly a foot wide, and only resembling a sheep run. Suddenly the advance-guard opened a hot fire, and the bugle sounded "halt!"

A few paces in front of me, my favourite sailor and fisherman, Howarti, was in the line, carrying a metal box upon his head. In addition to his musket, which was slung across his shoulders, I had given him one of my double breechloading pistols, which he carried in his belt.

The word was suddenly passed that "Howarti was speared!"

Lances now flew across the path, and the line opened fire into the grass upon our right, according to orders.

I immediately went up to Howarti. I found him

sitting upon the ground by the side of his box, in the act of reloading his pistol with a Boxer cartridge. A lance had struck him in the fleshy part of the right arm, just below the point of junction with the shoulder, and, passing through his body, it had protruded from his stomach. Upon feeling the wound, Howarti had dropped his load, and drawing his pistol, he shot the native dead, as he leapt from his ambush to recover the lance which was sticking in the poor fellow's body.

Here was another of my best men sacrificed. Howarti had always been a true, good man, and he had just exhibited his cool courage. He had himself pulled the spear from his body.

My wife had followed me immediately upon hearing that Howarti was injured. He had reloaded his pistol, but in reply to my question whether he could sit upon a donkey, he fainted. I roughly bandaged him for the present moment, and we laid him upon an angareb (stretcher-bedstead), but the men were so heavily laden that it was difficult to find supporters. Lieutenant Baker kindly took one end upon his shoulder, and with the assistance of the advance guard, we carried him forward. The bugle sounded the "advance."

Again the lances flew across the path, but a few

shots with the sniders cleared the way, and leaving the narrow route, we broke our way through the tangled grass, and ascended the slope to the plantain forest. Here, thank goodness, there was no grass. The bugle sounded "halt" in the middle of the plantains.

Sentries having been posted, every man was now employed in felling the tall plantain-trees, and in arranging them to form a wall around the camp.

One blow of a sharp, heavy sabre will cut through the stem, thus in a short time, as we all worked, a clearing of about an acre was made, and by sunset we had piled them so as to form a tolerable protection from lances.

Throughout the day it had never ceased raining, thus every one was soaking and miserable. Of course we had no tent, but some invaluable mackintosh camp sheets. I had examined Howarti's wounds, which I knew were mortal. The air as he breathed was rattling through the gash in his stomach. I washed and bandaged him carefully, and gave him a dose of brandy and laudanum.

No one had a drop of water to drink, neither did any one know the direction of the well; but, as all were cold and wet through, no person suffered from thirst. Fortunately, we had matches in a small silver case that had resisted the damp; and after some difficulty and delay, fires were blazing through the little bivouac, and the soldiers and women were crouching round them.

We were comfortable that night, as we had beds to lie upon; but I felt sure it would be for the last time, as it would be necessary to destroy much luggage, the men being too heavily laden.

All was at length still; the soldiers, who were all tired, went to sleep, with the exception of the sentries, who were well on the alert.

As I lay on my bed, I thought of the morrow. I knew we should have a trying time, as the whole country would now be thoroughly organized against us. Our start from Masindi had taken them by surprise—thus we had not met with much resistance; but to-morrow would be a fighting day, and I made up my mind to leave the cattle to themselves, as it would be simply impossible to drive them.

The night passed without an attack.

On the following morning, 15th June, poor Howarti was evidently about to die, but the plucky fellow faintly said that he could ride a donkey if assisted. It was impossible to carry him, as the path was too narrow for four people to walk beneath a stretcher.

He was placed upon a donkey, and supported with difficulty by a man at his side.

I was obliged to pile upon the fire a number of things that we could not carry, including the large oaken stand of the astronomical telescope.

It was 7.30 A.M. before we started.

The troublesome cattle at once began to stray, and I immediately ordered them to be abandoned. I felt certain that in the event of a general attack they would have created great confusion, by probably rushing down the line and overturning the men.

It was the greatest relief to be rid of the animals: thus we marched on merrily at about two and a half miles an hour, through the usual narrow path amidst gigantic grass (now about nine feet high) and thick forest.

In about an hour and a half we arrived at a descent, towards a bottom in which there was a broad, open swamp, with a stream running through the centre.

The advance-guard was not more than a hundred yards from the bottom, and the line was descending the hill in close order, when a sudden uproar broke out, as though all the demons of hell had broken loose. Yells, screams, drums, horns, whistles from many thousand concealed enemies, for an instant startled the troops! A tremendous rush in the grass gave notice of a general attack from an immensely powerful ambuscade. The officers did their duty.

Every load was upon the ground, and in a moment alternate files were facing to the right and left, kneeling just as the lances began to fly across the path. The bugles rang out "fire," and the fight commenced on our side.

I saw several lances pass within an inch or two of my wife's head; luckily we were kneeling on one knee. The file-firing was extremely good, and the sniders rattled without intermission. The grass was so dense, that simple buck-shot would be reduced to a very limited range, although excellent at close quarters. The servants quickly handed the elephant breechloaders, and a double shot to the right and left was followed by the loud explosion of the picrate of potash shells against some unseen objects, either men or trees.

A quick repetition of the picrate shells seemed to affect the spirit of the attack. I imagine that the extremely loud explosion of the shells in the midst, and perhaps also in the rear of the enemy, led them to suppose that they were attacked from behind.

It is difficult to say how long the attack continued, but a vast amount of ammunition was expended before the lances ceased to fly through the line, and the drums and horns were at length heard at a greater distance in the rear. The bugle at once sounded the "advance," and I marched the men forward, crossing the stream at the bottom, and gained the open, where we found ourselves in a kind of swampy field of about ten acres. "Ha!" exclaimed many of the soldiers, "if we could only get them on a clear space like this."

The men were mustered. Poor Howarti was dead, and they had left him in the grass by the roadside, as it was impossible to transport him.

The rear-guard had been hotly pressed, and the natives had rushed upon the path, close to the sniders, which had punished them severely. Had we depended upon muzzle-loading muskets, the party must have been quickly destroyed; the sharp fire of the sniders at close quarters must have caused immense loss at the first onset.

I now determined to lighten the loads considerably. It was difficult to carry the angarebs, as the legs caught in the high grass. I spoke a few words to my men, who declared that they were not afraid of the natives if they were not so heavily laden.

We collected wood and made a fire, upon which

I ordered everything to be burnt that was really cumbersome. The bedsteads were broken up; a case of good French cognac was committed to the flames; Lieutenant Baker's naval uniform, with box, &c.; the cocked hat frizzled up on the top of the bonfire. The men were provided with raw hides, upon which they slept at night; these were now wet through and cumbersome: I therefore ordered them to be thrown into the high grass and abandoned.

The brandy bottles burst upon the fire. A sergeant of the "Forty Thieves," named Fadlullah, had been attending to the heap of burning materials, and I saw him stoop over the flames, as though intending to save one of the liquor bottles for himself. At this moment several burst and saturated his loose cotton trousers with blazing spirits. The man vainly endeavoured to extinguish the fire, and he danced wildly about, until I seized and threw him down in the swamp, and quickly drew the wet green grass over him and subdued the flames. He was severely burnt about the legs, from which the skin slipped off in large flakes.

I now had to doctor him, when every man's legs ought to have been in the best order. Fortunately I had a little oil (for the lamp), and the wounds were quickly dressed and bandaged with cotton wool and lint.

The force was now much relieved, as the loads had been lightened. During the operation of burning the supplies, the best shots of the "Forty Thieves" had been stationed to pick off any natives who attempted to spy our movements by ascending the lofty trees.

I now gave the order for the advance, and the march recommenced. In a few minutes we were once more buried in the gigantic grass jungle.

We had hardly entered the covert when the shouts and blowing of horns and beating of drums once more commenced. This was the signal to ambuscades in front that we were moving forward.

In the course of an hour's march, the rear bugle had sounded "halt" at least half a dozen times, as two of the donkeys were weakly, and could not be driven on without difficulty.

Again the rear bugle sounded "halt!" I immediately sent the sergeant of the bodyguard, Mohammed-el-Feel, to shoot the donkeys, and to throw their loads into the high grass. Two shots announced the end of the donkeys.

The bugle sounded "advance," and we at length travelled comfortably. The weather was fine : we rejoiced in the sun, as it dried our reeking clothes.

Suddenly the advance-guard opened fire! then the rear-guard was closed upon by a sudden rush of the enemy, and the whole line commenced file-firing into the thick covert.

I ordered the bugler to sound "forward," and "cease firing," as the men were getting a little wild.

One of "The Forty," Ali Goboor, had been wounded by a lance through the leg, but he managed to limp along.

We now began to understand the places at which we were sure to meet an ambuscade. Whenever we descended a slope towards a marshy bottom, there was certain to be a large force concealed behind the lofty reeds that grew in the swamp. I ordered the advance-guard to fire a few shots low down in the reeds whenever they should approach these places. By this plan we generally induced the enemy to throw their spears before we were in the midst; in which case we opened a heavy fire into the grass, and marched straight forward.

The ambuscades had been carefully planned. A row of grass of perhaps two or three yards in thickness was left standing in its natural position along the path ; behind this vegetable wall, the grass had been either cut down or torn up, so as to afford a clear space for the natives to take a good run when throwing their lances. They accordingly waited until we should enter the snare, and they calculated their opportunity for making a combined attack when they considered that our line of march was exactly opposite. Of course they could not see us through the thick screen of grass any more than we could distinguish them.

We were at an additional disadvantage, as we were always exposed to attacks from fresh enemies ; the route was occupied throughout, thus they were not cowed by the defeats of every ambuscade in the rear.

Considering the great numbers of spears that had flown like flashes of light through the line, it was astonishing that we had not had more numerous casualties. Several men had been struck on their knapsacks, which had served as shields.

We at length came to an exceedingly awkward place, that I felt sure would be well occupied. Upon our right lay a row of rocky hills, to which we were marching parallel. We had to descend through forest to lower ground. To reach this it was necessary to pass between numerous blocks of granite that completely commanded the path. Each block was about twenty or twenty-five feet high, and several much exceeded this height. The base was the usual high grass and forest.

I ordered the men not to fire unless they should see the enemy, and to take a good aim.

Presently, as we descended through the pass, the attack commenced. Two spears struck Colonel Abd-el-Kader, one in the fore-arm; the second ripped his tough leather gaiter, and glanced off.

The sniders were ready, as the enemy were obliged to show their heads above the rocks, and one fellow, who was exactly above us, either lost his nerve, or received a bullet, which allowed his lance to come rattling down the rocks as a complete failure. I ordered the bugler to continue to sound "forward" (Illah Réh), as it was advisable to push through this awkward place as quickly as possible.

Directly that we were out of the pass, I tied up Abd-el-Kader's arm, and we continued the march until we halted at 2.5 P.M., in a piece of open cultivated ground, where I determined to bivouac for the night.

I had resolved always to finish the day's journey by one march, as it would afford time for erecting a protection of thorns and branches of trees to prevent a sudden night attack.

Fortunately the weather was fine. Abd-el-Kader was now faint and weak from loss of blood. I attended to his wound, which was an ugly gash, and gave him a good dose of brandy, and advised him to go to sleep.

Lieutenant Baker and the other officers assisted in erecting the defence of thorns. All the wet clothes were spread out to dry in the sun, and everything was got ready for the night. I did not care for myself, but I was sorry for the hardship that my wife must endure, without a bed or tent. My men cut two forked poles, upon which they lashed a horizontal bar, which supported a camp-sheet to protect her from rain or dew. A pile of long green grass was laid on the ground beneath, upon which was stretched a mackintosh camp-sheet, and a good thick blanket.

We had been most fortunate in having only a loss of one killed and two wounded since we left Masindi.

My men had fired away an enormous amount of ammunition during the march, as they appeared to become more and more nervous as they advanced. Every thick clump of reeds that rose a few feet higher than the surrounding grass was supposed to conceal an enemy, and it was immediately raked by a hot fire from the advance guard.

ATTACK ON THE REAR GUARD BY AMBUSCADE—DEATH OF A BRAVE SOLDIER. Vol. ii. p. 343.

On 16th June, the night having passed quietly, we started at 6.30 A.M., and marched silently.

There was a curious feeling upon first waking in the morning, when we rose and buckled on the ammunition-belts. Every one was aware that his nerves must be upon the stretch, and that his finger must be ready for the trigger, from the commencement till the end of the march, to act against unseen enemies.

Upon arrival at a stream in a muddy bottom, we were immediately attacked by a strong force in ambuscade. Some of the enemy exposed themselves boldly, and rushed upon the soldiers just in front of the rear-guard. Several were shot by the sniders, but one fellow, with unusual pluck, speared a soldier whose musket had missed fire, through the chest. This poor fellow, thus mortally wounded, grappled with his assailant, and tugging the spear from his own wound, he drove it through the native's heart.

The rear bugle sounded "halt," while the knapsack and cartouche-belt were detached from the gallant soldier, whose body was left by the side of his enemy.

We marched until 10.15 A.M., having fought nearly the whole way, and expended a frightful amount of ammunition. We had now arrived at our old halting-place, Chorobézé, twenty-seven miles from Masindi.

My men had become so extravagant of their cartridges that I was forced to interfere. If this nervousness should continue, we should be soon left without ammunition, and every soul would be massacred.

I therefore mustered the troops, and examined all their pouches. Some of the advance-guard had fired away eighty rounds each, only during the morning's march!

Many had fired fifty rounds! The muskets had not used so many, owing to the greater difficulty of loading, but they also had been frightfully extravagant.

The men had come to the conclusion that the only plan of marching in safety through the high grass, which was full of unseen enemies, was to constitute themselves into a sort of infernal machine, that would be perpetually emitting fire and bullets on all sides.

This was all very well with an unlimited supply of ammunition, but we had no idea of what might still be in store for us. We were now slightly more than fifty miles from Foweera. Fortunately, in our journey from the river to Masindi, I had timed every march within five minutes, and I had all particulars in my note-book; therefore I could guess the position pretty closely during the morning's advance.

Having mustered all the men, I turned out all the ammunition from their pouches. The cartridges were all counted.

I now examined all the reserve ammunition.

The total, including that from the men's cartouche-boxes, was—

Cartridges for snider rifles	. . .	4,540
,, ,, muskets	. . .	4,330
		8,870

I now addressed the men, and abused them most forcibly, calling them "old women," and several other uncomplimentary epithets for soldiers. I divided among them forty rounds each, and I swore solemnly by their prophet, "that I would not give them another cartridge from this spot (Chorobézé) until we should reach Major Abdullah's detachment at Fatiko."

I explained that if any man should fire away his ammunition, he should continue the march with an empty pouch—Wah Illahi!

I gave the most positive command, that in future

not a shot should be fired without orders, unless spears actually were thrown, on which occasions the troops would fire a few shots exactly into the spot from which the weapons had arrived; but on no account was a bullet to be fired at random.

I dismissed the men with this warning, and set them to work to construct a night defence as usual.

It was a most fortunate peculiarity of the Unyoros that they did not attack at night-time. This was a grievous fault upon their side. If they had surrounded us every night, they would have kept us awake, and not only would have tired the men out, but they would have caused a useless expenditure of ammunition.

On 17th of June, we started at 6.15 A.M., with the intention of reaching Koki. I recognised several villages, but we passed them without halting. We at length arrived at a fine, broad route, that was sufficiently wide for a dog-cart. This had evidently been recently prepared, and there could be no doubt that it was arranged as a snare that would lead us into some powerful ambuscade. At the same time, the compass showed that the broad path led in the right direction.

I halted the force, and went to the front to examine the road. There was no other path. It was therefore incumbent upon us to keep to the broad route, although we knew that it must lead us to a trap prepared for our destruction.

It was like walking upon ice that was known to be unsafe. We advanced.

For about half an hour we marched without opposition. This was a longer interval than usual to be free from an attack. At length we arrived where the broad road suddenly terminated. The advance-guard halted.

We searched for a path, and at length discovered the original narrow route a few paces to our left.

This had been purposely concealed by grass and boughs.

We had hardly entered this path when we were suddenly attacked. A horsekeeper was wounded by a spear, which passed through his leg, behind the knee, and cut the sinew, thus rendering him helpless. He was immediately placed upon a donkey. The unfortunate lad who led the horse a few paces before me now uttered a wild shriek, as a spear passed completely through his body. The poor boy crept to me on his hands and knees, and asked, "Shall I creep into the grass, Pacha?—where shall I go?" He had not another minute to live.

A spear struck another horsekeeper on the hip, and

the soft iron point turned up against the bone in a curve like a fish-hook.

A sharp fire dispersed the enemy, who retired to a distance, yelling and blowing their whistles. The wounded horsekeeper could manage to walk forward.

There is a peculiar bird in the forests of Unyoro which utters a shrill cry, with these notes :—

The natives imitate this cry with their whistles of antelope's horn. I had noticed that previous to an attack from an ambuscade, we had always heard the call of this bird.

My Baris declared that the bird warned us of the danger, and cried, "Co-co-mé! Co-co-mé!" which in their language means, "Look out! look out!"

My soldiers said that the bird exclaimed, "Shat-mo-koor! Shat-mo-koor!" which is the order, "Make ready!" They accordingly always brought their rifles on full cock when they heard the signal.

There was something puzzling this day respecting the distance. According to my calculation, we should have reached Koki. Still we marched on through high forest and the interminable grass. My wife was dreadfully fatigued. The constant marching in wet boots, which became filled with sand when crossing the small streams and wading through muddy hollows, had made her terribly foot-sore. She walked on with pain and difficulty. I was sure that we had passed the village of Koki, which was surrounded by much open ground and cultivation; and I now felt certain that the broad road, that had been constructed to mislead us, had taken us by the rear of Koki, which we had thus over-shot.

We were marching forward in perfect silence, when I heard a bird cry "Co-co-mé! Co-co-mé"!

That instant the spears came among us, and the rifles replied as quick as lightning. The English practice of rabbit-shooting in covert is very useful in this kind of warfare, as you must fire a snap shot into the spot exactly as the spear flies by you. Thus a good shot can hit the thrower just as a rabbit is knocked over in jumping across a drive.

The bugle of the advance-guard sounded "halt." I never liked to hear that order, as something must have gone wrong.

I immediately walked forward, and found that Lieutenant Mohammed Mustapha had been wounded.

The spear had struck him just behind the shoulder-joint of the left arm, and had passed over the blade-bone and spine previous to making its exit by the right arm. This was a very nasty wound, and he was bleeding profusely. I made a couple of pads, and, placing one upon each hole, we bandaged him tightly.

I now went up to my poor old horse, "Zafteer." The unfortunate animal was carrying a heavy load, and a large hunting-spear had struck him just behind the saddle. The weapon was so sharp and heavy, and had been thrown with such force, that it had penetrated a double blanket, and had not only passed clean through the horse's body, but had also cut through a blanket-fold upon the other side.

A large portion of the bowels protruded, and were hanging a foot below the horse's belly. The intestines were divided, thus death was certain.

As the old horse could still walk, and did not know its own danger, I ordered the advance. I intended to halt at the first convenient point.

In about a quarter of an hour we saw increased light in the distance, and we presently emerged upon a large open vale surrounded by forest. This cheerful space extended over about ten acres, in the centre of which was a well of good water, about fourteen feet deep, and so wide that a man could descend by steps hewn out of the gravel. This was a grand place for the halt.

My first duty was to remove the load, together with the saddle, from my good old horse. I returned the bowels, and having placed a strong pad over the wounds, I passed the roller round his body, and buckled it tight over the pads.

This operation was hardly completed, when a severe shivering fit seized the poor animal, and he fell to the ground to die.

With great sorrow I placed my pistol to the forehead of the faithful old Zafteer, and he died, having carried and laid down his load, together with his life, at the end of the march by the well.

I was much distressed at this loss. It seemed that I was to lose all my best and most faithful followers —the good Monsoor, whom to this hour I regret as a brother; the ever-ready and true Howarti; Ferritch Baggāra; the unfortunate Ramadān, besides others who were very valuable; and now my old horse was gone.

We slept that night by his body, and warmed ourselves by a fire that consumed his load—for there was no one to carry it. My despatch-box helped to cook our scanty dinner. We had marched sixteen miles.

My troops had behaved remarkably well. The scolding that I had given them had produced a good effect. Very little ammunition had been expended, and the firing had been exceedingly steady.

Although we had not been attacked at night, I never omitted the precaution of a defence of strong thorns and branches of trees.

Had this march through a frightful route of forest and high grass been made in the Bari tribe, we should not have had a night's rest.

We marched at 6 A.M., with sunrise, on 18th June. The weather had been fine since the first day of soaking rain on the start from Masindi: we were thankful for this blessing, as there was no shelter for any one.

It would be fatiguing to narrate the incidents of the continual ambuscades. Every day we were attacked, and the enemy was repulsed many times. "Co-co-mé! Co-co-mé!" was now well understood by the troops; and although we had men wounded, the enemy invariably got the worst of the encounter. Up to the present we had been most fortunate in bringing on all our people, but I was anxious lest some should receive wounds that would actually incapacitate them from marching. Should a man be killed outright, how much soever he might be regretted, still there was an end of him; but there was no end to the difficulty of transporting wounded men in our helpless condition, without carriers.

We had rather hot work during this day's march, and four soldiers had been wounded by spears.

My wife was dreadfully tired, and sometimes the pace was too severe for her. At length she was so fatigued that she declared she must halt for rest. It was impossible to halt in the thick jungle and grass; therefore, as I had observed a large grove of plantains on the crest of the hill before us, I gave her my hand to assist her in the ascent, and we shortly entered the dark forest of bananas, which was, as usual, clear and free from grass.

All the women were glad to rest, as the poor things were carrying heavy loads. We halted in the midst of the plantains, and every one sat down, except the numerous sentries whom I placed in concealment in various positions. I fully expected that natives might be following us, in the hopes of picking up the load of some wounded man that had been left behind.

Not a word was spoken, or even whispered.

My men were very bloodthirsty. They had been atrociously treated by the natives, and had suffered much. They longed to get their enemies fairly before them, and the "Forty Thieves" were now keenly looking out for the approach of the wily Unyoros.

We heard distant voices; they were coming nearer. A sharp clicking of locks might be heard, as the men got ready.

Ali Sadik was one of my best shots in "The Forty." I now saw him taking a steady aim. Sāat Choush, who was the champion shot of "The Forty," had also raised his rifle, and almost immediately several shots were fired, and the troops rushed forward! Two natives had been knocked over, and some of the men returned, dragging in a body by the heels.

I now scoured the immediate neighbourhood, and discovered a quantity of dhurra that was just ripened. This was immediately gathered as a great prize.

During this interval, my men had been engaged in a most barbarous ceremony, that perfectly disgusted me.

These superstitious people had an idea, that every bullet they might fire would kill an Unyoro, if they could only devour a portion of their enemy's liver.

. They had accordingly cut out the liver of the dead man, and having divided it among them, they positively *had eaten it*—raw! They had then cut the body into pieces with their sword-bayonets, and had disposed them upon the limbs of various bushes that overhung the path, as a warning to any Unyoros who should attempt to follow us.

I would not have believed that my "Forty Thieves," whom I had considered to be nearly civilized, could have committed such a barbarity. The truth was, that in the high grass they could not see the effect of their shots; therefore they imagined that the horrid rite of eating an enemy's liver would give a fatal direction to a random bullet.

We marched, and having had several encounters with the enemy in jungle, if possible, worse than before, we halted at Kaseega.

One of my best men, Serroor, had a narrow escape; a lance went through his neck, almost grazing the jugular vein.

On 19th June, we marched at 6.5 A.M. This was one of the worst journeys, as the ravines were numerous, and the forest dark and tangled. It was difficult for our solitary horse (Jamoos) to carry his load, as it became continually hooked in the hanging loops of the wild vines. We were quickly attacked by various ambuscades, in one of which my wife suffered the loss of a great favourite. This was poor little Jarvah, who went by the name of the "fat boy." Two spears struck the unhappy lad at the same moment—one of which pinned both his legs as though upon a spit; the other went through his body. This loss completely upset my wife, as the unfortunate Jarvah had upon several occasions endeavoured to protect her from danger. He was killed only a few paces behind her.

In one of the ambuscades, just as the enemy had been repulsed, Faddul, the strongest man in the "Forty Thieves," who was close to me, carrying his knapsack on his back, his rifle slung across his shoulders, and a box of 500 snider cartridges (64 lbs.) upon his head, walked up to me during the halt and reported himself as badly wounded.

A spear had struck him obliquely in the posterior, and had taken a direction towards the groin. The man was literally bathed in blood, which ran from him in such a stream that a large pool was formed at his feet as he stood before me.

The instant that the box of snider ammunition was taken from his head, he fell apparently lifeless to the ground.

I thought that he had bled to death.

His rifle and knapsack were removed, and I examined his pulse and heart. I could not feel any movement. All I could do was to pour some brandy very slowly down his throat, and to leave him on the side of the path as another good man lost to the expedition.

We marched forward, and in about ten minutes we arrived at an open field of sweet potatoes. The change from dark jungle and dense grasses of giant height, to the fresh and clear space cannot be understood, unless by those who experienced the difficulties of the march.

I halted the advance-guard in the centre of the open field, and waited for the rear to close up.

As it arrived, I saw a man staggering forward, supported by two soldiers. Upon nearer approach, I recognized my strong friend, Faddul, thus risen from the dead! The brandy had revived him sufficiently to show some signs of life, and the rear-guard had thus brought him along with them. We laid him down to rest beneath a tree that grew in the middle of the cultivation.

We were now in a sad difficulty. There were numerous roads, or rather very narrow paths, which converged from all quarters upon this potato ground. No one knew the direction. The Baris were completely at fault. The farther the people explored the immediate neighbourhood, the more helpless they became.

This was a serious matter. Up to the present time we had been most fortunate in keeping to the right path.

I now called my renowned pathfinder, Abdullah, of "The Forty."

Abdullah made a survey of the surrounding tracks, and then returned to me with the news that he had discovered the route. This he immediately pointed out.

A general exclamation of derision from the officers and many of the men was the only reward Abdullah received for his important discovery, as his path was in quite an opposite direction to the route they had anticipated.

The compass corroborated Abdullah's road, but before I adopted it, I asked him why he declared so positively that he knew the way? He replied, that when on the march from Foweera, he had observed a peculiarly-shaped tree, upon which was fastened a native cojoor, or spell. That tree was on rising ground above a ravine, and he could now show me both the ravine and the magic tree.

I accompanied him to the spot, and certainly the tree was there, with some pieces of ragged bark-cloth and some grass tied to the stem. I had often seen talismans that were fastened to the trees, and I suggested to Abdullah that there were many of them along the road. He was so confident in accepting every responsibility as guide, that I followed him without hesitation, and the march continued. The wounded Faddul was supported as before.

In a short time I myself recognized the path as being very near to Kisoona, which place we suddenly entered after a march of thirty-five minutes from the potato field. The advance-guard fired a volley at some natives, who rushed into the grass upon our unexpected arrival.

We were now in open ground, with good native huts for shelter, and a large extent of cultivation, where an unlimited supply of potatoes could be obtained.

As the rear-guard closed up, I mustered all officers and men. Having spoken a few words of encouragement, and complimented them upon their extreme steadiness since I had lectured them at Chorobézé, I congratulated them upon having advanced so far, under God's protection, through such numberless enemies, with comparatively so little loss. We were now only twenty-one miles from Foweera, and we knew the road. The news of our arrival would almost immediately reach Rionga, and I should fortify this spot and remain here for some days to allow my wounded to recover their strength. During this time all hands would be employed in preparing potatoes for store, by cutting them in slices and drying them in the sun.

I now ordered the band to strike up with the greatest vigour, to show the natives who might be within hearing, that we were in the best of spirits.

My officers and men were all delighted, and overwhelmed me with compliments. I only replied by begging them always to trust in God, and to do their duty.

I immediately started off a party to dig potatoes, while Lieutenant Baker and myself, with a number of men, slashed down with sabres the extensive grove of plantain trees, so as to have a perfectly clear space around the camp.

We made a strong defence at Kisoona, and the rest of several days was invigorating to the wounded men, and enabled my wife's feet to recover sufficiently to continue the march on the 23rd June.

I had arranged that the drums and bugles should sound the morning call at 5 A.M. daily, as though in a permanent camp. This was to assist me in a plan for avoiding ambuscades on the day of marching from Kisoona.

On the 22nd I gave orders that every man should

be ready to march punctually at 5 A.M., the instant that the morning call should have sounded.

The natives, hearing the call to which they had been daily accustomed, would have no suspicion of our intended departure; therefore they would not have sufficient time to organize and man their ambuscades.

On the morning of 23rd June we evacuated the camp in the semi-darkness, the instant that the drums and bugles had ceased, and we thus obtained an excellent start that saved us much trouble. The attacks later in the day were feebler than usual, and after a march of fourteen miles we arrived at a well of water at 2.5 P.M., at which spot we halted for the night. During this march we had only one man wounded.

We were now within Rionga's country, but I nevertheless made a defence of thorns and branches of trees for the night.

On 24th June we started at 6.5 A.M., and after a march of seven miles, during which we were undisturbed, we arrived at the old camp of Suleiman's company at Foweera on the Victoria Nile, where we had expected to find shelter and good houses.

Everything had been destroyed by fire! Nothing remained but blackened ashes.

CHAPTER X.

BUILD A STOCKADE AT FOWEERA.

MY losses from the 8th June to the 24th had been ten killed and eleven wounded. Every officer and soldier had thoroughly done his duty, having displayed admirable coolness and courage upon many trying occasions. None but black troops could have endured the march of about eighty miles with heavy weights upon their heads, in addition to their usual accoutrements.

I at once set to work to build a new station, and with the old wood that had formed the fence of Suleiman's zareeba, I commenced a defensive arrangement.

There was very little heavy timber that was adapted for a stockade. I therefore formed a protection by sinking deep in the ground, at intervals of three feet, two strong posts about seven feet above the surface. These upright timbers, standing opposite to each other at a distance of about ten inches, were filled with long poles laid one over the other horizontally. At two corners of the square fort were flanking works of the same construction, which would sweep each face of the defence.

In a very few days my men had completed a strong and neat stockade around a number of small temporary huts which formed our new station.

Having thus housed my troops, it was necessary to prepare for the future. I fully expected that Major Abdullah had fallen into the snare prepared for him by Kabba Réga: thus I should have no other force to rely upon, except the few men that now formed my small but tough little party. If so terrible a calamity should have occurred as the destruction of Abdullah's detachment, I should not only have lost my men, but I should become short of ammunition; as my stores and arms would have fallen into the hands of the enemy. This doubt caused me much grave anxiety.

It was strange that we had not received some communication from Rionga, whose island was only fifteen or sixteen miles above stream from Foweera. Our side of the river appeared to be quite uninhabited, and simply consisted of the interminable groves of bananas, that had belonged to the inhabitants at a time when the district had been thickly populated.

The Victoria Nile, opposite the Foweera station, was about 500 yards wide. At this season the river was full. The huts that we had erected on the north side, upon our arrival from Fatiko, had been destroyed by the natives. This did not look as though much friendship existed.

Upon hearing our drums and bugles on the day of our arrival at Foweera, a few natives had come to the high rock opposite, and had commenced a bawling conversation, that was only slightly understood by one of our women and Molōdi the Madi.

Molōdi knew Rionga, as he had visited him at a former time, together with a party of Abou Saood's people. His very slight knowledge of the language was sufficient to explain to the natives across the river that I wished to communicate with Rionga.

The people on the north happened to belong to Kabba Réga, and they were enemies of Rionga; thus we were addressing the wrong parties.

It was highly necessary to make some arrangements for crossing the river. There were no canoes on this side, and it would be dangerous to trust to rafts, as there were waterfalls about three or four hundred yards below stream upon our left. I determined to construct boats.

We felled three large dolape palms (*Borassus Ethiopicus*), which were the only trees of that species in this neighbourhood. These palms are well adapted for canoes, as the bark, or rather the outside wood, is intensely hard for about an inch and a half, beneath which the tree is simply a pithy, stringy substance, that can be rapidly scooped out.

Two of the logs, when shaped, were each twenty-six feet in length; the third was smaller.

Throughout the march from Masindi we had managed to carry an adze, a hammer, and a cold chisel. The adze now came into play, together with the handy little axes of the " Forty Thieves."

Among my troops was a Baggara Arab, who was a " canoe-builder." This was one of the best men of " The Forty," and it was now for the first time that I heard of his abilities as a boat-builder.

The men took an immense interest in the work; but as too many volunteers might interfere with the principal shipwright, I sent them all into the forest to collect plantains. I gave orders that every man should prepare 14lbs. of plantain flour for the journey, in case it should be necessary to march to Fatiko.

The canoes progressed, and a slice of about a foot

wide having been taken off horizontally from stem to stern, the soft inside was scooped out with an adze, and with lance-heads bent to form a half circle.

In a few days the logs were neatly hollowed, and were then carried down and launched upon the river. The long, narrow canoes would have been very dangerous without outriggers, therefore I determined to adopt the plan that I had seen in Ceylon; and as Lieutenant Baker well represented the omniscience of naval men in everything that concerns boats, nautical stratagems, incomprehensible forms of knots, rigging, &c., &c., I left all the details of the canoes to his charge. In a short time we possessed three admirable vessels that it was quite impossible to upset. I now required a few rafts for the transport of baggage, as it would be awkward to cross the river by small sections should an enemy oppose our landing on the precipitous bank on the opposite shore. I therefore arranged that we should cross in two journeys. The party now consisted of 97 soldiers including officers, 5 natives, 3 sailors, 51 women, boys, and servants, and 3 Europeans; total, 158 persons.

There was no ambatch wood, but I thought we might form rafts by cutting and then drying in the sun the long tough stems of the papyrus rush. These, if lashed together in small bundles, could be shaped into rafts similar to those used by the Shillook tribe.

Lieutenant Baker took the three sailors and a few intelligent soldiers, and set to work.

The 29th June had arrived without any news of Rionga. The country appeared to be quite devoid of inhabitants on the south banks, neither did the natives show themselves on the north. We were masters of the situation, but there was an uncomfortable feeling of loneliness in our position of outcasts. We were very hungry, as we had not tasted animal food since the 14th inst.; there was no game, neither were there any doves or birds of any kind, except occasional vultures, which, after sitting upon a dead tree and regarding us for some time, went off with a low opinion of our respectability.

We lived upon boiled plantains and red peppers, together with various wild plants that are wholesome, but not nice, when boiled as spinach. Unfortunately, our small supply of salt was exhausted, therefore we were obliged to burn grass and make potash from the ashes as a substitute.

We had a small quantity of brandy, but we reserved this in case of illness or other necessity.

My men generally made two journeys daily, together with the women, to collect green plantains, and they immediately commenced peeling and drying them in the sun upon their return to camp.

On the evening of the 29th they came home in great spirits, having captured a prisoner. They had tied his arms cruelly behind his back, and had led him to camp by a cord secured to his neck.

This man had been discovered in company with two others who had escaped to the other side of the river in a canoe.

I ordered his arms to be released, and cross-examined him, Molōdi acting as interpreter.

The prisoner seemed quite confident upon seeing my wife and myself. "Don't you remember me?" he exclaimed; "was it not I who many years ago carried the travelling-bag for the lady on your journey to Fatiko? Was it not *you* that shot the antelopes on the march, and gave me meat to eat when I was hungry?"

Here was an extraordinary piece of good luck! My men had actually captured an old friend in the thickets, who had formerly marched with us in the reign of Kamrasi.

This fellow now gave us the news. Rionga wished to see me, but he had been so cheated and deceived by the slave-hunting companies of Abou Saood, that he was afraid to trust himself among us; he was friendly disposed, but he did not know my intentions concerning himself.

The prisoner declared that the treachery of Kabba Réga had been planned from the beginning. The 300 natives who had accompanied my party from Masindi, with the post to Fatiko, had attacked and killed some of my men, but he knew no particulars; only that they had not gone on to Fatiko with my people. This was a great relief to my anxiety, as in that case Abdullah must be safe with his detachment. I ordered the prisoner to be detained, but to be well treated.

We had rain nearly every day.

At daybreak on 1st July, after a heavy night's rain, a voice from the high wet grass, about a hundred yards distant, cried out to the sentries in Arabic, "Don't fire! I am a messenger from Rionga to Maleggé!" (my former nick-name).

The man, cold and shivering, was brought before me. He had travelled by canoe during the night, but had been afraid to approach the sentries until daylight.

Being assured of my good-will, he informed me that a nephew of Rionga's was in the grass waiting for my reply. He immediately ran out, and soon returned to the camp with his companion.

As these people spoke Arabic, I now explained the whole affair, and assured them of my repeated refusal to attack Rionga, when I had been pressed to do so both by Kamrasi, and by his son, Kabba Réga. There could be little doubt that, had I allied with him against Rionga, the battle of Masindi would never have taken place ; and the lives of some of my best men would have been spared. Thus Rionga had been the chief cause of trouble.

I would now depose Kabba Réga, and appoint Rionga as the vakeel or representative of the Egyptian government, provided he would swear allegiance.

I sent a present to Rionga of an entire piece each of Turkey red cloth, blue twill, and four handkerchiefs; at the same time I explained that we were very hungry, and required cattle and corn.

Before the messengers returned, I inspected the troops, who marched round the camp in their best scarlet uniforms, to the sound of the drums and bugles. This exhibition appeared to create a great impression on Rionga's people, who would report us fit for service on their return to their chief.

Thirty of the men were suffering from ulcerated legs, caused by the sharp, poisonous edges of the high grass.

THE VICTORIA NILE—AT RIONGA'S ISLAND.

In a couple of days, two large canoes arrived from Rionga with presents of some corn, sweet potatoes, and a cow and sheep. We killed the beef immediately, as we were ravenously hungry.

On 16th July, we started, in nine canoes that had been supplied by Ronga, to visit him at his station. The troops marched by land on the south bank.

After paddling for about fifteen miles along the grand Victoria Nile, which in the narrowest part was at least 300 yards wide, we arrived at 5 P.M. at a desolate spot, exactly opposite to the tail of the large island upon which Rionga resided.

Nothing had been prepared for our reception, therefore we landed in the forest, and my men set to work to collect firewood for the night. The troops who had marched overland had not arrived. Fortunately we had some flour and a bottle of currypowder; therefore we dined off dhurra-porridge and curry, and lay down on our camp-sheets to sleep.

This was a thorough negro welcome; nothing to eat!

The next morning, at about 7 A.M., the troops with Colonel Abd-el-Kader arrived; they had suffered much from high grass and thorns, as they had been obliged to break their way through the jungle, in the total absence of a path.

A number of Rionga's natives now arrived to assist in making our camp. All hands set vigorously to work building huts, in an excellent position that I had selected on the river's bank.

On 18th July, messengers came early to inform me that Rionga would arrive that morning to give me a warm welcome.

I had already sent him, from Foweera, a beautiful cloak of gold brocade, together with a new tarboosh and sky-blue turban.

At about 8 A.M., drums were beating on the island, and horns were blowing in all directions; these were signals that the renowned Rionga was on the move. We shortly perceived numerous large canoes pushing off from the island, and making for our landing-place, which I had already cleared.

A cow, sheep, and a load of corn were first delivered as a present. These were followed by Rionga, and a large staff of his principal headmen.

He was a handsome man of about fifty, with exceedingly good manners. He had none of the stiffness of Kamrasi, nor the *gauche* bearing of Kabba Réga, but he was perfectly at his ease. He at once thanked me for the handsome suit in which he was

RECEPTION OF RIONGA.

To face p. 372, Vol. i.

dressed, without which, he assured me that it would have been difficult for him to have appeared before me in a becoming manner. The troops were drawn out to receive him, and the conversation at once turned upon Kabba Réga and Abou Saood.

He had an intimate knowledge of all that had taken place, which had been reported to him by his spies; and he declared that Abou Saood had long ago arranged a plan with Kabba Réga for our destruction should we arrive from Gondokoro.

Rionga was well aware how often I had refused to attack him, and he confessed that I had been his saviour by the arrest of Suleiman, who would have joined the forces of Kabba Réga to have crushed him.

I took a great fancy to Rionga, as he was so perfectly free and easy in his manner. He told me several anecdotes of the escapes he had had from snares laid for him by Kamrasi; and he seemed quite rejoiced that I, who had always declined to molest him before I had known him personally, should now have taken him by the hand.

He declared that he would always remain the faithful representative of the Khedive's government, but at the same time we must immediately *exchange blood;* without which ceremony, the people would not rise in his favour. He said, "If the natives of this country, and also the Langgos and the Umiros, shall hear that I have exchanged blood with the Pacha, they will have thorough confidence, as they will know that he will always be true to me, and I to him; but without this irrevocable contract, they will always suspect some intrigue, either upon your side or mine."

Rionga proposed that we should drink blood on the following morning, as no time should be lost: he revelled with childish delight in the despair that would seize Kabba Réga and his chiefs when they should hear the news that the Pacha and his friend Rionga had exchanged blood.

The preparation for the ceremony was to commence that evening. We were to drink a large quantity of plantain cider. "Not such stuff as Kabba Réga gave you," exclaimed Rionga; "but a drink such as a friend will partake with you." I was not to eat anything on the morrow, until the sun should be in a certain position in the heavens, at which time he would call upon me. I was to exchange blood with Rionga; Colonel Abd-el-Kader and Lieutenant Baker were to go through the same interesting ceremony with his minister and his son at the same time.

I recommended him at once to summon the chiefs of the Langgos and the Umiros, as I should wish to secure their alliance and allegiance without loss of time.

Many large jars of the best quality of plantain cider were now brought from the island.

The night passed in nothing but singing and dancing, as Rionga gave an entertainment in honour of our arrival, and as a preliminary to the ceremony of exchanging blood on the following morning.

At about 9 A.M. the unpleasant task was to be performed. Rionga arrived and begged me to accompany him within a tent, together with Lieutenant Baker, Colonel Abd-el-Kader, and Kamissua and Majōbi.

Several of his first-class people were admitted as witnesses; these were Inqui, Kimata, Ulendu, Singoma, Kibera, and some others.

Fortunately I had a small lancet in the handle of my knife; therefore I made a slight incision on my left fore-arm, from which a few drops of blood flowed. Rionga immediately seized my arm and greedily sucked the scratch. I had to perform upon his arm, and I took care to make so slight a puncture that only a drop of blood appeared; this was quite enough for my share of the ceremony. We were now friends for ever, and no suspicion of foul play could possibly be entertained. Lieutenant Baker and Abd-el-Kader went through the same operation with their respective partners, and cemented an indissoluble friendship.

It was rather a disgusting performance, but at the same time it was absolutely necessary for the success of the expedition. I had now really secured a trustworthy man, who would act as my vakeel.

When we emerged from the hut, a minstrel appeared, who played upon a species of harp, and sang praises of myself and Rionga ; and, of course, abused Kabba Réga with true poetical licence.

I gave the minstrel a considerable present of beads, and he went away rejoicing, singing and twanging his instrument to the discomfiture of all our enemies.

It was fortunate that I had been able to carry so much as 300lbs. of beads. The soldiers could now purchase fish and potatoes.

On the 23rd July, two great sheiks were introduced by Rionga : " Gonah," the chief of a Langgo district, and " Okooloo," a renowned warrior of the Umiros.

The naked body of Okooloo was covered with small tattoo marks, each of which I was assured represented a victim to his lance.

If he had really killed half that enormous number of men, he must have considerably reduced the population, and he could have been doing little else during his life. Samson's feat of killing 1,000 men was hardly to be compared to the slaughter that had been accomplished by Okooloo.

The prospect of a general attack upon Kabba Réga with fire and lance was delightful to the taste of this warlike old chief, who would, at the end of the campaign, have no more room on his own skin, and would have to keep the list of his game either upon the back of a son or a favourite wife.

I soon made friends with these tribes. A few red and yellow handkerchiefs, and two or three pounds of red and white beads, were sufficient to gain their alliance. I proclaimed Rionga as the vakeel of the government, who would rule Unyoro in the place of Kabba Réga, deposed. Rionga was accepted by acclamation; and if the young traitor, Kabba Réga, could have witnessed this little *projet de traité*, he would have shivered in his shoes.

Rionga was a general favourite, and the natives were sincerely glad to see him at length supported by the government. Throughout his life he had striven bravely against every species of treachery and persecution; the day of his revenge had arrived.

I did not wish to overrun Unyoro until the grass should be fit to burn; this would not be until the end of November.

I therefore arranged that I would leave Abd-el-Kader with sixty-five men in a powerful stockade that I had constructed on the edge of the river in this spot, N. lat. 2° 6′ 17″, to support Rionga, and to organize the native forces, while I would take forty men (sniders) and march to Fatiko, to inquire into all that had happened during my absence. It would be necessary to form a corps of irregulars under the command of Wat-el-Mek, which I should immediately send to occupy Unyoro.

Rionga told me that he should immediately attack M'rooli in company with the Langgos and Umiros, who would quickly overrun the country now that Kabba Réga was unsupported by the slave-hunters.

He at once collected fifty natives to carry our loads to Fatiko.

On 27th July, having left all beads, &c., with Colonel Abd-el-Kader for the purchase of provisions, we took a cordial leave of Rionga, and started, in six canoes, at 12.30 P.M.; paddling down the stream, we arrived at our deserted zareeba at 3.12 P.M. We found the camp quite undisturbed; no one appeared to have entered it since we had left it some days ago. The palm outrigger canoes were lying in the same spot, secured to the rushes; and all that had belonged to us was rigidly respected.

Rionga had given us a sheep to eat during our march of seventy-nine miles from Foweera to Fatiko. This did not seem very generous, but his cattle had been mostly carried off by the slave-hunters under Suleiman.

Fortunately, just as we entered our old station, I shot a guinea-fowl, which made a good curry, and saved our store of dried fish for the uninhabited wilderness before us.

The best fish (as I before mentioned in "The Albert N'yanza") is the *Lepidosiren annectens*, and this fat and delicate meat is excellent when smoked and dried.

We slept in our old camp, and early on the following morning we prepared to cross the river.

Rionga's people did not quite trust the inhabitants on the other side; I accordingly sent a strong party of rifles across first to occupy the high rocky landing-place.

On the return of the canoes, we were just preparing to cross with the remainder of the party when I observed eight natives walking very fast along the forest-covered cliff on the other side. We immediately gave the alarm to our men who occupied the rocks. The telescope now discovered that the arrangement of the hair of these natives was the fashion of Shooli and Fatiko.

The eight strangers, who had not before observed us, now halted in astonishment, and presently they shouted, in good Arabic—

"Are you the Pacha's soldiers? We are sent by Abdullah to look for the Pacha!"

This was great good fortune; then Abdullah was alive, and I hoped my detachment was all right!

We crossed the broad river, and upon close arrival, we discovered that two of the messengers were well known to us, one of whom was Jarro, the interpreter of the great sheik, Rot Jarma.

The first gleam of pleasure with which I had welcomed these messengers quickly changed to considerable anxiety.

I was now informed that the attempt to destroy us by poison, and subsequently by a treacherous attack at Masindi, was mainly due to the intrigues of Abou Saood, who had originally advised Kabba Réga to resist me should I arrive in his country. This traitor Abou Saood had considered that we should be certainly massacred when once in the heart of Unyoro. He had therefore assumed a despotic command of Fatiko and all the neighbouring countries shortly after my departure; and he had given orders to the natives and to the sheik, Rot Jarma, that "no supplies of corn should be provided for Major Abdullah's troops."

Rot Jarma had been faithful to the government, and his people had carried corn to Major Abdullah. Abou Saood had therefore ordered his men to attack Rot Jarma. They had accordingly surprised him while believing in the protection of the government, and had captured his cattle, together with a number of slaves. In that attack the brigands had lost five men, whose guns had been subsequently taken to Kabba Réga for sale by the natives we had seen at Masindi.

Abou Saood then, enraged at the loss of five men, together with their guns, had sent for Wat-el-Mek from Faloro, and gave him the command above the well-known Ali Hussein, with orders to carry fire and sword through the country.

Major Abdullah had vainly expostulated. Abou Saood had personally threatened him; and Ali Hussein and an officer named Lāzim, with some others, had gone armed into the government camp, and had actually seized natives who had taken refuge with Abdullah, from whose house they were thus dragged by force in defiance of authority.

When the news arrived from Foweera that I had punished Suleiman for the murder of the prisoner, both Abou Saood and his people had declared, that they "would secure Major Abdullah in a forked pole, or shéba, and treat him in a similar manner." They had also threatened to attack the government camp.

Major Abdullah had written to me at Masindi requesting instructions; he had intrusted the letter to a native of Faieera. This man had most unfortunately arrived at Masindi late in the evening upon which the troops had been poisoned. On the following morning he was a witness to the murder of poor Monsoor and Ferritch Baggára; and when the general action commenced, he climbed up a tree at no great distance from the station, and cried out that "he was the bearer of a letter from Abdullah."

The bullets whizzed so thickly about him that he descended from his post, and then, being alarmed lest he might be killed by the natives should his mission be discovered, he had run away as fast as possible, and had returned 160 miles to Fatiko. Thus I never received Major Abdullah's letter.

The letter-carrier, having seen our handful of men surrounded by many thousands of the enemy in Masindi, and knowing that the perfect organization of Unyoro would bring countless enemies upon us, who would occupy the routes by ambuscades, had considered our position hopeless.

The report was spread "that we were all destroyed:" thus Abou Saood was delighted.

Some days later, my party arrived that had left Masindi on the 23rd May with the post for Fatiko, together with the prisoner Suleiman.

These people had suffered terribly, and had lost eleven men killed, exclusive of one who had died on the way from fatigue.

The treacherous plan arranged by Kabba Réga had failed, and the natives had attacked them before the time appointed. This will be described hereafter.

Suleiman was no longer a prisoner, but he commanded the Fabbo station for Abou Saood.

Wat-el-Mek had received my letter, and he wished to serve the government; but Abou Saood had prevented him; and now that I was supposed to be dead, it would be impossible.

This man, Wat-el-Mek, had nevertheless behaved well, as he had immediately demanded 100 men from

Abou Saood, and fifty men from Abdullah, in order to march to Unyoro, join Rionga, and with a native army he would have searched for us throughout the country.

Abou Saood had refused to give the 100 men, therefore we had been left to our fate.

The result of the story was that I must hurry on to Fatiko; Rot Jarma had sent his messengers to discover me whether dead or alive, and should I not march quickly, Abdullah might be attacked and overpowered, and the slave-hunters would possess themselves of all the ammunition and stores.

. . . . . .

. . . This was not very refreshing news, after all the troubles we had gone through.

Had I received this important intelligence during my stay with Rionga, I should not have left Colonel Abd-el-Kader with sixty men behind me. It would not do to waste time by halting; and should I send to recall Abd-el-Kader immediately after my departure, the effect upon Rionga would create suspicion. The withdrawal of the troops would destroy all confidence on the part of his native allies.

I gave the order to march forward at once.

My horse, Jamoos, now the only survivor of all those that I had brought from Cairo, was in good condition, but he suffered from a woeful sore back, occasioned by the heavy load that he had carried from Masindi. My wife was therefore obliged to walk, as the mud was too deep for the solitary donkey, who was weak and ill.

For more than a mile and a half we had to wade through flooded marshes nearly hip deep; the heavy rains had made the country boggy and unpleasant.

We had one sheep for the journey of seventy-nine miles, but this was missing upon the second day's march, and we subsequently discovered that it had been stolen and eaten by our guide and the carriers supplied by Rionga. We were thus reduced to dried fish in the place of our lost mutton, for which we felt inclined to go into mourning.

Although we had been badly fed of late, and for twenty-three days had been without solid animal food (from the march from Masindi), we were nevertheless in excellent health; and always hungry.

We marched well through the uninhabited wilderness of forest, high grass, and swamps, and arrived at the village of Sharga, ten miles from Fatiko, on August 1st, 1872.

The people had collected in considerable numbers to receive us, and we were presented with a fat ox for the troops, thirteen large jars of merissa, and a very plump sheep for ourselves.

The soldiers were delighted, poor fellows; and we likewise looked forward with no small pleasure to a good stew.

Numerous sheiks had collected to receive us, and a formal complaint and protest was made against Abou Saood and his people.

An attack had been already planned, and Abdullah and his small detachment of 100 men would be overpowered. They were already disheartened, as they believed that we were dead, and they had been daily taunted with this fact by the brigands, who asked them, "what they were going to do now that the Pacha was killed."

Abou Saood, having given his orders to Wat-el-Mek, and to the ruffian Ali Hussein, had withdrawn to the station of Fabbo, twenty-two miles west of Fatiko, to which place he had carried all the ivory. He was not fond of fighting, *personally*.

The natives corroborated the information I had received from Rot Jarma's messengers. They declared that not only had women and children been carried off, but that the slave-hunters under Ali Hussein had cut the throats of many of their women before their eyes, and had dashed the brains of the young children upon the rocks in derision of my power; saying, "Now see if the Nuzzerāni (Christian) can protect you!"

They declared that Wat-el-Mek really wished to join the government, but that when he got drunk, both Abou Saood and others could induce him to behave badly.

There were several hundred people present at this meeting; and the sheiks wound up in a cool and temperate manner, by advising me "not to judge from what they had told me, but simply to march early on the following morning to Fatiko, and to receive the report direct from my own commandant, Major Abdullah.

"If he contradicts us, you may say that we are liars; then never believe us again."

This was the conclusion of the palaver.

The morning of 2nd August arrived, and we started at 6.20 A.M., and marched fast over a beautiful country of dells, woods, and open park-like lands, until we ascended the hill that rose towards the high plateau of Fatiko.

As we passed the numerous villages we were joined by curious bands of natives, who by degrees swelled our party to nearly a thousand persons. There was no doubt that these people expected to witness a row, as they knew that Abdullah had been threatened. It was therefore highly probable that we might be attacked, as the slave-hunters would imagine that my small force of forty men was the last remnant of my detachment.

No one at Fatiko had an idea of my existence: thus we should arrive as though risen from the dead.

I halted the men on a large flat rock about a mile and a half south of Fatiko. Here they changed their clothes, and dressed in their best scarlet uniforms and white linen trousers.

We again marched forward, until, upon gaining the racecourse-like plateau, we perceived the station in the distance.

The bugles now sounded the "assembly," to apprise Major Abdullah of our approach. We then marched to the bugles and drums, while the natives, who delight in music, struck up an accompaniment on their whistles. My wife was riding the horse, as his back was nearly recovered.

With the telescope, I now perceived a great stir in Major Abdullah's camp. The men were running to and fro; presently red dots appeared; these rapidly increased, until a thin line of scarlet showed me that his troops were drawn up outside the camp to receive us.

We arrived at 9.30 A.M. The first formalities having been gone through, the troops embraced their friends; and I shook Major Abdullah warmly by the hand, and asked him for immediate news. He merely replied: "Thank God, sir, you are safe and arrived here; all will go well now that you are alive again. I have kept a journal, and when you have rested, I will hand you my report in writing."

My old dragoman, Mohammed, had burst out crying with joy at our arrival; and he assured me that it was most fortunate that I had arrived, as affairs had become worse than ever.

The natives that had accompanied us had ascended the large flat rock which commanded the station (and which now forms the citadel), upon which they had squatted down like a flock of cormorants, to observe all that passed.

No one had come to salute me from Abou Saood's station, which was almost a portion of that belonging to the government, as it was only separated by a level turf ninety yards across.

The absence of the vakeel and his people was a studied insult, as it was his duty to have at once appeared, with his men in line to receive us.

A hut having been swept out, I entered to change my dress, as I wished to inspect the troops. I never wore a uniform in this country, except upon state occasions ; but a simple Norfolk shirt of thick white cotton, and trousers of the same material. This, with an Egyptian silk coffeeah arranged over my old helmet hat, was sufficient for Central Africa.

I ordered Major Abdullah to form the troops in line, as I wished to inspect them.

At the sound of the bugle, they formed two deep on the beautiful turf outside the slight fence which surrounded the camp. My horse, having been rubbed down and quickly saddled, was led through the narrow wicket ; having mounted, I rode down the line and made a short inspection of the troops, who appeared to be in excellent health.

I was just returning to the camp, and was about to dismount, as I could not ride through the extremely narrow wicket, when I was begged by Major Abdullah to wait a little longer, as the people of Wat-el-Mek were now approaching with their numerous flags, to salute me according to the usual custom.

Seven large silk crimson flags upon tall staffs

headed with lance points, and ornamented with balls of black ostrich feathers, marked the intervals of the advancing line of ruffians.

They were about 270 strong, and they now formed a line in very open order, exactly facing the government troops, at about forty yards' distance. Two principal officers, Wat-el-Mek and the celebrated Ali Hussein, were exceedingly busy in running up and down the line, and forming their men, so as to make the greatest display of force. Wat-el-Mek was dressed in bright yellow with loose flowing trousers. Ali Hussein was in a snow-white long robe with black trousers. The officers were distinguished by clean clothes, but the men were clad in various costumes, generally formed of tanned leather.

By way of complimenting me, they had brought out two *large cases of ammunition*—each a load for a native!

These boxes were placed with a guard beneath a tree. My wife, who had as usual come to watch the proceedings, now begged me to dismount, as she had noticed the cases of cartridges, and she feared I might be treacherously shot.

Of course I remained on horseback until the company had completed their arrangements. They now stood in position with their officers in their respective places, but no one moved forward.

I could not believe that they would have the audacity to attack the government troops; but having waited for some time face to face, without the slightest "salaam" having been made by the officers of Abou Saood, I ordered Major Abdullah to retire to the camp with his troops, and to disperse.

I then requested him to send for Wat-el-Mek, as I wished to speak with him immediately.

With much patience, I waited within the station for about half an hour; during which time, five different officers had gone to call Wat-el-Mek, and each had returned with a message that "he would come presently."

At length, two of his people, who had in my absence insulted and threatened to attack Major Abdullah, arrived in the camp with a message, "that both the vakeels *were sick*." I ordered these men to be detained.

I could no longer stand this insolence, as I at once understood that they refused to appear. Accordingly, I instructed Major Abdullah to go himself with a few soldiers, and should Wat-el-Mek refuse to obey my order to accompany him, he should put him under arrest.

The bugle summoned the men who had dispersed,

and they immediately formed two deep in the small open space within the camp, to receive instructions. At this time, Lieutenant Baker voluntered to go and speak to Wat-el-Mek, who would (he thought) be more likely to listen to him than to Major Abdullah, who had so frequently been insulted by the slave-hunters during my absence.

I agreed that it would be advisable; at the same time he must be accompanied by some troops. I therefore began to address the men who were standing before me, and I instructed them to obey Lieutenant Baker implicitly, and upon no account to——

My instructions were interrupted by a volley of musketry concentrated upon the mass of scarlet uniforms!

Without the slightest provocation we were thus treacherously attacked, and heavy file-firing continued upon the station. The bullets were whistling through the straw huts, and seven of my men, including Molōdi, were struck within a few seconds.

My wife, who was always ready in any emergency, rushed out of her hut with my rifle and belt.

The soldiers had already commenced firing by the time that I was armed and had reached the front, by the edge of the light fence of wattles, that were inferior to the weakest hurdles.

I now observed the enemy about ninety yards distant; many of them were kneeling on the ground and firing, but immediately after taking a shot, they retired behind the huts to reload. In this manner they were keeping up a hot fire.

I perceived a man in white upper garments, but with black trousers: this fellow knelt and fired. I immediately took a shot at him with the "Dutchman;" and without delay I kept loading and firing my favourite little breechloader at every man of the enemy that was decently dressed.

We should have lost many men if this hiding behind huts and popping from cover had been allowed to continue. I therefore called my "Forty Thieves" together, and ordered the bugler to sound the charge with the bayonet.

Pushing through the narrow wicket gateway, I formed some thirty or forty men in line and led them at full speed with fixed bayonets against the enemy.

Although the slave-hunters had primed themselves well with araki and merissa before they had screwed up courage to attack the troops, they were not quite up to standing before a bayonet charge. The "Forty Thieves" were awkward customers, and in a quarter of a minute they were amongst them.

THE SLAVE-HUNTERS ATTACK AT FATIKO—THE ADVANCE OF THE "FORTY THIEVES."

The enemy were regularly crumpled up! and had they not taken to flight, they would have been bayoneted to a man.

I now saw Wat-el-Mek in his unmistakable yellow suit; he was marching alone across a road about 180 yards distant.

He was crossing to my right; and I imagined, as he was alone, that he intended to screen himself behind the houses, and then to surrender.

To my surprise, I observed that when he recognized me, he at once raised his gun and took a steady aim.

I was at that moment reloading; but I was ready the instant that he had fired and missed me.

He now walked quickly towards a hut across to my right. I allowed about half a foot before him for his pace, and the "Dutchman" had a word to say.

The bullet struck his right hand, taking the middle finger off at the root, and then striking the gun in the middle of the lock plate, it cut it completely in halves as though it had been divided by a blow with an axe. He was almost immediately taken prisoner. One of "The Forty" (Seroor) was so enraged that he was with difficulty prevented from finishing Wat-el-Mek with a bayonet thrust.

I now ordered a general advance at the double; and the troops spread out through the extensive town of huts, which occupied about thirty acres.

As we ran through the town, I observed about 150 of the enemy had rallied around their flags, and were retreating quickly, but steadily, in the direction of the Shooa hill. They continued to turn and fire from the rear of their party.

Having reduced the distance to about 150 yards, the crimson silk banners afforded excellent marks for rifle practice. They fell to the right and left; the shots were directed a little low so as to hit the bearers. In a few minutes not a flag was to be seen! The fatal sniders poured bullets into the dense body of men, who, after waving to and fro as the shots thinned their number, at length ran off without any further effort to maintain a formation.

For upwards of four miles Lieutenant Baker and I chased these ruffians with the "Forty Thieves." Many were killed in the pursuit; and upon our return to the camp at Fatiko at 2 P.M., we had captured a herd of 306 cattle, 130 slaves, 15 donkeys, 43 prisoners, 7 flags, together with the entire station.

The enemy had suffered the loss of more than half their party killed.

The actual fighting had been done by the "Forty Thieves;" and the men of Abdullah's detachment had behaved disgracefully. Instead of following the enemy in the retreat, they had fraternised with a crowd of natives in pillaging the extensive station.

I now had to clear all these fellows out. The officers appeared to have quite lost their heads; and the natives had carried off all the guns and ammunition from the dead men, and had sacked and plundered the powder magazine.

My wife had placed sentries on the high rocks which commanded a view of the entire country; she had also had the cattle driven within the fence; and she had secured the prisoners, including Wat-el-Mek, in two large huts, over which she had placed a guard. The officers had been so completely bewildered by the suddenness of the affair, that their wits had been exercised in an extraordinary direction. They had commenced firing Hale's rockets while we were in advance pursuing the enemy, and a couple of these screeching projectiles had actually passed over my head.

We had neither eaten nor drunk since the preceding evening, with the exception of some water that we had procured from a stream at the extreme limit of the pursuit; where we had lost the enemy, who had scattered in the forest.

With her usual forethought, my wife had ordered the cook to have breakfast ready; and having washed hands and faces, we sat down to a good curry of mutton, and excellent *café-au-lait*, the milk having been obtained from the captured cows.

We had worked fairly that morning, having marched ten miles from Sharga, then fought the rebels and run four miles in pursuit; and four miles on our return, through an exceedingly rough country.

My old friends, Gimōro and Shooli, were delighted to see us again. The native sheiks thronged round the entrance of our hut to congratulate us on the defeat of the rebels; and messengers had been already sent off to Rot Jarma and all the principal headmen of the country.

Wat-el-Mek was safe. I knew that most of the principal officers were either killed or wounded; but I was anxious to be assured of the fate of the arch-ruffian, Ali Hussein.

"Where is Ali Hussein?" I asked the natives.

"*Dead!*" cried a number of voices.

"Are you certain?" I asked.

"We will bring you his head, for he is not far off," they replied; and several men started immediately.

We were very hungry; and as curry is quickly eaten, we were not long at breakfast; this was hardly concluded when some natives rushed to the open door, and throwing something heavy on the floor of the hut, I saw at my feet the bloody head of Ali Hussein!

There was no mistake in the person. The villainous expression was as strongly marked upon the features in death as it had been in life.

The natives had appropriated his clothes, which they described as "a long white robe and black trousers." Ali Hussein had been struck by two bullets; one had broken his arm, and the other had passed through his thigh. He was alive when the natives discovered him; but as he had been the scourge of the country, he, of course, received no mercy from them.

CHAPTER XI.

NO MEDICAL MEN.

THE death of the unfortunate Dr. Gedge, my chief medical officer at Tewfikeeyah, added to the retirement of one of the Egyptian surgeons from Gondokoro, had left me with so weak a medical staff that I had been unable to take a doctor from headquarters. I therefore was compelled to perform all necessary operations myself, and to attend personally upon the wounded men.

In the late encounter, although I had not actually lost a soldier, seven were badly wounded. One had a broken thigh, and the bullet had remained in the leg. Two had smashed ankle-joints, in one of which the ball remained fixed among the bones. Some of the prisoners were also wounded, and one shortly died.

Wat-el-Mek's hand was much lacerated, in addition to ·the loss of the middle finger.

I dressed all the wounds with a weak solution of carbolic acid. After some trouble, I extracted the bullet from the broken thigh,[1] and set the bone.

Wat-el-Mek had two excellent English double-barrelled guns. That destroyed by the "Dutchman" was a gun by Blissett of London, which had been given to him by Captain Speke when he parted at Gondokoro: the other was my own old gun, that I had given to Ibrahim when I travelled with him during my first journey in Africa.

On the 3rd August I took evidence against Abou Saood. Mohammed Wat-el-Mek, and a prisoner named Besheer, who was an officer in the same company, both swore upon the Koran, that in firing at me "they had only obeyed the orders of Abou Saood, who had instructed them to attack me and the government troops should I attempt to interfere with their proceedings."

Wat-el-Mek declared upon oath that he had always wished to serve me, but he had been prevented by Abou Saood and others; and he had now been rightly punished. This, he said, was "God's hand." He had been in countless fights with natives during many

---

[1] This man was one of "The Forty;" and about two months after the wound he was again on duty, and only slightly lame.

years, and he was possessed of powerful charms and spells, including numerous verses from the Koran suspended from his arms : these had always protected him until the day when he had raised his hand against the government. His charms had at once failed him, and he had lost both his finger and the gun with which he had fired at me.

My officers and soldiers really believed that I had purposely cut his finger off, and smashed his gun by a rifle shot, to prove to him what I could accomplish with a rifle ; and thus to warn a man who would be useful to me, instead of killing him.

Wat-el-Mek now offered to swear upon the Koran fidelity and allegiance if I would pardon him ; and he would at once prove his sincerity by raising an irregular corps.

This man was a curious character ; his superstitious nature had been seized with the conviction that his present position was a special visitation of divine wrath. He was a courageous fellow, and he knew the country and the natives better than any man living. I had always wished to engage his services, and I considered this an excellent opportunity.

The officers now begged me to forgive him. He

was led away to a stream of clear water, where he went through the process of washing with a cake of soap, which was sorely needed. He was then dressed in clean clothes that were lent to him for that purpose, and the Koran was brought and laid open at a particular passage.

Placing his wounded hand upon the page, he repeated with great devotion the formal oath.[1]

I now gave him a few words of good advice, encouraging his preconceived idea that God had chastised him specially, and that the future would depend upon his own conduct.

Having thus secured this valuable man, whom I had always wished to engage at the commencement of the expedition, there was much to be done, and it will be necessary to make a few extracts from my journal that will better explain the position :—

"*August* 5, 1872.—I ought to hang Abou Saood, but much diplomacy is necessary. The rebels in their three stations, Fabbo, Faloro, and Farragenia, number about 600, exclusive of armed Baris.

"I have with me 146 men, including officers. Should I raise the whole country, the difficulty would be to prevent the natives from exterminating Abou Saood and the whole of his forces. Should such an

[1] Wat-el-Mek always behaved well from that time.

event occur, how should I be able to occupy this extensive country with so small a force? I have lately had a painful lesson in the treachery of Kabba Réga, who, when I had relieved him of his enemies, the slave-traders, immediately turned against *me*. These natives might probably do the same. Negroes respect nothing but force; and the force that now exists, if removed, will leave them free to act against the government. Already they have benefited by the fight with the slave-hunters, by running off with the arms and ammunition, together with a number of cattle, while our troops were engaged with the enemy."

I came to the conclusion that it would be unwise to get rid of the slave-hunters by physical force. Although I felt that they were entirely in my power, as I could bombard their stations with Hale's rockets if they should refuse to turn out, the natives would, in the event of a flight, most assuredly possess themselves of the guns and ammunition.

With 146 men, I could not take more than eighty men to act against 600, as the small force of sixty-six would be the minimum that I could leave to protect the Fatiko station. If with eighty men, together with a wild army of natives, I should attack Fabbo (in which I had heard that

Abou Saood was concentrating his people from the other stations), every one of the slave-traders would be massacred. It would be impossible for eighty men to fight, and to secure at the same time the 600 stand of arms that would be in the hands of the rebels. These, together with the muskets belonging to the Baris, would all fall into the possession of my native allies, who would immediately scatter and disappear with their prize.

Should I attack Fabbo, the result would simply arm the natives with 800 or 900 stand of muskets, together with a large amount of ammunition, which they might probably use against me at some future time.

I resolved to work diplomatically, and to keep the slave-hunters' party as a rod above the backs of the natives, until I should discover their real character.

It had been necessary to establish a corn tax[1] for the support of the troops. Possibly the natives, if

---

[1] The corn tax was thus established. Each house was taxed to pay a small basket of corn every full moon. All old and infirm people and also strangers were exempted from taxation. The headman of each village was responsible for the tax, and he delivered a bundle of small pieces of reed, the size of drawing pencils, which represented the number of houses belonging to able-bodied men. This tax was always paid cheerfully, in gratitude for the protection afforded by the government.

entirely relieved from their oppressors, might refuse to acknowledge government taxation! At all events I determined to proceed cautiously.

The first step was to summon Abou Saood and to hear his defence from his own mouth.

I had given the prisoners their choice, of either enlisting in the government service, or returning to Khartoum.

Of course they ought to have been shot in a batch; but I could not afford to shoot them. I had to catch and tame my wild beasts instead of destroying them.

A considerable number agreed to serve under Wat-el-Mek.

I wrote, on 5th August, a letter addressed to Abou Saood, summoning him to appear instantly at Fatiko: at the same time I promised him a free exit; without which written assurance I might as well have summoned the "man in the moon."

It was difficult to procure natives who would accompany the new irregulars with the letter, as news had arrived that Abou Saood's people were plundering and laying waste the neighbourhood of Fabbo.

At length I arranged that eight of the new levy, together with the native blacksmith and several others from Fatiko, who were well known in the Madi country, should go to Fabbo (22 miles) with my letter to Abou Saood. The blacksmith would protect the irregulars by explaining their new position to any natives who might desire to molest them.

I also sent a proclamation to be read publicly in the zareeba, summoning all subjects of the Khedive to declare their allegiance to the government.

On the following day (6th August) the blacksmith and his people returned from Fabbo thoroughly disgusted. Upon their arrival near the zareeba of Abou Saood they had cried out to the slave-hunters that they had brought "a letter from the Pacha to Abou Saood!" The slave-hunters had replied with a well-known form of abuse in that country, and had immediately fired a volley into the blacksmith and the eight men of their own people!

The blacksmith and his natives had lost no time in running back to Fatiko; and the eight irregulars having thrown themselves on the ground, had (the blacksmith supposed) at length explained who they were.

I mention these circumstances, as the European and American public will be the judges whether

I erred on the side of leniency or severity throughout this expedition. In Egypt and the Soudan I have no doubt that my name is hated, as a Christian that shed the blood of Mohammedans; but I trust the civilized world will acquit me of any bloodshedding except in the act of lawful self-defence. If the Mohammedans could have killed me, there would have been no crime.

It has been seen that not only were we treacherously attacked at Fatiko, but my messengers to Abou Saood were fired upon *while he was in the camp*.

The patience and forbearance that I was obliged to assume were far more trying to my feelings than the march from Masindi.

It has always been an intense satisfaction to me that I had reliable witnesses to every incident of the expedition; otherwise, I might perhaps have been suspected of some prejudice against Abou Saood and certain Egyptian authorities that, unknown to myself, might have discoloured the true aspect of affairs. I can only refer to Lieutenant Baker, R.N., and that gallant officer, Lieutenant-Colonel Abd-el-Kader, and many others, including all soldiers and servants who belonged to the detachment at Fatiko.

DESTRUCTION OF LIEUT. COLONEL TAYIB AGHA'S DETACHMENT AT MOOGI.

These persons subsequently gave their evidence, which they will be ready at all times to repeat.

On 7th August, at about 5 P.M., Abou Saood appeared with about forty of his men. He was afraid to enter my camp without a second assurance in writing that he should not be made prisoner.

Of course he swore that he had not given orders to fire at me; and he declared that his people of Fatiko had only fired because they were afraid that the natives who had accompanied me were about to attack them.

I asked him, "If that were the case, why had they not communicated with me, as I was only ninety yards distant?" He said his people had not fired at the government troops, but only at the natives who were upon the rock.

He could not quite explain in that case "how it was that 1,000 natives perched upon the rock close together, had escaped without a man being wounded, while not only were seven of the government troops knocked down by bullets, but the huts and furniture of our camp, including boxes in the magazine, &c., had been completely riddled with balls." He then began to lay the blame on Wat-el-Mek, and even had the audacity to declare that "he had nothing to do with slaves, but that he could not restrain his people from kidnapping." I never heard any human being pour out such a cataract of lies as this scoundrel. His plausibility and assurance were such that I stood aghast ; and after he had delivered a long speech, in which he declared that " he was the innocent victim of adverse circumstances, and that every one was against him," I could merely reply by dismissing him with the assurance that there was " only one really good and honest man in the world, who invariably spoke the truth ; this man was *Abou Saood.* All other men were liars."

On the following morning Abou Saood came to take leave. He pretended to devote himself to my service, and declared that he should now at once return to Fabbo and organize the best of his people into an irregular corps for the government, and he should act with energy as my vakeel, and assist me in every manner possible. He begged me not to believe a word that any one might say *except himself*, and he swore by the eyes and head of the Prophet (this was his favourite oath whenever he told the biggest lie) that there was no one so true to me as he, which he would prove by his acts. He then went back to Fabbo.

This is the last time that I ever saw Abou Saood. He took 200 men upon his arrival at Fabbo, and after having told his men to cut the throat of the sheik Werdella, who was a prisoner in the Fabbo camp under my special orders for protection, he went straight to Gondokoro to his friend Raouf Bey.

This officer, who commanded at head-quarters during my absence, although he heard from Abou Saood's people of the attack made upon me at Fatiko, and Abou Saood had arrived without either a passport or letters from myself, positively allowed him to depart to Khartoum.

At Khartoum Abou Saood spread every conceivable false report. Thence he travelled to Cairo, expressly to complain to the Khedive's government of the manner in which he had been treated by me.

Thus the greatest slave-trader of the White Nile, who was so closely connected with the Soudan government that he was a tenant who had rented a country WHICH DID NOT BELONG TO EGYPT, now applied to that government for protection against my interference with his murders, kidnapping, and pillaging, which were the accompaniments of his slave-hunting in Central Africa.

The fact of this renowned slave-hunter having the audacity to appeal to the Egyptian authorities for assistance, at once exhibits the confidence that the slave-traders felt in the moral support of certain official personages who represented public opinion in their hatred to the principal object of the expedition.

The various links in the chain which united the interests of Abou Saood with certain officers who were opposed to the spirit of the enterprize will be at once perceived.

From the very commencement, this man had been the chief intriguer who had endeavoured to ruin the expedition. He had fraternised with the Baris when they were at open war with the government. He had incited the tribes to attack me, and at length his own companies had fired at me by his orders. *He now sought the protection of the Egyptian government at Cairo.*

Although we shall not see Abou Saood again, it will be interesting to watch the close of his career, as the public will most probably form their opinion of the sincerity of the Egyptian government respecting the question of "slavery" by the ultimate fate of this renowned slave-hunter.

We shall now leave Abou Saood in Cairo, where he spread the false report of the massacre of Lady Baker and myself, which reached England and appeared in the newspapers in April 1873.

After Abou Saood's departure from Fabbo, the influence of Wat-el-Mek began to be felt, and many men flocked to the government standard. Nevertheless, that station was a scene of anarchy. The slave-hunters were divided among themselves. The party that followed Wat-el-Mek were nearly all Soudanis, like himself, but the Arabs were split up into companies, each of which had elected a separate leader. This dissension was exactly what I desired, and I played the game accordingly. As I have before stated, I wished to avoid physical force.

Ali Genninar, whom I had engaged at Masindi, was an excellent fellow, and before Abou Saood deserted the country, he had been the first man to arrive at Fatiko and unite with the government. He now collected sixty-five men, whom I at once enrolled, and having given them their government flags, I started them off without delay to support Rionga in Unyoro, and recalled Abd-el-Kader and his troops to Fatiko. At the same time I sent Rionga many valuable presents.

There were several terrible scoundrels at Fabbo, among whom was Salim-Wat-Howah, who, together with Lāzim, had threatened to shoot Major Abdullah in his own camp during my absence in Unyoro.

I had Lāzim in irons at Fatiko, but Salim-Wat-Howah, having been dressed in very dirty brown clothes, had escaped on the day of attack. This man

Salim was the head of the greatest villains at Fabbo, and he and his band of about one hundred men daily sallied out of the zareeba and plundered and burnt the neighbourhood in open defiance of Wat-el-Mek.

When these ruffians captured women, they now cut their throats and threw them into the Un-y-Amé river, explaining to the natives that they defied me to "liberate" them when their throats were cut.

Every day the natives flocked to me from Fabbo with the most dreadful tales of atrocities.

The time had now arrived when I could make the move that I felt sure would reduce the country into order.

The slave-hunters were in this position. I had sent Ali Genninar with sixty-five men to Unyoro, 200 had gone off with Abou Saood, 100 reprobates clung to Salim-Wat-Howah, and the remainder were true to Wat-el-Mek.

I therefore sent a message to Fabbo, which Wat-el-Mek would make public in the zareeba: "that, having received daily complaints from the natives of outrages committed by Salim-Wat-Howah and his company, it was my intention in forty-eight hours to visit Fabbo with the troops, together with the native witnesses to the outrages complained of."

I ordered "all those men who had enlisted in the government service, together with all others who were true to the Khedive, to retire from the Fabbo station to Faloro: thus Fabbo alone would represent the malcontents."

I felt sure that the dissension which had existed among the various parties would now break out anew, and that Salim-Wat-Howah, fearing a personal visit from me, which might reduce him to the headless condition of Ali Hussein, would follow the example of his master, Abou Saood, and fly from the country.

The hint that I had given respecting the retirement of the loyal people to Faloro, so that Fabbo would represent the disloyal, would be sufficient warning that physical force was intended, should other means fail.

The day upon which Wat-el-Mek published the proclamation was one of general consternation in Fabbo.

Wat-el-Mek left the station with his Soudanis.

Salim-Wat-Howah and his men suddenly sprang upon the vakeel, Suleiman, and having secured him, while others broke open the powder-magazine, they possessed themselves of three cases (1,500 rounds) of ball-cartridge, together with the flags of the station. With this prize they marched out of the zareeba with their slaves, who carried their luggage, and took the road towards Latooka, about nine days' march distant.

Without firing a shot, I had thus won the game. All the bad people had found the country too hot for them. The remaining men received certificates, and raised the corps of irregulars to 312 officers and men; all of whom were nominally under Wat-el-Mek, although Ali Genninar held a separate command in Unyoro. I now strengthened his party by a reinforcement.

From this date, the victory was gained, and I could only thank God for the great success that had attended all my efforts. The slave-hunting was now at an end throughout an immense district, as the slave-hunters had ceased to exist south of Gondokoro. Excepting Unyoro, the days of bloodshed were past. The "Forty Thieves," who had so gallantly stood by me through every difficulty, never again had an enemy before them. I was devoutly thankful for days of peace.

My task was now full of pleasure and gratification. I had established perfect confidence among the natives throughout the large country of Shooli. The Lira tribe had declared their allegiance, and we had friends upon all sides.

I had as usual planted gardens at Fatiko, which were flourishing. The natives no longer concealed their stores of corn; but dancing and rejoicing had taken the place of watchfulness and insecurity.

The children and women flocked to our camp; and marketing upon a large scale was conducted without a squabble. The two good men, Shooli and Gimōro, who were daily visitors, assured me that there was only one feeling throughout the country, of gratitude and good-will. This was a great reward to me for the many difficulties we had undergone; but now that the calm days of peace had arrived, I looked back with keen regret upon the good men that I had lost, especially to the memory of poor Monsoor. There was no person who would have enjoyed my success so much as that worthy man.

It is now time to speak of Suleiman and the party who had left Masindi on 23rd May with the post for Fatiko, together with the 300 Unyoro carriers who were to have transported Abdullah's detachment to Foweera.

The letter (concealed in a package) that I had sent to Eddrees, with orders that "the party should return at once to Fatiko should they suspect foul play," had reached them before they had crossed the Victoria Nile.

Mohammed, the Cairo dragoman, had strongly suspected treachery, owing to the unaccountable tardiness of the natives in pushing straight for Fatiko. Every day messengers had arrived from Masindi, and others had been returned in reply by the sheik Pittia, who had charge of the 300 Unyoro carriers.

When my letter had been received, Mohammed advised Eddrees to return at once to Masindi; but the latter, finding himself about fifty miles on the journey, concluded that it would be better to continue the march.

They had delayed so many days on the road, that the stock of flour intended for the whole journey would have failed, had they not spared their supply, and fed upon potatoes whenever they halted near cultivated ground.

On one occasion, a number of their men had as usual gone off to forage, and were employed in digging sweet potatoes, when they were suddenly attacked by the natives concealed in the high grass, and eleven men were speared; five of my troops and six of the irregulars. Fortunately some of these men had fired their muskets before they died, and the reports alarmed the remainder of the party, who were in a small village. There was not a native to be seen, but the drums and horns were sounding, and as the Victoria Nile was close at hand, they considered it would be advisable to cross the river before the natives should attack them in force.

It was necessary to release Suleiman, who was secured in a shéba. This man had been committed to the charge of Mohammed. Before Mohammed cut the raw hide strap which secured the forked pole, he made Suleiman swear by the prophet not to escape, but that he would deliver himself up to Major Abdullah at Fatiko.

The party, now reduced to twenty-five men, immediately started. Upon arrival at the banks of the river, they happened to come suddenly upon a native, whom they seized.

They soon observed a canoe on the other side of the river, in which were two men. They now made an arrangement for the capture of the canoe, which was to them a case of life or death.

The prisoner was dressed in the usual flowing robe of bark-cloth. His hands were tied behind him, and one of the party who could speak the language now concealed himself behind the bark-cloth robe, and holding the native tightly by the arms, he threatened him with instant death unless he called the two natives in the canoe.

At first he hesitated, but fearing the knife at his back, the point of which just pricked him to let him know that it was ready, he shouted to the men in the boat.

"Say you have a number of plantains, and you want to take them across the river," whispered his invisible prompter from behind.

The natives in the canoe hesitated. "Say you will give them each a bunch of plantains if they will ferry you over," again whispered the cunning Arab.

The canoe now pushed off from the bank, and paddled towards the apparently solitary native.

The irregulars were concealed in the high grass close to the bank, and as the canoe touched the shore, they shot the two natives dead, and immediately secured it.

They now unlashed the arms of the prisoner, and insisted upon his paddling the canoe across the river. Two journeys were necessary. The first was successful, and the regular troops, together with the post and Suleiman and others, were safely landed. During the second journey, as the canoe was passing a rock above some dangerous rapids, the native suddenly upset the boat by throwing his weight quickly to one side, and plunged the whole party in the river. Some of them were carried over the cataracts and drowned. The others, including Ali Genninar, were good swimmers, and they reached the shore.

Although the irregulars thoroughly knew the country, they now found themselves in the immense wilderness that separates Unyoro from the Shooli and Madi tribes.

In this sea of high grass they wandered for some days, lost; until they at length discovered the regular path, and, after great suffering, reached Fatiko.

Eddrees, who had been appointed vakeel, became a traitor, and upon meeting Abou Saood and his people, who had come out to receive the party upon their arrival, he holloed out, "Look sharp for your neck, Abou Saood: the Pacha has sent an order to arrest you."

A short time after this, Eddrees died of dysentery. Suleiman behaved in an honourable manner. Instead of going into Abou Saood's camp, he immediately presented himself before Major Abdullah, and confessed his sins, acknowledging that he had been justly punished. He surrendered himself into the hands of the commandant, according to the oath he had taken on the road.

Although Major Abdullah had now received the post, together with my orders, he thought it advisable, considering the danger of a collision with Abou Saood's people, to allow Suleiman his liberty on parole, and he had returned to his position of vakeel at Fabbo. Ali Genninar had at once offered to continue his duties as a government soldier.

A few days after the arrival of the post, the news was brought of the battle of Masindi, and that our escape from Unyoro was impossible.

The almost open hostility of Abou Saood and his numerous forces had paralysed Major Abdullah, who, fearing the responsibility of an outbreak, kept quiet, and trusted in Providence, until I had fortunately appeared.

There can be no doubt that the plan laid by Kabba Réga for securing the arms and effects of Major Abdullah and his detachment broke down through a premature attack on the part of the natives, who had neither the courage nor the patience to go to Fatiko on the chance of success in such a distant enterprise. . . . .

Suleiman had written me a letter imploring forgiveness. Wat-el-Mek arrived at Fatiko after the seizure of the ammunition by Salim-Wat-Howah, and he begged pardon for Suleiman, assuring me that he was truly penitent; that the devil had misled him, and Abou Saood was that devil. If I would only grant him a free pardon, no man would be more faithful; and the irregular force now established would be delighted at such an act of clemency.

Although Suleiman was a great ruffian, he was like everybody else in that respect. If I had refused the enlistment of all immoral characters in the middle of Africa, I should have had what is now known in England as a "skeleton regiment." I had already punished him severely. In every case of defiance of the government, the people had now seen that so small an organized force as 200 regulars, amongst innumerable enemies, and without any communication with head-quarters, had been able to beat down and crush every enemy, whether native or rebel. In times of real weakness, it is frequently necessary to be severe, that a grave example may establish authority; but after victory and success, I felt that an act of clemency might, even among half savages, be more binding than iron fetters.

I therefore told Wat-el-Mek that I could not give any promise until Suleiman should present himself before me at Fatiko. It was his duty to deliver himself up as a prisoner upon parole.

On 3rd October Wat-el-Mek arrived at Fatiko accompanied by Suleiman, who came to surrender.

The prisoner was dressed in a filthy brown woollen cloak, and his head was covered with a greasy and almost black tarboosh: he had the appearance of having slept on a dust-heap. This beggarly outside was a token of repentance and humiliation.

Suleiman was brought before me, and he immediately rushed forward and knelt to kiss my feet, exhibiting at the same time considerable emotion; which surprised me, as he was notorious as a stern, hard-hearted Kurd.

I said a few words to him, explaining that he must not think me impenetrable if I doubted his sincerity, as I had been already deceived, after having shown him much kindness: at the same time I did not wish to exert severity, if I could win him to obedience by good advice.[1] I offered him a free pardon if he would swear upon the Koran fidelity to the Khedive. Soould he deceive me, and become a rebel after this, he knew the consequences.

Suleiman now declared, and swore upon the Koran, that he had acted only upon orders he had received from Abou Saood. It was he who, in spite of my

[1] Suleiman always remained faithful from that moment, and became a dependable officer.

written command that the sheik Werdella should be spared, had ordered two of his slaves to take him from the Fabbo zareeba, and to cut his throat.

Both Wat-el-Mek and Suleiman, as late vakeels of Abou Saood, swore to their written evidence, to which they attached their seals in the presence of witnesses, that Abou Saood had given orders to his vakeels to harry the country and to capture slaves and cattle ; that none of the people employed by him received wages in money, but that they were invariably paid in slaves, valued at a certain sum.

"All the opposition that I had met with had been caused by Abou Saood."

Suleiman, having received a written pardon, made his salaam and retired. An hour later he was washed beautifully clean, and was gorgeously dressed in a Turkish costume of light-blue woollen cloth, trimmed with gold and black braid, with a new tarboosh, a handsome silk shawl in thick folds around his waist, and his sabre dangling by his side. This sudden metamorphosis from dirt and ashes to dazzling attire was symbolical of disgrace and humiliation, succeeded by pardon and restoration to office.

Suleiman was to continue as vakeel of the Fabbo station, under the command of Wat-el-Mek. In the magazines of Fabbo were 3,200 elephants' tusks.

These, I had no doubt, would be confiscated by the Khedive.

. . . .

A short time before the arrival of Suleiman, an extraordinary incident had occurred at the Fatiko camp.

One morning, when the bugles blew the usual call, it was discovered that the prisoner Lāzim had escaped, although he had been secured in irons.

Fortunately, it had rained slightly during the night; thus it would not be difficult to track his footsteps. I immediately sent for Shooli and Gimōro, whose village was only 700 yards distant, to whom I promised a reward of a cow, should they succeed in capturing the escaped felon. They quickly got upon the track of the fugitive, and followed like bloodhounds.

I have already described this fellow Lāzim as having been one of the ringleaders in the rebellion of the slave-hunters; and he was almost as notorious a character as Ali Hussein. He was originally himself a slave, and had escaped from his master at Khartoum many years ago, after which he became one of the most determined slave-hunters.

I felt sure that it would have been impossible for him to have escaped without the connivance of the sentry. I therefore ordered all the soldiers that had formed the various night-guards over the prisoner to be brought before me. As they stood in line, I simply told them that "the prisoner had escaped, and that one of the men now present was guilty of aiding and abetting. I could discover the rascal who had thus disgraced himself as a soldier by simply looking at his face."

Having carefully examined the countenance of each man, I felt confident that I had fixed upon the guilty person, as one individual quailed beneath my eye, and at length looked down upon the ground. This happened to be one of the worst characters in the force. I therefore at once ordered him to be flogged.

During the infliction of punishment, this fellow not only confessed that he had assisted in the escape of Lāzim, but he made a clean breast of several other delinquencies. He was accordingly put in irons, and condemned to break stones for the new roads.

In the evening Shooli returned, but without the prisoner. Before he gave his report, he begged me "not to be angry." He then described that he had tracked Lāzim's footsteps for a long way along the Fabbo road until he had at length met several natives, who were coming towards him. These men declared that they had met Lāzim, who had managed to get rid of his irons; but as he was unarmed, they knew that he must have run away. They accordingly asked him for his pass from me, as it was well known that I never allowed a man to go alone without a written order.

Lāzim of course was unable to produce a paper. The natives, therefore, insisted upon his returning with them to Fatiko, and, upon his remonstrating they seized him. A struggle ensued, and they at length knocked him upon the head with an iron mace and killed him. Thus ended one of the greatest scoundrels, and the government was relieved by his escape from custody, which had so quickly terminated his career.

CHAPTER XII.

I SEND TO GONDOKORO FOR REINFORCEMENTS.

On 25th November, 1872, I started Wat-el-Mek to Gondokoro with a force of irregulars, in addition to a captain and twenty regular troops in charge of the post. His party consisted of 100 men.

The fleet from Gondokoro had left on the 3rd of November, 1871 : thus it was natural to suppose that reinforcements had arrived from Khartoum, according to my written instructions on that date. I now wrote to Raouf Bey at head-quarters, to send up 200 men under the command of Lieutenant-Colonel Tayib Agha, of the Soudani regiment. I also wrote for a supply of cattle, as my stock had dwindled to a small herd of milch cows, and the people at Fabbo had no meat except the flesh of any game that might be killed.

A short time after the departure of Wat-el-Mek and his party for Gondokoro, Suleiman the vakeel arrived from Fabbo with the intelligence that a large body of Abou Saood's slave-hunters, including 3,000 Makkarika cannibals, had arrived on the Nile from the far west, with the intention of taking the ivory from Fabbo !

It appeared that Abou Saood had gone from Gondokoro to his station at the Bohr; from thence he had sent a party with a letter to Atroosh, the vakeel of the Makkarika station, about 250 miles distant, with orders that he should send a powerful force, with sufficient carriers, to take the ivory by violence from Fabbo.

Abou Saood had not expected that the people whom he had left at that station would have enlisted under the government standard. Thus he imagined they would at once fraternize with the invading force.

The natives of the country were thoroughly alarmed, as the cannibals were eating the children of the Koshi country on the west bank of the Nile, in about 3° latitude ; and should they cross the river, the Madis and Shoolis expected the same fate.

I ordered Suleiman (who had received a letter from Atroosh) to take a letter from me to Ali Emmeen, the vakeel of the invading force, instructing him to present himself before me at Fatiko instantly with an escort of his own people, limited to twenty-five men. At the same time I gave instructions to the natives upon no account to furnish boats for a larger party.

After some days' absence Suleiman returned, but without Ali Emmeen, who was afraid to appear. This vakeel had received my verbal assurance from Suleiman that, should any persons attempt the passage of the river without my permission, they would be instantly shot; at the same time, if he wished to convey the ivory to Gondokoro by the usual route, he could do so with an escort of regulars.

This was an awkward position for Ali Emmeen, who had expected to find allies at Fabbo, but who now found a faithful corps of irregulars with Suleiman at their head acting under my orders.

He accordingly took 100 men and returned about 180 miles to the camp of Atroosh for fresh instructions. The 3,000 Makkarika cannibals were left with the remainder of his company on the west bank of the Nile to feed upon the natives of Koshi until his return.

Every day people arrived at Fatiko with horrible reports of the cannibals, who were devouring the children in the Koshi district. Spies went across the river and brought me every intelligence. It appeared that the 3,000 Makkarikas had been engaged by Ali Emmeen under the pretence that they were " to go to Fatiko and fight a chief called 'the Pacha,' who had enormous flocks and herds, together with thousands of beautiful women and other alluring spoil;" but they had not heard that they were to carry 3,000 elephants' tusks to the station of Atroosh.

My spies now told them the truth. " Fight the Pacha!" they exclaimed : " do you not know who he is? and that he could kill you all like fowls, as he did the people of Ali Hussein? He has no cows for you to carry off, but he has guns that are magic, and which load from behind instead of at the muzzle!"

This was a terrible disappointment to the deluded Makkarikas, which at once spread dissension among them, when they found that they had been cajoled in order to transport the heavy loads of ivory.

A providential visitation suddenly fell upon them. The small-pox broke out and killed upwards of 800 bloodthirsty cannibals who had been devouring the country.

The Nile was reported to be about six miles in width opposite their station, in about 3° latitude, which is only a few miles from the Albert N'yanza. This visitation of small-pox created a panic which entirely broke up and dispersed the invading force, and defeated their plans.

We were now in frequent communication with Rionga, who was always represented in my Fatiko camp by the presence of one of his sheiks and several men.

Ali Genninar had made a combined attack upon Kabba Réga, together with Rionga and the Langgo tribe, and had utterly defeated him. His people were now deserting him in great numbers, and were flocking to the winning side. Kabba Réga had taken to flight, and was supposed to be hiding in the neighbourhood of Chibero, on the borders of the Albert N'yanza.

M'tésé, the king of Uganda, had invaded Unyoro from the south, and having heard of Kabba Réga's treachery towards myself, he had sent an army of 6,000 men under his general, Congow, to be placed at my disposal.

This friendship was the result of my diplomacy in having sent him valuable presents from Masindi, together with a letter warning him against Kabba Réga, who wished to prevent the goods of the north from reaching Uganda, in order that he might monopolize the trade in Unyoro.

The subsequent conduct of Kabba Réga had

proved this accusation, and M'tésé had heard with rage and dismay that I had been forced to burn all the numerous goods, which otherwise would have passed to him in Uganda.

On the 25th December the fort of Fatiko was completed. This was commenced on the 28th August; thus my men had been four months engaged in the work, owing to the extreme hardness of the subsoil, which was a compact gravel resembling concrete.

The three faces of the fort measured 455 yards of fosse and earthen rampart. The fosse was eight feet wide, eight feet deep, and the face of the rampart was protected by *chevaux-de-frise* of sharpened stakes. The west base of the fort was the rock citadel, which commanded the surrounding country. Upon this solid foundation I had built an excellent powder-magazine and store, of solid masonry. This fire-proof building was roofed with a thick cement of clay from the white-ant hills, that had been tempered for some weeks and mixed with chopped straw.

All my work was completed, and I could do nothing until the reinforcements should arrive from Gondokoro. The natives paid their trifling corn-tax with great good humour, and they generally

FORT FATIKO.

CHAP. XII.] *COMMENCEMENT OF HUNTING SEASON.* 435

arrived in crowds of several hundreds, singing and dancing, with large baskets of tullaboon upon their heads, with which they filled our rows of granaries.

The grass was now fit to burn, and the hunting season had fairly commenced. All the natives devoted themselves to this important pursuit. The chase supplies the great tribe of Shooli with clothing. Although the women are perfectly naked, every man wears the skin of an antelope slung across his shoulders, so arranged as to be tolerably decent. The number of animals that are annually destroyed may be imagined from the amount of the skin-clad population.

Although the wilderness between Unyoro and Fatiko is uninhabited, in like manner with extensive tracts between Fabbo and Fatiko, every portion of that apparently abandoned country is nominally possessed by individual proprietors, who claim a right of game by inheritance.

This strictly conservative principle has existed from time immemorial, and may perhaps suggest to those ultra-radicals who would introduce communistic principles into England, that the supposed original equality of human beings is a false datum for their problem. There is no such thing as equality among human beings in their primitive state, any more than there is equality among the waves of the sea, although they may start from the same level of the calm.

In a state of savagedom, the same rules of superiority which advance certain individuals above the general level in civilized societies will be found to exert a natural influence. Those who become eminent will be acknowledged by their inferiors. The man who is clever and wise in council will be listened to; the warrior who leads with courage and judgment will be followed in the battle; the hunter who excels in tracking up the game will be sent to the front when the party are on the blood-track. In this way superiority will be generally admitted. Superiority of intellect will naturally tend to material advancement. The man of sense will gather more than the fool. That which he gathers becomes property, which must be acknowledged by society as an individual right that must be protected by laws.

In tribes where government is weak, there is a difficulty in enforcing laws, as the penalty exacted may be resisted; but even amidst those wild tribes there is a force that exerts a certain moral influence among the savage as among the civilized: that force is public opinion.

Thus, a breach of the game-laws would be regarded by the public as a disgrace to the guilty individual, precisely as an act of poaching would damage the character of a civilized person.

The rights of game are among the first rudiments of property. Man in a primitive state is a hunter, depending for his clothing upon the skins of wild animals, and upon their flesh for his subsistence; therefore the beast that he kills upon the desert must be his property; and in a public hunt, should he be the first to wound a wild animal, he will have gained an increased interest or share in the flesh by having reduced the chance of its escape. Thus public opinion, which we must regard as the foundation of *equity*, rewards him with a distinct and special right, which becomes *law*.

It is impossible to trace the origin of game-laws in Central Africa, but it is nevertheless interesting to find that such rights are generally acknowledged, and that large tracts of uninhabited country are possessed by individuals which are simply manorial. These rights are inherited, descending from father to the eldest son.

When the grass is sufficiently dry to burn, the whole thoughts of the community are centred upon sport; but should a person set fire to the grass belonging to another proprietor, he would be at once condemned by public opinion, and he would (if such establishments existed) be certainly expelled from his club.

There was no more work undone in my charming Fatiko station. The roads from the three gates were so far completed as to form respectable approaches. The gardens had produced abundantly, and the troops were all in excellent health and good discipline. On Mondays and Fridays they were exercised at light-infantry drill for several hours. Every man had his post, which he occupied like lightning when the bugle suddenly sounded the alarm. The " Forty Thieves" held the rock citadel, as they could fire over the heads of those in the camp without fear of accident. The night alarm sounded unexpectedly, and as I went the rounds, every man was at his quarters without a whisper. The cleanliness and general order of the camp were perfect.

I now associated with the natives as a hunter. It was in this capacity that I had first won their hearts many years ago. We were so short of meat that I began to feel the necessity that first turned the hand of savage man against the beasts of the forest.

The chase throughout the Shooli country was carried on as a profession, and was conducted by general rules under an admirable organization.

The favourite method of hunting was by means of

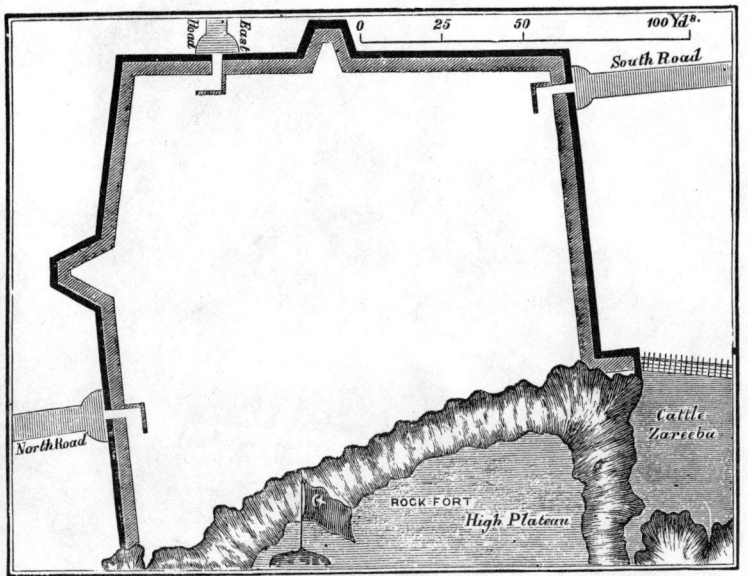

Fort Fatiko—Ground Plan.

nets. Every man in the country was provided with a net of strong cord. This was twelve yards long, and about eleven feet deep, if stretched to its maximum. The meshes were about six inches square. There was no promiscuous net-hunting, but the chief of the district organized the chase in the following manner :—

The big nogara was sounded, and the news rapidly spread that an assembly was desired at the village of their headman. At Fatiko the chief was Wat-el-Ajoos Omare. A few hours after the drum had summoned the headmen, natives might be seen approaching from all sides to the appointed spot at which the council was to be held.

After much talking, it was at length decided that the hunt should take place upon the manors of certain individuals whose property was contiguous. The day of the hunt was arranged, and the headmen of the villages retired to make the necessary arrangements.

Should a chief be hospitably disposed, he would frequently give a grand entertainment prior to the hunt. On such occasions upwards of a thousand natives would arrive from different villages, in their full-dress costume, consisting of plumes of ostrich feathers, leopard-skin mantles, and their faces painted a frightful colour with fresh cow-dung. On these occasions a large quantity of merissa was consumed, and one or two oxen were slaughtered, according to the wealth of the person who gave the festivity.

The sorcerer was an important personage at such entertainments, as it was necessary to assure good luck by a variety of magic ceremonies, that would not only protect the hunters from accidents, but would also bring the wild animals direct into their nets.

At length the day of the hunt had arrived, when several thousand people would collect at a certain rendezvous, about nine miles distant from Fatiko, on the Fabbo road, which is the best neighbourhood for game.

At a little before 5 A.M. I started on my solitary but powerful horse, "Jamoos," accompanied by Lieutenant Baker and Colonel Abd-el-Kader, with a few soldiers of "The Forty." Gimōro and Shooli, who were renowned hunters, were always with me when shooting. These excellent men had an extraordinary affection for each other, and they were well known as inseparables—the one was rarely seen without the other.

Descending the rocky terrace from the station at Fatiko, we were at once in the lovely, park-like glades, diversified by bold granite rocks, among which were scattered the graceful drooping acacias in clumps of dense foliage.

Crossing the clear, rippling stream, we clambered up the steep bank on the opposite side, and, after a ride of about a mile and a half, we gained the water-shed, and commenced a gradual descent towards the west.

We were now joined by numerous people, both men, women, and children, all of whom were bent upon the hunt.

The men carried their nets and spears; the boys were also armed with lighter weapons, and the very little fellows carried tiny lances, all of which had been carefully sharpened for the expected game.

The women were in great numbers, and upon that day the villages were quite deserted. Babies accompanied their mothers, strapped upon their backs with leathern bands, and protected from the weather by the usual tortoise-like coverings of gourd-shells. Thus it may be imagined that the Shooli tribe were born hunters, as they had accompanied the public hunts from their earliest infancy.

My two boys, Säat and Belläal, carried spare guns. These fine strong lads always attended me, and they had become useful gun-bearers. They were both plucky fellows. Little Amarn had been suffering for more than twelve months from an ulcerated leg; therefore he was spared from unnecessary fatigue, and was the pet boy at home.

As we proceeded, the number of natives increased, but there was no noise or loud talking. Every one appeared thoroughly to understand his duties.

Having crossed the beautiful Un-y-Amé river, we entered the game country. Extensive prairies, devoid of forest, now stretched before us in graceful undulations to the base of distant mountains. The country was watered by numerous clear streams, all of which drained into the main channel of the Un-y-Amé river, that became a roaring torrent during the wet season.

We now left the Fabbo path and struck off to our left for several miles, over ground that had been cleared by burning, which showed in many directions the crimson fruit of the wild ginger, growing half-exposed from the earth. This is a leathery, hard pod, about the size of a goose-egg, filled with a semi-transparent pulp of a subacid flavour, with a delicious perfume between pine-apple and lemon-peel. It is very juicy and refreshing, and is decidedly the best wild fruit of Central Africa.

The natives immediately collected a quantity, and we quickly pushed forward to the rendezvous, where, upon arrival, we found a great number of people were collected.

A line of about a mile and a half was quickly protected by netting, and the natives were already in position.

Each man had lashed his net to that of his neighbour and supported it with bamboos, which were secured with ropes fastened to twisted grass. Thus the entire net resembled a fence, that would be invisible to the game in the high grass, until, when driven, they should burst suddenly upon it.

The grass was as dry as straw, and several thousand acres would be fired up to windward, which would compel the animals to run before the flames, until they reached the netting placed a few paces in front; where the high grass had been purposely cleared to resist the advance of the fire.

Before each section of net, a man was concealed both within and without, behind a screen, simply formed of the long grass bound together at the top.

The rule of sport decided that the proprietor of each section of netting of twelve yards length would be entitled to all game that should be killed within these limits; but that the owners of the manors which formed the hunt upon that day should receive a hind-leg from every animal captured.

This was fair play; but in such hunts a breach of the peace was of common occurrence, as a large animal might charge the net and receive a spear from the owner of the section, after which he might break back, and eventually be killed in the net of another hunter; which would cause a hot dispute.

The nets had been arranged with perfect stillness, and the men having concealed themselves, we were placed in positions on the extreme flanks with the rifles.

Rifle-shooting was dangerous work, as the country was alive with people, who were hidden in every direction.

I took my position behind a white-ant hill in front of a stream which rippled in a hollow about forty yards beneath me.

Molodi had quite recovered from the wound he had received on 2nd August, and he carried the basket that contained our luncheon. This consisted of three bottles of milk and a few hard-boiled eggs, with a supply of salt and pepper.

There is nothing so good as milk for support during a long day's work, provided it is used with water, in a proportion of one-third milk. A bottle of rich milk will therefore produce three bottles of wholesome drink. This is far preferable to the use of

NET HUNTING IN THE SHOOLI TRIBE.

spirits, which are merely a temporary stimulant, and frequently are great enemies to good rifle-shooting.

Molodi's basket was arranged with a white napkin over the contents. As such a colour would attract attention, I ordered him to conceal himself and his basket behind a neighbouring ant-hill.

Mr. Baker was far away on my right; and Abd-el-Kader was upon the extreme right flank.

Everything was ready, and men had already been stationed at regular intervals about two miles to windward, where they waited with their fire-sticks ready for the appointed signal.

A shrill whistle disturbed the silence. This signal was repeated at intervals to windward.

In a few minutes after the signal, a long line of separate thin pillars of smoke ascended into the blue sky, forming a band extending over about two miles of the horizon.

The thin pillars rapidly thickened, and became dense volumes, until at length they united, and formed a long black cloud of smoke that drifted before the wind over the bright yellow surface of the high grass.

The natives were so thoroughly concealed, that no one would have supposed that a human being beside ourselves was in the neighbourhood. I had stuck a few twigs into the top of the ant-hill to hide my cap; and having cut out a step in the side for my feet at the required height, I waited in patience.

The wind was brisk, and the fire travelled at about four miles an hour. We could soon hear the distant roar, as the great volume of flame shot high through the centre of the smoke.

The natives had also lighted the grass a few hundred yards in our rear.

Presently I saw a slate-coloured mass trotting along the face of the opposite slope, about 250 yards distant. I quickly made out a rhinoceros, and I was in hopes that he was coming towards me. Suddenly he turned to my right, and continued along the face of the inclination.

Some of the beautiful leucotis antelope now appeared and cantered towards me, but halted when they approached the stream, and listened. The game understood the hunting as well as the natives. In the same manner that the young children went out to hunt with their parents, so had the wild animals been hunted together with their parents ever since their birth.

The leucotis now charged across the stream; at

THE BRUTES WITH FIRE.

the same time a herd of hartebeest dashed past. I knocked over one, and with the left-hand barrel I wounded a leucotis. At this moment a lion and lioness, that had been disturbed by the fire in our rear, came bounding along close to where Molodi had been concealed with the luncheon. Away went Molodi at a tremendous pace! and he came rushing past me as though the lions were chasing him; but they were endeavouring to escape themselves, and had no idea of attacking.

I was just going to take the inviting shot, when, as my finger was on the trigger, I saw the head of a native rise out of the grass exactly in the line of fire; then another head popped up from a native who had been concealed, and rather than risk an accident I allowed the lion to pass. In one magnificent bound it cleared the stream, and disappeared in the high grass.

The fire was advancing rapidly, and the game was coming up fast. A small herd of leucotis crossed the brook, and I killed another, but the smoke had become so thick that I was nearly blinded. It was at length impossible to see; the roar of the fire and the heat were terrific, as the blast swept before the advancing flames, and filled the air and eyes with fine black ashes. I literally had to turn and run hard into fresher atmosphere to get a gasp of cool air, and to wipe my streaming eyes. Just as I emerged from the smoke, a leucotis came past, and received both the right and left bullets in a good place, before it fell.

The fire reached the stream and at once expired. The wind swept the smoke on before, and left in view the velvety black surface, that had been completely denuded by the flames.

The natives had killed many antelopes, but the rhinoceros had gone through their nets like a cobweb. Several buffaloes had been seen, but they had broken out in a different direction. Lieut. Baker had killed three leucotis, Abd-el-Kader had killed one, and had hit a native in the leg with a bullet, while aiming at a galloping antelope. I had killed five.

I doctored the native, and gave him some milk to drink, and his friends carried him home. This was a very unfortunate accident, and from that day the natives gave Abd-el-Kader a wide berth.

Most of the women were heavily laden with meat: the nets were quickly gathered up, and, with whistles blowing as a rejoicing, the natives returned homewards.

The women were very industrious, and never went

home empty-handed; but if some were unfortunate in their supply of meat, they gathered immense bundles of firewood, which they carried many miles upon their heads to their respective villages. . . .

The time passed very happily at Fatiko, and the fact of my joining with the natives in their sports added to the confidence already established.

I frequently went into their villages to smoke a pipe, and to chat with the people : this always pleased them, and the children generally crowded round me, as I never went empty-handed, but a few beads or other trifles were always forthcoming as presents.

Gimōro had been very unfortunate in losing his children when young, and I understood that the mortality was very great among all infants from two years old to five.

I attribute this to the absurd custom of public night nurseries. According to the population of the village, there are certain houses built upon pedestals or stone supports about three feet from the ground. In the clay wall of the circular building is a round hole about a foot in diameter; this is the only aperture.

At sunset, when the children have been fed, they are put to bed in the simplest manner, by being thrust headforemost through the hole in the wall, assisted, if refractory, by a smack behind, until the night nursery shall have received the limited number. The aperture is then stopped up with a bundle of grass if the nights are cool.

The children lie together on the clay floor like a litter of young puppies, and breathe the foulest air until morning, at which time they are released from the suffocating oven, to be suddenly exposed to the chilly daybreak. Their naked little bodies shiver round a fire until the sun warms them, but the seeds of diarrhœa and dysentery have already been sown.

It may be readily imagined that accidents frequently occur in the great hunts already described, as it is quite impossible to speculate upon the species of animal that may be driven into the net. A fine little lad of about eleven years old was killed by a leopard within a mile of my Fatiko station. The grass had been fired, and the animals instinctively knew that they were pursued.

The boy went to drink at a stream close to some high reeds, when a leopard pounced upon him without the slightest warning. A native who was close to the spot rushed up to the rescue, and threw his spear with such dexterity that he struck the leopard through the neck while it had the boy in its mouth, killing it upon the spot. The boy was immediately brought to me, but the lungs were lacerated, and he died during the night.

On another occasion five men were wounded (two fatally) by a lioness, which fought so gallantly that she at length escaped from her assailants with two spears in her body.

I was not present on that occasion, but I have frequently admired the pluck of the Shooli natives, who attack every animal with the simple hunting-spear, which of course necessitates a close approach.

On 30th December I went out with a few natives on the Fabbo road, simply to shoot in order to procure meat for the camp. We were about ten miles from the station, and the game was so wild on the open prairies that we had found it impossible to approach within shot. We had seen great numbers of the beautiful leucotis antelope (rather larger than a fine fallow buck), also hartebeest (*Antelope bubalis*), all of which had quitted the clean ground which had recently been burnt, and had retired to the high grass upon a long sloping undulation.

Among our natives were two men who were the owners of the grass; they therefore proposed that we should place the guns in position, while they should march up to windward, and fire the grass in the usual manner.

Lieutenant Baker was placed about 300 yards to my left, and Colonel Abd-el-Kader about 150 paces to my right. As we faced the high grass we had the ground clear at our backs, as the young herbage was just sprouting after the recent burning.

As usual, I was concealed by a large ant-hill, behind which, my two boys Sāat and Bellāal squatted with my spare guns. About 100 yards before me, in a slight hollow, the grass was quite green, as the depression had until lately held water. This rank herbage would of course stop the fire upon its arrival from the sloping hill-face. About forty yards from me the grass was high and dry.

About half an hour after the guns were posted we heard the whistles, and shortly after, the smoke rose in various places, until at last a crescent of fire spread over the hill. The wind was very light, therefore the fire travelled slowly, and the game advanced at an easy pace. I now heard shots upon my left at the extreme flank, where I had posted a few of the best shots of the " Forty Thieves," including Ferritch Ajōke.

I saw the game breaking covert in herds of several hundreds in that direction. Presently Abd-el-Kader had a shot upon my right, and I observed several antelopes bounding along upon the clear space in our rear.

I was not in luck, but I now saw a splendid buck leucotis walking quietly through the grass, and slowly descending the slope to the green hollow, which would bring him straight towards me should he keep this direction.

Just at that moment I saw a long yellow tail rise suddenly from the green hollow, and an instant later I saw a fine lion, with tail erect, that had evidently been disturbed by the advancing fire.

The lion was down wind of the buck leucotis, which was now close to the unseen enemy, and was just descending the bank which dipped into the green hollow : this would bring the antelope almost upon the lion's back. The two animals suddenly appeared to touch each other as the leucotis jumped down the bank, and the lion sprang to one side, apparently as much startled as the antelope, which bounded off in another direction. The lion now disappeared in the high grass, with the head towards my position.

I whispered to my boys not to be afraid should the lion appear close to us, and at the same time I took the spare gun from Bellāal, and laid it against the ant-hill to be in readiness. This was a breechloader, with buckshot cartridges for small antelopes.

In a few minutes I heard a distinct rustling in the

high grass before me. The two boys were squatting on the ground to my right.

Presently a louder rustling in the grass, within forty yards in my front, was followed by the head and shoulders of a large lioness, who apparently saw the two boys, and with her hazel eyes fixed she advanced slowly towards them.

Not wishing to allow a closer acquaintance, I aimed at her chest, and fired the "Dutchman."

The lioness rolled completely over, backwards, and three times she turned convulsive sommersaults, at the same time roaring tremendously; but to my astonishment she appeared to recover, and I immediately fired my left-hand barrel. At this she charged in high bounds straight towards my two boys.

I had just time to snatch up my spare gun and show myself from behind the ant-hill, when the lioness, startled by my sudden appearance, turned, and I fired a charge of buck-shot into her hindquarters as she disappeared in the high grass upon my right.

I now heard her groaning in a succession of deep guttural sounds, within fifty yards of me.

In a few minutes I heard a shot from Abd-el-Kader, and he shortly came to tell me that the wounded lioness, with her chest and shoulder covered with blood, had come close to his hiding-place; he had fired, and had broken her ankle-joint, but she was still concealed in the grass.

Shooli and Gimōro now came up with some of the natives, as they had heard the lion roar, and feared some accident might have happened.

These were very plucky fellows, and they at once proposed to go close up and spear her in the grass, if I would back them up with the rifles.

We arrived at the supposed spot, and after a search we distinguished a yellowish mass within some withered reeds.

Shooli now proposed that he should throw his spear, upon which the lioness would certainly charge from her covert and afford us a good shot, if the guns were properly arranged.

I would not allow this, but I determined to fire a shot at the yellow mass to bring her out, if every one would be ready to receive her.

Lieutenant Baker was on my right, with a double-barrelled express rifle that carried a No. 70 bullet. This minute projectile was of little use against the charge of a lion.

I fired into the mass at about twenty yards' distance.

The immediate reply was a determined charge, and the enraged animal came bounding towards us with tremendous roars. The natives threw their spears but missed her. Mr. Baker fired, but neither he nor a left-hand barrel from the " Dutchman " could check her. Everybody had to run, and I luckily snatched a breechloading No. 12 smooth-bore loaded with ball from a panic-stricken lad, and rolled her over with a shot in the chest when she was nearly in the midst of us.

She retreated with two or three bounds to her original covert.

I had now reloaded the " Dutchman," and having given orders that every one should keep out of the way, and be ready, I went close up to the grass with Shooli, and quickly discovered her. She was sitting up like a dog, but was looking in the opposite direction, as though expecting an enemy in that quarter.

I was within twelve yards of her, and I immediately put a bullet in the back of her neck, which dropped her dead.

In her inside we discovered a freshly-eaten leucotis calf, which had been simply divided by her teeth in lumps of about two pounds each. This was quite fresh, and my soldiers and the natives

CHARGE OF A LIONESS.

divided it among them as a *bonne-bouche*. Nasty fellows!

The day's sport had been:—One lioness killed by myself; one leucotis buck by Mr. Baker; one leucotis buck by Abd-el-Kader; two does of the same species by Ferritch Ajōke; and the natives had speared three calves. Total, one lioness and seven antelopes, *all* of which were to be eaten.

We reached home at 5.40 P.M., not having had time to eat anything since the preceding evening. The lioness measured nine feet six inches from nose to tail extremity.

As this work is simply an account of the principal events connected with the Khedive's expedition, I cannot afford space for many sporting incidents. Game was very abundant, and we generally kept the station well supplied; at the same time I gave large quantities of flesh to the natives.

I sometimes sent a party of my "Forty" to hunt, in which sport they took a great interest, and the practice with the rifle improved their shooting.

The natives throughout the country were perfectly happy and contented, but the women had been somewhat disturbed by the accounts they had received of our encounter with the lioness. They held a meeting in Gimōro's village.

On the following day both Gimōro and Shooli arrived at my public divan looking rather dejected.

They informed me that the women, having held a meeting, had arrived at the conclusion, "that the Pacha must not be allowed to go out hunting, as he might possibly be killed by a lion or a buffalo." "What would happen to us?" continued the women, "if any accident should befall our father? Would not the slave-hunters immediately return to the country and destroy us, simply because he had protected us? Do we not now sleep in peace? and were we not always awake at night before he came among us?"

The women decided that I was to be kept in the camp as a cojoor or talisman, and that the natives were not to lead me into danger of wild animals.

This declaration of the ladies of Fatiko could hardly be called *petticoat* government, as their total independence of attire precluded any reference to such a garment; but it was a distinct assertion of women's right to protect the person who had protected them. They were excellent people, and were always well cared for and kindly treated by the men.

My fort at Fatiko was within call of two large villages—those of Gimōro and the sheik of the country: during my sojourn of seven months, I never heard a woman scream, neither was there any domestic or civil disturbance.

There were no police required in that country; there were no pickpockets, as there were no pockets to pick—which was one advantage in favour of nudity. A London police magistrate would have died of *ennui;* the constables could not even have sworn to a case of intoxication, merely as a matter of form to afford him employment. There were no immoral females to disgrace the public streets; neither were there any beggars, vagrants, organ-grinders, or perambulators to worry, deafen, or upset you. My country was a picture of true harmony. We had no complex machinery of law; there was no such difficulty as an estate in Chancery; no Divorce Court, or cases of *crim. con.* that necessitated an appeal. Adultery would be settled by flogging respondent and co-respondent, with a judicial separation after the punishment.

I had no ecclesiastical difficulties; no High Church, Ritualists, Low Church, Broad Churchmen, philosophers, Wesleyans, Baptists, Presbyterians, Roman Catholics, Episcopalians, Independents, nor even a Jesuit or a descendant of Israel to bring discord into my harmonious tabernacle.

My troops were Mohammedans, without an opposing sect; therefore, for lack of opposition, they were lukewarm believers.

The natives believed in nothing.

The curious fact remained, that without the slightest principle of worship, or even a natural religious instinct, these people should be free from many vices that disgrace a civilized community. I endeavoured to persuade the most intelligent of the existence of a Deity who could reward or punish; but beyond this I dared not venture, as they would have asked practical questions, which I could not have explained to their material understanding.

1 extract *verbatim* from my journal the short entry of 31st December, 1872 :—

" The close of the year finds us, thank God, at peace in this country, with every prospect of prosperity."

CHAPTER XIII.

ARRIVAL OF M'TÉSÉ'S ENVOYS.

On 15th January, 1873, the sentry on the rock citadel reported a party arriving from the Unyoro road. Shortly after, the reports of guns were heard, and it was made known that envoys had arrived from M'tésé, the king of Uganda, together with an escort of natives, and two of my soldiers from Rionga. M'tésé's people were armed with guns.

The envoys were quickly ushered into the new divan, which was a circular, lofty building, twenty feet in diameter, neatly plastered, and painted light grey with a mixture of wood-ashes.

Ali Jusef, the principal envoy, was a native of Sishuaali, on the coasts of the Red Sea entrance, and the Indian Ocean. I had several officers who were natives of the same country, including the gallant Ferritch Agha and Said Agha: thus I had excellent interpreters.

The envoys were beautifully clean, in white Bombay cotton clothes, and they were quite civilized, and as intelligent as Europeans. They appeared to have a thorough knowledge of the route to India, and the various tribes along the eastern coast of equatorial Africa.

These people gave me much useful information; and I shall, as usual in this work, simply extract from my journal the exact entry made at the moment whenever I received geographical reports from the natives : thus I shall give to the public the unpolished statements precisely as I heard them ; upon which data theoretical geographers may form their own opinions.

"The envoys report, that from Ujiji (pronounced by them Uyéyé) you can travel by lake direct to Magungo, the lake being the M'wootan N'zigé.

"The Victoria N'yanza is called by two names, 'Sessy' or 'Kuréwé.' Although large, it is small in comparison with the M'wootan N'zigé."

There was no news of Livingstone ; but, according to my request from Masindi, M'tésé had sent everywhere in search of him, and he had forwarded my two letters addressed to him in different directions.

The king, M'tésé, had written me a letter expressing great friendship, and declaring that when the news of Kabba Réga's treachery had reached him, he had sent an army under General Congow, to be placed at my disposal.

This army was now quartered at Mashudi,[1] waiting for my orders. M'tésé begged me to visit him as soon as possible, as he only had one desire, *i.e.* "to see my face," and that he "did not wish for presents."

This was a model African potentate; at the same time I could not possibly visit him, as my term of service would expire upon the 1st of April.

I was much disappointed at this impossibility, as M'tésé can do more for Central Africa than any other potentate. He behaved well to Speke and Grant, and he had been very true to me.

On 11th February, fresh envoys arrived from M'tésé, including my old friend Waysooah, who was as usual dressed very carefully in Indian costume, with a handsomely-worked cotton robe.

M'tésé had written me another letter in Arabic, begging me to send him one of my soldiers as my representative, if I could not come personally.

[1] Two days' march from Rionga's island.

The road was now declared to be practically open between Fatiko and Zanzibar by means of M'tésé's friendship.

This excellent man, who was now a Mohammedan, and kept an Arab secretary, had already sent to Ujiji in search of Livingstone, according to my request, and his messengers had returned with the news, "that he had been at Ujiji, and had crossed the lake to the west; since which, nothing had been heard of him."

M'tésé's people were still in search of Livingstone. Ujiji was declared to be on the " M'wootan N'zigé," *i.e.* the Albert N'yanza.

I give this information exactly as I received it.

I now wrote a letter to Dr. Livingstone, of which the following is a copy :—

"Fort Fatiko,
("N. lat. 3° 1'; E. long. 32° 36',)
"*February* 13*th*, 1873.

" My dear Livingstone,

" M'tésé, the king of Uganda, has been searching for you, according to my instructions sent to him in June 1872.

" He also forwarded my letters to be given to you when met with.

" His envoys have now visited me at Fatiko, with

the report that M'tésé's messengers heard of you as having formerly been at Ujiji; but that you had left that station and crossed the Tanganyika to the west.

"Nothing more is known of you.

"I have sent a soldier with the envoys who convey this letter; he will remain with M'tésé. This soldier (Selim) was one of Speke's men, who travelled from Zanzibar to Cairo.

"M'tésé will take the greatest care of you. He has behaved very well to the government.

"Since I wrote to you in June, Kabba Réga treacherously attacked me with many thousand men.

"I thrashed him thoroughly, and I have set up Rionga, the old enemy of his family, who is now sheik of the government.

"M'tésé sent Congow with several thousand men to assist the troops.

"I trust, my dear Livingstone, that this letter may reach you. Do not come down the lake. It is now well known that the Tanganyika is the Albert N'yanza; both known as the great lake M'wootan N'zigé.

"A steamer will, I trust, be on the lake this year.

"Ever yours most sincerely,
"SAM. W. BAKER."

On 13th February, after a few days' pleasant sojourn at Fatiko, M'tésé's envoys returned to Uganda, accompanied by my representative, Selim, who although a private, was a very intelligent Suāchli; he had formerly accompanied Speke from Zanzibar. I gave Selim instructions to impress upon M'tésé the necessity of assisting Livingstone without a moment's delay.

It is interesting to remember, now that the great traveller is dead, that the arrangements I had made for his assistance would have secured his safety, and would have enabled him to pursue his geographical investigations northward, without the slightest risk or difficulty, beyond the bodily fatigue which is inseparable from African travel.

My letter was not only delivered by M'tésé's orders into the hands of Lieutenant Cameron, R.N. at Unyamyembi, but *M'tésé actually sent me his reply through the weary distance to Gondokoro!* This reply was received by my successor, Colonel Gordon, and was forwarded to the Khedive, as a proof of the effect of the expedition under my command, in opening *through postal communication* in the heart of Africa. People who are unacquainted with the difficulties of Africa cannot sufficiently appreciate this grand result. The intelligent king, M'tésé, should receive a present from our government, as a reward for having exerted himself to assist an English consul in distress. The small sum of £200, judiciously expended would procure trifles that would be treasures to M'tésé, and would do more to open up Central Africa to travellers than any other means.

I fear this will be forgotten, and that M'tésé will be neglected after this truly philanthropic effort to relieve an English traveller and CONSUL when in difficulty.

I wrote a letter thanking M'tésé for all that he had done, and assuring him that our country would be grateful to him for any assistance that he might render Livingstone. At the same time that I thanked him for his aid to myself, I begged he would recall his army from Unyoro, as my troops, although few, were strong, and that, having already defeated Kabba Réga, I required no assistance.

I sent General Congow a present of a sword, and a few articles to M'tésé, in return for a specimen of beautifully-dressed skins, sewn together as neatly as the work of a French glover. . . .

The time wore on in considerable anxiety concerning the party that I had sent to Gondokoro under Wat-el-Mek for reinforcements.

I had allowed them forty-two days for their

return to Fatiko with the cattle and troops, but no intelligence had been received of their movements from the week they had started. Fortunately the abundance of game in the neighbourhood had supplied the troops with meat.

At length, after ninety-three days' absence, news was brought that Wat-el-Mek and the troops were close at hand. Shooli had arrived at daybreak to say that a native had seen them on the previous evening on the north side of Shooa hill, about seven miles from Fatiko.

At 2.30 P.M., on 8th March, we distinguished the white uniforms ascending the plateau at the north end of the Fatiko plain; and shortly after, the main body emerged from among the rocks and foliage, and formed on the level ground. I at once distinguished with the telescope the lieutenant-colonel, Tayib Agha, upon his well-known powerful white horse.

My troops in full uniform went out to meet the reinforcements, which quickly marched up and formed on the level turf outside the fort upon the north side.

I rode out and inspected the troops.

Not one head of cattle had arrived!

The lieutenant-colonel, Tayib Agha, had made a sad mess of his command during the march. He had quarrelled with Wat-el-Mek; and simply because some of the native carriers had absconded in a portion of the Bari country named Moogi, he had set fire to the villages in revenge! This was in a country where I had established peace.

The Baris had attacked the troops, and had not only killed twenty-eight of our men, but had actually stripped the bodies, and possessed themselves of clothes, arms, and ammunition. They had also captured the cattle.

Although Tayib Agha had about 280 men he actually retreated, and dared not attack the natives to recover either the bodies of his men, or their muskets!

I at once determined to leave Major Abdullah as commandant at Fatiko, and to take Tayib Agha back to Gondokoro, as he was not fit for an independent command.

The immense delay in sending up the reinforcements had been occasioned by the long voyage from Khartoum.

When Wat-el-Mek had reached Gondokoro, the troops *had not arrived* from Khartoum; therefore he was obliged to wait.

When at length they did arrive, they had been *thirteen months* on the voyage from Khartoum to Gondokoro, and had passed the rainy season with the slave-traders in the camp of Kutchuk Ali on the Bahr Giraffe; this river they reported as navigable, owing to my canals, which had continued open.

It was the old story of delay and indolence, unless I was personally present to force them forward.

I had now 620 men, therefore I reinforced Rionga and the various stations. I thus garrisoned strongly Fatiko, Fabbo, and Paniadoli—the stockade opposite Rionga's island, in N. lat. 2° 6′.

The country of Unyoro was now completely in the grasp of Ali Genninar and Rionga. Unyoro extends to the south of the equator on the shores of the Albert N'yanza, where Kabba Réga, who was now lost, was supposed to be hiding.

On 14th March I drew out the following orders for Major Abdullah, who would remain as commandant of Fatiko:—

" 1. Observe the rules at present existing respecting sentries.

" 2. Observe the rules at present existing for cleanliness of camp.

" 3. Plant negheel grass on ramparts during the rainy season.

" 4. Clean out the fort ditch once every month.

" 5. Each company of troops is to cultivate corn and vegetables at the commencement of the rains.

"6. Each company to be exercised at musketry drill for one hour daily.

"7. All troops to be exercised at light-infantry drill for three hours on Mondays and Fridays, upon which days there will be no other work.

"8. The corn-tax is to be regularly collected, so that three months' supply shall be the minimum in the camp granaries.

"9. The bugle to sound the night alarm once every month, to accustom the men to night quarters.

"10. The troops to occupy their stations at general quarters, according to present practice.

"11. Banana plants to be introduced upon every opportunity from Magungo.

"12. Coffee-berries[1] to be sown in nursery-beds, when received from M'tésé.

"13. The old huts to be cleared away and replaced by new, constructed in lines similar to those in the south camp.

"14. No ivory to be purchased in exchange for cattle, but only in barter for goods.

"15. *No slaves to be either purchased or taken.*

"16. The bugle to sound 'Extinguish fires' at 8 P.M."

Having left everything in perfect order in the

[1] I had written to him for a supply of coffee-seed.

new central territory, I was ready to start for Gondokoro on 20th March.

I had been two years and five months without any news or communication with either Egypt or Europe when the post arrived with Wat-el-Mek. About 700 copies of the *Times* had arrived at once. We had been introduced to the Tichborne case; and of course had, at the earliest stage of the trial, concluded that the claimant was Arthur Orton. The news that is almost stereotyped in English newspapers gave us the striking incidents of civilization. Two or three wives had been brutally knocked about by their husbands, who had received only a slight punishment. A prominent divorce case; a few Irish agrarian outrages; a trial in the ecclesiastical court of a refractory clergyman; the smash-up of a few public companies, with the profitable immunity of the directors; a lady burnt to death; a colliery explosion: several hundred railway accidents, which induced me to prefer walking; the Communists had half destroyed Paris; republican principles were fast spreading through England; the Gladstone ministry would last for ever; some babies had been poisoned, and the baby-farmer had been hanged; deceased wives' sisters were to marry their disconsolate brothers; England was to pay a tribute to America (for the freaks of the *Alabama*); drunkenness was on the increase; ladies were to become our physicians; &c. I was almost afraid to return home; but as I had some friends and relations that I wished to see again, I left my little paradise, Fatiko, and marched for Gondokoro, accompanied by my good natives, Shooli and Gimōro.

After the absurd conduct and the defeat of Tayib Agha at Moogi, I fully expected to have to fight my way through; but upon arrival in that district the natives knew me, and we were not molested. They even sent me six cows which had been lost by Tayib Agha on the road during his unlucky march.

I had taken under my especial protection a number of Bari women and young girls whom Wat-el-Mek and Tayib Agha had pressed into their service to carry loads during their journey from Gondokoro to Fatiko. There can be no doubt that these poor creatures never would have been returned to their country, had I not delivered them; but seeing their condition upon their arrival at Fatiko, I had ordered them to accompany me, and to show me the position of their homes during the march.

On arrival at the broad dry bed of a stream about two days' march from Gondokoro, we halted beneath the shade of a large tree for breakfast. The women and children now approached, and hesitatingly declared that this was their country, and their villages were near. They evidently doubted my sincerity in restoring them, which hurt me exceedingly.

"Go, my good women," I exclaimed, "and when you arrive at your homes, explain to your people that you were captured entirely against my will, and that I am only happy to have restored you."

For a few moments they looked around them, as hardly believing the good news. In another instant, as the truth flashed across their delighted minds, they rushed upon me in a body, and before I had time for self-defence, I found myself in the arms of a naked beauty who kissed me almost to suffocation, and with a most unpleasant embrace licked both my eyes with her tongue. The sentries came to my assistance, together with the servants, who withstood the grateful crowd; otherwise both my wife and myself would have been subjected to this painful thanksgiving from the liberated Bari women.

Their freedom having been explained, we gave each a present of beads as a reward for the trouble they had undergone, and they went away rejoicing upon the road to their own homes.

We arrived at Gondokoro on 1st April, 1873,

AFFECTIONATE RESULTS OF A SUDDEN FEMALE EMANCIPATION.

Vol. ii p. 474.

without the slightest disturbance during the march. This was the exact day upon which my term of service would have expired, according to my original agreement with the Khedive.

I halted the troops about half a mile from Gondokoro, to allow them to change their clothes, when I observed with the telescope some of the Englishmen approaching. Several of my welcome countrymen at length arrived.

"Where is Mr. Higginbotham?" I asked, as I was eager to see my excellent chief engineer and friend.

There was a slight pause before the reply—"*He died on the last day of February!*"

I was quite overpowered with the dreadful news! Poor Higginbotham! who had been my right hand throughout the early portion of the expedition! He was a man who so thoroughly represented the character that we love to think is truly English, combining all energy, courage and perseverance. He was gone!

We marched into Gondokoro. Fourteen months had made a change for the worse. I had left the station with a neat ditch and earthwork; the environs had been clean. It was now a mass of filth. Bones and remnants of old clothes, that would have been a fortune to a rag-and-bone shop, lay scattered in all directions. The ditch was filled up with sand, and the fallen bank washed in by the heavy rains, as it had never been cleansed during my absence.

The guns fired a salute; Raouf Bey and the troops appeared in good health; and I was shown into poor Higginbotham's house on the cliff above the river.

A beautiful new steamer of 108 tons, built of steel, with twin screws, was floating on the stream. This was the work of my Englishmen, who had taken a pride in turning out the best results that Messrs. Samuda Brothers and Messrs. Penn & Co. could produce.

I went on board to inspect the new vessel directly after breakfast. She had been admirably constructed, and being devoid of paddles, she would be able to glide through the narrow channels of the Bahr Giraffe like a fish.

Although the station was dirty and neglected, I must do Raouf Bey justice in acknowledging that he had paid much attention to the gardens on the islands, which were producing so abundantly that the troops received rations of vegetables daily.

Raouf Bey had also shown determination, and had accepted great responsibility in shooting a soldier for desertion during my absence.

THE NEW STEAMER 108 TONS, 20-HORSE POWER, THE "KHEDIVE."

It appeared that the reinforcements lately received from Khartoum were merely slaves that had been sold to the government, and had rapidly been trained for soldiers. Many of these people had originally come from the White Nile, therefore they were disposed to desert upon the first opportunity.

A considerable number had deserted, with their arms and ammunition. They had also stolen Raouf Bey's guns and rifles from his house, and had absconded to Belinian. Raouf Bey had called upon the Belinian to give up the deserters; but the Belinian natives had only replied to the summonses by making nightly demonstrations of attack against the station of Gondokoro, which had rendered sound sleep impossible for the last month. Raouf Bey had accordingly invaded Belinian, and had fought a pitched battle, in which the deserters who had joined the Baris fired upon the troops. Two of them were killed.[1]

I immediately sent for Allorron, who had now become a faithful sheik of the government. He confessed all his sins, and of course laid the whole blame upon Abou Saood, who he declared had

[1] On this occasion, the Baris being well supplied with muskets and ammunition, the troops of Raouf Bey suffered considerable loss.

deceived him, and instigated him against the government. I did not wish for any explanations upon the truth of which I could not rely. I therefore ordered him to go at once to Belinian, and inform the natives that, unless they gave up the deserters, I should pay them a visit with the "red shirts," who had now returned with me from Fatiko. At the same time I promised him three cows if he succeeded.

In a few days he returned with two deserters. These men were tried by court-martial, and having been found guilty, they were shot in the presence of the regiment.

Order and discipline were at once restored among the troops.

Now that I had returned with the "Forty Thieves," the natives of Belinian no longer visited the camp at night, but the country shortly became quiet and peaceful.

Wat-el-Mek, who had accompanied me from Fatiko, returned with reinforcements and a herd of cattle to his district. I parted with regret with my good men Shooli and Gimōro, to whom I gave some useful presents.

On 10th April I commenced a new fort with ditch and earthwork around the magazines, but the sandy

GONDOKORO OR ISMAILÏA.

SACRED TO THE MEMORY OF EDWIN HIGGINBOTHAM: DIED AT GONDOKORO, 28TH FEBRUARY, 1873.

nature of the soil will cause much trouble during the heavy rains.

I ordered Mr. Marcopolo to take stock, together with an Egyptian officer (Foād Effendi), of everything that remained within the magazine, and to take a receipt for his stores. This task occupied nearly a month.

The Englishmen had carefully packed everything that belonged to the No. 3 steamer and machinery, and had stowed her in a magazine that was given in charge of an officer, who gave a receipt for the contents.

Everything was ready by the 25th May for our return homewards. I erected a monument of red brick coated with pitch over my poor friend Higginbotham's grave, within my garden, near the spot where the missionaries were formerly buried.

We started on the 26th, having taken a farewell of my gallant "Forty Thieves," many of whom showed much emotion at parting. As I walked down the line of troops when I took official leave, my old soldiers broke the bounds of discipline by shouting: "May God give you a long life! and may you meet your family in good health at home!"

I felt a choking sensation in saying good-bye; but we were soon on board, and the steam was up.

The new steamer, the *Khedive*, took us in tow, and we travelled rapidly down the stream towards home in old England.

Although I had written the most important letters to the Khedive and to his minister in October 1871, I had, to my amazement, *not received one word in reply* by the post that had arrived from Egypt. I had apparently been looked upon as a dead man that did not require a letter. It appeared that my existence was utterly ignored by the Egyptian government, although I had received my letters in due course from England.

On arrival at the Bahr Giraffe, we found that the canals which I had formerly cut were much improved by the force of the stream. Although these passages were narrow, they had become deep, and we progressed with comparatively little trouble.

On 7th June, three sails were reported ahead on the horizon. We pushed forward with some curiosity, but unfortunately a sudd of vegetable rafts had closed the passage for a short distance, which required about an hour to clean; this delayed the chase.

That evening, as we had stopped for the night

at a spot known as the "Three Dubbas," we heard a woman's voice from the high grass addressing us in an imploring tone. I immediately sent a boat to make inquiries, as one of our native girls understood the language.

It appeared that the woman had the small-pox, and she had been therefore thrown into the high grass, and abandoned by the vakeel of the three vessels that we had observed in the distance. She described these vessels as being crowded with slaves.

I gave the unfortunate creature a supply of six days' food, together with a cooking-pot and some firewood, but I dared not introduce so horrible a disease as the small-pox among our party. She was thus left alone upon the dubba.[1]

On 8th June we steamed along, towards the tall masts and yards of the three vessels which we perceived upon the horizon.

The intricacies of the narrow channel were such that we did not overtake the slavers until sunset.

We then anchored for the night in a lake, while I sent a boat forward into the canal occupied by the three vessels to order the vakeel of the company to visit me immediately.

[1] At this season native fishermen visited the dubba, therefore she was most probably discovered on the following morning.

In a short time the boat returned with my old acquaintance Wat Hōjoly, the vakeel of the Bohr station belonging to Abou Saood.

I had always liked this man, as he was generally straightforward in his manner. He now told me, without the slightest reserve, that during my absence in the south, several cargoes of slaves had passed the government station at Fashoda by bribing the governor; and that he would certainly have no difficulty, provided that I did not seize him. He confessed that he had 700 slaves on board the three vessels, and according to orders that he had received from his master, Abou Saood, he was conveying them to their destination, a few days south of Khartoum, on the White Nile; at which point they could either march overland to the west *viâ* Kordofān, or to the east *viâ* Sennaar; whence they could pass unmolested to the Red Sea or to other markets.

The small-pox had broken out among the slaves, several of whom had died.

I was most thoroughly disgusted and sick at heart. After all the trouble and difficulties that we had gone through for the suppression of the slave trade, there could be no question of the fact that Abou Saood, the great slave-hunter of the White Nile, was supported by some high authority behind the scenes, upon whom he could depend for protection.

This was apparently the last act of the drama, in which the villain of the piece could mock and scoff at justice, and ridicule every effort that I had made to suppress the slave trade. His vessels were actually sailing in triumph and defiance before the wind, with flags flying the crescent and the star, above a horrible cargo of pest-smitten humanity, in open contempt for my authority; which Wat Hōjoly had been carefully informed did not extend north of Gondokoro.

I asked this plain-spoken agent whether he was quite sure that he could pass the government station? "Oh yes," he replied, "a little backsheesh will open the road; there is nothing to fear."

I was then informed by the same authority that Abou Saood had gone to Cairo to appeal to the Khedive's government against my proceedings, and to represent his TRADE as ruined by my acts.

This was a remarkable disclosure at the end of the last act; the moral of the piece was thus explained before the curtain fell. The slave-hunter *par excellence* of the White Nile, who had rented or farmed from the government, for some thousands sterling per annum, the right of TRADING in countries which did *not* belong to Egypt, was now on the road to protest against my interference with his *trade,* this innocent business being represented *by three vessels with seven hundred slaves that were to pass unchecked before the government station of Fashoda.*

I told Wat Hōjoly that I did not think he would succeed upon this occasion, but that I should certainly not lay hands upon him.

I had not received replies to my letters addressed to the Khedive, therefore I was determined not to exert physical force again; at the same time I made up my mind that the slave vessels should not pass Fashoda.

On the following morning we passed ahead, and the fearful stench from the crowded slave vessels reeking with small-pox followed us for quite a mile down the wind.

On 19th June, at 3.30 P.M., we reached Fashoda. The governor at once came on board to receive us.

This officer had been only recently appointed, and he appeared to be very energetic and desirous to assist me in the total extinction of the slave-trade. I assured the governor (Jusef Effendi) that I had entirely suppressed it in my territory, and I had also suppressed the river trade in 1870; but if the authorities were determined to connive at this abomination, I had been placed in a disgracefully false position, and had been simply employed on a fool's errand.

Jusef Effendi assured me that it would be impossible for vessels to pass Fashoda with slave cargoes now that he represented the government, as the Khedive had issued the most positive orders within the last six months against the traffic in slaves; therefore such instructions must be obeyed.

I did not quite see that obedience to such orders was absolutely necessary, as the slave trade had been similarly prohibited by proclamation in the reign of the late Saïd Pacha, but with no permanent effect.

There were two fine steamers lying at Fashoda, which had formed a portion of the fleet of six steamers that I had sent up from Cairo some years ago to tow my flotilla up the White Nile. This was the first time that I had ever seen them.

I now told Jusef Effendi that he would be held responsible for the capture of Abou Saood's three vessels, together with the 700 slaves; at the same time, it would be advisable to allow them to arrive at Fashoda before their capture should be attempted; as the fact of such an audacious contempt of law would at once implicate the former governor as having been in the habit of connivance.

Jusef Effendi appeared to be in earnest. He was an active and highly intelligent Circassian who held the rank of lieutenant-colonel.

My servants had discovered by chance, when in communication with Wat Hōjoly, that Salim-Wat-Howah, who had been one of the principal ringleaders in the attack upon the troops at Fatiko, and had subsequently knocked down Suleiman and possessed himself forcibly of the ammunition from the magazine, with which he and his party had absconded, was now actually concealed on one of the three slave-vessels. I had taken care not to mention his name to Wat Hōjoly, lest he should be left at some station upon the route, and thus escape me.

I now gave a written order to Jusef Effendi to arrest him upon the arrival of the slave vessels, and to send him to Khartoum in irons.

The news of Abou Saood's personal appeal to the government at Cairo was confirmed by the best authorities at Fashoda.

On 21st June I took leave of Jusef Effendi, and upon the 28th, at 11 A.M., we arrived at the large tree which is within five miles of Khartoum, by the short cut across the neck of land to the Blue Nile.

I stopped at this tree, and immediately wrote to Ismaïl Yagoob Pacha, the new governor of Khartoum, to telegraph *instantly* to Cairo to arrest Abou Saood.

I sent this note by a faithful officer, Ferritch Agha, with positive orders that he was to deliver it into the hands of Ismaïl Pacha.

This order was immediately carried out before any people in Khartoum had an idea of my return. Had I at once steamed round the point, some friend would have telegraphed my arrival to Abou Saood in Cairo, and he might have gone into concealment.

In the afternoon we observed a steamer rounding the distant headland at the point of junction of the two Niles. She rapidly approached, and in about half an hour my old friend, Ismaïl Yagoob Pacha, stepped on board my diahbeeah, and gave us a hearty welcome.

There was no letter either from the Khedive or Cherif Pacha, in reply to the important communications that I had written more than two years ago.

Ismaïl Yagoob Pacha was a friend of eight years' date. I had known him during my first expedition to the Nile sources as Ismaïl Bey, president of the council at Khartoum. He had lately been appointed governor, and I could only regret that my excellent friend had not been in that capacity from the commencement of the expedition, as I should have derived much assistance from his great energy and intelligence.

Ismaïl Yagoob Pacha is a Circassian. I have observed that all those officers who are superior to the average in intellect and general capacity belong to this race. The Circassians are admirably represented in Cherif Pacha, who is well known and respected by all Europeans in Egypt for his probity and high intelligence; and Riaz Pacha, who was lately the Minister for Public Instruction, is a Circassian much beloved and respected.

Ismaïl Yagoob had commenced a great reform in the Soudan, in his endeavour to put down the wholesale system of bribery and corruption which was the ruin of the country. He had also commenced a great work, according to the orders he had received from the Khedive, to remove the sudd or obstruction to the navigation of the great White Nile.

The Khedive had given this important order in consequence of letters that I had written on 31st August, 1870, to the Minister of the Interior, Cherif Pacha, and to his Highness direct on 8th October,

1871, in which communications I had strenuously advocated the absolute necessity of taking the work in hand, with a determination to re-establish the river in its original navigable condition.

Ismaïl Yagoob Pacha had been working with a large force, and he had succeeded in clearing, according to his calculations, one half of the obstruction, which extended for many miles:

There was no actual difficulty in the undertaking, which was simply a matter of time and steady labour.

The immense force of the main stream, thus confined by matted and tangled vegetation, would materially assist the work, as the clearing was commenced from below the current.

The work would become lighter as the head of the sudd would be neared.

A curious accident had happened to Ismaïl Pacha by the sudden break-up of a large portion of the sudd, that had been weakened by cutting a long but narrow channel.

The prodigious rafts of vegetation were hurried before the stream like ice-floes, and these masses having struck against a line of six noggurs, the vessels were literally swept away and buried beneath the great rafts, until they capsized and disappeared for ever in the deep channel.

Late in the evening Ismaïl Pacha took leave and returned in his steamer to Khartoum. We had enjoyed a long conversation, and I felt sure that the Soudan and Central Africa would quickly feel the benefit of Ismaïl Yagoob Pacha's administration, as he combined great energy and determination with nine years' experience of the requirements of his province.

On 29th June the new steamer, the *Khedive*, rounded the point at full speed with our diahbeeah in tow.

All the population of Khartoum thronged to the banks and the new quay to witness the arrival of the extraordinary steamer that travelled without paddles, and which had been constructed by the Englishmen at Ismailïa (Gondokoro).

The troops were in order, and as the *Khedive* drew alongside the quay we were warmly welcomed by Ismaïl Yagoob Pacha with the usual formalities.

A few days later, a steamer arrived from Fashoda with the three vessels in tow belonging to Abou Saood, which had attempted to pass the government station with more than 600 slaves on board, about 100 having died of the small-pox since I had left the Bahr Giraffe. The small-pox was still raging on board, therefore the vessels were taken to the north bank of the Blue Nile and placed in quarantine.

As the guard passed by with prisoners, I recognized my friend the vakeel, Wat Hōjoly, in irons. The unfortunate man had found a new governor at Fashoda instead of his old acquaintance; thus he did *not* pass free; as I had anticipated.

Walking next to the vakeel, heavily ironed, with his wrists secured in a block of wood similar to stocks, came the cream of ruffians, Salim-Wat-Howah, nailed at last.

This villainous-looking fellow was afterwards tried before the medjeldis, or tribunal, and by overpowering evidence he was found guilty of having first threatened to attack Major Abdullah in the government camp of Fatiko; and secondly, with having actually given the orders to fire, and having fired himself on 2nd August, 1872, when we had been treacherously attacked by Abou Saood's company.

I spoke in favour of Wat Hōjoly, as he had otherwise behaved well towards the government, and he was simply carrying out the orders of his master, Abou Saood.

It had been the usual custom in the Soudan to spare the employers, who were the most responsible parties, but to punish the small fry, such as vakeels, and the reis, or captains of vessels.

Ismaïl Pacha had made great improvements in Khartoum, and he had completed the new government house that had been commenced by his predecessor, Moomtazz Pacha, who was also a most intelligent Circassian. He had likewise made a great change by converting a large open space into a public garden, where it was his intention that the military band should play every evening for the amusement of the people.

Steam irrigation works were also commenced on the north side of the Blue Nile for the cultivation of cotton.

After a few days at Khartoum we took leave of our good friend, Ismaïl Yagoob Pacha, and started for Cairo by steamer.

I had left my two boys, Sāat and Bellāal, with Ismaïl Pacha, to be instructed either as musicians or soldiers, the latter profession being their great ambition. There was already a school established for the education of the more intelligent negro boys that might be liberated from the slave-traders.

Upon our arrival at Berber, I found a considerable improvement in the country. The Arabs were beginning to return to the fertile banks of the river, and to rebuild their sakeeyahs or water-wheels. This change was the result of a wise reform instituted by the Khedive, in dividing the Soudan into provinces, each of which would be governed by a responsible and independent official, instead of serving under a governor-general at the distance of Khartoum.

Hussein Khalifah was now the governor of Berber. He was the great Arab sheik of the desert who had so ably assisted Mr. Higginbotham in transporting the machinery and steamer sections by camels from Korosko to Berber across the great Nubian desert, for a distance of about 400 miles. The Arabs were much pleased at his appointment as governor, as he was one of their race.

In starting from Berber for Souakim, I had the great misfortune to lose by death one of my excellent Englishmen, David Samson. He had been ailing for some time, and the intense heat of July was more than he could endure in riding across the desert. Poor Samson died on the first day's march, and I had his body conveyed to Berber, where it was buried in the Coptic cemetery with every mark of respect.

This was a sad termination after a journey of nearly four years and a half, when he was on the hopeful road towards home.

We were nearly wrecked during the voyage from Souakim to Suez, as the engine of the sloop-of-war was out of repair. We then changed to another steamer, which carried away the cap of her rudder during a heavy sea and fresh northerly gale. Fortunately our English shipwrights were on board, and Lieutenant Baker, R.N., knew his work; thus we escaped drowning on a coral reef, which would assuredly have been our fate had we been left to the ignorance of the officers and crew.

We reached Cairo on 24th August at 4.30 P.M. On 25th I had the honour of presenting myself to his Highness the Khedive, to explain the large chart of his new territory that I had annexed in Central Africa.

I received from his Highness the Imperial order of the Osmanie, 2nd class, as a token of his approbation of my services. I had already had the honour to accept from his hands the order of the Medjidie, 2nd class, before I had started upon my mission. His Highness the Khedive now conferred upon Lieutenant Baker the order of the Medjidie, 3rd class.

I handed the botanical collection to his Highness the Khedive, which had been carefully prepared throughout the journey by Lady Baker. Unfortunately more than 300 specimens of plants had been destroyed by the conflagration at Masindi. The botanical specimens, together with samples of the fibres, skins, and the salt of the new territory, were ordered to be forwarded to the Vienna Exhibition.

The Khedive expressed his determination to judge Abou Saood by a special tribunal, composed of Cherif Pacha, Nubar Pacha, and Ismaïl Pacha, the Minister of Finance. I handed seventeen documents to Nubar Pacha, with evidence sworn to upon the Koran before witnesses, and properly sealed by Wat-el-Mek, Suleiman, the sheiks of the country, Major Abdullah, and others, against Abou Saood, charging him with various crimes, including treason in having given the orders that his Fatiko company should fire at me and the government troops. I took a receipt for these important documents.

I had also brought up several of the "Forty Thieves" as *viva-voce* witnesses, in addition to Lieutenant Baker, R.N., Lieutenant-Colonel Abd-el-Kader, Captain Mohammed Deii, and two servants, Suleiman and Mohammed Haroon. Thus all the evidence was in official order:—

1. 26th Jumay Owal, 1289, report of Major Abdullah (commandant of Fatiko): threatening conduct of Abou Saood's vakeels during my absence.

2. 28th Jumay Owal, 1289, the declaration of the regimental officers of Fort Fatiko.

3. 6th October, 1872, 1st Shabān, 1289, the declaration of the vakeels of Abou Saood (Wat-el-Mek and Suleiman), that they had acted according to orders received from Abou Saood.

4. 26th Jumay Owal, 1289, Major Abdullah's declaration against Abou Saood and his company at Fatiko.

5. 12th Jumay Ocher, 1289, declaration of the chiefs of the country, complaining of the kidnapping of women and children, massacres, &c., committed by Abou Saood and his companies.

6. Declaration of Abou Saood's men, containing declarations of Mohammed, Wat-el-Mek, and Besheer Achmet, that Abou Saood gave the order to fire at the Pacha and the government troops. Two large papers.

7. 29th Jumay Owal, 1289, letter from Abou Saood from Fabbo.

8. 29th Rebi Owal, 1289, Major Abdullah's reasons for not detaining Suleiman, and for not arresting Abou Saood.

9. 2nd Jumay Acher, 1289, letter from Abou Saood, Fatiko.

10. 29th Jumay Owal, 1289, order for confiscation of Fatiko after the attack made upon the troops.

11. Letter from officers of Fabbo.

12. 4th Regeb, 1289, report of Abou Saood's escape with government guns, &c.

13. 22nd Jumay Acher, 1289, letter from vakeel Suleiman, Fabbo.

14. 3rd November, 1872, *procès-verbal*; declaration of Suleiman and Abou Saood's people.

15. 1st Shabān, 6th October, 1873, copy of orders to Wat-el-Mek.

16. Mohammed the dragoman's declaration.

17. Wat-el-Mek's declaration that he and his people were always paid by Abou Saood in slaves, and that the conduct of the stations was according to his orders. Also that he had obeyed Abou Saood's orders in attacking me at Fatiko.

I insisted upon appearing personally as accuser against Abou Saood, but I was begged to return to England, and to confide him to the hands of the authorities, as his Highness declined to bring him before the public tribunal.

His Highness the Khedive had the kindness to confer promotion upon my faithful officer, Lieutenant-Colonel Abd-el-Kader, to the rank of kaimakām; and Captain Mohammed Deii to the rank of saccolāssi. He also granted a reward to the soldiers who had fought the battle of Masindi, and marched through eight days of ambuscades to Foweera.

A gratuity of a month's pay was given to every English engineer and mechanic, and they started for England.

After a delay of about six weeks in Egypt, his Highness afforded us a gracious and hospitable occasion of taking leave of himself and the young princes, to all of whom I am indebted for much courtesy and kindness.

CHAPTER XIV.

CONCLUSION.

THE foregoing chapters will have afforded a sufficiently distinct view of the expedition to enable the public to form their own opinion of the position of the slave trade.

It will have been seen that I had acted directly against that infamous traffic from the commencement of the work, according to the explicit instructions of my firman: at the same time I had made due allowances for the ambiguous position of the traders upon the White Nile, who were actual tenants of the government. Thus I never visited the interior of their camps, nor had I disturbed their stations in any way, but I had passed them as without the pale of my jurisdiction; at the same time I gave the vakeels due warning, and entirely prevented them from making use of the river as the highway of the slave trade.

In 1870, while I was camped at Tewfikeeyah, I entirely suppressed the river traffic; but the fact of my having overtaken three vessels with 700 slaves belonging to Abou Saood at the close of the expedition, on my return towards Khartoum, must be a damning proof of complicity on the part of certain government officials.

Thus it is plain that, while I was endeavouring to do my duty, others who should have been supporting me were actually supporting the slave-hunters. No people could have had the absurd audacity to attempt the passage of the river in front of Fashoda—a government station, garrisoned by two regiments, and provided with two steamers—unless they were in league with the officials.

My personal interference has rendered the slave trade of the White Nile impossible so long as the government is determined that it shall be impossible. At the close of the expedition, the higher officials had been changed, and the country appeared to be in good hands. The governor of Fashoda, Jusef Effendi, had captured the slave vessels of Abou Saood according to my instructions. Ismaïl Yagoob Pacha had been appointed governor of Khartoum. Hussein Khalifah, the Arab desert sheik, was governor of Berber, and various important changes had been made among the higher authorities throughout the Soudan, which proved that the Khedive was determined upon reform.

One grand and sweeping reform was absolutely necessary to extinguish the slave trade of Central Africa, and this I had the honour to suggest:—" That all the present existing traders or tenants of the White Nile should be expelled from the country, precisely as I had expelled them from the territory under my command." The government would then assume the monopoly of the ivory trade of the White Nile, and the natives would in a few years be restored to confidence.

So long as the so-called traders of Khartoum should be permitted to establish themselves as independent piratical societies in the Nile Basin, the slave trade would continue, and the road through Darfur and Kordofān would be adopted in place of the tabooed White Nile.

Should the White Nile companies be totally disbanded, the people now engaged must return to their original agricultural pursuits in the Soudan, and their labour would tend to an increase of the revenue, and to the general prosperity of the country.

I have already published so much on the subject of the slave trade in " The Albert N'yanza," that I fear to repeat what I have before so forcibly expressed. I have never changed my original opinions on this question, and I can only refer the public to page 313, vol. ii., of that work, whence I take the following extract :—" Stop the White Nile trade; prohibit the departure of any vessels from Khartoum to the south, and let the Egyptian government grant a concession to a company for the White Nile, subject to certain conditions, and to a special supervision. . . .

. . . " Should the slave trade be suppressed, there will be a good opening for the ivory trade ; the conflicting trading parties being withdrawn, and the interest of the trade exhibited by a single company, the natives would no longer be able to barter ivory for cattle ; thus they would be forced to accept other goods in exchange. The newly-discovered Albert Lake opens the centre of Africa to navigation. Steamers ascend from Khartoum to Gondokoro in lat. 4° 55'. Seven days' march south of that station the navigable portion of the Nile is reached, whence vessels can ascend direct to the Albert Lake ; thus an enormous extent of country is opened to navigation, and Manchester goods and various other articles would find a ready market in exchange for ivory at a prodigious profit, as in those newly-discovered regions ivory has a merely nominal value.

"Beyond this commencement of honest trade I cannot offer a suggestion, as no produce of the country except ivory could afford the expense of transport to Europe.[1]

"If Africa is to be civilized, it must be effected by commerce, which, once established, will open the way for missionary labour; but all ideas of commerce, improvement, and the advancement of the African race that philanthropy can suggest, must be discarded until the traffic in slaves shall have ceased to exist.

"Should the slave trade be suppressed, a field would be opened, the extent of which I will not attempt to suggest, as the future would depend upon the good government of countries now devoted to savage anarchy and confusion." . . . .

"Difficult and almost impossible is the task before the missionary. The Austrian mission has failed, and their stations have been forsaken; their pious labour was hopeless, and the devoted priests died upon their barren field."

By a reference to that work also,—"The Albert N'yanza"—it will be seen that in the present expedition I carried out the plans that I had proposed at the termination of my first journey.

[1] The proposed railway from Cairo to Khartoum will overcome this obstacle.

I have no doubt that missionaries will take advantage of the change that has resulted from the suppression of the slave trade and the establishment of a government. At the same time, should they attempt a settlement in the neighbourhood of Gondokoro, they must be prepared with an inexhaustible stock of patience when dealing with the Baris.

The Madi and Shooli tribes would be found tractable and more capable of religious instruction. It is my opinion that the time has not yet arrived for missionary enterprise in those countries; but at the same time a sensible man might do good service by living among the natives, and proving to their material minds that persons do exist whose happiness consists in doing good to others. The personal qualifications and outfit for a single man who would thus settle among the natives should be various. If he wished to secure their attention and admiration, he should excel as a rifle shot and sportsman. If musical, he should play the Highland bagpipes. He should be clever as a conjuror, and be well provided with conjuring tricks, together with a magic lantern, magnetic battery, dissolving views, photographic apparatus, coloured pictorial illustrations, &c., &c. He should be a good surgeon and general doctor, &c.; and be well supplied with drugs, remembering that natives have a profound admiration for medical skill.

A man who in full Highland dress could at any time collect an audience by playing a lively air with the bagpipes, would be regarded with great veneration by the natives, and would be listened to when an archbishop by his side would be totally disregarded. He should set all psalms to lively tunes, and the natives would learn to sing them immediately.

Devotional exercises should be chiefly musical.

In this manner a man would become a general favourite; and if he had a never-failing supply of beads, copper rods, brass rings for arms, fingers, and ears, gaudy cotton handkerchiefs, red or blue blankets, zinc mirrors, red cotton shirts, &c., to give to his parishioners, and expected nothing in return, he would be considered a great man, whose opinion would carry a considerable weight, provided that he only spoke of subjects which he thoroughly understood.

A knowledge of agriculture, with a good stock of seeds of useful vegetables and cereals, iron hoes, carpenter's and blacksmith's tools, and the power of instructing others in their use, together with a plentiful supply of very small axes, would be an immense recommendation to a lay missionary who should determine to devote some years of his life to the improvement of the natives.

In the magnificent equatorial portions of Africa there is a great field for British enterprise, and much might be accomplished by lay missionaries, who would at the commencement avoid theological teaching, until by other means they should have gained an ascendency over the minds of the natives. By slow degrees confidence might be established; and much may be effected by good example. . . .

The geography of Central Africa, that has made great strides within the last few years, will now be rapidly extended. The fact of an established government under the direction of my able successor, Colonel Gordon, R.E., is sufficient to assure the most sceptical that the future will be rich in geographical discoveries. It is hoped that the steamer which I carried up to Gondokoro will be transported to the Albert N'yanza early in the year 1875. It is impossible to foretell the result of steam communication on the great inland sea M'wootan N'zigé.

I do not love to dwell upon geographical theories, as I believe in nothing but actual observation; but I cannot quite disbelieve my native informants, who assured me that they had travelled to Ujiji by canoe from Chibero on the Albert N'yanza.

By the latest intelligence from Lieutenant Cameron, dated Ujiji, 28th February, 1874, the mean of many observations for altitude of the Tanganyika Lake, taken with mercurial barometer, aneroids, and boiling-water thermometers, gives 2,573 feet above the sea-level.

The corrected altitude of the Albert N'yanza, taken by me at Vacovia, N. lat. 1° 14′, March 14, 1864, is 2,720. The uncorrected or the absolute observation of the instrument was 2,448.

Whenever Lieutenant Cameron shall return home, it will be interesting to observe the results of his corrected observations, as they already so closely approach the level of the Albert N'yanza.

As the Khedive's expedition under Colonel Gordon will shortly have the advantage of a steamer on the Albert Lake or M'wootan N'zigé, the question of a connection between the two lakes will be definitely settled.

When that question shall have been resolved, geographers must turn their attention to the great river Sobat, which is by far the most important affluent of the Nile.

Although during my recent expedition I have not travelled over much new ground, the advantages to geography are considerable, owing to the professional observations of Lieutenant Baker, R.N., to whom I confided the entire charge of the topographical department. Some slight corrections have been made in observations for longitude taken during my first expedition; and as every place is now rigidly attested on the map, that portion of Central Africa is most thoroughly investigated, and the astronomical positions of all principal points and stations are incontestable.

The fact of this thorough exploration, and the establishment of the Egyptian government, now afford a firm base for all future travellers. The good work of one man can be carried on by his successor. Formerly it was impossible to render the necessary support to an explorer in Central Africa. A distant country cannot plunge into war with a savage potentate of the equatorial Nile Basin because he has either captured an explorer or devoured a missionary.

There was only one step practicable if the improvement of Africa were to be attempted. Egypt was the only country that could form a government by the extension of her frontier to the equator. This would insure the safety of future travellers where hitherto the life of an individual had no guarantee.

This annexation is now effected, and our relations with the Khedive assure us that the heart of Africa will be thrown open to the civilizing influence of the North.

When the railway shall be completed from Cairo to Khartoum, there will be direct communication by rail and river. Countries that are eminently adapted for the cultivation of cotton, coffee, sugar, and other tropical productions will be brought within the influence of the commercial world, and the natives, no longer kidnapped and torn from their homes, will feel the benefits of industry, as they now feel the blessings of protection.

It is well known that the greatest difficulties lie in the first footsteps of a great enterprize; but those difficulties are overcome, and patience and perseverance will at length perfect the good work. The impression of civilization must be gradually and slowly engraved upon Central Africa, and those who work in this apparently hopeless undertaking must not be appalled by the difficulties of the task.

In the share that I have taken during nine years passed in Africa, I have simply represented one of those atoms of which Great Britain is composed. I deeply regret that personally I have not had the honour of serving my Queen, but I trust that indirectly I have worked out that principle, which England was the first to initiate, expressed in the word "Freedom," which, we maintain, is the natural inheritance of man.

Mingled with the regret that I was not in the service of her Majesty, is the pleasure that I feel in testifying to the able manner in which the Royal Navy was represented, throughout a long and trying expedition, by Lieutenant Julian Alleyne Baker, R.N. This energetic young officer rendered me the greatest assistance, and has left a vivid impression on the minds of the natives, and of the Egyptian troops, of the activity, and the straightforward, manly character that has always distinguished British sailors in whatever duty they have had to perform, whether on sea or land.

I return my acknowledgments of the faithful and courageous services of Lieutenant-Colonel Abd-el-

Kader, and other officers who accompanied me through every difficulty with patience and devotion.

I also thank Mr. Marcopolo, my intelligent and trustworthy secretary and chief storekeeper, at the same time that I acknowledge the services of those industrious English engineers and mechanics who so thoroughly supported the well-known reputation of their class by a determination to succeed in every work that was undertaken. Their new steamer, the *Khedive*, remains upon the White Nile an example of their energy and capability.

Lastly, I must acknowledge the able assistance that I have received, in common with every person connected with the inland expedition, from my wife, who cared for the sick when we were without a medical man, and whose gentle aid brought comfort to many whose strength might otherwise have failed. During a period of fourteen months, with a detachment of 212 officers and men, exclusive of many servants and camp-followers, *I only lost one man from sickness*, and he was at an out-station.

In moments of doubt and anxiety she was always a thoughtful and wise counsellor, and much of my success through nine long years passed in Africa is due to my devoted companion.

The foundation for a great future has been laid: a remote portion of the African race hitherto excluded from the world's history has been brought into direct communication with the superior and more civilized races; legitimate trade has been opened; therefore, accepting commerce as the great agent of civilization, the work is actually in progress.

Fortified posts extend to within two degrees of the equator. The alliance with M'tésé, the king of Uganda, enabled me not only to communicate by letter (addressed to Livingstone) in the distant country of Unyamyembé, but a reply was sent by Lieutenant Cameron, together with large presents of ivory, to me at Gondokoro,[1] as I have been informed by a letter from Colonel Gordon.

The Khedive of Egypt, having appointed Colonel Gordon, R.E., has proved his determination to continue the work that was commenced under so many difficulties. The Nile has been opened to navigation; and if the troubles that I encountered and overcame shall have smoothed the path for my able and energetic successor, I shall have been well rewarded.

[1] The letter and the ivory from M'tésé were received by Colonel Gordon.

The first steps in establishing the authority of a new government in a tribe hitherto savage and intractable were of necessity accompanied by military operations. War is inseparable from annexation, and the law of force, resorted to in self-defence, was absolutely indispensable to prove the superiority of the power that was eventually to govern. The end justified the means.

At the commencement of the expedition I had felt that the object of the enterprise—" the suppression of the slave trade,"—was one for which I could confidently ask a blessing.

A firm belief in Providential support has not been unrewarded. In the midst of sickness and malaria we had strength; from acts of treachery we were preserved unharmed; in personal encounters we remained unscathed. In the end, every opposition was overcome: hatred and insubordination yielded to discipline and order. A paternal government extended its protection through lands hitherto a field for anarchy and slavery. The territory within my rule was purged from the slave trade. The natives of the great Shooli tribe, relieved from their oppressors, clung to the protecting government. The White Nile, for a distance of 1,600 miles from Khartoum to Central Africa, was cleansed from the abomination of a traffic which had hitherto sullied its waters.

Every cloud had passed away, and the term of my office expired in peace and sunshine. In this result, I humbly traced God's blessing.

FINIS.

After my departure from Egypt, Abou Saood was released, and was appointed assistant to my successor.

APPENDIX.

THE fact quoted at the end of the concluding chapter respecting the release of Abou Saood became known to me when the manuscript was almost completed. The astonishment that I felt will doubtless be shared by the public, who will draw their own conclusions.

It is useless to shut the eyes to the support thus openly given to the greatest slave-hunter of the White Nile.

It will be interesting to refer to the instructions that I had received from the Khedive in the firman which granted me the necessary powers for the command:—

"Considering the savage state of the people who inhabit the countries of the White Nile;

"Considering that neither government, nor law, nor security exists in those countries;

"Considering that humanity necessitates the suppression of the slave-hunters, *who are to be found there in great numbers* &c. &c. . . . ."

. . . It will be seen that the firman commences with an admission that the tribes are savage; that no security exists; and that the slave-hunters are in great numbers.

The curious anomaly is presented, that "the slave-hunters who are to be found there in great numbers" were all subjects and *tenants of the Egyptian government!* Thus the government expedition under my command was to suppress the Arab companies who farmed the right of trading by an annual rent paid to the governor-general of the Soudan.

Without any exception, every White Nile trader was a tenant of the Soudan government: thus the government was in the position of a participator in illegal profits.

This painful fact, coupled with the positive instructions that I had received, will account for the intrigues and opposition of the Egyptian public.

My orders, signed by the Khedive, continue thus:—

"An expedition is organized to subdue to our authority the countries situated to the south of Gondokoro;

"*To suppress the hunting of slaves,*" &c. &c.

I was thus commanded to annex the country which was already farmed out to slave-hunters!—and "to suppress the hunting of slaves," which was to ruin the tenants of the government!

Is it possible to conceive a greater anomaly? or a house more completely divided against itself?

I do not attempt to explain this apparently hopeless mystery. We have to search somewhere for sincerity.

If the slave-traders had been punished by the government at the close of the expedition, the effect upon the White Nile companies would have been positive. Instead of this, we find that after a long expedition to suppress the hunting of slaves, the chief slave-trader, Abou Saood, remains in the ascendant!

Since the completion of my manuscript, I have heard that the slave trade of the White Nile revived after my departure from the country! We have seen that I overtook three vessels, with 700 slaves, on the return voyage, that were about to pass Fashoda. The re-appearance of the slave

APPENDIX.

trade since my departure is an unquestionable proof that in spite of the Khedive's orders the authorities are determined to uphold this abominable traffic; and I refer with regret to page 312 in vol. ii. of "The Albert N'yanza":—

"Egypt is in favour of slavery. I have never seen a government official who did not in argument uphold slavery as an institution absolutely necessary to Egypt."

This was written in 1866, and the fact is corroborated in 1874.

In the career of Abou Saood, it will have been seen that he is first introduced as a tenant of the Soudan government, who farmed the right of trading (*i.e.* slave-trading) from the Soudan governor, who had *no right* to any lands upon the White Nile beyond the Shillook.

Thus the Soudan government and the slave-trader are discovered in close connection at the opening of the book, sharing profits from the spoil of a country that belonged to neither.

The second appearance is the arrival of Abou Saood at Gondokoro with 1,400 head of cattle, which he had captured in defiance of my authority, from the Shir tribe. This act caused the massacre of the government detachment at the Shir station.

The third appearance is in the capture of three vessels belonging to Abou Saood, with 600 slaves, on the way from his Bohr station, *towards Khartoum*, at the close of the expedition.

The last appearance is the appointment of Abou Saood to a post in the present expedition!

Thus the great slaver of the White Nile is rewarded.

In spite of the assurance that I received from the Khedive and from Nubar Pacha that he should be fairly judged upon the evidence that I produced, the prisoner was released.

It is not improbable that Abou Saood may succeed Colonel Gordon in the command of the expedition to "*suppress the slave trade.*" The government may require black troops for the army. The new territory has added some millions of subjects to the Khedive; these will be liable to the law of conscription. Abou Saood would be an excellent recruiting officer in Central Africa, as the kidnapping of slaves has been a useful apprenticeship.

The support given to Abou Saood at the close of the expedition, corroborates the suspicions that I had always entertained concerning the connivance of government officials at the slave trade.

We have already seen that Kutchuk Ali, one of the greatest slave-hunters of the White Nile, had been appointed by Djiaffer Pacha to command the government expedition on the Bahr Gazal.

We can therefore readily understand that Abou Saood, who has already been rewarded, was supported in his intrigues throughout the expedition. If he was supported by a contract with the government at the commencement, and also rewarded at the end, it is fair to suppose that he was supported throughout.

Although I had written most important letters to the Khedive, and also to his minister, Cherif Pacha, on 8th October, 1871, which necessitated a reply, I never received an answer. I had reported the conduct of Abou Saood in having captured herds of cattle from the Shir. I had also reported the conduct of my regimental officers in having purchased slaves in large numbers. I had also represented in severe terms the conspiracy of the officers to abandon the expedition, and I had begged for an immediate reply.

From that day I never received any written communica-

APPENDIX.   519

tion from the Khedive or his ministers during my command in Central Africa. Thus no notice was taken either of the piratical acts of Abou Saood, or of the conspiracy of the officers.

A few extracts from the valuable work of Dr. Schweinfurth will throw a light upon the spirit which animated the authorities, all of whom were incensed at my having presumed to understand the Khedive's orders literally respecting the suppression of the slave trade.

In page 485, vol. ii., he writes:—"The ill-feeling and smothered rage against Sir Samuel Baker's interference nurtured by the higher authorities, breaks out very strongly amongst the less reticent lower officials. In Fashoda, and even in Khartoum, I heard complaints that we (the Franks) were the prime cause of all the trouble, and if it had not been for our eternal agitation with the Viceroy, such measures, would never have been enforced."

In page 477, vol. ii., he continues:—" Notwithstanding that Sir Samuel Baker was still on the upper waters of the river, the idea was quite prevalent in all the seribas, that as soon as the 'English Pacha' had turned his back upon Fashoda (the government station in the Shillook country), the mudir (governor) would relapse into his former habits, and levy a good round sum on the head of every slave, and then let the contraband stock pass without more ado. But for once the seriba people were reckoning without their host. The mudir had been so severely reprimanded by Baker for his former delinquencies, that he thought it his best policy, for this year at least, to be as energetic as he could in his exertions against the forbidden trade."

In page 470, vol. ii., Dr. Schweinfurth writes:—" I knew that Sir Samuel Baker was upon the Upper Nile, and did not doubt that his presence would have the effect of making the government take the most strenuous measures against any import of slaves."

Page 429, vol. ii.:—" Before Sir Samuel Baker's expedition put a stop to it altogether, the slave trade that was carried on down the river was quite insignificant compared to the overland traffic." "For years there has been a public prohibition against bringing slaves down the White Nile into Khartoum, and ever and again stronger repressive measures have been introduced, which, however, have only had the effect of raising the land traffic to a premium; but as a general rule, the Egyptian officials connive at the use of this comparatively unimportant channel of the trade, and pocket a quiet little revenue for themselves by demanding a sum varying from two to five dollars a head as hush-money."

In page 429, vol. ii.:—"The expedition of Sir Samuel Baker has stopped this source."

In page 410, vol. ii., Dr. Schweinfurth writes:—" Already had Sir Samuel Baker, with praiseworthy energy, commenced scouring the waters of the Upper Nile, and by capturing all slave-vessels and abolishing a large 'chasua' belonging to the mudir (governor) of Fashoda, had left no doubt as to the earnestness of his purpose," &c.

In page 83, vol. i.:—"Beyond the true eastern shore, the Dinka are said to be settled in extensive villages, and at that time still furnished an inexhaustible supply of slaves to the marauding expeditions of the garrison of Fashoda. In 1870 Baker succeeded in putting an end to this disorder, the knowledge of which penetrated to the most remote tribes."

The evidence of so trustworthy a traveller as Dr. Schweinfurth is exceedingly valuable, as he was in the Western Nile districts at the time that I was actively engaged; thus he had opportunities of witnessing the results of my interference, and the hostility exhibited by the authorities. He is simply in error concerning the importance of the slave trade of the river, which he much underrates, as will have already been seen by the fact of 700 slaves being stowed away upon only three vessels belonging to Abou Saood.

These vessels, that were captured by my orders at Fashoda, on their way towards Khartoum, were an example of the truth foretold by the traders with whom Dr. Schweinfurth was travelling in the west—"that as soon as the English Pacha had turned his back upon Fashoda, the governor would relapse into his former habits, and levy a good round sum on the head of every slave, and then let the contraband cargo pass without more ado."

There were always well-known slave routes through Kordofān, but these channels became of extreme importance when I rendered the slave traffic of the river impossible.

It is quite unnecessary to write more on the subject of the slave trade. I believed that the Khedive of Egypt was sincere when he gave me the orders to suppress this horrible traffic; and I trust, from the simple and straightforward description of the expedition, that the world will acknowledge that I did my duty, at the same time that I exhibited the utmost leniency towards the ruffianly lessees of the Soudan government.

I still believe that the Khedive is sincere at heart in wishing to suppress the slave trade, but he requires unusual moral courage to enter the lists single-handed against Egyptian public opinion.

Abou Saood was the incarnation of the slave trade. I begged that he might be tried before the Medjildis or public tribunal in Cairo in my presence. The Khedive declined to bring him before the public council, but offered to try him by a special and *secret* tribunal.

The greatest slave-hunter of the White Nile WAS REWARDED!

MISSIONARY LABOUR.

My opinion has been frequently asked on this subject, and many have endeavoured to persuade me that a rapid change and improvement of the natives may be effected by such an agency. I cannot resist by argument such fervent hopes; but if good and capable men are determined to make the attempt, they may now be assured of peace and security at Gondokoro, where they will have the advantage of the good name left by the excellent but unfortunate members of the late Austrian mission.

GEOGRAPHY.

I have not changed my opinions that have already been expressed in "The Albert N'yanza," except that, from the native testimony, I presume there must be a channel which connects the Tanganyika with the Albert N'yanza. This channel may easily have escaped the notice of Dr. Livingstone and Mr. Stanley when skirting the reedy northern shores of the Tanganyika lake.

Without a guide, it would be a work of much time and difficulty to discover the true channel among the labyrinth-like inlets that characterize the vast beds of floating water-grass.

Many years ago, when at Magungo, on the Albert N'yanza, I could not at first believe that the raft-choked entrance of the Victoria Nile in apparently dead water was indeed the mouth of that important river. My subsequent experience in the marshy and lacustrine Bahr Giraffe has confirmed my impressions of the extreme difficulty of deciding upon the non-existence of a channel until after a lengthened investigation.

I cannot conceive that the Lualaba of Livingstone can be included within the Nile Basin. Livingstone decided the level of the Tanganyika lake to be within 72 feet of my level of the Albert N'yanza. With the same instruments he determined the altitude of the Lualaba to be lower than the Albert N'yanza, thus showing the impossibility of a connection between that river as an affluent with the lake.

I will not presume to assert that the Lualaba is a source of the Congo, as I have a strong objection to geographical theories or assertions unless proved by actual inspection; but if Livingstone's observations for altitude are correct, it is impossible that the Lualaba can be connected with the Nile.

Dr. Schweinfurth's discovery of the Wéllé river flowing towards the west, between the 3rd and 4th deg. N. lat., is a clear proof that no river can be running from the south to the north-east towards the Nile Basin, otherwise the Wéllé river would be intersected.

My friend, Djiaffer Pacha, the former governor-general of the Soudan, having originally been an admiral in the Egyptian navy, was highly scientific, and a great geographer. He was of opinion that the sources of the Nile could not possibly be south of the equator. I heard him explain his reasons in a most emphatic manner to a select circle of admiring Beys, who bowed down to his superior learning and intelligence. He argued that the idea of the Nile sources being to the south of the equator militated against common sense. "Some people," he said, "are so opinionated that they persist in their belief in the southern sources; but I will prove to you that such a theory must be the result of ignorance. You all know, my friends, what is meant by a 'globe'?" As none of his hearers had ever seen one, they remained silent.

"A globe, my friends, is a sphere which represents the true figure of the earth. If you will take a spherical body in your hands, and draw a line around it at the exact centre, you will find that it represents two inclines from that centre, or equator; one of which tends to the north, the other to the south.

"You will readily understand that a river cannot run uphill" ("hear, hear" from the audience); "therefore a man of only moderate capacity will be convinced of the correctness of my theory, that the sources of the Nile cannot be south of the equator. If the sources were south, they would run down towards the south, and follow the inclination of the globe. *It would therefore be impossible that the water should run up the hill from the south to cross the equator, and then start down the northern inclination of the globe* to reach Egypt and the Mediterranean."

Djiaffer Pacha's geographical lecture perfectly satisfied his hearers, who exclaimed "Sahhé" (it is true), and they wondered that no man except their own governor-general had before discovered this palpable fact in physical geography!

The Egyptian ex-admiral's science was a warning against an indulgence in theories.

In page 186, vol. ii., Dr. Schweinfurth[1] writes:—"Its course [the Lualaba], indeed, was towards the north; but Livingstone was manifestly in error when he took it for a true source of the Nile, a supposition that might have some semblance of foundation, originating in the inexplicable volume of the water of Lake M'wootan (Albert N'yanza), but which was negatived completely as soon as more ample investi-

[1] "The Heart of Africa."

gation had been made as to the comparative level, direction, and connection of other rivers, especially of the Wéllé."

Although Dr. Schweinfurth was unprovided with astronomical instruments, we may place thorough reliance in the integrity and ability of this traveller, who has taken the greatest pains to arrive at true conclusions. I am quite of his opinion, that the Wéllé is outside the Nile Basin, and drains the western watershed.

In a letter from Dr. Livingstone addressd to Sir Bartle Frere, dated Lake Bangweolo, 27th Nov., 1870, he writes:—
"The Tanganyika, whose majestic flow I marked by miles and miles of confervæ and other aquatic vegetation for three months during my illness at Ujiji, is, with the lower Tanganyika, discovered by Baker, a riverine lake from twenty to thirty miles broad."

It is thus clear that Livingstone considered that the Tanganyika and the Albert N'yanza were one water. On 30th May, 1869, dated Ujiji, he writes to Dr. Kirk:—
"Tanganyika, N'zigé Chowambé (Baker?) are one water, and the head of it is 300 miles south of this."

"The majestic flow" of confervæ remarked by Livingstone on the Tanganyika is beyond my comprehension, if that vast lake has no outlet at the north.

In Livingstone's letter of 27th Nov., 1870, he writes:—
"Speke's great mistake was the pursuit of a foregone conclusion. When he discovered the Victoria N'yanza he at once leaped to the conclusion that therein lay the sources; but subsequently, as soon as he and Grant looked to the N'yanza, they turned their backs on the Nile fountains. Had they doubted the correctness of the conclusion, they would have come west into the trough of the great valley, and found there mighty streams, not eighty or ninety yards, as their

White Nile, but from 4,000 to 8,000 yards, and always deep."

I was surprised that Livingstone could make such an error in quoting Speke's White Nile from the Victoria N'yanza as eighty or ninety yards in width! At M'rooli, in latitude N. 1° 37″, I have seen that magnificent river, which is at least *a thousand yards* in width, with a great depth. I have travelled on the river in canoes, and in the narrowest places, where the current is naturally increased, the width is at least 300 yards.

From my personal experience I must strenuously uphold the Victoria Nile as a source of enormous volume, and should it ever be proved that the distant affluents of the Tanganyika or the M'wootan N'zigé are the most remote, and therefore the nominal sources of the Nile, the great Victoria N'yanza must ever be connected with the names of Speke and Grant as one of the majestic parents of the Nile Basin.

Latterly, when speaking of the Lualaba, Livingstone writes to Sir Henry Rawlinson :—" The drainage clearly did not go into Tanganyika, and that lake, though it probably has an outlet, lost all its interest to me as a source of the river of Egypt."

We are, therefore, completely in the dark concerning the flow of water from the Lualaba south of the equator, and of Schweinfurth's Wéllé north of the equator, but both these large rivers were tending to the same direction, north-west. The discovery of these two rivers in about the same meridian is a satisfactory proof of the western watershed, which completely excludes them from the Nile Basin. If the Tanganyika lake has no communication with the Albert N'yanza, the old Nile is the simple offspring of the two parents—the Victoria and the Albert lakes.

When the steamer that I left at Gondokoro in sections

APPENDIX. 527

shall be launched upon the Albert N'yanza, this interesting question will be quickly solved.

Early in November 1871, when I was on the Nile south of Regiāf, I noticed the peculiar change that suddenly took place in the river. We were then in N. lat. 4° 38″, below the last cataracts, where the water was perfectly clear and free from vegetation, with a stream of about three and a half or four miles per hour.

Suddenly the river became discoloured by an immense quantity of the *Pistia Stratiotes,* of which not one plant was entire.

This aquatic plant invariably grows in either dead water or in the most sluggish stream, and none existed in the part of the river at N. lat. 4° 38″.

I examined many of the broken plants, which, instead of floating as usual on the surface, were mingled in enormous quantities with the rushing waters. None were rotten, but they had evidently been carried down the numerous rocky waterfalls which occupy the interval between N. lat. 3° 34″ and 4° 38″, and were thus bruised and torn asunder.

The extraordinary influx of damaged aquatic plants continued for many days, and unmistakably denoted the rise in the level of the Albert N'yanza at that season (say 1st Nov.). Above the falls, in N. lat. 3° 32″, there is very little current in the broad deep Nile; and in about N. lat. 3° this river is several miles in width, with no perceptible stream. In those propitious calms the *Pistia Stratiotes* grows in vast masses along the shores, and the annual rise of the lake creates a current which carries the plants towards the cataracts, and consequent destruction.

By this sign I conclude that the maximum of the Albert N'yanza would be during the month of November.

Languages.

The following list of words will afford a fair example of the differences in language of the various tribes between Gondokoro and the equator:—

	Loboré.	Bari.	Shooli.	Unyoro.
A fowl	Ă-ōō.	Chŏkŏrē.	Gwéno.	Ŭnkōkō.
A mat	Găllăcă.	Térō.	Kabōōné.	—
Flour	Ărăfōō.	Bōlŏ.	Mōcha.	Obsănŏ.
Fire	Arsi.	Kēmang.	Māi.	Moora.
Water	Yēē.	Fēēum.	Pee.	Māizi.
Milk	Léh.	Léh.	Chāk.	Amăttăi.
A cow	Tee.	Kitāng.	Deāng.	Inté.
A bull	Mōnikō.	Mōni.	Tū-ān.	—
A dog	Orké.	Diong.	Gunoah.	—
Rain	Yēē.	Koodoo.	Kcrt.	Injooré.
The sun	Yetăkăli.	Narlong.	Tschen.	Musānné.
A chief	Orpi.	Măttăt.	Ruort.	Mătōngăli
A sheep	Kăbeelo.	Kabisho.	Ramo.	Imbūzi.
A goat	Indree.	Keené.	Dēāll.	Imbūzi.
The moon	Īmbāh.	Yārfăh.	Dooé.	Quézi.
The stars	Beebi.	Kātchikoo	Lakori.	Nynērzi.
Flesh	Isăh.	Lŏkŏrē.	Rengo.	—
Dhurra (corn)	Āsīh.	Kēēmăk.	Gyah.	—
A basket	Evōch.	Soodah.	Adooku.	—
Beads	Meeoh.	Sooksook.	Teko.	Unguānzé.
Coracan Eleusine	Loqué.	—	Kāāl.	Būrrŏi.

		Unyoro.		Unyoro.
A tree	Bisālé.	Halt	Indēēndă.
Far off	Arrāiée.	Go away	Tāisa Gĕnda.
Near	Aiēe.	Come here	Igghia.
Not far	Ămpi.	Sit down	In-kărră-hānzé
A house	Ĕngōōi.	Get up	Im-mōōkka.
Plantains	Bitōki.	A man	Moosegga.
Beans	Kōli.	A woman	Mookăzzé.
Butter	Măggită.	A girl	Miss-sooki.
A canoe	Obwāto.	A boy	Um-wana.
A paddle	Engāiee.	A thief	Mōōsŭmă.
A mountain	Orsōzi.	Fish	{ Lubāri or Ĕnchŏa.
The earth	Intăkă.		
The sky	Iggŏhr.	Wood	Bītī.
A road or path	Mŭhāmla.	Eggs	Yōōli.
Go on	Togĕndi.		

Domestic Animals.

It is a singular fact that, although the domestic ox, sheep, and fowls are found everywhere among the negroes of Central Africa, there is no trace of the original stock among the wild animals of the country. The question arises—where did they come from?

Dogs are domesticated, and are used by the natives in their hunts. Those of Central Africa are miserable pariahs, but they are nevertheless much prized by their owners.

After the attack at Fatiko by the slave-hunters, which resulted in the dispersion of their party, upwards of 170 dogs became houseless. The natives asked my permission to capture them, and, having spread their hunting-nets, they drove the dogs as they would wild animals, and daily secured a great number, which they trained to hunt the calves of antelopes and the great grass-rat (*Aulacodus Swindernianus*).

Negroes have no sympathy with the young of wild animals, and I have never seen a pet animal or bird in their villages. Although I offered two cows for every young elephant they might catch, I never could prevail upon them to spare the little ones. Five were speared ruthlessly in one day, within two or three hours' march of Fatiko. A negro is never seen without his spear, and he finds the greatest pleasure in sticking it into either something or somebody.

Diseases.

Small-pox is prevalent. Cholera rarely attacks the country, but it is known. Dysentery is very common in the White Nile districts, but it is rare in the highlands. This complaint is generally fatal at Gondokoro. Great caution should be used, and impure water avoided. Marsh fever is the general complaint of the low ground, but is rare in the highlands of Fatiko and Unyoro.

I have never met with typhoid fevers in Central Africa, although they are common at Khartoum.

Measles, whooping-cough, scarlatina, croup, diphtheria, are quite unknown.

Blindness is only the result of extreme age, and is very rare. I never saw a case of mania, nor have I ever met more than one idiot in Central Africa. The brain appears to be exercised as a simple muscle of the body, and is never overstrained by deep thought or by excessive study. There are no great commercial or parliamentary anxieties; no struggles to keep up appearances and position in society against the common enemy, "small means;" no hearts to break with overwhelming love; but the human beings of Central Africa live as animals, simply using the brain as a director of their daily wants. Thus in their simple state they never commit suicide, and never go mad. Their women never give birth to cripples or monsters, as the sympathetic uterus continues in harmony with the healthy brain.

I have seen only two dwarfs. These were in Unyoro, one of whom was described by Speke (Kimenya): he is since dead. The other was at the court of Kabba Réga, named Rakoomba. We measured this little fellow, who was exactly three feet and half an inch in height, at the age of about eighteen years.

The teeth are remarkable throughout Central Africa. I have examined great numbers of skulls, and I never found a decayed tooth. Many tribes extract the four front teeth of the lower jaw. The bone then closes, and forms a sharp edge like the jaw of a turtle.

Mammalia.[1]

The principal animals and birds in the Shooli country are:—

	Native name.
Gazella dama	Lajooar.
Nanotragus hemprichianus	Amoor.
Cervicapra leucotis	Teel.
Cervicapra ellipsiprymna	Apoolli.
Cervicapra arundinacea	Oboor.
Alcelaphus bubalis	Poora.
Tragelaphus scriptus	Rōda.
Hippotragus Bakeri	Aboori.
Camelopardalis giraffa	Ree.
Phacochœrus Æliani (Rüpp) (Wart-hog)	Kool.
Bos caffer	Joobi.
Elephas Africanus	Létch.
Rhinoceros bicornis	Oomooga.
Felis leo	Lobōhr.
Felis leopardus	Quātch.
Wild dog, probably (*Lycaon pictus*)	Orara.
Jackal	Roodi.
Hyœna crocuta	Lalūha.
Manis Temminckii	Mooāk.
Hystrix sp.	Chō.
Viverra genetta	Gnongé.
Felis caracal	Quorra.
Herpestes striatus	Juang.
Struthio camelus	Oodo.
Leptoptilus crumenifirus	Kicoom.
Hyrax sp.	Dooka.
Aulacodus swindernianus, or great reed-rat	Neeri.
Eupodotes sp.	Apōdo.
Numida meleugris (?)	Owéno.
Francolinus sp. (?)	Awéri.

The zebra exists in the Shooli country, but is very rare. Hippopotami are to be found in the Asua river.

On the borders of the White Nile we find the *Cervicapra megaceros* and the beautiful *Damalis Senegalensis,* which I

---

[1] Mr. Sclater, of the Zoological Society of London, has furnished me with the scientific names of the antelopes and other mammals.

had supposed was a new species when I first secured it on the banks of the Bahr Giraffe.

Nothing new has been actually discovered during the expedition, and there can be nothing existing as an animal that is not well known to the natives, with whom I constantly associated; therefore there is little hope of unknown species, excepting the wild dog known by the Shooli as "Orara."

The botanical collection, made entirely by Lady Baker, was handed to the Khedive of Egypt, therefore I regret that I cannot describe it.

Liberated Slaves.

Upon arrival at Gondokoro with our party, we were shortly visited by the Bari father of little Cuckoo, who had travelled seven hundred miles with us. In a year and a half Cuckoo had grown immensely, and, being in a good suit of clothes, he was with difficulty recognised by his savage-looking parent, who had parted with him as a naked, ash-smeared little urchin of between six and seven years old.

I am sorry to say that Cuckoo did not meet his father with an affectionate embrace, but he at first positively refused to go with him; and when compelled to accompany him as a prodigal son and wanderer, he dug his knuckles into his eyes and began to cry. Poor little Cuckoo knew that the days of beef and good cooking had passed away. He expressed his determination to run away from his father and to return to us; but as his home was on the west bank of the Nile, we never saw little Cuckoo again.

The boys and young women whom I had liberated from the slave-hunters, and who had acted as domestic servants, were well cared for at the close of the expedition, and I secured them situations with well-known respectable families in Cairo and Alexandria. Amarn, the Abyssinian boy, who in intelligence had been far in advance of the negro lads, accompanied his mistress to England at his express request, where he is now regularly installed in our own household. The ulcerated leg, from which he had suffered for two years in Africa, was soon cured by the kind attention of the surgeons of St. George's Hospital, shortly after his arrival in London.

A Few Hints.

I shall give the following hints as they occurred to me, and as I noted them down at the time when in Africa:—

Medicine Chest.—Should be of teak, covered with zinc, with copper edges and corners. The bottom should be first covered externally, to enable the wet to drain off without touching the wood. The expensive canteens purchased of Messrs. Silver and Co., although covered with metal on the top and sides, had no metal beneath; thus they were a prey to damp and insects.

All bottles in medicine chest should have numbers *engraved* on the glass to correspond with an index painted on the inside of the lid. Insects and damp quickly destroy gilding or ordinary paper labels.

Seidlitz powders and all effervescent medicines should be packed in wide-mouthed, stoppered bottles, but never in papers.

Matches.—Bryant and May's " Victoria Matches " will stand the damp of the tropics beyond all others.

Tarpaulins.—Should be true mackintosh; but no other preparation of india-rubber will stand the heat of the tropics. No. 2 canvas painted is better than any preparation of tar, which sticks when folded together.

All tarpaulins should be 12 feet square, with large metal eyelet holes and strong lines. If larger, they are too heavy.

Bottles—All wine or liquor bottles should have the necks dipped in bottle-wax thickly. Metallic capsules will be bitten through and the corks destroyed by cockroaches.

Milk.—Crosse and Blackwell's "liquid cream" is excellent. That of the Anglo-Swiss Company was good at the commencement, but it did not keep sweet after two years.

Shoes and Boots.—Shoes are better than laced boots, as the latter give much trouble. The soles should not be too thick, and should be studded with sharp nails. Two pairs of long, brown leather boots to reach above the knee are useful for riding. All shoes should be kept in light canvas bags, tightly tied at the mouth to protect them from insects.

Dry Stores.—Should all be hermetically sealed, and great care should be observed in soldering the tin cases. This is frequently neglected, and the result of careless soldering is ruin to all biscuits, flour, sago, macaroni, &c.

Ammunition.—All cartridges should be taken from England loaded; and for private use they should be hermetically sealed in boxes containing one hundred each if small, or fifty if large.

Five hundred snider cartridges, in teak boxes lined with soldered tin, weigh 64lbs. each, and can be carried on the journey by one native.

Casks of wood are unsuited for African travel; small beetles perforate them. Galvanized iron flattened kegs are useful for carrying water through the desert. For camels which carry four casks they should contain ten gallons each; for mules, eight gallons.

Plates, &c.—All plates, cups, saucers, dishes, &c., should be enamelled on metal.

Saucepans, kettles, &c.—Should be copper.

Drinking cups should be silver, to contain one pint or more, and to fit into each other.

A tankard with a very strong hinge to the lid is invaluable to keep out flies, but the servants will probably wrench the lid off.

Boxes.—Do not attempt to spare money in boxes. They should be of the stoutest block tin, or of copper, well painted. Tradesmen are apt to do you in the hinges.

All boxes should lock with *brass* locks. Shun padlocks. A master-key should open all your boxes, even should you have a thousand. Each box should have a pierced metal label slung with wire upon each iron handle. Painted numbers quickly wear out.

My boxes measured *twenty-two* inches long, twelve inches deep, fourteen broad. These were quite invaluable throughout the expedition.

Guns and rifles must depend upon individual tastes. Never possess such an antiquated affair as a muzzle-loader.

Hollow bullets are quite useless for thick-skinned animals. I like No. 10 rifles, with chambers to contain a cartridge with ten drachms No. 6 powder. Such a rifle must weigh fifteen pounds to shoot accurately.

Axes.—All axes, picks, hoes, &c., should have *oval holes*, but *nearly* circular, to receive the handles. Natives will break any civilized method of fitting.

Every soldier should carry a very small, long-bladed, but narrow hatchet of soft steel.

Feathers.—Preserve all feathers of game, taking care to strip them from the stems, for making pillows.

The large wing-feathers of geese, bustards, &c., make dusting-brushes, fans, quill toothpicks, &c.

Hale's rockets.—Those which explode are invaluable. Six and three-pounders are large enough, and are handy to carry.

Norton's pumps were of no use except in sandy or gravelly soil, and they did not equal my expectations.

Blue lights are quite invaluable if fitted with percussion caps. They should be packed in a strong tin box, with partitions to contain a dozen; to be placed near your bed at night.

Lamps.—Should burn either oil or candles.

Burning glasses are very useful if really good. The inner bark of the fig-tree, well beaten and dried in the sun, makes excellent tinder.

Musquito gaiters or *stockings* should be wide, of very soft leather, to draw over the foot and leg quite up to the thigh joint. These are a great comfort when sitting during the evening.

Tanned goods.—All tents, awnings, sails, nets, lines, &c., should be tanned, to preserve them in African climates.

Books.—All journals and note-books should be tinted paper, to preserve the eyes from the glare, which is very trying when writing in the open air upon white paper.

Seeds.—Should be simply packed in brown paper parcels sewn up in canvas, and should *never be hermetically sealed*.

Blood.—When meat is scarce do not waste the blood. Clean out the large intestine of an animal if far from camp. This will contain a considerable quantity, and can be easily secured by a ligature at each end.

Fish can be preserved without salt, by smoke. They should be split down the *back* (not the belly) from head to tail, and be smoked upon a framework of sticks immediately when caught. Four forked sticks, driven into the ground as uprights to support two parallel poles, crossed with bars, will form a framework about three feet high; the fire is beneath. All fish and flesh is thus preserved by the natives when hunting.

Salt.—When efflorescent on the surface of the soil, scrape with a spoon or shell, and collect it with as little sand as possible. Cut a hole two inches square in the bottom of a large earthen pot, cover the hole with a little straw, then fill the pot with the salt and sand. Pour water slowly over this, and allow it to filter into a receiver below. Boil the product until the water has evaporated, then spread the wet salt upon a cloth to dry in the sun.

Potash.—If you have no salt, treat wood ashes or those of grass in the same way.

Oil.—All seeds or nuts that will produce oil should be first roasted like coffee, then ground fine upon a flat stone, and boiled with water. The oil then rises to the surface, and is skimmed off. Unless the nuts or seeds are roasted, the boiling water will not extract the oil.

Crutches.—To make impromptu crutches to assist wounded men upon a march, select straight branches that grow with a fork. Cut them to the length required, and lash a small piece of wood across the fork. This, if wound with rag, will fit beneath the arm, and make a good crutch.

In this manner I brought my wounded men along on the march from Masindi.

Tamarinds.—Whenever possible, collect this valuable fruit. Take off the shell, and press the tamarinds into lumps of about two pounds. They will keep in this simple form for many months, and are invaluable in cases of fever—cooling when drunk cold, and sudorific when taken hot. If taken in quantity, they are aperient.

THE LAST LETTER OF MR. EDWARD HIGGINBOTHAM, ENGINEER-IN-CHIEF TO THE EXPEDITION, WHO DIED 28TH FEB., 1873. RECEIVED AT FATIKÓ.

"ISMAILÏA, *Feb. 2nd*, 1873.

" EXCELLENCY,

" Wat-el-Mek arrived here on the 23rd December, 1872, bringing your welcome letter of the 14th November. I need not say how glad I am to hear that you are all well and have had good health since your departure.

" I have been very anxious about you, as there were all kinds of rumours afloat here.

" I write down the news, the different items in the order they have occurred.

" On the 20th August, 1872, the traders arrived from the West with a considerable quantity of ivory.

" On the 29th August, Aboo Soud made his appearance, with sixty or seventy of his people, and immediately all kinds of rumours were in circulation. That you had been obliged to retreat from Unyoro with the loss of half the men; Abd-el-Kader killed. That you had returned to Fatiko, and would be here in a short time, and the whole expedition would then return at once to Khartoum.

" It also became at once known that you had fought with Aboo Soud's people, and killed a great number of them, but the cause I could not find out. I questioned several of the men, but could gather no details of the affair. It was very evident they did not wish to give any information respecting the matter.

" Seeing nothing of Aboo Soud, I next day went to see

Raouf Bey, and found Aboo Soud there, 'Atrush,'[1] and several others. I remained there some time, but could learn nothing beyond what I had heard the day before. Seeing this, I asked Aboo Soud why the government troops and his people had fought together. He replied that he had not been present, and knew nothing whatever about the matter. That after the fight you had sent for him, and asked him to take down in writing what had occurred. That he had refused, on the grounds that he had not been present, and that he was only Aboo Soud and you were a Pacha.

"He then left you and returned to Fobbo, and afterwards marched for here, as he found, after what had occurred, that it was impossible to procure porters to carry the ivory from the different stations. His intention in coming here was to try and persuade 'Atrush' and the natives from the West to return with him to Fobbo to bring the ivory here.

"I then asked him for letters, when, much to my surprise, he replied that he had none. I at once put it down for certain that he had come here without your knowledge or consent.

"After the arrival of Aboo Soud, the general feeling here was one of satisfaction. Every face looked brighter. You were coming here, and we were all to start for Khartoum at once; in fact, the expedition was at an end.

"Aboo Soud took up his quarters at your old place (Hellet-el-Sit), and was engaged for several days in dividing the ivory brought from the West.

"Raouf Bey wished to go out to capture cattle, and asked Aboo Soud and the men of Atrush to accompany him. However, the expedition did not come off for some reason, I

---

[1] Atrush, the vakeel of Abou Saood's stations in the Makkarika country west of the Nile.

believe because the men of Atrush were afraid of having anything to do with us, after hearing the news brought by Aboo Soud. Whether Aboo Soud really asked 'Atrush' and his people to return with him to Fobbo I do not know; report says that he did, and they refused to have anything to do with him hereafter. They broke up their camp at once, and marched, many of the men declaring their intention of making for their 'Zareeba,' and then marching across country with their women, children, and slaves, to join the stations on the Bahr Gazelle.[1]

"On September 9th a 'diahbiah' arrived from Khartoum belonging to Aboo Soud, but not letters.

"On the 11th September, Aboo Soud, with all his people and boats, left for the 'Bohr.'[2]

"On the 6th November a boat arrived at Khartoum, belonging to a merchant; ten months and a half on the journey. He met Aboo Soud on his way to Khartoum.

"On the 8th November six boats arrived with corn for the Government. They belonged to Aboo Soud, and had contracted at Khartoum to deliver a certain quantity of corn here. These boats, after discharging the corn, returned to the 'Bohr.' Ten months on the journey.

"On the 27th December, 1872, one of a fleet of twenty-two boats arrived; the remainder we were to expect every day. They have since arrived, bringing 400 men, and corn; all Soudanis. The 'sackoylarsi' died on the way.

"They brought, of course, the latest news, which you will now receive.

"The new steamer was finished a few days ago, and very well she looks. The men are now engaged in packing the

---

[1] Thus to escape with the slaves *viâ* the routes of Darfur and Kordofān.
[2] The "Bohr" is one of Abou Saood's largest stations on the White Nile.

smaller one, and repairing your 'diahbiah.' We find it impossible to drag her up, as we are afraid of pulling her in pieces in doing so. However, we are making the best job of her we can.

"As regards the carts, I am afraid we cannot rely on their being of the slightest use. Everything made of European timber appears to perish rapidly here. All the 'Kyassa' boats, and the three wooden 'diahbiahs' built at Cairo, are worthless, and obliged to be broken up. They have been dragged up, caulked, and patched, only to sink again. They are all wrecks, and we are breaking them up. The timber we get from them is for the most part unfit to burn on the steamer, it is so rotten.

"Even the barge, built by the Englishmen twelve months ago, of new timber, will be worthless in another six months.

"Only '*Soont*' seems to stand the climate, all other timber becomes rotten at once.

"The fleet of twenty-two boats and the merchant's boat return to-morrow, with the exception of four. They remain here to do the general work, and to replace the ones being broken up.

"I have also kept here a crew of eight men for your 'diahbiah.' All the old boatmen are returning; there has been great sickness amongst them.

"Two of the workmen have died since you left, and a third is useless from a sore leg. There is now no sawyer.

"The health of the Englishmen, as well as my own, has been but indifferent, but quite as well as could be expected taking into consideration the fact that we are living at Ismailïa. Soon after Wat-el-Mek's arrival I was attacked with inflammation of the lungs, and have been laid up since; —a very disagreeable illness; but am getting better.

"Wat-el-Mek will, of course, explain his long delay here, about which you will be very anxious. He expects to leave to-morrow.

"We have had a wonderfully wet season, quite different from the year before; the whole place flooded at times; the river sometimes covering the islands for days together.

"I need not say how glad I shall be to meet you all again.

"Remember me kindly to Lady Baker and Mr. Baker, and believe me to be,
"Excellency,
"Your most obedient servant,
"E. HIGGINBOTHAM.

"*His Excellency* SIR SAMUEL BAKER, PACHA,
"*Commander-in-Chief, &c. &c. &c.*

"The 'reises' of the fleet of boats which has arrived, all agree that the 'Sud' is a far less formidable affair than the year we passed through, there now being plenty of water where it was before dry. There is also little or no grass."

GEOGRAPHICAL NOTES.

Meteorological Register kept by Lady Baker.

Place.	Date.	Thermometer. 6 A.M.	Thermometer. Noon.	Rainfall.	Wind.	Remarks.
Ismailia	1871. Aug. 1	70	80	..	variable	Light.
	,, 2	73	82	..	,,	
	,, 3	72	80	·29	,,	
	,, 4	72	82	..	,,	
	,, 5	74	82	..	,,	
	,, 6	73	84	..	,,	
	,, 7	74	80	·01	,,	
	,, 8	74	80	..	,,	
	,, 9	74	78	..	,,	
	,, 10	72	76	·22	S.W.	Light.
	,, 11	72	82	..	W.	
	,, 12	74	85	..	N.E.	
	,, 13	74	74	·22	N.	
	,, 14	70	84	..	N.	
	,, 15	75	83	..	S.W.	
	,, 16	74	80	·21	N.E.	
	,, 17	77	74	·56	N.E.	
	,, 18	72	80	..	E.	Light.
	,, 19	74	75	·07	variable	
	,, 20	72	82	..	N.E.	
	,, 21	72	82	..	variable	
	,, 22	73	84	..	N.	
	,, 23	70	84	..	S.W.	
	,, 24	73	85	..	N.	
	,, 25	75	85	..	N.	Light.
	,, 26	75	90	..	variable	
	,, 27	74	85			
	,, 28	73	85			
	,, 29	77	86			
	,, 30	76	86			
	,, 31	75	85	·12		
	Sept. 1	72	87	..	N.E.	
	,, 2	69	72	1·78	S.W.	
	,, 3	70	83			
	,, 4	72	85	..	N.	
	,, 5	72	86			
	,, 6	71	80	1·10	S.	
	,, 7	70	86	..	N.	Light.
	,, 8	75	84			
	,, 9	74	74	1·02	S.E.	
	,, 10	72	84			
	,, 11	72	87	..	N.	
	,, 12	73	86			
Belinian	,, 13	72	84			
	,, 14	72	84			
	,, 15	73	78	..	N.W.	
	,, 16	70	75			
	,, 17	70	80			
	,, 18	70	78	3·20		
	,, 19	68	77	..	variable	

APPENDIX. 545

METEOROLOGICAL REGISTER kept by LADY BAKER—continued.

Place.	Date.	Thermometer. 6 A.M.	Thermometer. Noon.	Rainfall.	Wind.	REMARKS.
Belinian	1871. Sept. 20	72	82			
	,, 21	74	81	..	W.	
	,, 22	72	80			
	,, 23	72	82	..	N.	
	,, 24	72	83	..	W.	
	,, 25	70	85			
	,, 26	76	85			
	,, 27	70	78			
	,, 28	72	82	..	N	
	,, 29	72	82	..	N.W.	
	,, 30	73	82	..	N.	
	Oct. 1	73	84	..	N.	
	,, 2	71	85	..	S.	
	,, 3	72	84			
	,, 4	72	85			
	,, 5	73	84			
Ismailia	,, 6	74	90			
	,, 7	75	90			
	,, 8	75	86	..	S.W.	
	,, 9	74	80	·20		
	,, 10	70	90	..	variable	
	,, 11	75	86	..	W.	
	,, 12	74	88			
	,, 13	75	86	·19	S.W.	
	,, 14	72	82	1·04		
	,, 15	70	84	·08	S.	
	,, 16	70	85	..	variable	
	,, 17	70	89	..	N.	
	,, 18	70	87	..	N.W.	
	,, 19	73	86	..	N.	Light.
	,, 20	74	88	..	N.	
	,, 21	74	87	..	S.E.	
	,, 22	75	84	..	S.	
	,, 23	75	82	..	S.	
	,, 24	72	82	..	S.	
	,, 25	71	84	..	S.	
	,, 26	72	82	..	variable	
	,, 27	72	84	..	S.	
	,, 28	72	82	..	W.	
	,, 29	70	86	..	variable	
	,, 30	74	86	..	N.	
	,, 31	74	86	..	N.	
	Nov. 1	72	86	..	S.	Light.
	,, 2	74	87	..	N	
	,, 3	74	82	..	S.	
	,, 4	72	85	..	variable	
	,, 5	72	86	..	S.	
	,, 6	76	86	..	S.	
	,, 7	74	87	..	variable	
	,, 8	73	86	..	S.	
	,, 9	73	86	..	variable	

546   APPENDIX.

METEOROLOGICAL REGISTER kept by LADY BAKER—continued.

Place.	Date.	Thermometer. 6 A.M.	Noon.	Rainfall.	Wind.	REMARKS.
Ismailia	1871. Nov. 10	74	88	..	S.	
,,	,, 11	74	88	..	N.E.	
,,	,, 12	72	84	..	S.	
,,	,, 13	76	86	..	N.	
,,	,, 14	74	85	..	variable	
,,	,, 15	75	86			
,,	,, 16	70	86			
,,	,, 17	73	86	..	S.	
,,	,, 18	73	85	..	N.	
,,	,, 19	73	86	..	N.E.	
,,	,, 20	73	90	..	S.	
,,	,, 21	72	92	..	S.	
,,	,, 22	70	88	..	N.	
,,	,, 23	70	90	..	variable	
,,	,, 24	70	90	..	S.	
,,	,, 25	70	90	..	S.	
,,	,, 26	72	90	..	S.	
,,	,, 27	72	89	..	W.	
,,	,, 28	73	89			
,,	,, 29	71	89	..	S.	
,,	,, 30	70	90	..	E.	
,,	Dec. 1	72	90	..	N.	
,,	,, 2	76	88	·40	N.	
,,	,, 3	76	77	..	S.W.	
,,	,, 4	75	83	·20	S.W.	
,,	,, 5	72	84	..	W.	
,,	,, 6	72	87	..	variable	
,,	,, 7	70	90	·12	N.E.	
,,	,, 8	74	92	..	N.	
,,	,, 9	76	93	..	N.	
,,	,, 10	72	90	..	variable	
,,	,, 11	76	92	..	S.	
,,	,, 12	74	94	..	S.	
,,	,, 13	74	87	..	S.	
,,	,, 14	70	90	·26	S.	
,,	,, 15	72	88	..	S.E.	
,,	,, 16	70	87	..	S.	
,,	,, 17	70	90	..	S.W.	
,,	,, 18	75	90	..	variable	
,,	,, 19	72	93	..	,,	
,,	,, 20	70	90	..	S.	
,,	,, 21	70	90	..	variable	
,,	,, 22	74	90	..	W.	
,,	,, 23	72	88	..	variable	
,,	,, 24	72	88	..	S.	
,,	,, 25	68	87	..	N.	
,,	,, 26	70	90	..	N.	
,,	,, 27	70	88	..	N.	
,,	,, 28	69	86	..	variable	
,,	,, 29	66	90	..	W.	
,,	,, 30	66	88	..	variable	
,,	,, 31	66	88	..	,,	

APPENDIX. 547

METEOROLOGICAL REGISTER kept by LADY BAKER—*continued.*

Place.	Date.	Thermometer. 6 A.M.	Thermometer. Noon.	Rainfall.	Wind.	REMARKS.
	1872.					
Ismailia	Jan. 1	69	90	..	variable	
,,	,, 2	70	90	..	,,	
,,	,, 3	69	90	..	,,	
,,	,, 4	70	92	..	,,	
,,	,, 5	70	90	..	,,	
,,	,, 6	70	88	..		
,,	,, 7	70	88	..	N.	
,,	,, 8	63	80	..	N.	
,,	,, 9	63	82	..	N.	
,,	,, 10	65	84	..	N.	
,,	,, 11	68	92	..	N.	
,,	,, 12	70	90	..	W.	
,,	,, 13	70	90	..	variable	
,,	,, 14	70	88	..	,,	
,,	,, 15	70	88	..	,,	Light.
,,	,, 16	70	88	..	W.	
,,	,, 17	69	88	..	S.	
,,	,, 18	69	90	..	N.	
,,	,, 19	66	90	..	variable	
,,	,, 20	72	92	..	N.	Strong.
,,	,, 21	72	92	..	S.	
,,	,, 22	80	86	..	S.	
,,	,, 23	74	90	..	variable	
,,	,, 24	80	92	..	,,	
,,	,, 25	75	89	..	,,	
,,	,, 26	77	92	..	S.	
Lat. 4° 38' N.	,, 27	77	88	..	variable	Light.
	,, 28	77	88	..	N.	
	,, 29	70	92	..	N.W.	
	,, 30	77	88	..	N.	Light.
	,, 31	75	90	..	variable	
	Feb. 1	75	90	..	N.	
	,, 2	72	84	..	N.	
	,, 3	72	86	..	S.	Light.
	,, 4	74	84	..	variable	
	,, 5	70	90	..	S.	
	,, 6	70	92	..	E.	
	,, 7	70	80	..	S.	Strong.
	,, 8	71	84	..	variable	Strong.
	,, 9	64	84	..	N.	
Lat. 4° 28' N.	,, 10	64	84	..	N.	
Lat. 4° 18' N.	,, 11	66	88	..	variable	
Lat. 4° 7' N.	,, 12	66	90	..	N.	Light.
Lat. 4° 1' N.	,, 13	70	90	..	N.N.W.	
Loboré.	,, 14	68	88	..	N.W.	
	,, 15	70	86	..	N.W.	
	,, 16	74	87	..	N.N.W.	
	,, 17	71	81	..	variable	
	,, 18	71	87	..	W.	
	,, 19	69	90	..	variable	
	,, 20	72	88	..	N.	Strong.

548   APPENDIX.

METEOROLOGICAL REGISTER kept by LADY BAKER—*continued*.

Place.	Date.	Thermometer. 6 A.M.	Thermometer. Noon.	Rainfall.	Wind.	REMARKS.
	1872.					
Lat. 4° 1' N. Loboré.	Feb. 21	71	83	..	S.S.E.	Strong.
	,, 22	68	88	..	S.E.	
	,, 23	71	85	..	N.	
	,, 24	77	80	..	N.	
	,, 25	69	80	..	variable	
	,, 26	69	86	..	N.	
	,, 27	71	86	..	S.	Strong.
	,, 28	70	82	..		
	,, 29	71	80	..	N.	Strong.
	March 1	66	80	..	N.	
	,, 2	70	89	..	variable	
	,, 3	69	89	..	,,	Strong.
	,, 4	69	88	..	E.	
	,, 5	68	88	..	S.E.	
Lat. 3° 7' N. Snooa.	,, 6	69	90	..	S.E.	
Lat. 3° 1' N. Fatiko.	,, 7	69	89	..	variable	
	,, 8	69	88	..	N.	
	,, 9	68	85	..	N.	
	,, 10	68	85	..	E.	
	,, 11	68	85	..	E.	
	,, 12	70	84	..	variable	
	,, 13	70	85	..	E.	Strong.
	,, 14	70	74	..	S.E.	
	,, 15	65	77	..	S.E.	
	,, 16	68	81	..	E.	Strong.
	,, 17	70	85	..	S.E.	Strong.
	,, 18	70	86	..	variable	
	,, 19	70	86	..	E.	
	,, 20	68	80	..	E.	
	,, 21	66	80	..	variable	
	,, 22	68	82	..	E.	
Lat 2° 16' N. Atada.	,, 23	65	80	..	N.E.	
	,, 24	65	80	..	E.	
	,, 25	66	78	..	variable	
	,, 26	64	80	..	N.	
	,, 27	68	82	..	N.	
	,, 28	68	82	..	E.	
	,, 29	64	84	..	N.E.	
	,, 30	64	76	..	S.E.	
	,, 31	64	76	..	N.E.	
	April 1	64	80	..	S.	Light.
	,, 2	66	78	·23	S.E.	
	,, 3	64	80	..	S.E.	
	,, 4	65	79	1·50	E.	
	,, 5	64	78	..	S.E.	
	,, 6	65	80	·07	E.	
	,, 7	64	79	..	E.	
	,, 8	65	80	·16	E.	
	,, 9	66	78	..	N.E.	
	,, 10	64	73	·73	variable	

APPENDIX. 549

METEOROLOGICAL REGISTER kept by LADY BAKER—*continued*.

Place.	Date.	Thermometer. 6 A.M.	Thermometer. Noon.	Rainfall	Wind.	Remarks.
	1872.					
Atada	April 11	66	80	·75	S.	Started for Masindi.
	,, 12	66	73	·23	S.	
	,, 13	65	76	·50	variable	
	,, 14	64	76	..	E.	
	,, 15	66	78	..	variable	
	,, 16	64	80	...	E.	
	,, 17	65	79	..	S.E.	
	,, 18	68	80	..	S.E.	
	,, 19	64	78	·23	S.E.	
	,, 20	65	80	..	S.E.	
	,, 21	64	80	·48	S.E.	
	,, 22	65	78	..	S.	
	,, 23	65	78	..	S.	Light.
	,, 24	64	78	..	E.	
{Lat. 1° 45′ N. Masindi.}	,, 25	64	78	·23	E.	Arrived at Masindi.
	,, 26	64	78	..	E.	
	,, 27	64	78	·26	E.	
	,, 28	64	72	..	E.	
	,, 29	64	72	·18	E.	
	,, 30	64	73	·64	S.E.	
	May 1	62	71	·14	W.S.W.	
	,, 2	64	72	..	S.W.	
	,, 3	62	72	..	S.E.	
	,, 4	60	73	..	variable	Light.
	,, 5	60	74	..	S.W.	
	,, 6	62	70	..	S.	
	,, 7	61	70	..	S.	
	,, 8	60	71	..	S.E.	
	,, 9	62	75	..	S.E.	
	,, 10	60	71	..	S.	
	,, 11	60	71	..	S.	
	,, 12	61	73	..	S.	
	,, 13	62	75	·82	S.	
	,, 14	60	71	..	S.E.	
	,, 15	60	73	..	W.	
	,, 16	60	71	·51	S.W.	
	,, 17	60	70	·10	S.W.	
	,, 18	60	70	·56	S.	Light.
	,, 19	59	70	..	S.W.	
	,, 20	60	71	·22	S.W.	
	,, 21	59	70	..	S.W.	
	,, 22	59	70	·30	W.	Strong.
	,, 23	60	72	·36	S.	Strong.
	,, 24	59	71	·10	N.E.	
	,, 25	59	71	..	N.W.	
	,, 26	65	69	·30	variable	
	,, 27	63	72	·80	W.	Light.
	,, 28	64	69	·23	W.	
	,. 29	64	72	1·00	W.	
	,, 30	62	72	..	S.	
	,, 31	60	70	·60	S.	

550   APPENDIX.

METEOROLOGICAL REGISTER kept by LADY BAKER—*continued*.

Place.	Date.		Thermometer.		Wind.	RAIN.—REMARKS.
			6 A.M.	Noon.		
	1872.					
Masindi	June	1	64	74	S.	
	,,	2	64	69	S.W.	
	,,	3	64	74	S.	
	,,	4	65	76	S.	
	,,	5	62	70	W.	Strong.
	,,	6	64	70	W.	
	,,	7	64	70	N.E.	
	,,	8				
	,,	9				
Fatiko	,,	10				
	Aug.	11	65	75	N.	Rained hard.
	,,	12	65	75	N.	
	,,	13	65	86	N.	Light.
	,,	14	64	75	N.	Rained heavily at night.
	,,	15	64	83	N.	Rained in the night.
	,,	16	63	83	N.	
	,,	17	63	83	N.	
	,,	18	65	78	S.	Rained in the night.
	,,	19	63	78	N.	Rained in the night.
	,,	20	65	83	N.	
	,,	21	65	84		
	,,	22	65	79	S.	Heavy rain at night.
	,,	23	66	84	S.	Light rain.
	,,	24	64	80	N.	Rained at night.
	,,	25	65	80	N.	Heavy rain.
	,,	26	66	80	N.	Rained in the night.
	,,	27	66	80	N.	Heavy rain.
	,,	28	66	80	N.	Rained in the night.
	,,	29	64	80	N.	Showery.
	,,	30	65	83	N.	Rained all night.
	,,	31	65	83	N.	
	Sept.	1	63	78	N.	{ Light rain from 1 P.M. till 5 P.M., and at night.
	,,	2	66	79	N.	Rained all the afternoon.
	,,	3	66	80	N.	
	,,	4	63	80	N.	Heavy rain at night.
	,,	5	66	80	S.	Light rain during the day.
	,,	6	66	79	W.	Showery.
	,,	7	65	79	N.	A shower in the night.
	,,	8	66	79	N.	A shower in the night.
	,,	9	66	86	variable	
	,,	10	62	86	,,	
	,,	11	63	79	N.	Heavy rain early.
	,,	12	66	86	S.	
	,,	13	65	86	S.	
	,,	14	66	86	N.	
	,,	15	66	86	variable	A shower.
	,,	16	66	86	E.	Rained during the night.
	,,	17	63	84	E.	Heavy rain at night.
	,,	18	66	86	N.W.	Slight rain at night.
	,,	19	66	86	variable	
	,,	20	63	80	N.	A shower.
	,,	21	66	86	N.W.	

APPENDIX. 551

METEOROLOGICAL REGISTER kept by LADY BAKER—*continued*.

Place.	Date.	Thermometer. 6 A.M.	Thermometer. Noon.	Wind.	RAIN.—REMARKS.
Fatiko	1872. Sept. 22	66	88	variable	
	,, 23	66	74	N.	Light rain during the night.
	,, 24	66	80	N.	
	,, 25	66	80	variable	
	,, 26	65	80	S.E.	Slight rain at night.
	,, 27	66	84	N.W.	
	,, 28	66	86	N.W.	
	,, 29	65	85	S.E.	Heavy rain at night.
	,, 30	63	84	S.E.	Heavy rain at night.
	Oct. 1	65	84	variable	Rained during the night.
	,, 2	66	84	N.W.	
	,, 3	66	86	S.E.	
	,, 4	66	86	E.	
	,, 5	72	86	E.	
	,, 6	70	88	E.	
	,, 7	72	90	S.E.	
	,, 8	72	90	E.	
	,, 9	72	80	N.	
	,, 10	63	81	N.	Light rain at night.
	,, 11	63	84	variable	Light rain at night.
	,, 12	66	84	,,	{ Heavy shower in afternoon, and light at night.
	,, 13	66	84	,,	Rained during the night.
	,, 14	66	86	,,	
	,, 15	66	84	,,	A shower at night.
	,, 16	65	86	E.	Light rain at night.
	,, 17	66	77	N.	Light rain at night.
	,, 18	66	86	N.	A shower at night.
	,, 19	66	79	variable	Rained during the night.
	,, 20	64	79	N.	{ From 3·30 P.M. till 6 P.M., and during the night.
	,, 21	65	81	N.	
	,, 22	66	81	N. light	
	,, 23	66	86	E. strong	
	,, 24	72	90	variable	
	,, 25	72	90	N.	
	,, 26	72	86	N.	
	,, 27	64	77	variable	Rained during the night.
	,, 28	62	79	,,	Heavy rain during the night.
	,, 29	63	80	,,	{ Rained for 2 hours heavily in the evening.
	,, 30	61	79	,,	{ Rained for 1½ hour in the evening.
	,, 31	65	82	S.E.	
	Nov. 1	66	86	S.E.	
	,, 2	65	84	E.	
	,, 3	65	84	E.	
	,, 4	66	90	N.	
	,, 5	72	90	E. by S.	
	,, 6	64	88	{ S.E. strong	
	,, 7	65	90	S.E.	
	,, 8	66	88	E. strong	

METEOROLOGICAL REGISTER kept by LADY BAKER—*continued.*

Place.	Date.		Thermometer.		Wind.	RAIN.—REMARKS.
			6 A.M.	Noon.		
Fatiko	1872. Nov.	9	72	90	E.	
	,,	10	72	90	variable light	
	,,	11	66	88	E. strong	
	,,	12	61	86	,,	
	,,	13	61	86	,,	
	,,	14	61	88	,,	
	,,	15	66	90	,,	
	,,	16	66	86	N. light	Heavy rain in afternoon and shower at night.
	,,	17	63	72	N.E.	Light rain for 2 hours in the night.
	,,	18	60	75	variable	
	,,	19	63	84	S.E.	
	,,	20	66	84	E.	
	,,	21	61	84	E. strong	
	,,	22	63	86	,,	
	,,	23	66	90	E. light	
	,,	24	65	90	,,	
	,,	25	66	80	variable	Light rain for 3 hours in the night.
	,,	26	61	84	S.E.	Heavy rain for an hour in the evening.
	,,	27	65	82	S.	Steady light rain all night.
	,,	28	65	79	S.E.	Rained during the night.
	,,	29	65	84	S.E.	Heavy rain in the evening.
	,,	30	66	84	S.	
	Dec.	1	66	86	variable	Rained during the night.
	,,	2	66	88	E.	
	,,	3	66	88	E.	
	,,	4	72	86	variable	
	,,	5	66	80	S.E.	
	,,	6	66	86	variable	Heavy rain for 2½ hours.
	,,	7	66	86	,,	
	,,	8	66	84	,,	Light at night.
	,,	9	66	80	E.	Rained for 2 hours in afternoon, and at night.
	,,	10	66	84	variable	A light shower.
	,,	11	66	84	,,	
	,,	12	72	88	S.E.	
	,,	13	72	88	S.E. strong	
	,,	14	62	86	S.E. strong	
	,,	15	63	88	S.E.	
	,,	16	66	86	S.E.	
	,,	17	63	88	S.E.	
	,,	18	60	86	S.E.	
	,,	19	61	86	S.E.	
	,,	20	61	86	S.E.	
	,,	21	66	88	S.E.	
	,,	22	63	89	S.E.	
	,,	23	66	88	variable	

APPENDIX. 553

METEOROLOGICAL REGISTER kept by LADY BAKER—*continued*.

Place.	Date.	Thermometer. 6 A.M.	Noon.	Wind.	RAIN.—REMARKS.
Fatiko ..	1872. Dec. 24	66	88	S.E.	
	,, 25	72	88	S.E.	Light shower in the evening, and heavy rain from 3·30 P.M. till 6 P.M.
	,, 26	66	79	N.	Light shower in the morning.
	,, 27	66	81	N.	Light in the afternoon.
	,, 28	66	79	N.	
	,, 29	63	79	variable	
	,, 30	66	79	,,	
	,, 31	66	79	,,	
	1873. Jan. 1	66	79	N. strong	
	,, 2	61	80	variable	
	,, 3	63	84	,,	
	,, 4	66	86	E.	
	,, 5	66	86	E.	
	,, 6	66	88	E.	
	,, 7	66	88	N.	
	,, 8	66	88	variable	
	,, 9	66	86	N.	
	,, 10	63	79	N.	
	,, 11	61	79	N.W.	
	,, 12	63	80	N.W.	
	,, 13	66	88	N.E.	
	,, 14	66	79	N.E.	
	,, 15	63	66	N.W.	
	,, 16	63	77	N.W.	
	,, 17	66	81	variable	
	,, 18	66	86	E.	
	,, 19	66	86	E.	
	,, 20	64	86	E. strong	
	,, 21	64	86	,,	
	,, 22	63	88	,,	
	,, 23	68	88	variable	
	,, 24	70	90	E.	
	,, 25	65	88	E	
	,, 26	63	88	S E.	
	,, 27	63	90	N.W.	
	,, 28	68	68	N.E.	
	,, 29	66	88	S.E. strong.	
	,, 30	66	88	E. strong	
	,, 31	68	88	,,	
	Feb. 1	66	88	variable	
	,, 2	66	88	E. light	
	,, 3	68	84	variable	Rained twenty minutes in afternoon.
	,, 4	64	86	,,	Light rain at night.
	,, 5	72	86	E.	
	,, 6	72	90	variable	
	,, 7	72	90	E.	

Meteorological Register kept by Lady Baker—continued

Place.	Date.	Thermometer. 6 A.M.	Thermometer. Noon.	Wind.	Rain.—Remarks.
Fatiko	1873. Feb. 8	72	88	E.	
	,, 9	68	88	E.	
	,, 10	66	90	E.	
	,, 11	66	90	E.	
	,, 12	66	90	E.	
	,, 13	66	86	E. strong	
	,, 14	72	88	variable	
	,, 15	72	92	,,	
	,, 16	68	92	E.	
	,, 17	68	90	E.	
	,, 18	72	90	E.	
	,, 19	68	88	N. strong	
	,, 20	72	86	,,	
	,, 21	63	84	,,	
	,, 22	66	86	N.N.W.	
	,, 23	68	88	N.W.	
	,, 24	72	88	N.W.	
	,, 25	77	86	variable	
	,, 26	75	90		
	,, 27	72	90	S.E.	
	,, 28	68	86	S.E.	
	March 1	68	86	variable	Slight shower in afternoon.
	,, 2	68	88	,,	A shower.
	,, 3	66	88	,,	A heavy shower.
	,, 4	66	86	E.	A shower.
	,, 5	65	88	variable	
	,, 6	66	86	,,	Light shower at 4·30 P.M.
	,, 7	66	90	S.E.	Two showers.
	,, 8	68	90	N.W.	
	,, 9	75	90	variable	
	,, 10	72	88	N.W.	
	,, 11	66	88	N.W.	
	,, 12	72	88	N.	
	,, 13	68	86	variable	
	,, 14	66	88	S.	A shower.
	,, 15	68	84	S.E.	
	,, 16	68	84	N.W.	Light shower.
	,, 17	66	72	variable	Heavy rain at night.
	,, 18	72	81	N.W.	
	,, 19	68	84	N.W.	
	,, 20	66			
On the march	,, 21				
	,, 22				
	,, 23	66	93	S.W.	
	,, 24				
	,, 25				
	,, 26	72	95	variable	
	,, 27	81	84		
	,, 28	72	93	E.	A heavy shower.
	,, 29	72	95	variable	A heavy shower.
	,, 30	72	93	,,	
	,, 31	75	92	,,	
Ismailia	April 1	75	95	,,	

APPENDIX. 555

METEOROLOGICAL REGISTER kept by LADY BAKER—*continued*.

Place.	Date.		Thermometer.		Wind.	RAIN —REMARKS.
			6 A.M.	Noon.		
Ismalia	1873. April	2	72	93	variable	
	,,	3	75	93	E. strong	Slight rain.
	,,	4	72	95	,,	Slight rain.
	,,	5	75	86	S.W.	
	,,	6	75	91	S.W.	
	,,	7	79	93	S.	
	,,	8	75	88	variable	Light rain.
	,,	9	75	88	S.W.	
	,,	10	77	97	N.W.	
	,,	11	75	97	E.	
	,,	12	77	95	S.	
	,,	13	79	91	W.	
	,,	14	75	91	S.	
	,,	15	77	93	S.W.	
	,,	16	77	77	variable	
	,,	17	72	91	,,	
	,,	18	75	77	S.W.	Light shower.
	,,	19	72	93	N.	Steady rain.
	,,	20	75	86	S.	
	,,	21	75	91	,,	Rain at night.
	,,	22	75	95	variable	Light steady rain.
	,,	23	75	88	S.	A heavy shower.
	,,	24	72	79	variable	Steady rain all night.
	,,	25	75	88	,,	
	,,	26	75	88	S.	Heavy rain at night.
	,,	27	77	79	S.	Light rain.
	,,	28	73	84	variable	
	,,	29	75	88	S.	
	,,	30	75	79	variable	Light rain at night.
	May	1	72	88	,,	
	,,	2	75	91	N. light	
	,,	3	75	88	S. strong	
	,,	4	75	80	variable	{Light rain for three hours in morning.
	,,	5	75	91	,,	Light shower.
	,,	6	77	91	S.	Shower at night.
	,,	7	72	81	S.	{Heavy rain from 3 A.M. till 9 A.M.
	,,	8	75	91	S.	
	,,	9	79	93	S.	
	,,	10	75	88	S.	Heavy shower at night.
	,,	11	75	90	variable	
	,,	12	77	90	S.	A shower at night.
	,,	13	75	73	N.E.	Heavy rain from 9 A.M. till 4·30 P.M.
	,,	14	74	88	S.	
	,,	15	74	88	S. light	
	,,	16	75	95	,,	
	,,	17	75	88	,,	
	,,	18	74	75	N.E.	Slight rain.
	,,	19	73	84	S. light	
	,,	20	73	91	variable	Slight shower.
	,,	21	73	84	S.	

556   APPENDIX.

METEOROLOGICAL REGISTER kept by LADY BAKER—*continued*.

Place.	Date.		Thermometer.		Wind.	RAIN.—REMARKS.
			6 A.M.	Noon.		
	1873.					
Ismalia	May	22	74	84	S.	
	,,	23	75	88	S.	
	,,	24	73	88	S.	Heavy rain all night.
	,,	25	75	88	S.	Heavy rain all night.
White Nile,	,,	26	70	88	S.	
on passage	,,	27	70	79	S.	Heavy rain in the night.
to Khar-	,,	28	75	86	variable	
toum.	,,	29	79	88	,,	A shower.
	,,	30	77	86	,,	
	,,	31	75	84	S.	
White Nile	June	1	75	84	S. light	
	,,	2	75	84	S.	
	,,	3	75	86	S.	
	,,	4	75	80	N.W.	Light rain all day.
Bahr Zaraffe	,,	5	75	84	,,	
	,,	6	75	84	S.	
	,,	7	75	84	variable	Heavy rain in afternoon.
	,,	8	75	84	S.	
	,,	9	75	86	variable	Very heavy rain.
	,,	10	75	86	S.	
	,,	11	75	86	S.	
	,,	12	75	86	S.	
	,,	13	79	86	S.	
	,,	14	79	86	S.	
	,,	15	79	86	S.	
	,,	16	77	86	N.	
	,,	17	77	86	variable	
	,,	18	77	88	S.	
White Nile	,,	19	75	86	S.	
	,,	20	75	86	N.	Heavy rain at night.
	,,	21	79	87	S.	
	,,	22	77	86	S.	Heavy rain at night.
	,,	23	79	86	S.	
	,,	24	79	88	S.	
	,,	25	75	86	N. strong	Light rain.
	,,	26	79	88	S.	
	,,	27	79	88	variable	Light rain.
	,,	28	75	86	N.	
Khartoum..	,,	29	79	90	S.	
	,,	30	79	90	S.	
	July	1	79	90	S.	
	,,	2	79	92	S.	
	,,	3	82	91	S.	
	,,	4	84	92	S.	
	,,	5	79	91	variable	
	,,	6	84	93	W.	
	,,	7	79	85	S.	

APPENDIX. 557

Mean Temperatures and Results from Lady Baker's Memoranda; arranged by Lieut. J. A. Baker, R.N.

Place.	Year and Month.	Thermometer at 6 A.M.			Thermometer at Noon.			Rainfall.	Number of Days on which Rain fell.	Prevailing Wind.	Number of Days on which this Wind blew.	Remarks.
		Min.	Mean	Max.	Min.	Mean	Max.					
Ismailia	1871. Aug.	70	73	77	74	82	90	1·7	8	variable	11	Also N.W. 5 days; and W. 6 days.
	Sept.	68	71	76	72	:	87	7·1	4	N.	12	And N. 6 days.
	Oct.	70	:	75	82	:	90	1·51	4	S.	14	
	Nov.	70	:	76	82	:	90	Nil	:	S.	7	And N. 7 days.
	Dec.	66	:	76	77	:	94	·98	4	S.		
Ismailia and Fatiko	1872. Jan.	63	:	80	80	:	92	Nil	:	N.	9	And variable 15 days; and S. 4 days.
Fatiko and Atada	Feb.	64	:	75	80	:	90	Nil	:	N.	10	And S. 4 days.
Atada and Masindi	March	64	:	70	74	:	90	Nil	:	E.	10	And S.E. 6 days; and N. 5 days.
	April	64	:	68	72	:	80	6·19	14	E.	12	And S.E. 9 days; and S. 5 days.
Masindi	May	59	:	65	69	:	75	6·04	14	S.	10	{ And S.W. 7 days; and S.E. 4 days; and W. 4 days.
	June	62	:	65	70	:	76	:	:	S.	:	{ Only the first 7 days in June were noted.
Fatiko	Aug.	63	:	66	75	:	86	:	:	N.	17	Only from August 11th.
	Sept.	62	:	66	74	:	88	:	:	N.	11	And 4 days N.W.
	Oct.	61	:	72	77	:	90	:	:	N.	9	And E. 6 days; and S.E. 3 days.
	Nov.	60	:	72	72	:	90	:	:	E.	14	And S.E. 6 days.
	Dec.	60	:	72	79	:	89	:	:	S.E.	14	
	1873. Jan.	61	:	70	66	:	90	:	:	E.	12	{ And N. 4 days; N.W. 4 days; N.E. 3 days.
	Feb.	63	:	77	84	:	92	:	2	E.	12	
Ismailia	March	65	:	75	72	:	95	:	11	variable		
	April	72	:	79	79	:	97	:	12	S.	9	And S.W. 5 days
	May	70	:	79	73	:	93	:	13	S.	20	
White Nile and Khartoum.	June	75	:	79	80	:	90	:	7	S.	20	And N. 4 days.
	July	79	:	84	85	:	93	:	:	S.	:	Only for the first 7 days in July.

Meteorological Register.—Towfikia, Lat. 9° 25′ 15″. 1870.

Month.	Mean Temperature, Fahr.		Rainfall.	
	6 A.M.	Noon.	Days heavy.	Days light
May	73·3	92·2	3	4
June	72·3	86·5	5	6

Meteorological Register kept at Towfikia, on the White Nile, Latitude 9° 25′ 15″ N., in 1870, by Lieut. Julian A. Baker, r.n., during Sir S. W. Baker's Khedive Expedition.

Date.		Aneroid.	Thermometer.	Wind.	Force.	Weather.	Remarks.
		Inches.					
July 23	– A.M.	28·56	73°	S.	2	c	
	– P.M.	·55	80	S.W.	7	t q r	
,, 24	– A M.	·60	73	S^{ly}	2	c o	
	– P.M.	..	..	S^{ly}	3	o r	
,, 25	6 A.M.	·65	71	S^{ly}	2	c	
	6 P.M.	·58	80	S^{ly}	2	b c	
,, 26	6 A.M.	·62	73	calm	0	b c	
	6 P.M.	·55	78	S.	1	b c	
,, 27	– A.M.	·65	73	S.	1	b c	
	6 P.M.	·51	79	calm	0	b c	Rained heavily in night.
,, 28	6 A.M.	·62	72	S.W^{ly}	2	b c t	
,, 29	6 A.M.	·60	75	S.W.	2	b c	
	– P.M.	..	..	N^{ly}	3	c r	{ Hard rain for two hours in the afternoon.
,, 30	6 A.M.	·56	73	S.	2	b c	
	6 P.M.	·50	73	S.	2	c r	Rained from 12½ to 2½ P.M.
,, 31	6 A.M.	·57	78	calm	0	c	
	noon	·54	78	S.	2	b c	
	6 P.M.	·47	78	calm	0	b c	Means of 9 days' observations: aneroid 28·57, thermometer 75° 1′.
Aug. 1	6 A.M.	·56	73	,,	0	b c	
	noon	·56	79	S.W.	1	b c	
	6 P.M.	·55	74	S.W.	2	c o r	Drizzle from 2 to 5 P.M.
,, 2	6 A.M.	·60	73	calm	0	c	
	noon	·60	77	S.E.	2	b c	Drizzle from 7 to 9½ A.M.
	6 P.M.	·52	78	S.W.	4	b c	
,, 3	6 A.M.	·56	73	calm	0	o c	Rain from 8 to 9 A.M.
	6 P.M.	·53	78	S.W.	1	b c	
,, 4	6 A.M.	·58	75	calm	0	b c	
	6 P.M.	·48	79	S.	2	b c	
,, 5	6 A.M.	·52	75	calm	0	b c	
	6 P.M.	·42	83	,,	0	b c	
,, 6	6 A.M.	·54	74	,,	0	b c	
	noon	·50	83	,,	0	b c	Rain from 1 to 2 A.M., r c q l t.
	6 P.M.	·50	75	N.W.	1	c o	Drizzle from 2 to 5 P.M.

APPENDIX. 559

METEOROLOGICAL REGISTER kept at TOWFIKIA, on the WHITE NILE — *continued.*

Date.			Aneroid.	Thermometer.	Wind.	Force.	Weather.	REMARKS.
			Inches.					
Aug.	7	6 A.M.	28·56	73°	N.	1	b c	
		noon	..	..	N.W.	3	b c	Slight rain 7 to 8 P.M.
,,	8	6 A.M.	·55	72	calm	0	b c	
		– P.M.	..	..	N.W.	2	b c	
,,	9	6 A.M.	·54	76	calm	0	b c	
		6 P.M.	·48	79	S.E.	3	c r	Rain from 5½ to 6 P.M.
,,	10	6 A.M.	·56	73	N.W.	3	c	
		noon	·56	74	N.W.	5	c d	Slight drizzle in afternoon
,,	11	6 A.M.	·56	74	calm	0	b c	Means of 11 days' observations : aneroid 28·54 thermometer 76°.
Sept.	4	6 A.M.	·62	73	,,	0	c	
,,	5	,,	·60	75	,,	0	b c	Rain from 2½ to 3¼ P.M.
,,	6	,,	·57	77	,,	0	b c	
		noon	..	..	N.E.	4	c r	Rain from 9 to 12 A.M.
		6 P.M.	..	..	S.E.	3	r	Rain from 5½ to 7 P.M.
,,	7	6 A.M.	·63	74	calm	0	b c	
		noon	..	..	S.E.	3	b c	
		6 P.M.	·52	78	calm	0	b c	
,,	8	6 A.M.	·60	75	,,	0	b c	
,,	9	,,	·61	75	,,	0	f	Rain from 9 to 9½ A.M.
		noon	..	..	S.	6	b c	
,,	10	6 A.M.	·54	76	S.	1	b c	
		6 P.M.	·58	76	calm	0	b c	
,,	11	6 A.M.	·63	74	,,	0	b c	
		6 P.M.	..	..	S.E.	2	b c	Rain from 2 to 2¼ P.M.
,,	12	6 A.M.	·65	76	N.E.	1	b c	
		noon	..	..	N.E.	5 to 8	c p q	Hard rain 2 to 3 P.M.
		6 P.M.	..	..	N.E.	1	b c	
,,	13	6 A.M.	·67	74	calm	0	b c	
		noon	..	..	S.	4	b c	
		6 P.M.	..	..	S.	3	b c	
,,	14	6 A.M.	·64	75	N.	1	b c	
,,	15	,,	·62	76	N.	1	b c	Means of 12 days' observations : aneroid 28·61, thermometer 75° 3'.

GENERAL AVERAGE OF ANEROID AND THERMOMETER.

For	9 days in July	.. ..	28·57	..	75·1
,,	11 ,, August	.. .. ..	·54	..	76·
,,	12 ,, September	.. .. ..	·61	..	75·3
	32		28·573	..	75·5

APPENDIX.

Observations for Determination of Heights made during Sir S. W. Baker's Khedive Expedition made by Lieutenant Julian A. Baker, R.N.

Date		Place.	Aneroid.	Air Temperature.	Hypsometers, Nos.			Heights.	
					4633.	9582.	9584.	A.	B.
			Inches	°	°	°	°	Feet.	Feet.
1870. July, Aug., Sept.		Towfikia ..	28·573	75·5	..	..	..	..	1559
1871. July	20	Gondokoro ..	..	76·	209·3	209·4	209·4	1481	1391
1872. January	21	,, ..	..	85·	209·15	209·2	209·2	1622	1542
,,	25	River Level (?) ..	26·55	..	..	..	..	..	3794
,,	,,	Base of Gebel Regiaf	26·52	..	..	..	..	..	3828
,,	,,	Top of Gebel Regiaf ..	26·20	..	..	..	..	..	4186
,,	28	Sheik Beden's ..	..	90·	209·	209·1	209·1	1696	1623
February	9	Koojo ..	..	87·	208·85	208·9	208·9	1806	1725
,,	10	Halt ..	..	90·	208·35	208·5	208·5	2052	1982
,,	11	Gomayshee ..	..	90·	207·85	208·	208·	2346	2277
,,	14	Labore ..	..	94·	207·55	207·7	207·7	2542	2471
March	1	At junction of Asua and Attabbi	..	87·	208·7	208·6	208·6	1982	1867
,,	3	Camp ..	..	87·	207·68	207·75	207·75	2481	2411
,,	4	On River Unyama	..	90·	207·35	207·4	207·4	2702	2620
,,	5	Shooa ..	..	95·	206·2	206·3	206·3	3386	3316
,,	11	Fatiko ..	..	80·	205·8	205·8	205·8	3587	3542

APPENDIX.

,,	18	First camp ..	26·92	90·	206·	206·1	206·1	3469	3422
,,	19	Second camp	26·80	91·	205·8	205·85	205·85	3622	3563
,,	20	Third camp	26·50	79·	205·2	205·2	205·2	3932	3900
,,	21	Fourth camp	26·55	82·	205·25	205·3	205·3	3894	3863
April	5	Foweera	26·76	86·	205·8	205·8	205·8	3626	3542
,,	15	Kisoona	26·76	71·	205·75	205·8	205·8	3525	3478
,,	,,	Kasija	26·48	79·	205·25	205·3	205·3	3874	3801
,,	16	Koki	26·51	80·	205·3	205·4	205·4	3821	3757
,,	19	Chorobezi	26·70	77·	205·65	205·7	205·7	3625	3557
,,	28	Masindi	..	67·	205·2	205·25	205·25	3813	3785
1873 March	20	Near Shooa Hill	..	88·	206·65	206·6	206·6	3167	3081
,,	21	On the River Unyama	..	91·	207·6	207·6	207·6	2587	2500
,,	23	Afuddo	28·13	84·	208·15	208·2	208·2	2204	2116
,,	27	Laboré	27·79	92·	207·6	207·7	207·7	2532	2442
May	26	Gondokoro	..	83·	209·1	209·2	209·2	1616	1510
July	8	Khartoum	28·96	108·	209·6	209·6	209·6	1462	1189
August	6	Oquack*	27·43	95·	206·9	206·9	206·9	3026	2814
September	2	Cairo†	30·30	87·	211·8	211·19	..	87	76

* Sanatorium about forty-five miles from Souakim, on the Red Sea.
† At a spot known by survey to be above the sea-level 81·3 feet.

The corrections required to be applied to the readings of the hypsometers were found at the Kew Observatory to be as follows:—

Date.	No. 4693.		No. 9582.		No. 9584.	
	At 205°.	At 212°.	At 205°.	At 212°.	At 205°.	At 212°.
1869. May	−0.05	+0·10	..	..	..	..
1868. November	..	..	+0·15	+0·20	+0·20	+0·20
1873. December	..	·00	..	−0·10	..	−0·10

The following corrections have been used in reducing the heights in column B; they are based upon the latest verifications:—

	No. 4693.	No. 9582.	No. 9584.
At 212°	0·00	− 0·10	− 0·10
,, 211	− 0·02	− 0·11	− 0·10
,, 210	− 0·04	− 0·11	− 0·10
,, 209	− 0·06	− 0·12	− 0·10
,, 208	− 0·08	− 0·13	− 0·10
,, 207	− 0·11	− 0·13	− 0·10
,, 206	− 0·13	− 0·14	− 0·10
,, 205	− 0·15	− 0·15	− 0·10

The atmospheric pressure at the sea-level has, in calculating the heights in column B, been assumed the same as that shown on *Buchan's Isobaric Charts;* and the temperature of the air there, the same as that shown on *Dove's Isothermal Charts.*

The heights in column A were calculated on the spot, and are generally greater than those in column B.

Buchan's Isobaric Charts of the World furnish the following data for the pressure of the atmosphere at the sea-level, in inches of mercury at the temperature of 32° Fahrenheit, over the countries extending from Egypt to the Equator:—

Months.	Lat. 20° N.	Lat. 10° N.	Lat. 0.
January	30·0	29·9	29·8
February	30·0	29·9	29·8
March	30·0	29·9	29·8
April	29·9	29·8	29·8
May	29·8	29·8	29·8
June	29·7	29·7	29·9
July	29·7	29·7	29·9
August	29·7	29·7	29·8
September	29·8	29·8	29·8
October	29·9	29·9	29·8
November	30·0	29·9	29·8
December	30·0	29·9	29·8

APPENDIX. 563

Dové's Thermal Charts of the World furnish the following data for the mean temperature of the air at the sea-level, for the coast of the same region:—

Months.	Lat. 20° N.	Lat. 10° N.	Lat. 0.
January	69	77	79
February	77	80	83
March	80	85	85
April	86	86	83
May	86	83	82
June	86	86	80
July	90	85	79
August	86	85	79
September	86	82	79
October	86	82	79
November	77	82	80
December	72	77	77

The heights deduced would, of course, be more reliable if we could ascertain the values for atmospheric pressure and temperature at the sea-level for the day and hour on which each observation of the hypsometer or aneroid was made.

The hypsometer observations appear to be excellent. They have been used for checking the aneroid readings. For this purpose the equivalents of tension of vapour for the boiling points have been taken from the extensive table, based upon Regnault's determinations, given in Sir Henry James's *Instructions for taking Meteorological Observations*, and the difference of the corresponding aneroid readings from them taken. From these differences are deduced the following mean corrections for the aneroid:—

$$
\begin{aligned}
\text{At } 30 \text{ inches} &\quad - \cdot 50 \\
,, \ 29 \ ,, &\quad - \cdot 47 \\
,, \ 28 \ ,, &\quad - \cdot 45 \\
,, \ 27 \ ,, &\quad - \cdot 43
\end{aligned}
$$

And these corrections have been used in the calculations of the heights of Towfikia and Gebel Regiaf, which are the only ones which depend upon the aneroid.

2nd February, 1874.   R. STRACHAN, F.M.S.

APPENDIX.

RESULTS of the ASTRONOMICAL OBSERVATIONS made by LIEUT. J. A. BAKER, R.N., during the YEARS 1870, 1871, 1872, and 1873, in SIR S. W. BAKER'S EXPEDITION up the RIVER NILE, calculated by WILLIAM ELLIS, F.R.A.S., of the ROYAL OBSERVATORY, GREENWICH.

TABLE I.—*Results of the Observations for Latitude.*

(These Latitudes are deduced from meridian altitudes, excepting those at Towfikia, 1870, November 7, and November 10 (first result), which are obtained from altitudes taken a little distance from the meridian).

Date.			Name of Place.	Object observed.	Resulting Latitude North.		
1870.	Jan.	13	Khartoum	Sun	15	36	6
	Feb.	14	Fashoda	Canopus	9	54	14
	March	9	The Dubbah, Bahr Zaraffe	Canopus	7	47	38
	June	7	Towfikia	α Centauri	9	25	12
	Nov.	7	,,	Sun	9	25	25
	,,	8	,,	Sun	9	26	19
	,,	9	,,	Sun	9	24	5
	,,	10	,,	Sun	9	24	27
	,,	10	,,	Sun	9	24	59
	,,	19	,,	Sun	9	25	11
	,,	21	,,	Sun	9	25	1
1871.	Jan.	11	The Dubbah, Bahr Zaraffe	Sun	7	46	47
	Feb.	1	Three Dubbahs, Bahr Zaraffe	Sun	7	31	51
	July	28	Gondokoro	Moon	4	56	28
1872.	Jan.	20	,,	α Ursæ Majoris	4	54	58
	,,	20	,,	γ Ursæ Majoris	4	53	49
	,,	20	,,	α Crucis	4	53	43
	,,	24	Gebel Regiaf	α Crucis	4	45	22
	,,	27	Sheikh Beden's, just below the rapids	Canopus	4	37	49
	Feb.	8	On the march from Sheikh Beden's to Loboré	Canopus	4	37	8
	,,	9	Goboor	Capella	4	28	34
	,,	10	Marengo	Capella	4	18	33
	,,	11	Moogi	Canopus	4	6	37
	,,	15	Loboré	Canopus	4	1	5
	March	1	At the junction of Asua and Attabbi	Canopus	3	42	38
	,,	3	At camp in the forest	Canopus	3	22	11
	,,	5	Shooa	α Crucis	3	7	17
	,,	10	Fatiko	α Ursæ Majoris	3	1	21
	April	5	Foweera	α Lyræ	2	12	35
	,,	14	Kisoona	α Ursæ Majoris	2	2	52
	,,	16	Koki	α Ursæ Majoris	1	59	26
	,,	19	Chorobézi	α Crucis	1	56	29
	,,	28	Masindi	α Crucis	1	44	35
1873.	Jan.	22	Fatiko	β Aurigæ	3	2	14
	,,	22	,,	Canopus	3	0	33
	,,	23	,,	Capella	3	1	28
	,,	24	,,	Capella	3	2	18
	,,	25	,,	Capella	3	2	38
	,,	27	,,	Capella	3	1	39
	Feb.	6	,,	Canopus	2	59	15

APPENDIX. 565

The results contained in the preceding Table having been combined as necessary, the following table was formed:—

TABLE II.—*Concluded Latitudes.*

Name of Place.	Latitude North.	Number of separate Determinations.	Name of Place.	Latitude North.	Number of separate Determinations.
Khartoum	15° 36' 6"	1	Goboor	4° 28' 34"	1
Fashoda	9 54 14	1	Marengo	4 18 33	1
Towfikia	9 25 5	8	Moogi	4 6 37	1
The Dubbah, Bahr Zaraffe	7 47 13	2	Loboré	4 1 5	1
Three Dubbahs, Bahr Zaraffe	7 31 51	1	At the junction of the Asua and Attabbi	3 42 38	1
			At camp in the forest	3 22 11	1
Gondokoro	4 54 45	4	Shooa	3 7 17	1
Gebel Regiaf	4 45 22	1	Fatiko	3 1 26	8
Sheikh Beden's, just below the rapids ..	4 37 49	1	Foweera	2 12 35	1
			Kisoona	2 2 52	1
On the march from Sheikh Beden's to Loboré	4 37 8	1	Koki	1 59 26	1
			Chorobezi	1 56 29	1
			Masindi	1 44 35	1

TABLE III.—*Results of the Observations for Longitudes from Lunar Distances.*

(In the reduction of these observations the 'Nautical Almanac' distances have been corrected for the errors of the places of the Moon and Planets as determined from the Greenwich Observations).

Date.			Name of Place.	Object to which Moon was referred.	Whether the Moon was East or West.	Resulting Longitude East.
1870.	Oct.	29	Towfikia	Sun	E.	31° 29' 0"
,,	,,	31	,, ...	Sun	E.	31 15 15
,,	,,	31	,, ...	Antares	E.	32 42 0
,,	,,	31	,, ...	Saturn	E.	32 1 15
,,	Nov.	7	,, ...	Aldebaran	W.	31 33 45
,,	,,	7	,, ...	Jupiter	W.	31 43 30
,,	,,	8	,, ...	Jupiter	W.	31 24 45
1872.	Jan.	18	Gondokoro	Fomalhaut	E.	30 48 15
,,	,,	18	,, ...	Jupiter	W.	32 8 0
,,	March	15	Fatiko	Jupiter	W.	32 37 0
,,	,,	16	,, ...	Sun	E.	31 46 15
,,	,,	16	,, ...	Jupiter	W.	32 58 0
,,	,,	17	,, ...	Aldebaran	E.	32 9 0
,,	,,	17	,, ...	Aldebaran	E.	32 6 30
,,	,,	17	,, ...	Jupiter	W.	32 52 15

At one place (Fatiko) two observations of eclipses of Jupiter's satellites were made, the results of which are given in the next Table:—

TABLE IV.—*Results of the Observations for Longitude, from Eclipses of Jupiter's Satellites, made at Fatiko.*

(In the reduction of these observations the 'Nautical Almanac' times have been used without correction, no corresponding observations having been found.)

Date.	Phenomena.	Resulting Longitude East.
1872. March 17	Reappearance of 1st satellite	32 37 45
1873. Feb. 6	Disappearance of 3rd satellite	32 35 45

Combining together the results of Tables III. and IV., the following values of longitude are found:—

TABLE V.—*Concluded Longitudes.*

Name of Place.	Longitude East.	Number of separate Determinations.
Towfikia	31 44 13	7
Gondokoro	31 28 8	2
Fatiko	32 27 49	8

In addition to the above, several differences of longitude were measured by means of two chronometers.

TABLE VI.—*Chronometric Differences of Longitude.*

Names of Places.	Resulting Differences of Longitudes.
Khartoum, east of Fashoda	0 21 0
Fashoda, east of Towfikia	0 30 45
Khartoum, east of Towfikia	0 51 45
Towfikia, east of the Dubbah. Bahr Zaraffe	1 3 15
Towfikia, east of Three Dubbahs, Bahr Zaraffe	1 3 15

The interval between the observations made before leaving Khartoum, and after arriving at Towfikia (taking Fashoda on

APPENDIX.

the way) was fourteen days, and the rates determined at Khartoum agree well with those afterwards found at Towfikia. The first three results of the preceding Table should therefore be good.

The last two differences depend on rates determined before leaving Towfikia, carried on twenty-nine days for "The Dubbah," and fifty-two days for "Three Dubbahs," there being no after determination of rate. These differences are therefore less worthy of confidence, although it may be noted as a favourable circumstance that in each case the two chronometers employed gave fairly accordant results.

INDEX.

A.

Abbas Pacha, Achmet Rafik's service under, i. 323.
Abbio, the old sheik of Loboré, offers assistance, ii. 48 *et seq.*; sends his son as a hostage, ii. 60.
Abd-el-Kader, Lieutenant-colonel, first aide-de-camp, appointed to command of Sir S. Baker's bodyguard, the "Forty Thieves," i. 31; trustworthiness of, i. 90, ii. 13; boards a slaver, i. 126; an excellent diver, i. 182; explains matters to Allorron, i. 224; commands an attacking party, i. 265; storms a stockade, i. 273; visits slavers' station at Gondokoro, i. 283; promptitude of, i. 356, ii. 231; accompanies Sir S. Baker to Unyoro, ii 5; advises capture of the sheik Bedden, ii. 24; fires Bari villages, ii. 32; in charge of baggage, ii. 68; sent to Foweera with instructions, ii. 165; sent to remonstrate with Kabba Réga, ii. 179; escorts Kabba Réga to Sir S. Baker's dwelling at Masindi, ii. 236; drills troops daily at Masindi, ii. 295, 297; his interview with Kittā-kără after battle of Masindi, ii. 302; his dwelling on fire, ii. 319; his duties on the march to Rionga, ii. 324; wounded, ii. 341; rejoins Sir S. Baker in Rionga's district, ii. 371; in command at Foweera, ii. 378, 384; his testimony respecting the expedition, ii. 408; recalled to Fatiko, ii. 415; as a hunter, ii. 448; promotion of, ii. 497; honourable mention of, ii. 510.

Abdullah, Major, left in command of a station, i. 375; completion of station commanded by, i. 379; visit to station of, i. 383; recalled, i. 385; Achmet's camp attacked after departure of, i. 397; further particulars respecting his command, ii. 38; attacked by the Baris of Bedden, ii. 55; left in command at Fatiko, ii. 134; in charge of liberated slaves, ii. 221; awkward position of, at Fatiko, ii. 233, 388; in peril, ii. 363; relieved by Sir S. Baker, ii. 389; ordered to arrest Abou Saood, ii. 448; in command at Fatiko, ii. 469; orders for, ii. 470; otherwise mentioned, ii. 5, 440.

Abdullah, the Shillook, volunteers to accompany Sir S. Baker in exploring the White Nile, i. 140; guards corn at Tewfikeeyah, i. 178; sent to Tewfikeeyah with letter for the governor of Fashoda, i. 179; returns from Tewfikeeyah with intelligence respecting letter, ii. 180.

Abdullah, the cook, i. 7.
Abdullah Maseri, catches the thief, i. 253.
Abdullah, the pathfinder, ii. 322, 358.
Aboo Kooka, a native interpreter, ii. 292, 314.
Abou Kookah, station of, i. 219.
Abou-noos or Abdnoos (ebony), i. 240.
Abou Saood (Agād & Co.), his contract with the Egyptian govern-

570   INDEX.

ment, i. 159 ; surreptitiously disposes of slaves, *ib.*; appearance and character of, *ib.*; treacherously murders the sheik of Belinian, i. 232 ; arrives at Gondokoro, i. 280 ; brings stolen cattle, i. 281 ; joyfully welcomed to Gondokoro by Baris, i. 282 ; his cattle confiscated, i. 284 ; Sir S. Baker's official letter to, *ib.*; intrigues of, i. 287 ; carries off cattle, i. 315 ; responsible for Shir calamity, i. 316 ; anticipates failure of the expedition, i. 320 ; further intrigues of, i. 321 ; traffics with Baris of Belinian, i. 323 ; asks for permission to quit Gondokoro, i. 341 ; incites officers to conspire, i. 365 ; success of his intrigues, i. 398 ; swindles the government, i. 425 ; departure of, i. 429 ; his station at Latooka, i. 432 ; otherwise mentioned, i. 353, 364 ; his stations near Ibrahiméyeh, ii. 78 ; meeting at Fatiko with, ii. 90 ; his intrigues with Shooli natives, ii. 94 ; his proceedings at Fatiko, ii. 107 : his contract to supply the troops with provisions, ii. 108 ; his character, ii. 109 ; wantonly attacks the Koshi country, ii. 112 ; swears eternal fidelity, ii. 120, 129 ; his instructions to Suleiman, the vakeel, ii. 158 ; visits Kabba Réga and prepares a snare, ii. 160 ; conspires with Suleiman, ii. 168 ; his first appearance at Masindi, ii. 193 ; wantonly attacks Rot Jarma, who was under government protection, ii. 233 ; Rionga's information respecting, ii. 373 ; abominable treachery of, ii. 380 *et seq.*; evidence against, ii. 401, 425 ; summoned to Fatiko, ii. 406 ; his defence, ii. 409 ; his flight and false reports, ii. 411 ; some of his slavers overtaken, ii. 482 ; arrest of, ii. 487 ; documentary evidence against, handed to Nubar Pacha at Cairo, ii. 495 *et seq.*; latest information respecting, ii. 514 *et seq.*

Achmet Bash Choush, narrow escape of, i. 305.

Achmet Effendi, conduct of, i. 178 ; leisurely proceedings of, i. 187 ; appointed to command of a station, i. 375 ; energetic conduct of, i. 379 ; returns to camp with intelligence, i. 397.

Achmet Rafik Effendi, left behind with Niambore, i. 281 ; natives threaten, i. 315 ; information respecting his conduct in the Shir matter, i. 318 ; negligence of, i. 323 ; anxiety for, i. 328 ; killed by Baris, i. 332.

African horse sickness, i. 362 ; diplomacy, ii. 23 ; paradise, ii. 85 ; love of music, ii. 92, 505 ; slavery, ii. 209 ; notions about honesty, ii. 210.

Afuddo, sport at, ii. 77.

Agād Achmet Sheik (head of the firm of Agād & Co.), his contract with the Egyptian government, i. 149 ; his grievances, i. 150, 156 ; modification of the terms of contract with, i. 157 *et seq.*; death of, i. 281 ; otherwise mentioned, i. 4, 132, 148, 425.

Agricultural enemies, i. 136 ; strike, i. 137 ; experiments, ii. 255.

Akiko Hill, bearings taken at, ii. 78.

Albert N'yanza (M'wootan N'zigé), arrangements for navigating the, i. 32 ; junction of Victoria Nile and, i. 143 ; White Nile flowing from the, ii. 74 ; mountains on west shore of, opposite Magungo, ii. 134 ; native information respecting Baréga, a country bordering on the, ii. 147 ; sighted from neighbourhood of Masindi, ii. 179 ; information from M'tésé's envoys respecting, ii. 198 ; sighted from Masindi, ii. 214 ; east shore of, ii. 262 ; Makkarika cannibals near the, ii. 432 ; native information respecting, ii. 462 ; Unyoro bounded by the, ii. 470 ; altitude of, taken by Sir S. Baker at Vacovia, ii. 507 ; future observations of the, *ib.*; connection of Tanganyika lake with, ii. 522 ; Dr. Schweinfurth on Livingstone's theories respecting, ii. 524 ; highest altitude of, ii. 527.

INDEX. 571

Alexandria, distance between Gondokoro and, i. 10.
Ali Amouri, representatives of, at Wat-el-Shambi declare their inability to supply troops with food, i. 217.
Ali Bey, governor of Fashoda, claims to have taken measures for suppressing the slave trade, i. 33; makes a razzia upon the Shillooks, i. 86; his interview with Sir S. Baker, i. 89; his method of taxing a district, i. 93; his intrigues against the Shillook king, i. 102; summoned to an interview with Quat Kare, i. 119 *et seq.;* dismissed and disgraced, i. 157; otherwise mentioned, i. 148.
Ali Emmeen persuades the Makkarika tribe to take hostile measures against Sir S. Baker, ii. 430; refuses to appear before Sir S. Baker, ii. 431; his representations to the Makkarikas, ii. 432.
Ali Genninar makes submission, and offers his services, ii. 227; supersedes Eddrees, ii. 244; Kabba Réga steals guns and ammunition of, *ib.;* in command in Unyoro, ii. 416; narrowly escapes drowning, ii. 421; and Rionga defeat Kabba Réga, ii. 433; and Rionga obtain complete possession of Unyoro, ii. 470.
Ali Goboor ("Forty Thieves") wounded by a lance, ii. 339.
Ali Hussein, an *employé* of Abou Saood, description of, ii. 102; treachery of, ii. 103; intercepts provisions, ii. 128; superseded by Wat-el-Mek, ii. 381; death of, ii. 398.
Al Jusef, an envoy from M'tésé, king of Uganda, arrives at Fatiko, ii. 461.
Ali Nedjar ("Forty Thieves"), death of, ii. 14; otherwise mentioned, i. 348, 420, 448; ii. 13.
Ali Sadik ("Forty Thieves"), a crack shot, ii. 354.
Allorron, a Bari chief, promises allegiance to the government, i. 221; hostile conduct of, i. 223; his connection with Abou Saood, i. 225; prejudiced against expedition, i. 228; refuses to supply cattle or food, i. 235; his aversion to the government, i. 236; his cattle confiscated, i. 255; his interview with Sir S. Baker, *ib.;* his negotiations with the Baris of Belinian, i. 277; assists Abou Saood, i. 283, 321; desires peace, i. 429; repentance and reformation of, ii. 477.
Amarn, an Abyssinian boy, rescued from a cruel master, i. 354; intelligence of, ii. 6; on a march, ii. 44; ill with an ulcerated leg, ii. 442; brought to England by Lady Baker, ii. 533.
Ambuscades, i. 345; ii. 339.
Ammunition, reckless waste of, ii. 342, 344.
Antelopes, i. 65, 68, 71, 73, 85, 87; ii. 446, 448, 451, 453.
Ants, i. 135, 234.
Ant-hills, i. 40, 65, 68, 71.
Apothecaries' Hall, medicines and drugs for the expedition obtained from, i. 18.
Artilleryman, death of an, i. 60; prophecy of an, i. 60; fulfilment of prophecy of an, i. 75.
Artillery for expedition, i. 16.
Assaballa, capture of slaver belonging to. i. 132.
Asua (River), an affluent of the Nile, direction of the, i. 143; impassable during the rainy season, ii. 3; junction of the Attabi with the, ii. 70.
Atbara (River), an affluent of the Nile, direction of the, i. 143.
Atroosh, a vakeel, station of, ii. 121; instructed by Abou Saood to attack Fabbo, ii. 430.
Attabi (River), water of the, quite clear, ii. 70.
Austrian mission station at Gondokoro, i. 222, 237.

B.

Baggara Arabs, followers of Ali Bey, help to levy taxes, i. 89; canoe-builder, ii. 365.
Baggera, immense size of the fish called, i. 444.

572   INDEX

Bahr Gazal (River), expedition of Djiaffer Pacha to the, i. 25, 44 ; navigable channels in the, i. 70 ; slave-vessel from the, seized, i. 132 ; scarcity of wood near the, i. 140 ; absence of current in the, i. 141 ; geographical particulars respecting the, i. 142 ; geographical theories respecting the, i. 398.

Bahr Giraffe (River), a branch of the White Nile, ascent of the, i. 38 ; particulars respecting the, i. 39 ; whole fleet in a *cul-de-sac* on the, i. 47 ; attempt of officials to prevent expedition from passing the, i. 148 ; wreck on the, i. 173 ; unnavigable character of the, i. 196 *et seq.* ; dam constructed across the, i. 204 ; return journey *viâ*—canal perfectly navigable, ii. 480 ; otherwise mentioned, i. 35, 37, 79, 89, 126, 133, 143 ; ii. 36.

Bahr Ingo (River), effluents at eastern corner of, ii. 118.

Bairam, the, a Mahommedan festival, i. 180.

Baker, Sir Samuel, firman of Khedive appointing him commander of the expedition to suppress the slave-trade of the White Nile, and to annex the Central Nile Basin, i. 7 ; English party under his command, i. 12 ; preliminary arrangements of, i. 12–20 ; unpopularity of his expedition, i. 25 ; surveys lacustrine region, i. 50 ; contemplates returning to Shillook country, i. 69 ; detects the nefarious practices of Ali Bey, the governor of Fashoda, i. 87 ; his interview with Ali Bey, i. 89 ; liberates slaves, i. 95 ; descends the Sobat, i. 96 ; assembles the entire fleet at Tewfikeeyah, i. 97 ; his first interview with Quat Kare, i. 100 ; conciliates the Shillooks, i. 104 ; his proceedings at Tewfikeeyah, i. 107 ; adjusts matters between Quat Kare and Ali Bey, i. 122 ; explores the old White Nile, i. 140 ; sends letter of remonstrance to Djiaffer Pacha, i. 148 ; his limited jurisdiction, i. 151 ; explanation of preceding limitation, i. 154 ; determines to assume monopoly of the ivory trade, i. 159 ; leaves Tewfikeeyah, i. 170 ; discovers the great White Nile, i. 201 ; constructs a dam across the Bahr Giraffe, i. 204 *et seq.* ; his operations at Gondokoro, i. 220 *et seq.* ; difficulties with the sheik Allorron, i. 246 ; officially annexes Bari country, i. 248 *et seq.* ; issues general order, i. 262 ; makes war with the Baris, i. 265 *et seq.* ; Abou Saood, i. 284 *et seq.* ; commences a campaign against the whole Bari tribe, i. 322 ; administers absolute justice, i. 353 ; and Baris of Regiāf, i. 367 ; further military movements of, i. 387 *et seq.*; his interview with the sheik Beddēn, i. 403 ; makes peace with the Baris, i. 419 ; advances south, ii. 1 ; meets Beddēn as appointed, ii. 17 ; quells a mutiny, ii. 35 ; arrives at Ibrahimëyeh, ii. 75 ; at Fatiko, ii. 83 ; notifies termination of Agād & Co.'s contract, ii. 110 ; arrives at Unyoro, ii. 136 ; meets Quonga, ii. 137 ; issues proclamation to volunteers, ii. 141 ; his native nickname, ii. 151, 218 ; pays an official visit to Kabba Réga, ii. 181 ; further interview with Kabba Réga, ii. 189 ; Abou Saood's portrait of, ii. 195 ; annexation of Unyoro, ii. 243 ; residence at Masindi, ii. 225 *et seq.;* general attack upon, by Kabba Réga, ii. 294 ; battle of Masindi, and defeat of the Unyoros, ii. 297 ; difficulties of the march to Foweera, ii. 304 *et seq.;* attempted assassination of, ii. 315 ; retreats from Masindi, ii. 327 ; meets Rionga, ii. 372 ; returns to Fatiko, ii. 378 ; arrives at Fatiko, ii. 389 ; defeats the rebels, ii. 397 ; summons Abou Saood to Fatiko, ii. 406 ; his reputation in Egypt and the Soudan, ii. 408 ; slave-trade entirely suppressed, and the slave-hunters driven from the country, ii. 416 ; formation of irregular corps, *ib.* ; the country at

INDEX.

peace, *ib.*; the government established throughout, *ib.*; tender solicitude of Fatiko ladies for, ii. 458; sends a letter to Dr. Livingstone, ii. 464: returns to Gondokoro, ii. 474; starts for home, ii. 480; returns to Fashoda, ii. 484; returns to Khartoum, ii. 490; returns to Cairo, ii. 492; interview with the Khedive, ii. 494; decorated by the Khedive, *ib.*; concluding remarks, ii. 499 *et seq.*; general remarks on Abou Saood, slave trade, and geographical details, *vide* Appendix, 515 *et seq.*

Baker, Lady, accompanies her husband, i. 12; takes charge of liberated slave-girl, i. 70; receives a gift from the Empress of the French, i. 146; accompanies Sir S. Baker to Belinian, i. 332; trains native girls to household duties, i. 358; witnesses an engagement, i. 379; courageous conduct of, ii. 272, 285; admirable forethought of, ii. 323, 397; on the march to Rionga, ii. 328, 330; in action, ii. 335; hardships endured by, ii. 342, 353, 360, 385; her presence of mind, ii. 393; botanical collection prepared by, ii. 494; invaluable services of, ii. 511; meteorological register kept by, ii. 544 *et seq.*

Baker, R.N., Lieutenant J. A. joins expedition, i. 12; his professional experience valuable, i. 28; assists in floating grounded steamers, i. 52; shoots a *Baleniceps Rex*, i. 59; shoots a buffalo, i. 65; takes part in lake survey, i. 67; Sir S. Baker's confidence in, i. 70; contributes to a remarkable "bag," i. 80; goes out antelope-hunting, i. 85; ill with fever, i. 86; visits camp of Ali Bey, i. 94; renders able assistance in exploring, i. 144; ill with fever, i. 164; shows an excellent example of industry, i. 173; value of his nautical knowledge, i. 182; suffers frequently from fever, i. 200; erects a flag-staff, i. 248; display of magic lantern by, i. 251; marches with troops to Belinian, i. 269; assists in forcing gateway of stockade, i. 273; visits slave-traders' camp, i. 283; narrow escape of, i. 306; assists in capture of cattle, i. 334; occupies an island abounding with corn, i. 378; returns from Gondokoro, i. 397; shoots an elephant, i. 432; makes observations from summit of Mount Regiàf, ii. 16; antelope-hunting, ii. 77; marches to Fatiko, ii. 84; visits Kabba Réga, ii. 217; assists in drawing plan of stockade, ii. 278; clears away trees, ii. 360; superintends canoe-building, ii. 366; decorated by the Khedive, ii. 494; geographical observations of, ii. 508; honourable mention of, ii. 510; mean temperatures arranged by, ii. 557; meteorological register kept by, ii. 558 *et seq.*; observations for determination of heights made by, ii. 560.

Baleniceps Rex, shooting the, i. 45, 59, 63, 189.

Bamba, the magic throne, held in great veneration, ii, 277, 316.

Baréga, statement of native envoys respecting situation and people of, ii. 147.

Baris form alliance with the Loquia, i. 308; steal corn, i. 318, 330, 332; a female foreign minister amongst the, i. 331; treachery of, i. 338, 341, 343; renew hostilities, i. 343; attack an exploring party, i. 378; attack Major Abdullah's party, i. 379; general attack by, i. 389; a friendly tribe of, i. 401; sue for peace, i. 417; geological aspect of country of the, i. 406; peace established with the, i. 419; political morality, i. 421.

Baris of Beddēn, friendly demeanour of the, i. 401; visit Ismailia, i. 402; moral influence of elephant hunt upon, i. 416; dependence upon, ii. 5; refuse to act as carriers, ii. 23; hostility of, ii. 25; make night attack, ii. 29; villages of, destroyed, *ib.*; treachery of the, ii. 55; attack Major Abdullah, ii. 57.

INDEX.

Baris of Belinian, sheik of, murdered by Abou Saood, i. 232; particulars respecting, i. 244; sheik of, declines to attend conference, i. 258; night march to Belinian, i. 269 et seq.; well armed, i. 322; the attack on Belinian, i. 324 et seq.; war with, i. 326–351; blamed for war, i. 418; shelter deserters, ii. 477.

Baris of Gondokoro, sheik of, i. 221; expelled by the Loquia, i. 226; cattle of, i. 233, 334; unfriendly conduct of the, i. 235 et seq.; stockades of, i. 243; the sheik's drum, ib.; weapons of, ib.; warlike character of, ib.; form an alliance with those of Belinian, i. 244, 268; tamper with the troops, i. 254; confiscation of cattle of the, i. 255; agreement with, i. 257; proposals of, i. 259; further confiscation of cattle of the, i. 261; completely abandon the troops, ib.; make night attempt to recover the cattle, i. 262; attack working party, i. 263; war with, i. 264; women of the, i. 277; constant attacks by, i. 287, 305; wily method of attack of, i. 307.

Baris of Regiāf, in alliance with those of Belinian, i. 367; hostile attitude of the, i. 368; rich in corn, i. 371; occupation of territory of the, i. 375.

Bari system of farming, i. 405; products, i. 431; method of catching-elephants, i. 434; guides, ii. 323, 324, 357.

Bark cloth, Kabba Réga's robe of, ii. 189; preparation of, ii. 229.

Baroondi (Speke's "Urundi"), ii. 263.

Bartholomé, M., a French trader, i. 231.

Bartooma, (M.), ii. 148.

Bazaine, Marshal, soldiers who had fought under, i. 16, 396.

Bedawi, the guide, i. 43.

Beddēn, Bari chief, visits Sir S. Baker at Ismailia, i, 402; otherwise mentioned, i. 420, 421; subsequent treacherous conduct of, ii. 17 et seq.

Belinian, attack upon, i. 268 et seq.; Baris of, vide Baris; river of, i. 334; mountain of, i. 346.

Bellāal, a negro boy, ii. 295, 441, 492.

Berber, i. 16, 21; frightful change in the aspect of country near, i. 134, 163; improvements at, ii. 492.

Besheer, swears information against Abou Saood, ii. 401.

"Bismillah!" wonderful effect of exclaiming, i. 443.

Bizemont, Visconte de, French lieutenant de vaisseau, arrives at Khartoum to join expedition, i. 146; withdraws from expedition on receiving intelligence of battle of Sedan, i. 162.

Black troops, i. 51.

Blue Nile, the, i. 31.

Bohooma, curious Unyoro customs respecting the, ii. 148.

Bohr tribes, i. 220; station, ii. 108, 430.

Bokāmba, ii. 281.

Bōnnĕggĕsăh, ii. 281.

Bonosoora, the, Kabba Réga's bodyguard, ii. 256; their pay, ii. 276.

Booāmba, a cannibal district, ii. 263.

Boulti (*Perca Nilotica*), i. 51, 443.

"Boxer" hollow bullets, i. 438.

Buffaloes, i. 43, 65, 87.

C.

Cairo, delays at, i. 19; start from, i. 21; horses from, i. 30; disappointments at, i. 33; artillerymen from, i. 60; criminals from, employed as soldiers, i. 105; ploughs from, i. 137; postal communication with, i. 163; Abou Saood's proceedings at, ii. 411, 483, 486; Sir S. Baker's return to, ii. 492.

Cairo - Khartoun railway, ii. 503, 509.

Camels, i. 22; return to Cairo of sloops transporting, i. 26; great need of, i. 23 et seq.

Cameron, Lieutenant, ii. 466, 512.

Camp at Tewfikeeyah, i. 100; at Gondokoro, i. 228; regulations at Gondokoro, i. 228.

Canals, i. 41, 47, 49; ii. 480.

Cannon, deterrent effect of, upon natives, i. 416, 420.

Cattle of Baris confiscated, i. 255, 261;

INDEX. 575

activity of Bari, i. 334 ; of Abou Saood confiscated, i. 284 ; carried off by Abou Saood, i. 315.

Central Africa, extreme fertility and healthy climate of, i. 2 ; number of slaves annually taken from, i. 4 ; slavers' atrocities in, i. 5, ii. 119, 199, 386, 414 ; leased to slave-traders, i. 153 ; future steam transport of, ii. 75 ; game laws in, ii. 437 ; missionary labour in, ii. 522 ; geography of, *ib.*; languages of, ii. 528 ; domestic animals of, ii. 529 ; diseases of, *ib.*; hints to travellers in, ii. 533.

Ceylon, farming in, i. 138 ; canoes, ii. 366.

Cherif Pacha, sympathizes with slave suppression, i. 9 ; no reply from, ii. 487 ; admirable representative of the educated Circassian, ii. 488 ; member of secret tribunal, ii. 495.

Cherri-Merri, an African boy, ii. 253, 272, 309.

Chibero, ii. 263, 433, 507.

Choráb, a travelling sack used for carrying flour, ii. 61.

Chorobézé, ii. 178, 344.

Co-co-mé, the supposed cry of a bird in Unyoro, ii. 348, 352.

Cojoor (magic), i. 429 ; ii. 206, 238, &c.

Congo (River), possible junction of, with the Lualaba, i. 143 ; ii. 523.

Congow, General, M'tésé's commander-in-chief, ii. 281, 433, 463, 467.

Conspiracy amongst Sir S. Baker's officers, i. 363.

Corn-tax paid by natives, ii. 405, 434.

Cotton, Shillook, i. 115 ; at Gondokoro, i. 431.

Cow, a vicious, i. 335.

Crews, difficulty in getting together, i. 31.

Crocodile, man carried off by a, i. 44 ; jammed between rafts, i. 57 ; a friendly, i. 64 : man seized by a, i. 290, 291 ; woman carried off by a, i. 292 ; shot, i. 293.

Croix, St., deserted mission station at, i. 219.

Cuckoo, an African boy, ii. 7, 44, 84 ; wishes to discard his father, ii. 532.

D.

Damalis Senegalensis, antelope found south of the Sobat, i. 68, *n.*

Darfur, annual importation of slaves *vid*, i. 4 ; settlement on the frontier of i. 25.

Death of Dr. Gedge, i. 171 ; from sickness, i. 48, 56, 60, 75, 218 ; of Monsoor and Ferritch Baggara, ii. 298 ; of Ramadan and Hafiz, ii. 320 ; of Howarti, ii. 330 ; of a gallant soldier, ii. 343 ; of the "fat boy," ii. 356 ; of Mr. Higginbotham, ii. 475 ; of Mr. David Samson, ii. 493.

Deang, a native village, ii. 154.

Debono, Andrea, an ivory merchant trading in Central Africa, ii. 114.

Delays and difficulties at Cairo, i. 19 ; occasioned by opening of Suez Canal, i. 19 ; at Khartoum, through negligence and secret opposition of Egyptian officials, i. 24 ; occasioned by Nile obstructions, *vide* Sudd ; occasioned by insufficient means of transport, i. 147 ; occasioned by negligence or opposition of subordinates, i. 176, 186, 188 ; at Gondokoro, ii. 2 *et seq.*; through Beddēn's breach of faith, ii. 17 *et seq.*; &c.

Desertion, cases of, capture and mock execution of a deserter, i. 81, 82 *et seq.*; six soldiers desert, i. 215 ; capture of a deserter, ii. 63 ; two deserters shot at Gondokoro, ii. 476, 478 ; a deserter killed in a fight with Baris of Belinian, ii. 477.

Dhurra (*Sorghum vulgare*), description of, i. 239 ; scarcity of, i. 317 ; in large quantities at Belinian and and Regiāf, i. 320, 371 ; occupation of an island abounding with, i. 378 ; occupation of a village containing, i. 387 ; ordered from Khartoum, i, 399 ; native method of storing, i. 371, 394, 407.

Diahbeeah charged by a hippopotamus, i. 46 ; a dwelling for

INDEX.

Sir Samuel and Lady Baker, i. 107, 166.
Dinka country depopulated by slavers, i. 111 ; natural advantages of the, i. 117 ; natives of the, i. 300.
Disaffection amongst the troops, i. 352.
Djiaffer Pacha, governor-general of the Soudan, places too much confidence in his officers, i. 23 ; arranges for a year's delay at Khartoum, i. 24 ; his expedition to the Bahr Gazal, i. 25 ; former experience of, i. 28 ; supplies Sir S. Baker with some *very* irregular cavalry, i. 29 ; employs Kutchuk Ali, an infamous slave trader, i. 44 ; letter from, i. 85 ; and Quat Kare, i. 102; neglects to obtain necessary vessels, i. 147 *et seq.*; and Ali Bey, i. 149 ; and the grievances of the ivory-traders, i. 152, 157 ; false position of, i. 155 ; antecedents of, i. 161 ; applied to for supplies of men and food, i. 399 ; his lecture on the sources of the Nile, ii. 523 ; otherwise mentioned, i. 15, 30, 32.
Djoor (River), musicians from Pongo on the, i. 96; and the western outlet of the Bahr Gazal, i. 142.
Dolape palm (*Borassus Ethiopicus*), pleasing appearance of, i. 96, ii. 76 ; used for canoe building, ii. 365.
Domestic arrangement at Gondokoro, i. 358, ii. 7 ; at Masindi, ii. 225.
Dome palm (*Palma Thebaica*), i. 96.
Dongola, sailors from, i. 134.
Drift vegetation, i. 40 *et seq.*

E.

Eddrees, a vakeel of Abou Saood, and formerly a member of Ibrahim's party, visits Sir S. Baker, ii. 137 ; offers his services to the government, ii. 140 ; at Foweera, ii. 166 ; ill with dysentery, ii. 244 ; receives secret instructions from Sir S. Baker, ii. 259 ; death of, ii. 421.

Egypt, natives of, engaged in slave-hunting, i. 3 ; building materials from, i. 98 ; mechanics from, i. 109.
Egyptian soldiers, formerly convicted felons, i. 16, 105 ; employed in cutting canals, i. 51 ; unhealthy constitutions of, i. 75, 98 ; miserable spirit of, i. 110, 133, 172 ; desertions amongst, i. 215, 253.
Egyptian mechanics. i. 27, 109 ; procrastination, i. 26 ; fanaticism, i. 59 ; cotton (galleen), i. 357 ; artillerymen, ii. 58.
Egyptian government and Abou Saood, ii. 411, 483, 486, 495 *et seq.*, 514, *et seq.*; and the slave trade, ii. 483, 485.
Elephants, sudden appearance of, at Gondokoro, i. 406 ; two elephants shot south of Regiâf, i. 412 ; specific gravity of, i. 414 ; Lieutenant Baker shoots a bull elephant near the camp, i. 432 ; nocturnal visit of, i. 433 ; strength of, i. 434 ; elephant gathers fruit of the hēglik, i. 435.
Ellis, F.R.A.S., Mr. W., results of Lieutenant Baker's astronomical observations arranged by, ii. 564.
Ellipsyprymna antelopes, i. 85.
Engineering workshops at Tewfikeeyah, i. 109 ; operations at Gondokoro, ii. 480, 511.
English mechanics, i. 360 ; engineers, ii. 36, 480, 511 ; news received in Central Africa, ii. 472 ; endurance and enterprise, ii. 35 ; party returns to Gondokoro for the purpose of constructing steamers, ii. 36.
Explosive shell invented by Sir S. Baker, effect of the, i. 55, 56, 64.

F.

Fabbo, keen competition for purchase of ivory between traders at, and those of other stations, ii. 115 ; Suleiman in command at, ii. 383 ; Abou Saood carries ivory to, ii. 385 ; rebels at, ii. 403; slavers' atrocities at, ii. 413; garrisoned, ii. 470.
Faddul ("Forty Thieves") wounded, ii. 356.

INDEX. 577

Faddul-Moolah, dives for a hippopotamus, i. 64.
Fadlullah ("Forty Thieves") severely burnt, ii. 337.
Faloro, slavers' station at, ii. 281; rebels at, ii. 403.
Farragenia, station at, ii. 81; rebels at, ii. 403.
Fashoda, arrival of Sir S. Baker's party at, i. 33; governor of, *vide* Ali Bey; and Bahr Giraffe junction, great difference in duration of journeys between, i. 188; Sir S. Baker's return to, at close of expedition, ii. 484.
Fatiko, first arrival at, ii. 83; Abou Saood's encampment at, ii. 87; geographical position of, ii. 91; natives of, ii. 93, 132; return of Lāzim's slave-hunting party to, ii. 106; government station at, ii. 120, 129; bad news from, ii. 233; postal party leaves Masindi for, ii. 248; perilous journey of post for, ii. 322, 383, 417; Sir S. Baker's return to, ii. 389; treachery of slavers at, ii. 391; defeat of rebels at, ii. 397; completion of fort at, ii. 434; great hunt with natives at, ii. 440; night nurseries at, ii. 449; peace and harmony established at, ii. 459; garrisoned, ii. 470.
Fazoklé, ii. 114.
Ferritch Agha, Lieutenant ("Forty Thieves"), promotion of, i. 298; Sir S. Baker's opinion of, i. 349; his former service in Mexico under Bazaine, ii. 5; nationality of, ii. 461; despatched with letter to Ismaïl Pacha, ii. 487.
Ferritch Ajoke, a Pongo soldier ("Forty Thieves"), deserts and is taught a salutary lesson i. 81 *et seq.*; subsequent career of, i. 298, 349.
Ferritch Baggara ("Forty Thieves"), Sir S. Baker's opinion of, i. 349; fatal mission of, ii. 292; murder of, ii. 299; tribute to the memory of, ii. 351.
Fig-tree (*Ficus Indica*), halt beneath a, ii. 45; Sir S. Baker's tent at Masindi pitched under a, ii. 184.
Fleet for transport of expedition, i. 15; vexatious delays at Khartoum in connection with the, i. 24; purchase and preparation of vessels for the, i. 27; stuck fast in the sudd of the Nile, i. 67; steamer of the, aground, i. 103; enters the White Nile, i. 216.
Flogging for desertion, i. 84; for theft, i. 105, 254; for neglect of duty, i. 168; for disobedience of orders, i. 218, 254; for pillage, i. 356; of Suleiman, ii. 173; of a soldier for connivance at Lāzim's escape, ii. 427.
Foquatch, ii. 135.
Fort at Gondokoro, i. 311 *et seq.*; ii. 434.
"Forty Thieves," The, Sir S. Baker's company of picked men, formation of the corps, i. 31; distinctive dress of, i. 299; take no part in the military conspiracy, i. 364; horrible superstition amongst, ii. 355; parting with, ii. 479; gallant and distinguished services of, i. 169, 200, 217, 228, 233, 254, 265, 269, 270, 272, 275, 297, 308, 310, 312, 325, 330, 334, 343, 356, 372, 378, 381, 410, 439, 443; ii. 13, 26, 33, 68, 84, 151, 298, 301, 308, 322, 355, 478.
Foweera, station at, i. 153, 322; arrival at, ii. 361; stockade at, ii. 362.
Francolin partridges, found in abundance on the banks of the Bahr Giraffe, i. 38.
Frere, Sir Bartle, extract from a letter of Dr. Livingstone addressed to, ii. 525.
French, H.I.M. the Empress of the, sends Lady Baker a token of her sympathy with the expedition, i. 146; volunteers join the expedition, *ib.*; volunteers return to Europe after the battle of Sedan, i. 163.
Fuel, scarcity of, i. 39; laying in supplies of, i. 44, 86, 96.

G.

Galla country, torrents from the, emptying into the Sobat, i. 35.
Gallas, the, former conquerors of Unyoro, ii. 149, 177.

578   INDEX.

Galvanized iron, adaptability of, for building purposes in tropical countries, i. 428.
Game laws in Central Africa, ii. 437.
Gardens at Tewfikeeyah, i. 107; at Gondokoro, i. 229; at Masindi, ii. 224, 254; at Fatiko, ii. 417.
Gebel Forké (M.), scenery near, ii. 52.
Gebel Kuku, bearings of, ii. 78.
Gedge, Dr. Joseph, chief medical officer, joins expedition, i. 12; starts from Cairo, i. 20; overtakes main body, i. 95; illness of, i. 145; death of, i. 171.
Geographical discussions with native chiefs, ii. 147; information obtained from M'tésé's envoys, ii. 462; notes, ii. 543.
Georgis, Dr., Greek physician to the forces, attends Dr. Gedge, i. 146.
Ghattas, an ivory and slave-trader, boats of, overtaken on Bahr Giraffe, i. 80.
Ghebbelli tobacco, ii. 28.
Gimōro, the guide, ii. 94, 129, 417, 441, 478.
Giraffe-hunting, i. 86.
Gobbōhr, halt at, ii. 45.
Gonah, a Langgo chief, ii. 376.
Gondokoro, arrival of expedition at, i. 220; desolation and change in the aspect of the country surrounding, i. 221; slave-trading operations at, i. 225; station at, i. 228; gardening at, i. 229; attack upon the station at, i. 308; fort at, i. 311; completion of fort at, i. 357; domestic arrangements at, i. 358; drought at, i. 363; corn supply for, i. 376; native visitors to, i. 422, 432; return to, at close of the Bari campaign, i. 424; peace and harmony at, i. 429, 447; distilling at, i. 431; fortified posts communicating with, ii. 1; dangerous delays at, ii. 3; return of English engineers to, ii. 36; reinforcements from, ii. 429; Sir S. Baker's final visit to, ii. 475; the steamer *Khedive* built at, ii. 476; final departure from, ii. 479.
Googoos, native term for corn storehouses, i. 239, 371, 394, 407.

Goose, the crimson-headed, i. 135.
Gordon, Lieutenant-Colonel, Sir Samuel Baker's successor, ii. 466, 512.
Grinding corn, Egyptian notions about, i. 110.
Guides, experience of, i. 37; entirely at fault, i. 110; Bari guides, ii. 323, 324, 357, &c.
Guinea fowl, i. 135; ii. 379.

H.

Hadj, a Mohammedan festival, i. 49.
Hafiz, the farrier, murder of, ii. 320; otherwise mentioned, ii. 312, 315.
Hansall, Mr., Austrian consul at Khartoum, i. 24.
Heglik (*Balanites Egyptiaca*), fruit of the, i. 431; elephants attracted by the fruit of the, i. 434.
Hemp (*Hibiscus*), Sir S. Baker persuades Baris to cultivate, i. 431; Bari use of, *ib*.
Herpestris, a genus of cat, i. 136.
Higginbotham, Mr. Edwin, engineer-in-chief, joins the expedition, i. 14; command entrusted to, i. 15; letter from, i. 85; illness of, i. 173, 184; energy of, i. 182; constructs a dam across the Bahr Giraffe, i. 204; last parting with, ii. 10; death of, ii. 475; grave of, ii. 479; last letter from, ii. 538; distinguished services of, i. 20, 27, 29, 32, 51, 52, 60, 69, 204, 231, 269, 270, 273, 311, 317, 359, 366, 427, 433.
Hillet-el-dolape, a native village destroyed by the governor of Fashoda, i. 96.
Hippopotamus hunting, i. 38; diahbeeah charged by a, i. 45; exciting hunt of a, i. 54, 80; frightful effect of the "Baker" explosive shell upon, i. 56, 64, 207; furious attack by a, i. 209 *et seq.*; an impenetrable, i. 436.
Hippotragus antelope, i. 68.
Hippotragus Niger, i. 68, 180.
Hitchman, Mr., an English shipwright, i. 13.

INDEX. 579

Hoes, used by Unyoro natives, ii. 197, 307.
"Holland" rifle, i. 191, 413.
Howarti, the fisherman, catches fish by exclaiming "Bismillah!" i. 443; death of, ii. 320; otherwise mentioned, i. 193, 439; ii. 5, 15, 351.
Hussein Halifa or Khalifah, Arab sheik intrusted with management of desert transport, i. 163; appointed governor of Berber, ii. 493.

I.

Ibn Batuta, extract from the writings of, affording evidence of the great antiquity of the ceremony observed upon the death of a king of Unyoro, ii. 203.
Ibrahiméyeh, station at, ii. 2; arrival at, ii. 75; sport at, ii. 77.
India-rubber tree on the banks of the Sobat, i. 96.
Irregular troops, review of, i. 29; enlistment of, ii. 2, 145, 153.
Ismailia, the new name given to the district when Sir Samuel Baker annexed the country formerly known as Gondokoro; *vide* Gondokoro.
Ismail Yagoob Pacha, governor of Khartoum provinces, his character and sympathy with the expedition, i. 148; instructed to telegraph to Cairo for the arrest of Abou Saood, ii. 487; his improvements at Khartoum, ii. 492.
Ivory, government robbed of, by Abou Saood, i. 425; statistics respecting the transport of, ii. 111; brisk competition for, ii. 116; trade in Uganda, ii. 208; carried to Fabbo by Abou Saood.

J.

Jarda, a Belinian chief, friendly relations with, i. 331; and his diplomatic sister, i. 336; proposes an alliance, i. 338.
Jangy, unfairly elected king of the Shillooks, i. 103, 122; deposed, i. 171.

Jarvah, the "fat boy," ii. 6; death of, ii. 356.
Jarvis, Mr., chief shipwright, i. 12, 109, 427.
Juba (River), particulars respecting, ii. 119.
Jusef Effendi, governor of Fashoda, interview with, ii. 484.
Jusef, station of, destroyed by natives, ii. 107.

K.

Kabba Réga, king of Unyoro, particulars respecting his succession to the throne of Kamrasi, ii. 98, 138; presents for, ii. 139, &c.; message to, by Quonga, ii. 143; policy of, ii. 149, 311, 312; sends messengers, ii. 152; his projected attack upon Rionga frustrated, ii. 158; inhospitable conduct of, ii. 164; obtains throne by the murder of Kabka Miro, ii. 178; officially visited by Sir S. Baker, ii. 181; description of, ii. 187; his dread of the slave-traders, ii. 189; his hatred of Rionga, ii. 191, 197, 220, &c.; sends presents, and complains of Abou Saood, ii. 198; spies upon Sir S. Baker's movements, ii. 217; his hatred of M'tésé, ii. 221; impromptu visit of, ii. 224; visits Sir S. Baker's new residence at Masindi, ii. 236; his idea of human happiness, ii. 240; present at formal annexation of territory, ii. 243; steals guns and ammunition, ii. 245; desires monopoly of ivory trade, ii. 251; suspected of foul play, ii. 259; sullen behaviour of, ii. 275; sends poisoned merissa to the troops, ii. 287; attacks the government station, ii. 294; sues for peace, ii. 309; diabolical treachery of, ii. 321, 369; Rionga's information respecting, ii. 373; defeat and flight of, ii. 433; disappearance of, ii. 470; otherwise mentioned, ii. 363, 404.
Kabka Miro, rightful heir to Kamrasi, murdered by Kabba Réga, by the help of the slave-traders, ii 138, 178.

Kābbŏyú, ii, 263.
Kadji Barri, ii. 269, 272.
Kamrasi, father of Kabba Réga, death of, ii. 137 ; Sir S. Baker's visit to Unyoro in the reign of, ii. 198, 310.
Karagwé, ii. 147, 151, 198.
Karka, a female slave liberated by Sir S. Baker, i. 358.
Kaseega, halt at, ii. 355.
Keedja, ex-chief of Atada, visits Sir S. Baker near Masindi, ii. 140.
Kerrison, Sir Edward, valuable rifle lent by, i. 72.
Khartoum, slave merchants of, i. 3, 4, 150, 259, &c.
Khartoum, diminished population of, i. 24 ; injurious effect of quartering troops at, i. 25 ; flight of boatmen from, i. 30 ; departure from, i. 31 ; Sir S. Baker meets with vessels from, i. 86 ; letter sent from Tewfikeeyah to, i. 132 ; return to, i. 146 ; second departure from, i. 164 ; distance between Gondokoro and, i. 223 ; return of vessels to, i. 360 ; difficulties of communication between Gondokoro and, i. 361, 445 ; sick and incapable sent off to, i. 377 ; vessels return to, i. 397 ; otherwise mentioned, i. 15, 17, 21, 22, 32, 36, 37, 66, 69, 81, 123, 125, 139, 145, 318, 320, 425 ; reinforcements from, ii. 3, 477 ; Ismaïl Pacha's improvements at, ii. 492.
Khedive of Egypt, his Highness Ismaïl Pacha, firman of, appointing Sir S. Baker, i. 6 ; humane conduct of, i. 9 ; his orders neutralized, i. 26 ; and the Khartoum merchants, i. 150 ; sincerity of, i. 154, ii. 521 ; officer's letter of complaint forwarded to, i. 366 ; formal complaint to, i. 399 ; letter to, i. 426 ; publicly prohibits slave-trading, ii. 485 ; energetic measures of, ii. 493 ; receives and decorates Sir S. Baker at Cairo, ii. 494.
Khor, The, i. 198.
Kinyon ("Crocodile"), a Bari lad, ii. 6.
Kirk, Dr., extract from a letter from Dr. Livingstone to, ii. 525.
Kishākka, on the Kittangūlé, ii. 263.

Kisoona, Suleiman summoned to, ii. 161 ; arrival at, ii. 359.
Kittākără, an Unyoro chief, made prisoner, ii. 166 ; gentlemanly demeanour of, ii. 177 ; intercedes for Kabba Réga, ii. 302 ; otherwise mentioned, ii. 151, 238, 256, 259, 265, 268, 271, 278, 307, 310, 312.
Kittangūlé (River), course of the, ii. 263.
Koōjoōk, halt at, ii. 45.
Koorshood Agha, i. 187.
Kordofan, annual importation of slaves from Central Africa *viâ* Darfur and, i. 4.
Korosko, desert transport from, i. 15 ; difficulty of obtaining a steamer to tow flotilla to, i. 20.
Koshi country invaded by Makkarika cannibals and Ali Emmeen, ii. 430.
Kutchuk Ali, a slave-trader appointed to an important command by Djiaffer Pacha, governor-general of the Soudan, i. 25 ; outrages committed by his people, i. 44 ; arrival at station of, i. 81 ; otherwise mentioned, i. 125, 132, 148, 187.

L.

Lacustrine region, survey of, i. 50 ; formation of soil in, i. 77 ; further details respecting, i. 53, 142 *et seq.*
Langugo, country, ii. 117 ; natives, ii. 118 ; chief, ii. 376.
Latooka, station at, i. 425 ; deserters to, i. 433 ; rebels retire to, ii. 416 ; otherwise mentioned, ii. 71, 75, 107.
Lay missionaries for Central Africa, ii. 505.
Lāzim, an *employé* of Abou Saood, ii. 104 ; capture of, ii. 413 ; escape of, ii. 426 ; death of, ii. 428.
Le Blanc, Monsieur, i. 163.
Leopard, boy attacked by a, ii. 450.
Lepidosiren annectens, a very useful and agreeable fish for food, ii. 379.
Leucotis antelopes, ii. 446, 448, 451, 453, &c.
Lifeboat, loss of section of a, i. 175 recovery of section of a, i. 184.

Lion - hunting, a disappointment whilst, i. 39 ; fight with a lioness, ii. 453.

Lira, a country rich in ivory, ii. 117 ; donkeys found in, *ib.*

Livingstone, Dr. David, erroneous theory of, i. 142 ; Sir Samuel Baker's inquiries after, ii. 151, 261, 282, 462 ; intelligence of, ii. 464 ; Sir S. Baker's letter to, sent by M'tésé's envoys, *ib.;* researches of, ii. 523 ; on the Tanganyika, ii. 524 ; on the Lualaba, ii. 526.

Lobbŏhr, country of the, i. 119.

Loboré, transport of luggage to, ii. 17 *et seq.;* advance to, ii. 31 *et seq.;* preparations for the march to, ii. 39 ; start for, ii. 43 ; arrival at, ii. 47 ; language of, ii. 48 ; natives of, ii. 49 ; customs, ii. 64 ; knowledge of the lever, ii. 65 ; dishonesty amongst natives of, ii. 66 ; carriers, ii. 69, 125 ; natives kill a buffalo, ii. 89 ; words, ii. 528.

Lokara, Kabba Réga's commander-in-chief, ii. 144, 146, 151.

Lokko (" Oom Nickla "), a Bari chief, i. 338 *et seq.*

Loquia, Bari tribe, invade Allorron's district, i. 226 ; capture cattle belonging to hostile tribe, i. 357 ; otherwise mentioned, ii. 221, 255, 259, 308, 311.

Lualaba, (River), position and course of, i. 143 ; discussions respecting the, ii. 523.

M.

Machinery, arrangements for transport of the, i. 18.

Machoonda, the Albert N'yanza beyond the, ii. 263.

Madi tribe, ingenious method of chaining prisoners amongst the, ii. 65 ; villages of the, destroyed by Abou Saood, ii. 70 ; attack slavers, ii. 97.

Magazine at Tewfikeeyah, i. 98.

Magnetic battery, beneficial effects of a shock from the, i. 61 ; considered magical by the natives, i. 405 ; exhibited to Kabba Réga, ii. 237 ; exhibited to M'tésé's envoys, ii. 283.

Magungo, mountains of, ii. 135 ; natives of, ii. 321 ; lake journey to, ii. 462 ; otherwise mentioned, ii. 522.

Mahomet Tewfik Pacha, the Khedive's eldest son, Sir S. Baker names his first settlement in the Shillook country after, i. 105.

Makkarikas, a cannibal tribe induced by Ali Emmeen to invade the Koshi country, ii. 430 ; attacked by small-pox, 432.

Marcopolo, Mr., chief storekeeper, arrives at Cairo, i. 27 ; his duties at Tewfikeeyah, i. 106 ; honourably mentioned, ii. 511 ; otherwise mentioned, i. 12 ; ii. 10, 37, 479.

Marengo, ii. 46.

Marshes, cutting through the, i. 49 *et seq.*

Mashudi, Rionga's stronghold, ii. 305 ; M'tésé sends an auxiliary army to, ii. 463.

Masindi, capital of Unyoro, disarming of slave-traders at, ii. 180 ; description of, *ib.;* character of soil at, ii. 197 ; government house at, ii. 198, 213, 225 ; M'tésé's envoy to Kabba Réga at, ii. 198 ; messengers from Faieera arrive at, ii. 233 ; nightly murders at, ii. 257 ; arrival of Karagwé merchants at, ii. 260 ; difficulty in obtaining food at, ii. 265 ; warlike demonstration of natives at, ii, 269 ; fort constructed at, ii. 278 ; in flames, ii. 296 ; battle of, ii. 297 ; night incendiarism at, ii. 317 *et seq.;* station at, fired, ii. 327 ; retreat from, *ib.;* night bivouac near ii. 333.

Matonsé, an Unyoro chief, visits Sir S. Baker, ii. 147 ; taken prisoner, ii. 166 ; conceives a dislike for Monsoor, ii. 238 ; present at hostile demonstration of natives, ii. 268 ; brings poisoned merissa from Kabba Réga, ii. 286 ; Monsoor goes to summon him before Sir S. Baker before battle of Masindi, ii. 290 ; blamed by natives for the battle of Masindi, ii. 309.

Masons at Gondokoro, i. 427.
McWilliam, Mr., chief mechanical engineer of steamers, i. 12, 109, 214, 427.
Meri, a Bari chief, i. 424.
Merissa, a kind of fomented drink, Marsala *versus*, i. 405 ; jars of poisoned merissa sent by Kabba Réga, ii. 286.
M'fumbiro, ii. 286.
Military arrangements for the expedition, i. 16; during the Bari war, i. 387 ; for reduction of the force, i. 399 ; previous to advancing south from Gondokoro, i. 427 ; ii. 1 *et seq.*; in respect of irregular troops, i. 29 ; ii. 145, 153.
Minich, the steamer, tows vessels out of harbour, i. 20.
Mohammed Deii, Captain and aide-de-camp ("Forty Thieves"), appointed to Sir S. Baker's bodyguard, i. 31 ; sent with a party to recall Abdullah's detachment, i. 384 ; accompanies Sir S. Baker to Unyoro, ii. 5 ; on the march to Loboré, ii. 43 ; his mission to Suleiman, ii. 169 ; promoted at close of expedition, ii. 497.
Mohammed-el-Feel, Sergeant of "Forty Thieves" i. 301 ; ii. 338.
Mohammed Haroon, Sir S. Baker's servant, i. 268.
Mohammed Mustapha, Lieutenant, wounded, ii. 349.
Mohammed Wat-el-Mek, Abou Saood's vakeel, parentage of, ii. 114 ; invades Koshi district, ii. 112 ; in concealment, ii. 113 ; entertains Speke and Grant, ii. 114 ; character of, ii. 115 ; geographical discoveries of, ii. 117 ; command of irregular corps offered to, ii. 248 ; appointed Abou Saood's commander, ii. 381 ; his anxiety to serve the government, ii. 383 ; capture of, ii. 395 ; his evidence against Abou Saood, ii. 401 ; his superstition and vow of fidelity, ii. 402 ; his useful influence, ii. 412 ; retires from Fabbo, ii. 415 ; intercedes for Suleiman, ii. 423 ; sent to Gondokoro for reinforcements, ii. 429 467 ; returns to Fatiko, ii. 468 ; brings news from Europe, ii. 472 ; returns finally to Fatiko from Gondokoro, ii. 478.
Mohammed the camel-driver, delighted at meeting Sir Samuel and Lady Baker, i. 432.
Mohammed the sailor, ii. 5, 14.
Mohammed, a former Cairo dragoman of Sir S. Baker, unexpected meeting with, ii. 83 ; gives valuable information, ii. 96 *et seq.* ; fidelity of, ii. 389 ; sent with Fatiko post, ii. 418 ; otherwise mentioned, ii. 147, 156, 231.
Monsoor, Lieut. ("Forty Thieves"), Sir S. Baker's favourite officer, de scription of, i. 200 ; visits slavers' camp with Sir S. Baker, i. 283 ; promotion of, i. 298 ; promptitude and fidelity of, i. 356, ii. 231 ; accompanies Sir S. Baker to Unyoro, ii. 5 ; cheerful industry of, ii. 43 ; accompanies Sir S. Baker to Kabba Réga's presence, ii. 217 ; native confidence in, ii. 252 ; his demeanour in a critical situation, ii. 268 ; sent to Kabba Réga for food, ii. 286 ; departs on a fatal mission to summon Matonsé, ii. 290 ; murder of, ii. 298 ; anniversary of his death, ii. 307 ; regret for, ii. 351, 417 ; otherwise mentioned, i. 334, 383, 389, 393, 401.
Moogé, encampment at, ii. 47 ; sheik of, ii. 50.
Moomtazz Bey, governor of Souakim, i. 22.
Moostoora, little native girl protected by Lady Baker, i. 131 ; sent to Khartoum to be educated, ii. 10.
Molodi, a Madi, ii. 265, 275, 322, 364, 444, 447.
Morbé, a Bari chief, elected the responsible sheik of the Baris, i. 257.
Morgian Agha, Lieutenant, ii. 5, 179.
Morgian Sherrif, Captain, gallant conduct of, i. 327 ; previous military experience of, ii. 5.
Morgian the guide and interpreter, i. 277, 279, 307, 343, 401 ; ii. 84, 265.
M'rooli, distance of Albert N'yanza

INDEX.   583

from, ii. 149 ; proposed combined attack upon, ii. 378.
M'tésé, the powerful and excellent king of Uganda, his conversion to Mohammedanism, ii. 98 ; invades Unyoro, ii. 453 ; sends envoys to Fatiko, ii. 463 ; opens communication between Fatiko and Zanzibar, ii. 464 ; friendship and energy of, ii. 466 ; letter to, ii. 467 ; his reply to Sir S. Baker's letter, ii. 512 ; otherwise mentioned, ii. 144, 148.
Mustapha Ali, flogged for engaging in prohibited traffic with natives, i. 218.
M'wootan N'zigé, *vide* Albert N'yanza.

N.

Native carriers, ii. 164, 179, 180, 385.
Négheel, a fine kind of grass, i. 226.
Negroes, class feeling amongst, i. 300 ; improvement of the condition of, i. 302 ; peculiar character of, i. 421 ; *vide* Central Africa.
Nersho, a respectable native educated by the Austrian missionaries, ii. 46.
Neka, an Unyoro chief, ii. 238, 247.
Niambore, a friendly sheik, i. 281 ; is the bearer of bad news, i. 314.
Nile (River), vessels start from Cairo for voyage up the, i. 20 ; character of obstruction in the, i. 37 (for further information, *vide* Sudd) ; affluents of the, i. 147 ; basin of the, i, 6, 8, 143 ; particulars respecting the, ii. 77.
Nile, the Blue, i. 143.
Nile, White, *vide* White Nile.
N'kolé, ii. 263.
Noba, a superior African caste, i. 300.
Nubar Pacha, favourable to expedition, i. 9 ; documentary evidence against Abou Saood handed to, ii. 495 *et seq.* ; member of secret tribunal for trial of Abou Saood, *ib.*
Nubian desert, transportation of lake steamers across the, i. 9, 20, 163 ; ii. 493.
Nubian sailors, i. 134.

O.

Okooloo, an Unyoro warrior, ii. 376.
Orchid, curious specimen of, ii. 161.
Origin of the White Nile slave-trade, i. 259.
Ostrich-hunting, i. 112.

P.

Paniadoli garrisoned, ii. 470.
Parrots regarded by natives with awe, i. 404.
Pigs, wild, i. 54.
Pistia Stratiotes, a river-weed, description of the, i. 47 ; in immense quantities in the Nile, ii. 527.
Pittia, a native interpreter, brings a message from Beddēn, ii. 24 ; otherwise mentioned, ii. 22, 147, 149, 151, 164, 418.
Plantain grove, halt in a, ii. 353.
Pongo, desertion and mock execution of a soldier, a native of, i. 82, 298 ; slave sent as a present to Sir S. Baker, i. 97 ; musicians from, i. 132.
Poncet, Jules, a French trader, i. 184, 218.
Prince of Wales, H.R.H. his sympathy with the expedition, i. 5.
Princess of Wales, H.R.H., native admiration of, ii. 239.
Prisoner, an old friend recognized in a, ii. 368.
Prolypterus, a species of fish, a great take of, i. 51.
Provisions for the expedition, i. 18 ; scarcity of, ii. 367, 385.
' Purdey " rifle, i. 72.

Q.

Quat Kare, king of the Shillooks, interview with, i. 101 ; his favourite wife, i. 102 ; intrigues against, i. 103 ; stoical conduct of himself and wives, i. 104 ; invited to a meeting with Ali Bey, i. 118 *et seq.* ; his case referred to the Khedive, i. 123 ; entertained by Sir Samuel Baker, i. 124 ; his three

INDEX.

sons sent to Khartoum, i. 132; restored to power, i. 171; assists in recovery of a sunken vessel, i. 132; New Year's gift to, i. 185.

Quay constructed at Tewfikeeyah, i. 105.

Queen, H.M., photograph of, exhibited at Masindi, ii. 239.

Quonga, a favourite adviser of Kamrasi, brings a conciliatory message from Kabba Réga, ii. 169; present to, ii. 177; otherwise mentioned, ii. 137, 138, 142, 146, 151, 238.

R.

Rahonka, an Unyoro chief, first appearance of, ii. 151; kills a refractory carrier, ii. 154; escape of, ii. 166; otherwise mentioned, ii. 159, 164, 185, 238, 268, 272, 278, 310, 312.

Rain-maker, Lokko, the old, ii. 40.

Ramadan, the Mohammedan festival, i. 173, 180.

Ramadān appointed schoolmaster at Masindi, ii. 253; carries musical box to Kabba Réga, ii. 312, 315; murder of, ii. 320; regret for, ii. 351.

Ramsall, Mr., an English boiler-maker, i. 13.

Raouf Bey, Colonel, disgraceful negligence of, i. 178; his friendship for Abou Saood, i. 286; his inefficiency, i. 311, 323; forwards letter of complaint from the officers, i. 364; Sir Samuel Baker's instructions to, before leaving Gondokoro for Unyoro, ii. 10; ordered to take charge of prisoners, ii. 248; connives at flight of Abou Saood, ii. 411; his conduct in his command at Gondokoro, ii. 476; otherwise mentioned, i. 32, 44, 53, 56, 70, 98, 134, 176, 187, 189, 192, 197, 218.

Rawlinson, Sir H., extract from a letter from Dr. Livingstone to, ii. 526.

Red Sea, perilous navigation in the, i. 21, ii. 494.

"Reilly" breechloader, i. 53.

Regiāf (Mount), the Baris of, i. 367; observations from summit of, ii. 16; curious rock at base of, *ib.*; sudden change in the Nile at, ii. 527.

Rionga, an Unyoro chief (the inveterate foe of Kamrasi), ii. 138; proposed attack on, ii. 150; his ancient feud, ii. 188, 191, 197, 220; contemplated alliance with, ii. 304; communication with, ii. 305; orders for the march to, ii. 324; the march from Masindi to, ii. 327 *et seq.*; arrival in district of, ii. 361; Sir Samuel Baker receives a message from, ii. 369; present for, ii. 370; gives a truly negro welcome, ii. 371; meets Sir Samuel Baker, ii. 372; goes through the ceremony of exchanging blood with Sir S. Baker, ii. 375; popularity of, ii. 377; proclaimed king of Unyoro *vice* Kabba Réga, *ib.*; Ali Genninar despatched with troops and present for, ii. 413; defeats Kabba Réga, ii. 433; holds Unyoro jointly with Ali Genninar, ii. 473.

Rockets, native notions respecting, ii. 224; *vide* Hale's rockets.

Rot Jarma, the great Shooli sheik, visits Sir S. Baker, ii. 126; fidelity of, ii. 381, 384; further mention of, ii. 95, 233, 381, 384.

Route arrangements, i. 15.

Rumanika, king of Karagwé, sends merchants to Masindi to purchase ivory, ii. 260.

S.

Sāat, a negro boy, ii. 6, 13, 295, 441, 493.

Saat Choush ("Forty Thieves"), champion shot, ii. 354.

Said, native boy, catches some fish of the *Silurus* species, i. 233.

Saïd Agha, a native of Sishuaali, ii. 461.

Saïd Pacha, slave trade formerly prohibited by, ii. 485.

Salim-Wat-Howah, an *employé* of Abou Saood, ii. 413; exploit of,

ii. 415 ; in hiding, ii. 481, 486 ; capture of, ii. 491.
Salt-making, "Forty Thieves" employed in, i. 430.
Samson, Mr. David, joins expedition, i. 13 ; death of, ii. 493.
Sand-banks, ii. 13.
Sangrado, i. 60.
Schweinfurth, Dr., sends his notes on the Western Nile Basin to Sir Samuel Baker, i. 145 ; his remarks on Sir Samuel Baker's proceedings, ii. 519, 520 ; geographical discoveries of, ii. 523 ; on the course of the river Lualaba, ii. 524.
Sedan, battle of, arrival of intelligence of the, i. 162.
Selim, the Suāchli, sent as an envoy to M'tésé, ii. 466.
Senaar, the, an Egyptian war-sloop, i. 21.
Seroor ("Forty Thieves"), narrow escape of, ii. 355.
Sesamé, an African wood, i. 239, 338.
Sessi lake, ii. 284.
Shadoof, an Egyptian machine for hand irrigation, i. 296.
Shallows in the Bahr Giraffe, i. 195.
Sharga, a native village, ii. 385.
Sheik, sad death of an old blind, i. 118 ; "the red sheik," i. 393.
Shell, the "Baker" explosive, i. 55, 56, 64 ; novel use for a, ii. 11.
Sheroom, a Bari guide, i. 269, 279, 307, 343, 429.
Shillooks, arrival in the country of the, i. 33 ; return to country of the, i. 69 ; plunder of the, by slave-traders, i. 87 ; the false king of the, i. 91 ; present from chief of the, i. 97 ; visit from king of the, i. 99 ; misrule of the, i. 104 ; opinions about the expedition amongst the, i. 111 ; friendly traffic with the, i. 113 ; honesty of the, i. 114 ; canoes used by the, i. 116 ; placed in charge of corn, i. 178 ; assist in raising sunken vessel, *ib.* ; rafts of the, ii. 367 ; otherwise mentioned, i. 98, 103.
Shipwrights, English, i. 12, 13, 108.
Shir tribe, a detachment of government troops destroyed by the, i. 314 ; expedition against the, i. 428 ; a chief of the, proposes to sell his son, ii. 211.
Shooa, mountain of, i. 78 ; no tracks of large animals between Latooka and, ii. 71 ; hill, Wat-et-Mek's detachment seen near, ii. 468.
Shooli natives, ii. 93 ; docility of, ii. 95; hunting season of, ii. 435 ; peace and harmony established with, ii. 436 ; conservative principles amongst, *ib.;* general hunting arrangements of, ii. 439 ; their skill as hunters, ii. 451.
Shooli words, ii. 528 ; animals and birds, ii. 531.
Shooli the guide, ii. 129, 417, 440, 468, 478.
Sickness, thirty-two cases of, at one time, i. 48 ; more cases of, i. 49 ; from marsh fever, i. 52, 58 ; many Egyptians down with, i. 61 ; artillerymen nearly all attacked with, i. 98 ; deaths from, *vide* Death.
Silber and Fleming, i. 13.
Silurus, a species of fish, i. 234.
Sishuaali, officers natives of, ii. 461.
Slave hunters of Khartoum, *vide* Khartoum ; Arabs employed as, i. 3 ; Egyptian subjects employed as, *ib.* ; traces of, i. 42, 44, 59 ; in the Dinka country, i. 111 ; further details respecting, ii. 70, 78 ; render all the native tribes hostile, ii. 112 ; devastations of, ii. 136 ; escape with slaves, ii. 167 ; at Foweera and Kisoona, ii. 198 ; frightful atrocities of, ii. 119, 386, 414 ; determined opposition of, ii. 208 ; kept as a rod for natives, ii. 405 ; plunder the neighbourhood of Fabbo, ii. 406 ; fire upon Sir Samuel Baker's messengers, ii. 407 ; captured at Fashoda, ii. 490.
Slave trade, suppression of the, i. 8. 14, 25, 96, 259 ; ii. 499 *et seq.;* revival of the, ii. 516 ; greatly desired by the troops, i. 352 *et seq.*
Slaves, discovery of, i. 127 ; emancipation of, i. 29, 164 ; female slaves married to the soldiers, i. 130 difficulty of managing liberated, i.

165; masses of, at Abou Saood's stations, ii. 122, 148; released, ii. 182; restored to their homes, ii. 207; purchased for needles, ii. 209; liberated, ii. 532.
Slave vessels confiscated, i. 129, 164; ii. 432.
Small-pox amongst the Makkarikas, ii. 432; amongst slaves, ii. 482.
Snakes, i. 50.
"Snider" rifles, i. 395; considered magical by the natives, i. 429.
Sobat (River), junction of the, i. 34; origin of the, i. 35; return to the, i. 96; direction of the, i. 143, ii. 118.
Soont (*Acacia Arabica*), i. 117, 140; ii. 117, 541.
Souakim, desert journey between Berber and, i. 22; governor of, *vide* Moomtazz Bey; otherwise mentioned, i. 16, 21, 28.
Soudan, the, miserable vessels of, i. 56; rule in, i. 103; cotton, i. 115; confusion in, i. 157; ancient funeral rites in, ii. 203; no help from, i. 399; otherwise mentioned, i. 3, 16; Ismaïl Pacha's improvements in the, ii. 488.
Soudan government, i. 23; opposition of, i. 26; insincerity of, i. 153.
Soudani regiments, superiority of, i. 288; demand an increase of rations, i. 317; prefer Central Africa to Khartoum, i. 377; otherwise mentioned, i. 59, 98, 357.
South, the march, ii. 1 *et seq.*
Speke and Grant, ii. 114, 148.
Sponge-bath used as a boat, ii. 163.
Sport, i. 38, 43, 65, 80, 179, 184, 189, 193, 220, 231, 234, 379, 409; ii. 11, 51, 131, 133, 446.
Stable at Tewfikeeyah, i. 106.
Steamers fixed by floating rafts or vegetation, i. 57; breakdown of one of the, i. 97.
Steel corn-mills, i. 111.
Stockades, assault on the, i. 327, 342.
Stores, ordering of, i. 14; packing of, i. 17; damaged by rain, i. 56; destroyed by rats and ants, i. 107; deliberate theft of, i. 218.
Sudd, the, or Nile obstructions, preparations for cutting through, i. 110, 172; six vessels wrecked in the, ii. 488; delays caused by, i. 56, 58, 140, 193, 215.
Suez, i. 21.
Suez canal, i. 19.
Suleiman, the missionary, i. 228.
Suleiman Effendi, i. 176; ordered to clear the channel, i. 177.
Suleiman, Sir S. Baker's servant, i. 408.
Suleiman, a vakeel of Abou Saood, ii. 136; receives formal notice of termination of Agād & Co.'s contract, ii. 139; present to, ii. 144; promises to assist Kabba Réga, ii. 150; ivory held by, ii. 153; murders a native, ii. 155, 159; his intrigues and vengeance, ii. 159; ordered to furnish carriers, ii. 165; his interview with Colonel Abd-el-Kader, ii. 166; in league with Rahonka, ii. 168; trial of, ii. 171; publicly flogged, ii. 173; and Rionga, ii. 373; in command at Fabbo, ii. 388; with the Fatiko post, ii. 419; surrender and pardon of, ii. 421 *et seq.*
Sunstroke, a death from, i. 48.

T.

Taka, mutiny at, i. 355.
Tamarind tree, forests of the, i. 431.
Tanganyika lake (supposed to be part of the great Albert N'yanza), i. 143, 263, 464, 507, 522; *vide* Albert N'yanza.
Taxes in the Soudan, i. 23.
Tayib Agha, Lieutenant-Colonel, conduct of, i. 175; and the wrecked vessel, i. 185; desired to lay in fuel, i. 187; behindhand on arriving with the vessels, i. 192; letter left in a bottle at the "Dubbah" for, i. 194; disgraceful loitering of, i. 271; Sir S. Baker awaits arrival of, i. 274; misses the path when in command of detachment marching to Belinian, i. 375; folly of, i. 317; cautioned, i. 318; defeat of, ii. 468; superseded, ii. 469.
Teel (*Leucotis*), ii. 131.

INDEX. 587

Tetel (*Antelope Bubalis*), ii. 51, 53, 79, 133, 451.
Tewfikeeyah, government station at, i. 100 *et seq.*; slaver sighted off, i. 125; farming, i. 134 *et seq.*; sport at, i. 136; mean temperature at, during May, June, and July, i. 138; return to, in October 1870, i. 164; station at, dismantled, i. 170; sudden fall of the thermometer at, i. 139.
Thief, a nocturnal, i. 167; discovery of the, i. 254; escape of the, *ib.*
Timber, scarcity of, i. 108.
Timsah, lake ("Crocodile Lake"), i. 190.
Tobacco cultivation in Unyoro, ii. 162.
Tomby, an interpreter, i. 231, 259.
Trieste, fir poles from, i. 18.
Troops, discontent amongst the, i. 245; laziness of the, i. 319; difficulty of maintaining proper discipline amongst the, i. 325 *et seq.*; laxity of discipline among the, i. 355 *et seq.*; conspiracy amongst officers of the, i. 365 *et seq.*; better spirit amongst the, i. 423; mutinous gathering of the, ii. 33; review at Fatiko of the, ii. 91; gallant and soldierly conduct of, ii. 351; reported extermination of the, ii. 383; gratuity to, ii. 497; *vide* Military arrangements.
Tullaboon (*Eleusine Coracana*), ii. 181.

U.

Uganda, M'tésé's capital, Abou Saood's people visit, ii. 98; threatened transfer of seat of commerce from Masindi to, ii. 144; manufacture of bark-cloth at, ii. 230.
Ujiji (pronounced Uyéyé) and Magungo, lake communication between, ii. 462; Livingstone heard of at, ii. 464.
Umbogo (the "Buffalo"), speaks Arabic, ii. 162; gives information respecting Abou Saood's treachery, ii. 168; particulars respecting, ii. 199; his views upon the question of soap, ii. 200; explains the uproar in Masindi, ii. 231; antecedents of, ii. 257; his report respecting native attack, ii. 307; otherwise mentioned, ii. 280, 290, 293, 302, 305, 314.
Umiro, tribe of the, defeat Abou Saood's people, ii. 102; massacre a party of slave-traders, ii. 105; as hunters, ii. 135; cattle of the, ii. 152.
Ume-el-Ete, a Mohammedan festival, i. 445.
Unyanyembé, Sir Samuel Baker's letter to Livingstone reaches, ii. 466; communication opened with, ii. 512.
Un-y-Amé (River), proposed general depôt for steamers near the mouth of the, ii. 75; channel of the, near Fatiko, ii. 130; murdered women flung into the, by slavers, ii. 413; great hunt near the, ii. 442.
Unyoro, ivory trade in, ii. 4; preparations for the journey to, ii. 129; the march to, ii. 139; scenery between Fatiko and, ii. 130; country of, devastated by slave-traders, ii. 136; natives of, ii. 150; chiefs visit Sir S. Baker, ii. 151; chivalrous ceremony in, ii. 177; extraordinary and ancient ceremony at the death of a king of, ii. 201; perfect organization in, ii. 213; liberation of slaves in, ii. 221; commerce established in, ii. 250; benefits conferred on natives of, ii. 277; natives attack government station at Masindi, ii. 294; Rionga proclaimed king of, ii. 317; further attacks by natives of, ii. 335; extent of, ii. 470; in the hands of Rionga, ii. 473; words, ii. 528.

V.

Vegetable obstructions in the river Nile, *vide* Sudd.
Vegetables raised at Tewfikeeyah, i. 108.
Victoria Nile, course of the, i. 143; march to Suleiman's station on the banks of the, through beautiful

scenery, ii. 136; width of, at Foweera, ii. 364; Rionga's stronghold on the, ii. 371; crossing the, ii. 379; mouth of the, ii. 522; Livingstone's erroneous statement respecting the width of, ii. 526.
Victoria N'yanza (Něraă Bali), information obtained from natives respecting the, ii. 284; erroneous theories respecting the, ii. 526; Victoria Nile of the, i. 143.
Vienna Exhibition, Sir S. Baker's botanical collection made during this expedition forwarded by the Khedive to the, ii. 495.
Vivisection of cattle by slave-hunters, ii. 428.

W.

Wady Halfah, time for ascending cataracts of the, i. 19.
Wani, the reputed sheik of the mountain, visits Sir S. Baker at Belinian, i. 338 *et seq.*
Wani the dragoman, i. 48.
Wat-a-jook, a native village on the Sobat, i. 96.
Wat-el-Shambi, destination of certain boats, i. 197; arrival at, i. 217.
Wat-el-Ajoos Omare, sheik of Fatiko, ii. 126; a hunt with the people of, ii. 439.
Waterbuck (*Redunca Ellipsyprymna*) in the Shir country, i. 434; on the river Asua, ii. 72.
Water-grass rafts, i. 41; fleet inclosed by, i. 52; cutting through, i. 189 *et seq.*
Watūta, M'wootan N'zigé passes through, ii. 263.
Wat Hojōly, a vakeel of Abou Saood, attempts to pass Fashoda with slaves, ii. 482 *et seq.*; taken prisoner at Fashoda, ii. 491.
Wāysŏŏa, envoy from Uganda, arrives at Masindi, ii. 281.
Wéllé (River), particulars respecting, ii. 523, 525, 526.

White ants, remarkable exodus of, ii. 157.
White Nile (Masāba), i. 10; slave trade of the, i. 23, 259; junction of the Sabot and, i. 34; between the Sobat junction and Gondokoro, i. 35; obstructed vegetable drift, *ib.*; totally unnavigable, i. 48; exploration of, i. 70; rats of the, i. 106; uninteresting districts of the, i. 108; English enterprise in the forests of the, i. 109; exploration of the Old, i. 140; ivory-traders rent the territory of the, i. 196; great necessity for clearing the main channel of the, i. 196, 399; discovery of the Great, i. 201; fleet enters the, i. 216; changed aspect of the, at Gondokoro, i. 221; sudden rise and fall of the, i. 233; the greatest enemy to the expedition, i. 361; reconnaissance of the last cataracts of the, i. 400; Livingstone's erroneous theories respecting, ii. 527.
Whitfield, Mr., shipwright, i. 13.
Wild-duck shooting, i. 53.
Wood, Mr., Sir S. Baker's secretary, i. 12; returns to Egypt, i. 132.
Woolwich tubes, superiority of, ii. 40.
Wreck, recovery of a, i. 181; of six vessels in the sudd, ii. 488.

Z.

Zafteer, a favourite horse, death of, ii. 351.
Zanzibar, native trade with, ii. 99; opening of communication between Fatiko and, ii. 464.
Zareebas (or kraals), description of Bari, i. 240; artfully concealed by high grass, i. 328; troops protected by, i. 330; owners of, also farmers, i. 405.
Zinc boat, a portable, i. 67.